John Riddell

Comments in Refutation of Pretensions Advanced for the First Time

And Statements in a Recent Work

John Riddell

Comments in Refutation of Pretensions Advanced for the First Time
And Statements in a Recent Work

ISBN/EAN: 9783337429423

Printed in Europe, USA, Canada, Australia, Japan

Cover: Foto ©Suzi / pixelio.de

More available books at **www.hansebooks.com**

COMMENTS
ON
THE KEIR PERFORMANCE
WITH
DRUMPELLIER'S EXPOSITION

COMMENTS

IN REFUTATION OF PRETENSIONS ADVANCED FOR THE FIRST
TIME, AND STATEMENTS IN A RECENT WORK

"THE STIRLINGS OF KEIR AND THEIR FAMILY PAPERS,"

WITH AN

EXPOSITION OF THE RIGHT OF THE STIRLINGS OF DRUMPELLIER TO THE
REPRESENTATION OF THE ANCIENT STIRLINGS OF CADDER

BY

JOHN RIDDELL, Esq.

ADVOCATE

AUDI ALTERAM PARTEM

Printed for Private Circulation
BY WILLIAM BLACKWOOD AND SONS
EDINBURGH: MDCCCLX

1314970

PREFATORY NOTE.

OF this Work, Three Hundred Copies have been printed for private circulation among the Members and Friends of the Drumpellier Family, and some Public Libraries.

At the same time, a sufficient number of Copies will remain in the hands of the Printers for a reasonable period, in order that each of those who were presented by Keir with copies of the "STIRLINGS OF KEIR AND THEIR FAMILY PAPERS," may have an opportunity of obtaining one also of the "DRUMPELLIER EXPOSITION," on application in person, or by letter, to Messrs WILLIAM BLACKWOOD AND SONS, George Street, Edinburgh.

EDINBURGH, *August* 1860.

PREFACE.

At a very early period of his professional career, more than forty years ago, the framer and writer of the following Exposition was applied to and consulted by William Stirling, younger of Drumpellier, on the part of his father, Andrew Stirling, then of Drumpellier, in respect to certain gentilitial rights and claims, including the representation of the ancient Stirlings of Cadder, which, by invariable tradition, had vested in their family.

On examination of the documentary and other evidence which Mr Stirling adduced, backed with more either then familiar to, or shortly afterwards recovered by him, the writer saw that the case was not only an honest one, but possessed incidents remarkable in their way, some of them even of a tragical or affecting character.* This, coupled with the interest of certain legal questions mooted, especially excited his ardour and zeal, and he not only accepted the offer to conduct the case, but actively entered upon the discharge of its duties.

---

[1] See Preface, p. x.

* This is fairly admitted by the recent Keir compilation, where it is prominently announced at the outset that "not the least interesting part of the following narrative (including the Cadder and Keir histories and genealogies) is the story of the ill-fated heiress of Cadder,"[1] and with which the writer may conjoin the far more tragical and affecting one of the unfortunate Buchanans of Leny—the instrument or cause of the catastrophe being much the same in both instances, as will be seen in the present Exposition.

PREFACE.

In acquiring the Cadder property in 1541 (by what means will be afterwards shown), the Stirlings of Keir became possessed of the Cadder charter-chest, rich in muniments and writs illustrative of the history and descent of that ancient family, and, doubtless, containing evidence that would at once confirm the Drumpellier claim on the one hand, or, on the other hand, set it aside. In either case—while it was natural and just to all to secure every means of information—the matter might thus eligibly be settled, and legal proceedings avoided; and, with this view, Mr William Stirling undertook the task of obtaining permission to inspect the Cadder writs, which, from what had passed between him, Mr Charles Stirling, the brother of the then Keir, and the Keir agent, he had entertained hopes might have been granted; but he here was doomed to disappointment, as will appear by the Correspondence in Chapter II. of this work.

An amicable accommodation, therefore, so sincerely sought by Drumpellier, being thus out of the question, the only alternative now left him in support or vindication of his gentilitial or preferable Cadder claims, was to betake himself to Law; of which resolution Keir forthwith, who had besides peremptorily announced his intention of opposing them to the utmost, was courteously apprised. And, accordingly, the writer, in pursuance of such object, was instructed to arrange and prepare a legal case for Drumpellier, which, in 1818, was duly submitted to and discussed by two legally constituted Courts. How triumphantly he then succeeded in establishing his desired Drumpellier-Cadder status and rights, will be seen in the course of the Exposition.

Nor is it the least striking feature of the case that, notwithstanding, as stated, the bold and peremptory threat of opposition by Keir against Drumpellier, he yet refrained from taking any step on these occasions, and actually, now conscious of the untoward dilemma into which he had brought himself by attempting what was *ultra vires*, calmly allowed

PREFACE.   v

him, if we may use the phrase, to "walk the course," and attain his object without the slightest legal demur and objection—a forbearance, too, which his family have wisely exercised down to the present moment.

The previous conviction and belief, therefore, of the Drumpellier family, in the justice and reality of their gentilitial rights and Cadder representation, being thus sanctioned and confirmed by the joint findings and awards of two public legal judicatories, *reddendo singula singulis*—as will be seen, where opposition by any party, thinking himself in the least aggrieved or compromised by the counter-procedure of another, was quite open and practicable—they at once might be held fairly conceded and admitted.

But further also, without any subsequent *rei interventus* either, to give a different cast to the case, or challenge or opposition whatever, the same undenied rights and status necessarily came, in 1859, over and above, to be hermetically sealed in favour of Drumpellier against the utmost efforts of cavil and disceptation, by the longest prescription of forty years that had elapsed since the epoch of the important legal proceedings stated in 1818; and *a fortiori*, too, if that require to be added by the later increase of time—still *cæteris paribus*—down to the present 1860, evidently rendering them quite impregnable and indefeasible.

His mind, as was natural, therefore, being deeply imbued with the preceding facts, it was not without some interest that the present representative of the Drumpellier family[1] learned in 1859—in the previous year stated—that a book had recently made its appearance under the title of "The Stirlings of Keir and their Family Papers."[2] When he succeeded in obtaining a perusal of this work, which he did at a public library (no copy having been forwarded to him or his family, though, as he understood, all others of the name had been supplied with them),

[1] Walter Stirling, Esq., Curzon Street, Mayfair, London.
[2] First circulated Dec. 28, 1858.

he found it had been printed under the auspices and for the behoof of Mr Stirling of Keir, the honourable Member for Perthshire, but compiled by his advisers and agent.

And it is with much regret that, on further examination, he discovered that these gentlemen had risked and sanctioned gross errors and misrepresentations in fact, to his prejudice. They have not only almost ignored the Drumpelliers and their rights and claims in what is pretended to be a full history of the Stirlings, but most unwarrantably, *without a shadow or tittle of evidence*, arrogated, on the other hand, for the first time, to their principal, a descent from the Stirlings of Cadder, with the chieftaincy, moreover, of the entire name, as their direct representative, notwithstanding the long undoubted and legally unchallenged preoccupation, as has been proved, of that identical status by Drumpellier—who yet is here even excluded from the field of competition—and in the face too of the actual abandonment by the Keir in 1818 of the Stirling contest with his family, though before peremptorily advanced and hostilely proclaimed—his after recreancy and prostration in that year, so irreconcilable with his vaunts—and, in other words, real discomfiture on the occasion.*

The presumption, if not audacity, of the procedure, in the peculiar circumstances, somewhat at first startled Drumpellier; but recollecting that his family status was truly impregnable to attack, and that he stood, as it were, upon a rock, and therefore confident that the attack of such subaltern work could be easily repulsed, it in the main commoved him but little. But what *did* give him concern, and the very idea of which occasioned him much annoyance, was, that the futile and unwarrantable pretensions enunciated in the above work made it incumbent upon him to appear before the public, which he was most unwilling to do, in order to make a full statement of the Drumpellier right, and at once unmask

---

* See, for all this, Chapters II. and III. of the Exposition.

and conclusively refute such unsupported and frivolous pretensions—pretensions which the Keir family, for obvious reasons, and so directly opposite to the Drumpellier conduct, never risked the mooting of in a court of law, but once, when incautiously brought upon the verge of it, actually eschewed and fled from the discussion, as if scared by the noise of their own footsteps.

The *rôle* or part, however disagreeable to the present Drumpellier at his advanced age, must be played by himself—and that *now*. It was due to the memory of those who had gone before—it was due to those who might come after him.

With this view, therefore, Drumpellier did the writer the honour of opening a communication with him, as the old friend and legal adviser of his family, and invited him, who was cognisant of the case from the beginning, and of all that had passed on the former occasion, to undertake the drawing up of a statement of the whole facts and evidence that could be honestly and legally adduced in support and elucidation of the Drumpellier rights. ^{In March 1859.}

He, indeed, has for some time previous to this been withdrawing himself from the practice of his profession; but this case, so connected with his earlier career, and the pleasurable associations of former days, as well as from the esteem he bears the applicant, possessed such peculiar attractions in his eyes, that he readily accepted the offer, and has undertaken to conduct and frame the Exposition required—the more so that, in the long interval, he had incidentally lighted upon some new pieces of evidence, besides further arguments and illustrations in its favour.

On entering upon his task, the Exponent found that the recent Performance, "The Stirlings of Keir and their Family Papers," professed to have been printed for private circulation. This by some has been supposed to preclude criticism, but even under this aspect such rule must have exceptions, and taken with the announced circulation to the extent

PREFACE.

of 150 copies, to parties curious in such subjects, including professed antiquaries of course, and some public libraries, it may be held to lose much of its private character, and to be the more open to public discussion. Were this vetoed, it is evident that, under such professed mask, most injurious statements might be risked, and the just rights and interests of parties assailed and denied with impunity, without the means of refutation and redress. Such results can never be sanctioned by the plainest rules of equity and justice. Besides which, it was the opinion of booksellers, no incompetent judges, in a much more favourable case for privileged privacy and public forbearance, as far back as 1781—rather a literary epoch—that "a book once *printed, and only given to friends, is in fact published,*" hence on a par with any publication.[1] Weighty reasons now as then may support the conclusion—and if so, *a fortiori*, the Keir Performance, whose circulation has not merely been restricted or confined to friends and relations, but flowed into more varied and public channels. The work in question, therefore, without farther preamble, may in every view be so treated.

The same appearing under the auspices and sanction of the honourable Member for Perthshire, with, however, the rather vague and undefined title of "The Stirlings of Keir and their Family Papers," bears to be more or less the handicraft or contribution of three respectable persons ; namely, Cosmo Innes, Esq., Advocate ; John Dundas, Esq., C.S., the present Keir agent ; and Mr William Fraser, Assistant-Keeper of the Register of Sasines ;[2] but more especially of the last mentioned —in fact, the announced *responsible* editor (a heavy *responsibility*, as may be seen), as well as deducer of pedigrees of branches of the Stirlings and other portions of the volume.[*]

[1] See Mason's Letters to Horace Walpole, Cunningham's recent edition of the Walpole Correspondence, vol. viii. p. 37.

[2] See Preface to the Keir Work, p. xii. note.

[3] See Ibid.

[*] The following is the statement the Editor gives of the efforts of the two other gentlemen, and their contributions to the work :—[3] "A part of the account of the Keir family was prepared by John Dundas, Esquire, C.S., who, amidst numerous professional claims on

PREFACE.

The Exponent confesses himself here somewhat in a dilemma, from three separate irons being thus put in the fire. When the authorship of a portion of the work is clear, it can easily be acknowledged, but when otherwise, it may be difficult; and with this view, in the emergency, and in the case of a quotation or argument therefrom, reference can only be made generally, so as to include the party, to the Keir Performance, or to its framers and compilers, under the style or description of the *Triumvirate*, which method, as will be seen, has been adopted.

The step is suggested, and indeed called for by common prudence, because, *e converso*, through an attempted specification of the author or writer, with ignorance, at the same time, of the respective merits and contributions of the Triumvirate, injury might unconsciously be done by ascribing to one what in truth was solely due to another; and hence, as authors—even the best—are deemed somewhat an *irritabile genus*, and neither, like Cæsar or Pompey, inclined "*ferre priorem*," or "*parem*," an awkward collision might thus arise, evoking perchance a new controversy—for which the writer might have the credit—that it would be as well to avoid.

Perhaps he also may be pardoned for remarking that Keir may have submitted himself with too much confidence to the gentlemen in question, who have undertaken their task rather too hastily,* of which, indeed, and strange inadvertencies, besides what is otherwise exceptionable, the Keir Performance bears witness, and whom, moreover, a *benevolent* and too ardent zeal to do the utmost for their principal may have blinded to the unbiassed merits of the case. Nor is it easy to believe that if the

---

his time, found leisure to interest himself in tracing the descent of a house with which his own family has long been connected (that of Keir obviously). Other portions of this volume have also been enriched by the kindness of Mr Dundas, in obtaining charters from the owners. Cosmo Innes, Esquire, ... *enlarged* Mr Dundas's account of the Keir family."

* A more just and eligible line of conduct, perhaps, the writer has afterwards suggested in the Exposition at p. 215.

latter had brought his intelligent mind to bear upon the subject—the materials for the purpose being so directly at his command—and made himself master of the Keir and Drumpellier's claims, he would have permitted the undue pretensions and allegations risked in the work circulated under his auspices to go forth to the world.

The writer humbly conceives that in this Exposition he has gone fully into details connected with the questions at issue in reference to the Stirlings of Cadder—now for the first time vainly attempted to be identified with Keir interests—perhaps too much so, and at too great length; but, at any rate, it is to be hoped, supplying *data* for due apprehension of the Drumpellier rights. Considering the impregnable and foreclosed position the Exponent occupies, as has been fully explained, ever since 1818, against all comers, he strictly was not required at all to notice the Keir Performance, or its invidious attacks, for it is out of the pale of law, besides refuted by the evidence—or rather utter want of evidence—of its own production. His having done so was merely to correct erroneous impressions that may, *ex facie*, unduly arise from the latter, and show how in reality his own case may stand.

So far the Exponent may now be regarded as *functus*; and, having fully accomplished his main object, he shall bid adieu to the topic, and in future abstain from making any such futile *brochure* or work the subject of comment or rejoinder, far less any of an anonymous kind, agreeably to existing approved practice. No party can here in the least complain; for if he think himself aggrieved, or to have a better claim to the Cadder status or representation than Drumpellier, or is able to qualify an interest in the matter (with all submission, however, it is thought rather difficult), he may at once have the most competent redress by betaking himself to the courts of law, and adopting 'the actual step of Drumpellier in 1818, which he therefore may consistently recommend, and that proved so successful to him, but hitherto quite precluded to Keir by the obvious irrelevancy and futility of his pretensions.

Before concluding, the writer must protest against the strange wayward fancy of ineptly and ludicrously stringing together in a pedigree, for its fictitious consolidation or aggrandisement, as father, or son, or in a near defined relationship, parties of old merely happening to have the same Christian name and surname, or the last exclusively, or even identifying them with one another, but who cannot legally be connected. The absurdity and irrelevancy must even strike a legal *tyro*. Yet we must add with regret, that the Keir Editor indulges in his lucubrations, in such practice, and here actually walks in the footsteps of Douglas.

We should remember, however, that true genealogy is an austere, stern potentate, governing by unswerving rigid laws, founded on truth only—knowing that thereby she can alone act with dignity and advantage; and not a reckless loose nymph or Bacchante, who, in her frolics, gives vent to every flattering tale and fable, to cajole and unduly elevate the credulous for her own profit and amusement of others, and to sallies of fancy and imagination. She would really seem the Empress Queen of the affections of our denounced genealogists, whom they are fain to follow in their peculiar sphere, instead of at once stopping their ears to her enthralling Circean music and fascinations, that have led so many astray.

CONTENTS.

CHAPTER I.

The recent Keir Performance, and preliminary remarks—Details evincing, *inter alia,* the necessity of the present Exposition, after provocation in that work, from the advisers of Keir, who is a stranger in the matter in question—General characteristics of the case, which is foreclosed in favour of Drumpellier, with other particulars, including armorial bearings, &c.*—Especially disclosing loose and secondary authorities of the Editor of the Keir Performance—His carelessness, besides often mere assumptions and misrepresentations, after the example of denounced Scotch genealogists—Exceptionable plan and conduct of the work—Confused and heterogeneous at the outset—The more objectionable when good models abroad might have been followed, such as the valuable recondite French histories and genealogies, and especially Sousa's magnificent history of the royal house of Portugal, a *chef-d'œuvre* of the kind—Two gross misrepresentations of the Drumpellier case in the Keir compilation—More precise details of the futile Keir opposition thereto in 1818,—so strikingly abandoned, after hostile vaunts, without any competition on their part—Family of Glorat, to whom Keir betook himself in his emergency, and sought to support him in secret against Drumpellier, proved but a frail reed, eventually unavailing—Indeed, now ungratefully stated in the Keir work, that there is "no evidence" of the exact or specific Glorat-Cadder descent, then so keenly backed by the Keir partisans against Drumpellier, and upon which alone these parties trusted for their purpose—Nevertheless, in the face of this, and insuperable obstacles, the former (while they here ignore Drumpellier, thus forcing him to self-defence) not only arrogate to the present Keir the Cadder representation, but usurp for him the Cadder armorial insignia with those of other families, to which he has no right, hazardously enough, as will be seen in the sequel—What is still more startling, they also suicidally and gratuitously abjure the original right of the Stirlings of Keir, and the *fibulati Strivelienses* (as they may be styled), to their heraldic buckles, but which the Exponent defends—while, moreover, giving them an extraneous descent—Remarkable absurdity of the Keir work as to the Cadder orthography, with another make-weight of little use, and palpable mistake of the arms of a distinct family for those of Stirling, ... 1-25

ADDENDA.

No. I.

(1.) Proof, *inter alia,* in the Keir Performance, of carelessness, and a striking, almost unprecedented, omission, or error, with respect to announced desirable evidence of the demise of the "ill-fated heiress of Cadder in 1588," together with adduction by the Exponent of original proof of the last genuine mention of the lady, . . 25, 26

(2.) And proof, again, that it (the Keir work) is careless in another particular, and ungrammatical, too, besides what will be elsewhere exposed, . . . 26, 27

---

* It has been judged proper and expedient, for a speedier and easier apprehension, to give here the titles and contents of the chapters more fully than in the text.

No. II.

The Stirlings of Craigbarnet or Craigbarnard, and evidence supplying a material deficiency at the outset of their pedigree in the Keir Performance, and substituting a true ancestor for the supposititious Duncan Stirling, foisted into the Glorat brief of service in 1818, to be afterwards noticed ; which, however, in truth enhances their antiquity, together with the high repute and importance of the Craigbarnet and Glorat families, of whom the latter are now heirs-male of the former, and inherit independently the direct representation of the noble houses of the Stewarts and Hepburns, *seriatim*, Earls of Bothwell, Lords Hailes, with other dignities, ... 27, 28

CHAPTER II.

THE DRUMPELLIER-CADDER "HEIRSHIP" AND REPRESENTATION.

State of the Cadder representation—That involves the question at issue—On the death of Andrew Stirling of Cadder, the last direct heir-male, in 1522—Primary steps of the Drumpellier family in 1817 and 1818 to assert their gentilitial rights and Cadder status—Relative correspondence between them and that of Keir in the above years—Abstract of their evidence then, with important conclusions, and additional corroborative proof —This chapter especially comprises, *inter alia* of importance—(1.) The correspondence between the Drumpellier and Keir families in reference to the Cadder descent and representation, with avowed determination of the latter to oppose the former ; and questions at issue from July 28, 1817, to February 20, 1818, including material journal (at pp. 45, 46), of William Stirling, younger of Drumpellier, 19th February in the same year, for which see p. 36 to 46—(2.) The printed statement or abstract of evidence in 1818 of the merits of the Drumpellier case, also bearing upon points at issue that were fairly communicated to Keir at the time—together with a few necessary explanations by the writer, for which see again p. 49 to p. 70, and—(3.) The remainder of the correspondence between the parties alluded to from March 6, 1818, to April 9, 1818 inclusive, and for which finally see p. 70 to p. 78, . . 29-96
The above correspondence is followed by conceived material inferences and conclusions, while the subject at large is closed by further evidence, illustrations, and arguments, corroborative of the Drumpellier claim upon the merits, besides what is adduced in the printed abstract cited in 1818, for which reference may be also made to p. 80 of this Chapter, down to p. 96.

ADDENDA.

No. I.

Decreet in 1535 in favour of Janet Stirling, heiress of Cadder, . . . 96-98
This comprises the incident of the ill-usage of the lady by Sir John Stirling of Keir, her forced and illegal union with James, his son, and undue conveyance, as may be inferred, of her estate, in 1541, to the latter, there being but little trust to be given to their statements and expositions in the matter, she being an unfortunate victim in their hands, much at their mercy, and subjected to their interested designs and machinations, or those of their tools.

No. II.

The strange suspicious collusive transaction is here discussed—or clandestine paction and settlement, with the mutual *quid pro quo*, in accordance with their views, between James Stirling of Keir and Thomas Bischop, in 1541, the import of which was accidentally derived by the Exponent from a copy taken long ago by a curious

CONTENTS.

antiquary, Mr Ramsay of Auchtertyre, from the Keir Inventory, but which the Keir Performance suspiciously again neither owns nor ventures to give from the original, which is carefully kept *in retentis*—Evident misrepresentation there as to adultery at the time—Probably used with more to coerce or frighten Janet of Cadder—who at any rate could not have been guilty of such alleged and pretended crime—into the designs of the parties, with other apprehended obvious remarks, both in reference to the document *ex facie*, to the lady and her situation, . . . 98-101

CHAPTER III.

CONSULTATIONS AND LEGAL STEPS OF PARTIES—WITH THE FINALE.

Minutiæ of legal procedure by the Drumpellier family in support of their Lettyr and Cadder rights and status—Including especially, at the outset, strenuous exertions of Keir for himself, and to thwart and oppose them—But, after much fruitless painful scrutiny and research, only evoking and conjuring up a ghastly and mysterious new personage, John Stirling of Bankeir, the true (though long-secreted) Keir representative, to the surprise and dismay of the Keir conclave—At length, as has been seen, desisted from—Explanation as to the said John, his status and peculiar history—The Keir advisers next induce Glorat legally and openly to oppose Drumpellier, though still acting clandestinely, and supplying him with the "sinews of war"—Drumpellier, however, in April 1818, successfully carries his service up to Lettyr, the main and more direct object, in the face of every opposing obstacle, but precluded from going into the merits of the Cadder question by a mere objection of Glorat in point of form, who, as well as Keir, dreaded such discussion—Drumpellier, however, here also eventually successful and unopposed, gained the full victory, Glorat even, in his turn, having abandoned the field—The case now, after the expiry, too, of the longest prescription of forty years and more, thus foreclosed to all against Drumpellier—Together with substantiation of other material facts formerly stated—Including gross misrepresentations in the Keir work against him and Janet of Cadder—With general remarks, &c., . . . 102-130

CHAPTER IV.

Is not Robert Stirling of Letter, the Drumpellier ancestor, identical with Robert Stirling, proved younger brother of William Stirling of Cadder in 1492 ?—What is required to fix this point ?—The inconsistent, and, as might be thought, suspicious mode of giving the Cadder writs and evidence in the Keir compilation—The transcendant and chivalrous Cadder crest in the above year, now unduly conjoined with an inferior one over the Keir shield of arms—Refutation again of the attack made in the same work upon the original and exclusive right of the *fibulati Strivelienses* to their armorial buckles—Palpable misrepresentation there of the antiquity of the Keir arms, not yet proved to have been borne prior to 1448—Further remarks on the subject of those of the northern Cawdors (including another misrepresentation there), who, in respect to their incidental armorial device, may be *in pari casu* with the Pelhams in England—With additional illustrations—And what may be the appropriate Stirling of Cadder and Keir bearings—That of the former preferable in just heraldry—While their representative was styled Stirling "of that Ilk," confirming their being chiefs of the Stirlings, in accordance with the Keir Performance, and a style now vested in Drumpellier as their heir, . . . 131-161

CHAPTER V.

KEIR PRETENSIONS, AND PEDIGREE.

Preliminary remarks, and exposition of undue assumption of the Stirling and Cadder status, as chief of the name, by Keir—With gross misrepresentations, &c. in the Keir Performance—Including usurpation there of the old Cadder crest, through which a fine and escheat of the work to the Crown is incurred by an Act of Parliament—The Keir origin and descent, though immaterial to the Drumpellier family, whose Cadder status has been fixed and recognised, nevertheless next gone into—The same uncertain—No clue thereto supplied by their first possessions, as in the Cadder and Drumpellier instances—John de Striwelyne, so simply styled (and never of Rathoran) in 1338, their presumed ancestor—Quite unappanaged, and solely indebted to his wife, a lady of family, for an interest in any lands, rather strangely settled exclusively upon her and her heirs—The settlement incidentally affords the only glimpse of John, of whose family, too, nothing transpires—A complete blank intervenes from thence down to 1414 and 1423—Refutation of erroneous representations and bare assumptions to the contrary in the Keir work—With impressions and inferences as to the Keir origin and descent *in hoc statu*—Luke Stirling of Ratherne (a small property, how acquired uncertain) an Armiger or Squire, and *artifex suæ fortunæ*, properly the Keir founder, a man of talent and respectability, from whom the Keir descent downwards is plain—the Keir family first baronial in 1473—Charge mooted against Sir William Stirling of Keir of being participant in the murder of James V., with some new evidence—Upon the whole, no proper proof yet of a Keir-Cadder descent, far less representation, that ought never to have been started—Keir origin still unascertained, and demanding investigation—New evidence meanwhile by the writer of the preceding Luke Stirling of Ratherne in 1414, and a property held by him, favourable to his rank and character, 162-186

ADDENDA.

No. I.

Full Copy in essentials of Grant by John de Ergadia, Lord of Lorn, to Mary, his father's sister, or his paternal aunt, of lands of Rathorane, &c., in 1338, with remarks upon its peculiar and unprecedented import, exclusive and privitive to the lady and irrespective of the husband, as shown or tested by other relevant instances, . . 187-189

No. II.

Proof refuting the Statement in the Keir Performance that John, Lord of Lorn, in 1338, nephew of Mary, wife of John de Strivelin, was " the last of the male line of the ancient Lords of Lorn," 189, 190

CHAPTER VI.

Futile attempts again of the Keir Performance, through their visionary ancestor, Sir William Stirling, before and after 1300—Who, though a broken reed, is unsuccessfully resorted to by the former in every emergency to connect the Keirs with the great *Vicecomites de Strivelin*—True deduction of the original ancestry and descent of the latter, the founders of the *fibulati Strivelienses*—Their ancient patrimonies, Uchiltrie and Cadder, so long in their line—Refutation of the preposterous efforts likewise of the Keir work to castrate or ignore as ancestors the earliest of the above *Vicecomites de Strivelin*, and to plant in their room certain motley nondescript Stirlings; and further still, to make the Keirs, still through their visionary ancestor, Sir William Stirling, their descendants and representatives, by a fabulous pedigree, eked back to 1130, the more to redound to the Keir antiquity and glory—All little worthy of serious discussion—Church tenure—The fief of Cadder, so long the heirloom of the *fibulati Strivelienses*, singularly a barony held of a bishop and archbishop, vested with the high powers of a Regality or Palatinate, of which there are a few parallel instances in England and Scotland—Sir John de Strivelin, the Scottish renegade and English knight and baron, who figured before the middle of the fourteenth century and afterwards—Crude and absurd notion, if intelligible, of his origin in the Keir work—With general remarks and conclusion, . . 191-217

CONTENTS. xvii

ADDENDA.

No. I.

Statement of the peculiar legal custom of "Saint Mungo," or "Saint Mungo's Widow," in the Diocese of Glasgow, curiously illustrated by legal practice in 1532, in the very case then cited from record of Marion Fleming, the widow of Alan Heriot, proprietor of lands there, and subsequent wife of Robert Stirling of Bankeir and Letter, the Drumpellier ancestor, reported by Sir James Balfour, Lord President then of the Court of Session, in his *Practiques of the Law of Scotland*, and deemed worthy of special notice by Chalmers in his *Caledonia*, ... 218, 219

No. II.

The See of Glasgow a Regality or Regal Barony, and Cadder holding of it as a Barony, proved by what follows, *ibid.*, ... 219, 220

No. III.

Allusion here to the Ragman Roll in 1292 and 1296, as yet inadequately given or illustrated, with a suggestion of its being a good *medium*, together with natural and accessible accessories, for minute and interesting accounts of Scotch families, . 220, 221

No. IV.

Singular instance of the Keir Editor in effect also ignoring the writer and others on the occasion of the Winton Service in 1840, precisely as the leading features and merits of the Drumpellier case in the Keir Performance, ... 221-223

This involves the progress of the case of the Service of the Earl of Eglinton, as heir-male of the Earls of Winton, from 1825 to 1840, how it originated, and who were throughout its main and sole legal conductors to the exclusion of any others, in refutation of what may follow from a narrow, inadequate, or biassed statement thereof in a recent work of the Editor.

CHAPTER VII.

Biographical and historical sketches and notices of the preceding Sir John Stirling of Keir and Thomas Bischop, who acted such important parts in reference to the Cadder Family and otherwise, both publicly and privately, ... 224-249

   I. Sir John Stirling of Keir (1503-1539), . . . 224, 234
   II. Thomas Bischop, Armiger (his chivalrous and due style), . 234-249

ADDENDA.

No I.

Remarkable instance, in the seventeenth century, of the dangerous influence and attractions of sons of Edinburgh burgesses with the higher and most beautiful of the fair sex, ... 250, also partly 253

CONTENTS.

No. II.

Respectability formerly of tailors in Scotland, and cases of members of good and even high families following, even as late as last century, secondary professions and trades, restricted now to the lower orders, exemplified in the instances of Hommyl in 1477, and families of Mowbray of Cockairney, Brodie, Seaton of Garltoun, and Primrose, ... 251-253

Drumpellier, Bankeir, and Lettyr Pedigree or Genealogical Table (marked No. I.), . 254

Genealogical Tree, deduced partly from statements in the recent work, *The Stirlings of Keir and their Family Papers*, and legal authorities of the Exponent (as explained in Exposition, p. 49, note *), in reference to the more immediate objects in view—the Cadder Family, including that of Carse—Sir William Stirling in 1270, 1295, the *putative* Keir ancestor—as also to the Keir family—showing how the descent and pedigree of the latter precisely stand at present (marked No. II.), . . 255, 256

GENERAL APPENDIX.

No. I.

Exposition of the errors, dishonesty, and malpractices of Douglas, the Peerage writer, in his statements and deductions of Scottish pedigrees, ... 257

No. II.

Original evidence of the first Hameldon or Hamilton settler in Scotland, and his possessing lands there, with incidental remarks about the origin of the Scotch Hamiltons, ... 258, 259

Explanatory Note as to case of Riddell against Brymer in 1811, in regard to the ignorance of a lawful impediment to a marriage *de facto* and putative, by *only* one of the parties, making their offspring lawful, though not upholding their union—involving, too, that of Sir James Stirling of Keir, Janet Stirling, Lady of Cadder, and their lawful son, John Stirling of Wester Bankeir, with authority showing that Scotch modern legal doctrine was likewise, last century, in favour of such legitimacy long subsequently to the Reformation in 1560, within which conclusively favourable epoch, however, the case of the latter comes, ... 259, 260

Since a statement made in the Contents, see p. v., line 2d from foot, the writer is most happy now to add, that a copy of "The Stirlings of Keir and their Family Papers" was, 10th of June 1859, sent Mr Stirling of Drumpellier, by the Honourable Member for Perthshire, with polite regret that he had not got it sooner (since its *first* circulation, as far back as September 6, 1858*)—owing to a mistake or omission of the Keir Editor, accidental according to the latter.

* See Keir Performance, Prefatory Note, p. iii., the true date, instead of Dec. 28, 1858, as in page referred to of Exposition.

CORRIGENDA ET ADDENDA.

Page 42, line 11.—For "second" heir, read "served" heir.

... 12, ... 3.—Even if it be explicitly proved that Craigbernard recognised Keir as chief, that might not be conclusive, *chief* not being held (as was maintained in a case) *nomen juris*, nor always *per se* denoting direct blood representation. The well-known Scotch designation "of that Ilk," pre-eminently applied to a family, and, as has been seen, to the Stirlings of Cadder, is much more significant and unequivocal in such respect.

... 107, note.—Further, to show the backneyed and confessed technical import of "natural and lawful," the Imperial Crown of France, by the organic decree in 1852, is eventually settled on Jerome Napoleon Buonaparte and his direct descendants, "natural and legitimate," certainly including the lawful only, and technically affixing such exact sense to the words.

... 132, line second from foot.—A charter in a private charter-chest, dated Linlithgow, June 2, 1479, to Robert Livingstone, son and heir-apparent of Henry Livingstone of Middlebinning, "*et Jonete Strevelyne, sponse sue*," is witnessed also by "*Magistris Humfridro Strivelyne*, et patricio were, vicario de benyng, Willelmi Strev . . . Ka . . ." (evidently, though partly obliterated by time, William Strivelin of Kader); the whole, we may conclude, a Livingstone and Stirling of Cadder family transaction.

... 150, paragraph 3.—Of course the argument of the *plain* bend in favour of Cadder is relevantly based upon Sir David Lindsay's Matriculation Register in the reign of James V., the unexceptionable ruling authority—irrespective of what may have in part erroneously preceded—and with which the subsequent heraldic practice and understanding are ever in conformity; the bend *ingrailed* being then, too, as clearly and uniformly the exclusive *distinctive* Keir bearing.

... 175, line 12.—For "delecto armigero nostro," read "dilecto armigero nostro."

... 206, paragraph 2.—There still remains, it seems, another gross misrepresentation to be exposed in the Keir work, it not being easy to exhaust them. At p. 66, ibid., it is actually affirmed that "the lands of Ochiltrees, in the parish and county of Linlithgow . . . . probably first became the property of *the family* (of *Keir, undoubtedly, it being here exclusively discussed*) in the 12th or 13th century!" when they certainly only first were acquired by them at the much later epoch of 1541, by the *noted* transaction, then sufficiently spoken to. Nor is this a solitary instance of the kind; there is, over and above, forsooth, the equally unfounded and flagrant one of the acquisition of Cadder by Keir at the same distant period, palpable enough in the page referred to. Neither has the Keir editor (in keeping with his usual fashion) adduced any authority of Ochiltrees being in the Stirlings in the 12th century, and he may be unaware of the curious and interesting deeds regarding it in the Chartulary of the Priory of St Andrews.—(See *Expos.*, pp. 194-5,) as he quotes not a word of it, or has more than the above of such ancient Stirling tenure of the fief by Cadder solely, not by Keir.

... 212, two last paragraphs, *ib.*—By authentic legal evidence adduced by Hodgson, in his recondite History of Northumberland, Sir John de Strivelin, the Scoto-Anglo Knight, was infeoffed 31st of Ed. III. (1357) in the Manour of Camboys, &c., and the 41st of the same monarch (1367), other lands, including Bedelynton, were granted "prefato Johanni de Strevelyn, et *Johanni filio suo* JAM DEFUNCTO,"[1] thus introducing us to his son of the same name, who had predeceased. Hodgson has equally established that the Knight, and Joan his wife, styled one of the three co-heiresses of Richard de Emeldon, in the first of Richard II. (1377), had lands in Holforth, which they settled upon John de Middleton, and Christian, his wife.[2]

It is proved, by an English record in the text,[3] that in 1364 the fealty "Johannis de Strivelyn, chivaler qui duxit *in uxorem Jacobam tertiam* filiarum Richardi de Emeldon defuncti de pro parte sua manerii de Jermuth."[4] This Jacoba must evidently be the same with the preceding Joan de Emeldon. And lastly, it is proved, by an inquisition (in perfect concurrence with Hodgson) by Wallis, in his history of the same county,[5] that Sir John died, 2d of Richard II. (1378), infeoffed, "cum uxore sua," who must still have been the same lady, in the Manor of Burnton there.

He was evidently opulent, and a large proprietor, independently of the inheritances of his two wives, Barbara de Swinburne, and Joan de Emeldon, both co-parceners, having acquired various grants of lands, from Edward III. (with whom he was in high favour), as well as certain parties in Northumberland, while utterly estranged from any Berwick burgesses or ancestry, so absurdly introduced with him as if connections, in the Keir Performance, under the head of the "Sir John de Striveling" in question.[6]

[1] Vol. ii., Part ii. p. 5.

[2] P.316, note.

[3] See Expos. p. 212.

[4] The same with Jessmouth.

[5] See vol. ii. p. 541.

[6] See Keir Performance, p. 195.

CORRIGENDA ET ADDENDA.

Barbara de Swinburne figures in Hodgson as eldest daughter and co-heiress of her distinguished family in 1327,[1] and, he adds, was succeeded by Sir John de Strivelin, certainly her spouse, from whom her property descended to the Middletons of Belsay. He has explicitly stated that the knight died without issue[2]—of course, by either of his wives, Barbara or Joan, the last of whom survived him; and represents the preceding John de Middleton and Christian his wife as taking Belsay and other parts of his property by what we would call a singular title,[3] under a special destination; but he seems not to be borne out by his evidence here. He infers that he had died childless in 1374; because, by an authority he adduces from an English record,[4] Edward III. is there proved, owing to such conceived reason, to have granted his lands of Flaxfleat in Yorkshire to Sir John de Surry. This, however, could not be, seeing it is legally established by Wallis, and elsewhere even admitted by Hodgson, that the knight did not die till 1378, the true year of his death; and the authority in question only imports a grant to Surry of Flaxfleat, which it states, "Johannes de Strivelin, chivaler, tenet (thus *at the moment*) *ad terminum vitæ*," without the least notice of his death as its inductive cause, that must have been in virtue of a transaction between the parties. Added to the above, Hodgson[5] further informs us that the "Tower of Belsay was the residence of John de Middleton, chevalier, in the reign of Henry V.; and as it has the arms of Middleton *impaling Strivelin* (which, it is to be regretted, he does not describe), I think it probable (he says) that it was built by him and *Christian* his *wife*, in the time of Edward III." These are the material persons who have been noticed, and hence Christian, from *such impalement of her* arms, evidently as John's wife, being a de *Strivelin*, must, instead of a stranger, have either been Sir John Stirling's daughter (as has been represented), or a near relative—supported, too, by his grants and devolutions of his property in her favour. Be this as it may, Hodgson[6] has legally established that the lady by the said John left issue John Middleton, who, by an inquisition in 1397, was found to be their heir.

Upon the whole, the matter here requires some more elucidation—it thus not being quite clear, as stated in the Exposition,[7] that Sir John left by Barbara Swinburne, his first wife, "female descendants, who continued his line;" and it being entirely English, may be best left to the study and scrutiny of an English antiquary, having access to the proper English records. "That he (the knight, in the mean time, contenting ourselves with this closing quotation from Hodgson)[8] resided much in the *county* (*Northumberlandshire*) is plain, from the figuring of his name as a witness to charters; and the high consideration in which he was holden may be inferred from his generally standing at the head of lists of witnesses."

Abstracting from his treason, he certainly was a distinguished, and probably meritorious person, besides his unimpeached descent (there being nothing of the burgess in it);[9] and his rank as an English baron, he was employed by Edward III. in Continental warfare, and intrusted by that monarch with the most important posts and commands in Scotland, where he acquired considerable fame. In particular, he gallantly measured swords with Sir William Douglas of Liddisdale, "the flower of chivalry," as he was pre-eminently styled, who, however, in 1338, as Fordun[10] transmits, though not until *after* "DICTUM *etiam conflictum apud* Craggis de Craggin, *cepit, ac devicit dominum Johannem de Strivelin ;*" as also his "*quingentos Strivelinos*"—a victory, doubtless, that gave additional laurels to the former. Winton, in his account of the battle,[11] states that Douglas then

"Fawcht wyth Jhon of Stryvelyne,
That wes of *Edynburch Capitane*,
And tuk hym thare wyth MEKIL PAYNE ;"

which identifies him with our Sir John, the Scoto-Anglo knight, who, shortly before, in 1335, had obtained from his now liege lord, Edward III., "*officium Vicecomitatus de Edeneburghe cum pertinentiis ac castrum nostrum ibidem custodiendi quamdiu nobis placuerit,*"[12] of course Edinburgh Castle, in a manner the key of the kingdom, of which he hence was keeper or captain. How he was liberated, after the "direful" battle at the Craigs of Craggin in 1338, or how his capture can be otherwise verified, is unknown.

Pages 255, 256, Pedigree marked No. II.—"Sir John de Striveling, Kngt., Lord of Curse and Alva," is made here the *father* of Marjory, married in 1357 to John Menteith, ancestor of the Monteiths of Carse; but this is erroneous, there having been, as can be legally proved, *intermediate* generations to Marjory; and such intimation is merely given because introduced into the Keir work, for the entirety of whose statements, as the writer has pointedly intimated, he is of course not answerable.

---

[1] History, vol. ii. Part ii. p. 233.
[2] Ibid., vol. i. Part ii. p. 357.
[3] Ibid.
[4] Abbreviatio Rotulorum Originalium in curia Scaccarii, vol. ii. p. 351.
[5] Vol. i. Part ii. p. 350.
[6] Ibid., pp. 302-3.
[7] See Expos., p. 209.
[8] History, vol. i. Part ii. p. 357.
[9] See Keir Performance, ut supra.
[10] See Scotochronicon, edit. Goodal, vol. ii. p. 339.
[11] See Macpherson's Edit., vol. ii. p. 227.
[12] Rot. Scot., vol. i. p. 382.

COMMENTS, &c.

CHAPTER I.

THE RECENT KEIR PERFORMANCE, AND PRELIMINARY REMARKS—DETAILS EVINCING, *inter alia*, THE NECESSITY OF THE PRESENT EXPOSITION, AFTER PROVOCATION IN THAT WORK. FROM THE ADVISERS OF KEIR, WHO IS A STRANGER IN THE MATTER IN QUESTION—GENERAL CHARACTERISTICS OF THE CASE, WHICH IS FORECLOSED IN FAVOUR OF DRUMPELLIER, WITH OTHER PARTICULARS, INCLUDING ARMORIAL BEARINGS, ETC.

SELDOM, perhaps, may Scotch antiquaries, especially those addicted to gentilitial or genealogical inquiries, family histories, or memorials, have been more interested than they doubtless were at a first survey of the work recently printed and circulated, entitled "THE STIRLINGS OF KEIR AND THEIR FAMILY PAPERS."

It comprises a thickish *smaller* quarto—*comparatively* speaking—of rather unsymmetrical proportions—"dumpy," we would almost say, so denounced by Byron in the case of the female form—for which we are indebted to the liberality and munificence of Mr Stirling of Keir, the eminent and accomplished representative of the above; and we certainly concur in hoping, with the editor,[1] that the "example thus set—probably the first work of the kind executed by a Scotch proprietor at his own sole charge—may yet be generally followed by the owners of other ancient charter-chests." Not only are such performances valuable and interesting in regard to their main object—the descents and connections of families, their fate and private fortunes—

[1] See work referred to, Preface, p. xv.

they often further contribute, by means of writs and muniments first disclosed, important facts and information in the broader and more public departments of history and law, especially consistorial. But then, such works must not be hastily or inadequately undertaken—careless or inaccurate—but, on the other hand, duly compiled and matured—grammatical withal, and without unfair bias, make-weights, and platitudes—charges to which, it is to be regretted, in a certain degree, the Keir Performance may be obnoxious,* and with a decided selection of what is truly new and material, else they may sadly disappoint expectations, and injure the very cause they design to serve.

Mere assumption and gratuitous inferences also—singularly not yet sufficiently exploded with us, and in which our antiquarian writers formerly indulged—should especially be substituted, in this more enlightened age, by strict and apposite reasoning built on sound and relevant facts, after the bright precedent and example set us by Lord Hailes, in all antiquarian discussions—including genealogy—to which flights of fancy, not unseldom their chief basis, are alien. He, and those distinguished in the same sure track, are the only authorities and models to be adopted on such occasions, to the complete exclusion of secondary manipulators like Douglas, Playfair, &c., and that much-to-be-deprecated class who did so much last century to bring Scotch pedigrees and private histories into discredit and disrepute. The first, the callous or unwitting bastardiser of the Hamiltons, the strange result of his undue venal attempts to enhance their Scotch antiquity,† is the Coryphæus of tricks and sad devices in his native genealogy, whose dishonest and unprincipled practices in that department are

---

* For example, in part, of such, on the grounds of carelessness and strange omissions, with grammatical error, see ADDENDA to this Chapter, under No. I., with relative particulars. It is proposed, in the course of this Exposition, to throw all notes, with their subjects and evidence, too long for paginal insertion, into the ADDENDA.

† WALTER FITZGILBERT DE "HAMELDON," of the county of Lanark, who swore fealty to Edward I. in 1296,[1] like so many of his Scotch compatriots, is the earliest ancestor legally proved of the Lanarkshire Hamiltons, or of Cadzow, or noble house of Hamilton, their pretended descent from an English Earl of Leicester antecedently, by genealogists, being too preposterous and untenable for a moment's notice. Douglas, however, while he also palms off this fable, in order to add a few inches to their Scotch antiquity makes the above patriarch Gilbert figure as early as 1272, by means of a grant then of the church of Cragyn to the Abbey of Paisley, witnessed, as he states, by "Gilbertus de Hambleton, Walterus, Seneschallus Scotie, Comes de Menteth."[2] There is nothing in support of the identity of the latter Gilbert with the preceding; and further still, upon examination of his authority, the Chartulary of Paisley,[3] it will be found that he merely figures in the grant, not, as above, first witness, even before the Earl of Menteth (there grossly misrepresented also by Douglas, as Stewart of

[1] See Ragman Roll, Bannatyne Club copy, p. 166.

[2] Referred to by Douglas as in the Chartulary of Paisley. See his Peerage, first edition, vol. i. p. 327.

[3] Maitland Club Publication, p. 32

capable of the fullest detection and exposition, and have recently, too, in a remarkable degree, been exposed by Chalmers in his *Caledonia*.*

And however, singularly enough, still a popular and even favourite authority of some, in all his guises, and quoted and relied upon in the recent Keir performance for a material Keir connection,† he may not be much exceeded, in his *peculiar* bent, even by Guthrie, the cotemporary English Peerage writer, ‡ so lashed and stigmatised by Churchill : [1]

> "*Is there not* GUTHRIE ?—Who, like him, can call
> *All opposites to truth*, and *conquer all ?*
> He calls forth *living* waters from *the rock :*
> He calls forth *children* from *the* BARREN *stock ;*
> He, far *beyond* the springs of *nature* led,
> Makes women bring forth after they are dead ;
> He, on a curious, new, and happy plan,
> In wedlock's sacred band joins man to man ;
> And, to complete the whole, most strange but true,
> By some rare magic makes them fruitful too ;
> Whilst from their loins, in the due course of years,
> *Flows the rich blood of* GUTHRIE'S ENGLISH PEERS."

[1] Poems under "The Author," edit. 1766, vol. ii. pp. 39, 40.

The preceding, at the outset, curiously too, may not either be inappropriate to what will transpire in the sequel from the Keir editor's lucubrations. In like manner, it may be said that he largely and miraculously, in genealogy,

> " Calls forth children from the *barren* stock,"

Scotland, which he was not, nor is so there styled), but in his wake as a humble churchman after others of his calling, a vicar, two chaplains, and the rector of a parish, under the significant description, "*Gilberto de Hameldon*, CLERICO," the import of which term, as a mere ecclesiastic or churchman, at the period, is sufficiently clear. To prevent the knowledge, however, of which untoward adjunct, the same notable writer—will it be credited ?—in his excerpt from the Chartulary, *entirely suppresses it*, and represents this Gilbert as a laic, and evidently of condition, from his *false* insertion or interpolation, as first witness in the testing clause. It need not be added that, if so descended from this clerical Gilbert Hameldon, according to Douglas, of which there is not the slightest evidence, the house of Hamilton would not only be of low, but of *spurious* origin. But this is not the only instance of such dishonesty or malpractices by the former,—more of the kind will be found against him in the next reference to his iniquities noticed in the text under No. I. in the general APPENDIX to this work. But for new original evidence of the first Hameldon or Hamilton, settler in Scotland, and his possessing lands there, see also ibid., No. II.

* For proof of all these charges, both by the writer and Chalmers against Douglas, see No. I. of APPENDIX referred to.

† See ibid., pp. 26-7, but carelessly, without giving the page in Douglas.

‡ *Douglas's Peerage* was published in 1764, thus only two years before the lines in reference to Guthrie by Churchill.

in his quasi-obstetric or philoprogenitive propensities,—after the precedent of Douglas, also,—to eke out or prolong a genealogy, or make it cohesive; while, in attempting *his* Cadder descent for Keir, and in certain misrepresentations, it may be added that he risks "all opposites to truth," and as victoriously "conquers all" in his teeming fancy.

It would indeed be a subject of deep regret, and to be lamented, were we now to countenance, or relapse into, such notable failings or propensities, reducing these matters of antiquity to a state of chaos or Cimmerian darkness; or, like the Keir editor—again after the fashion of Douglas,[1] moreover, in whose track he occasionally follows in mere assumptions and misrepresentations, though of course not in his expedients or dishonest devices—adduce trivial or denounced writers or authorities in substantiation of ancient facts. Of this class is that most distinguished and most credible writer, Mr John Fairbairn, so late as 1636, under whose wing alone, at some length, doubtless to the surprise and dismay of many, the Keir editor,[2] at the very outset of his work, *Icarus*-like, attempts his callow flight into the remote sphere of the origin of the Stirlings, and just with the similar success that might be expected. And further, Ferrerius, but a needy foreigner who misrepresented Scotch history to save himself from starving; and of whom Lord Hailes says (while elsewhere stigmatising him), that "it would be endless to remark all his errors; some of them, however, (being) so flagrant that they cannot be past unobserved."[3] Yet, strange again, the editor, or his coadjutors, pointedly adduce him, in a controverted point of history, to "exculpate" Sir William Stirling of Keir "from any direct participation in the murder of James III.:"[4] that worthy indeed, as here to be relied upon, who, in writing history, where truth and honesty have been deemed of some avail, inculcates this convenient doctrine, that "*Absit* TANTUM MENDACIUM *illum quod ab omnibus facile deprehenditur*"[5]—namely, to avoid that falsehood only, easily to be detected by all, with the implied converse, that otherwise you may falsify or be mendacious as you choose! He here, nevertheless, is a kind of sheet-anchor in the Keir Performance, and whom, with the secondary Abercromby in his *Martial Atchievements of the Scottish Nation*,[6] written, as late as 1711, popular chiefly with the vulgar, and Hawthornden,[7] it cites for the express purpose in view; and how cogently, and with what real effect, may be afterwards seen.

In probation, indeed, of the most ancient facts, the work resorts to the

---

[1] See his Works.

[2] See Keir Performance, under "Origin of the Stirlings," pp. 1, 2.

[3] See his Disquisition on *Regiam Majestatem*, Annals of Scotland, edit. 1797, vol. iii. p. 304.

[4] See Keir Performance, p. 26.

[5] See Lord Hailes's Annals, *ut supra*, pp. 299, 300.

[6] See Keir Work, pp. 25, 26.

[7] Ibid.

most modern *authorities*—if we can use the last term on the occasion—being fain, in explanation of "the ancient name of Stryveling," to quote the idle and childish supposition of Nimmo[1] (here rather synonymous with *Nemo* or *nil*), in his *History of Stirling*, published but in our day, in 1817, that it was from the term signifying "strife,"—seemingly, *par excellence*, as if strife was more peculiar to that town, and the other Scotch towns or cities less obnoxious to the charge! What greater platitudes and make-weights? And will it be credited that the obscure and twaddling Fairbairn—or *pulchra proles*, as he might have been Latinised by the punning practice of his century, notoriously introduced by James VI.*—with the modern Nimmo, are the sole writers whom the Keir Performance can adduce on the origin of Stirling or the Stirlings.

[1] See Keir Work, under the "Origin of the Stirlings," p. 2, note.

The same Keir work or compilation with which we have been favoured, under the auspices of the honourable member for Perthshire, professes to give, in the first place, a full pedigree of the Strivelins or Stirlings, especially including the chief and principal line of Cadder, which is also affirmed, from the reign of William the Lyon, to have "continued in the family" (that is, in *one* and the *same* original Stirling stock, from the context)[2] "without *interruption* to the present time." This, like similar assertions, as may transpire in the sequel, cannot justly be maintained, seeing Cadder actually, on the other hand, was interrupted in its original Stirling descent; it indubitably having diverged therefrom through a singular title in 1541, as will also be shown, for the *first* time, to the distinct race of Keir (as must be presumed *in hoc statu*), with whom only subsequently it has "without interruption" remained.

[2] See Preface to Keir Work, p. x.

The Keir editor, too, at the outset of his performance,[3] after stating the loss the Keir family had sustained of their old documents by the burning of the Tower of Keir in 1488 (comprised in their ancient patrimony of Auld or Old Keir,[4] subsequently alienated, in 1527, to undoubted Drumpellier ancestry, who were infeft therein for a time), adds, that "the Stirling family have *continued* in possession of the barony of Keir *ever since*"—which is thus, certainly, in part refuted; and, moreover, that they "acquired many other properties, each acquisition bringing with it the usual feudal progress of title-deeds, including those of their *earliest* inheritance of Cadder." This

[3] See Ibid., p. ix.
[4] To be afterwards fully proved.

* Greek also was sometimes here called into play, the cotemporary *Godscroft*, historian of the houses of Douglas and Angus, being then styled *Theagrius*.

passage, like others in the work, is not so distinctly or definitely worded as it might be. If it intends to intimate, as might appear, that Cadder was in fact their earliest inheritance, or rather patrimony, that is clearly refuted by the work elsewhere proving that they had acquired other properties antecedently to Cadder, in which, as has just been stated, they were only first seised under a singular title in 1541.

At the same time, the pedigree cited from the Keir Performance includes the stock of Keir proper, and a statement of each successive generation. Next thereafter is "an account of the branches of the Stirling family, and of several families connected with the Stirlings, at least by name."[1] But then this is *preceded* by what is too curtly and indistinctly entitled an "Abstract of *the charters*," &c.,* or premonitory kind of index, not amounting, on the whole, to an ordinary full inventory, subsequent to which, though with the strange and awkward *intervention* of the above pedigree and branches, only come the "*charters*," &c., *themselves*, in the shape of a heterogeneous mass of writs and muniments, in reference to sundry Stirlings of different origins, and, moreover, to distinct families; while, lastly, after this sort of hodge-podge, are the Keir births and marriages, &c., with their letters, that form, perhaps, the most curious and interesting portion of the work. With the latter, however, the present Exposition does not deal, only confining its criticism or remarks to the earlier or more ancient contents.

The better plan, in the case of this heterogeneous assemblage of writs and muniments—adduced, it must be confessed, rather in pell-mell confusion—and saving us the necessity, in consequence, too often to wander in quest of necessary facts and information through a species of labyrinth actually from p. 197 to 472 inclusive, might have been their arrangement in this way, under distinct and appropriate heads, according to their contents:—

I. The *oldest* at the outset, generally affecting the Stirlings;

II. Those exclusively the chief line of Stirling of Cadder downwards, with their cadets;

III. Those, in like manner, Keir;

IV. Those similarly as to Craigbarnet, &c., and not overlooking cadets either: and so on, whether in regard to other Stirlings, or strangers introduced

[1] See Keir Performance, Preface, p. ix.; and History, at p. 83 *et seq.*

---

* The "Abstract" in question, with its title, regularly should have been after the pedigree or account of the Stirlings, and intervening separate pedigrees again, and immediately before the heterogeneous mass of writs to which it directly and exclusively refers.

somewhat like make-weights, of whom there are not few in the same collection; while there might have been, besides, a separate *index materiarum*, or what is essential or deserving notice, historical, legal, or genealogical.

The mere index of names and places at the end of the Keir Performance, though certainly, in its way, so far useful and serviceable, being of course limited and restricted, does not meet or advance the objects in view.

A strange mode of reference or quotation, too, may be observed throughout the work. A writ or muniment is there *first* quoted by its number *before* the page wherein it is contained, though, in order to expiscate the former, you certainly must *first* find the latter. This seems against all reason and propriety—really, borrowing rather a homely illustration, like putting the cart before the horse.

It is remarkable that the French, though deemed more prone to light and superficial works, however lively and original, and flights of imagination, besides the Germans and Italians, supply us with the best examples and rules to be adopted in graver matters like the present, apparently out of their beat and sphere. They might here, as the *beau ideal*, have been submitted to the attention of the Keir compilers; in support of which, reference may be made to the elaborate and valuable histories of Montmorency and Laval in 1623 (besides later ones), of Chastillon previously in 1621, and of Dreux in 1631, all by Du Cheue; to which may be added the *Histoire Genealogique de la maison d'Auvergne* in 1708, by the distinguished antiquary Baluzius, as well as those of a still higher class of the princely houses of Brittany, Burgundy, and Dauphiny, not to add Lorraine, familiar to French authorities, all before the middle of last century, and some considerably so.[*]

The preceding are especially interesting and well digested. In the closing portion or volumes, besides engravings of seals and portraits of the leading

---

[*] Perhaps, under such a superior category, the best and fullest history is that of the Royal House of Portugal (immeasurably before Anselme's of the Maison Royale de France in 1726), by Sousa, that was published at Lisbon from 1735 to 1749, the time spent in the compilation. It comprises fourteen folio volumes, the last being a useful index, unfolding the various alliances and royal ramifications with all deserving attention. But further still, there are six other folio relative volumes containing the ever-delightful *Provas* or *Preuves*, precisely as in France; and among many antiquarian attractions are the legal vouchers for the marriage, in 1405, of Beatrix, daughter of John, king of Portugal, to Thomas, earl of Arundel in England. She was sister of the first Duke of Braganza, ancestor of that royal and imperial house. Brunet styles the above, filling in all twenty volumes, "Ouvrage capital dans son genre," and hence a good model to be adopted. Every one of the performances quoted have pedigrees or genealogical tables, indispensable to a speedy apprehension of the contents, with portraits of the most distin-

or distinguished parties discussed, are the ever-inestimable "PREUVES" and family writs, arranged in good order, such as might have been adopted in the Keir work. They are usually in value above what is in that compilation, constituting of themselves a full, varied chartulary of complete documents, never imperfectly given, or as in a summary translated form, and sometimes out of place, as occasionally in the latter; while they also not unfrequently let out original facts and information important to other countries, even including Scotland.

In the Keir work, too, there is a striking solecism in the utter want of genealogical tables or trees of any kind, so useful for a quick perception of the descents—whether of leading families discussed, or of others, certainly not few in number, though, as has been proved, never omitted abroad on such occasions, and as little with us either in peerage cases, or in those of the most ordinary kind.

Such marked deviation from so salutary a practice is to be regretted, as the malicious might suggest it was prudentially to exclude the more palpable detection of errors and misrepresentations in the work in question, where they certainly occur, and therefore requiring to be somewhat veiled and not made too apparent.

The Keir miscellany, as it may be styled, is, besides, graced and adorned by pictorial gems and illustrations, selected, as might be expected, with the taste and discrimination that distinguish the honourable member for Perthshire, including old and modern family portraits, autographs, coloured views of residences, their rural beauties and embellishments, blazonry, and coats of arms in all the hues and tints of the rainbow. But amid such gorgeous sights,

guished persons. This may be better, perhaps, than the indiscriminate expedient of giving such often without reference to fame and distinction. The Keir editor's recent lucubrations must indeed follow those of the kind thus noted, *longo intervallo.*

In the genealogy "of the sovereign house," de la Tour, published at Brussels in 1709—a remarkable and rather splendid performance of three folio volumes of the largest size, besides portraits, and abundant genealogical tables—the arms of the descendants are given together with their names, while behind their shields they are even represented, *in propria persona,* in their public or official dresses, whether as princes, bishops, abbesses, nuns, nobility, generals, &c. The effect is good, and might, to a certain degree, be adopted by us in future better-compiled Scotch family histories. Portraits in such works, in ordinary modern costume, have but a sorry appearance; and when of parties neither eminent nor famous, without disparagement of such in the Keir editor's lucubrations, occasionally suggest to us but ludicrous impressions—even of

"Tenth possessors of a foolish face,"

embalmed in Savage's noted lines, notwithstanding every laudable effort to restrain our muscles or a smile.

such dazzling and glittering attractions—the flower of the charter-chest, and flowers of the parterre—

—" Media de parte *laboris*,*
Surgit amari aliquid, quod in ipsis floribus angat." †

Of which, indeed, the Stirlings of Drumpellier have to complain. For in the middle portion of the *common* work or labour,[1] besides in no small degree elsewhere, however unmerited and uncalled for, there is much certainly of the *amari* in their regard. The former contains two gross errors and misrepresentations, so far as the proper and obvious import of words may go. (1.) That the family of Drumpellier, in fact, failed to establish their claim as the Stirling of Cadder heirs, through a question of identity, represented as submitted to a court in 1818 : and (2.) That they since then had no further prosecuted it.

[1] See Keir Performance, p. 179-181.

Than these there cannot be conceived more erroneous and unfounded charges, or more unjustly to their prejudice. They never here sustained any such defeat upon the merits of that claim, which was not then gone into, or otherwise, so as in the least to affect or compromise it. On the contrary, while they always courted and solicited the utmost discussion, so strong and irresistible was their Cadder right and status that none have ventured on that head to meet or join issue with them. The question, indeed, may be now barred and foreclosed in the manner to be stated ; but it was exclusively against the opponents of the family of *Drumpellier*—not against *them*—the result and victory in the matter being irretrievably in their favour.

It will be here incumbent to go somewhat into details.

When the Drumpellier-Cadder status was first mooted, and the family took legal steps to establish it, and courteously apprised that of Keir of such intention, they were met by them with bold language indeed, and an announced determined opposition. But they found upon inquiry, to their no small surprise, that they had here no case or interest ; neither did they in the least then, as now, *pretend to be of Cadder* ; and their legal agents or advisers, after a keen and protracted investigation, availing themselves also of what the Drumpellier had liberally imparted—a mode of conduct which, it is to be regretted, afforded a striking contrast to the pertinacious withholding of any information on the other side—at length abandoned the competition on

Announced determination by the Keir family to oppose steps by Drumpellier to establish his Cadder status in 1818.

---

* "*Leporum*" is the original here travestied, as well as two other words.   † "Some *bitter* bubbles up, and e'en on roses stings."—BYRON.

the part of their client, and forbore directly to move in a matter that has ever since been legally barred to him and his representatives.

But they soon abandoned their opposition, which was next attempted by Glorat, through Keir's means.

But then there was still a means indirectly on his part to thwart and impede Drumpellier in his object—though momentary, as it proved—by inducing the knightly family of Glorat, after some demur and disinclination—upon pretence of a counter-Cadder descent, which Keir then warmly backed and supported—legally to oppose the former, Keir supplying Glorat with the means and "sinews of war:" while thus himself, too, opening a masked battery against Drumpellier, though neither he nor his family appeared or sisted themselves as parties.

Efforts of both—by the former openly, and the latter clandestinely—but unsuccessfully—to prevent the vital service of Drumpellier to Robert of Letter, in 1818;

The combined efforts of the two opponents, the one publicly, the other clandestinely, through the mask or *ægis* of his ally, were in the main unsuccessful. They could not, after their utmost efforts to defeat it, prevent Drumpellier from attaining his chief and vital object of being served heir in 1818 of Robert Stirling of Bankier and Letter, who died in 1537, and truly in whose line, as will be proved in the sequel, was the *status* of heir and representative of Calder, which thus really came to be vested in Drumpellier, who, moreover, in virtue of further evidence, craved, in fact, that representation to be then discussed, and legally recognised in him.

and Glorat could only stave off merits of the Cadder question by a quirk of form.

This step, however—so much dreaded, for very obvious reasons, by his opponents—was precluded by a preliminary quirk, merely in point of form, resorted to by Glorat, who would not go into the question, in order to stave it off—his only expedient—and that was irrelevantly supported by the subordinate judge who presided. But the check thus prompted by the utter futility of his claim (Keir still being *sub rosa*), while what had preceded had, in the main, been in favour of Drumpellier, was, as premised, but momentary, in virtue of a reservatory protest on behalf of his rights, which he took upon the occasion to prosecute them "in *another* shape." This he accordingly did before a competent, and, it may be held, in the circumstances, better court (as will be also seen), where he prevailed, and indeed walked the course without the faintest opposition, and had the Cadder status, as well as principal arms of Cadder, which go *semel et simul* together with supporters, on the same ground duly recognised and secured to him. These were then, formally, with a statement and recognition also of his relative pedigree and right and *status* as the Cadder heir and representative, recorded in the "Register" of the Tribunal—which is ordained by a special

But Drumpellier, after that, successful and unopposed, obtained a full recognition of his Cadder rights and status.

Act of Parliament in 1672, to "be respected" so far, as "true and unrepealable." And so fully and finally ended the affair.

Keir, as premised, never would venture into the field; and as for Glorat, whom he had anxiously implored in his necessity—and to whom he was so much beholden for a time, though the latter, after demur and disinclination, had sported the notion of a Cadder descent, and taken out a competing brief to be served the Cadder heir in 1818 that was never prosecuted—it had been merely *ex facie* to enable him, as above, to oppose Drumpellier, for in reality he was not so. His asserted pedigree in the brief laboured at the outset under a vital and suicidal flaw, through interpolation, as his supposed Cadder ancestor, of a fabulous Duncan Stirling, depriving it of all force and effect, however otherwise ancient and respectable.* Glorat did no more than the above, and finally quitted the field.

From the known ability and *marked* line of conduct of the counsel whom he had consulted, and upon whom he mainly relied in a subsequent parallel case (which, with the preceding, will be minutely stated in a chapter hereafter), Glorat, if practicable, would doubtless, under his advice, as was *quite competent*, have opposed Drumpellier on the latter occasion; but being now fully aware of the weakness and futility of his claim, which, in a manner, he had twice before abjured or abandoned, and tired of his unavailing exertions, chiefly out of friendly motives, at the pressing entreaties of Keir, he at length no longer persisted, but quitted the field with the full and undisputed victory to Drumpellier. The undisputed victory, therefore, remained with Drumpellier.

But alas for this old knightly family of Glorat, the undoubted male Craigbarnet representatives, now when the scales otherwise preponderate—"*tempora mutantur, nos et mutamur*," &c. After their heir, Sir Samuel Stirling, Baronet, had been thus, in a manner, paramount on *one* side in the litigation in question, and there alone legally acted and contended on the footing of the Cadder *heir-male* and chief of the Stirlings,[1] at the earnest entreaty of Keir, who directly backed and supported him in such *status* and undertaking when himself unable to meet Drumpellier, and thus so far succumbed to him, what since has been the return or acknowledgment to Glorat, and how is he now represented? Would it be believed that the Keir performance[2] is at pains to inculcate that there is "*no* evidence of the exact relationship of the first *Stirling* of *Craigbernard* (Glorat's undoubted ancestor ¹ His brief, accordingly, will be fully given in a subsequent chapter. ² See ibid., p. 127.

---

* See evidence on this head, and his want of connection with Cadder, with due explanations, in the ADDENDA to the present Chapter, No. II., under title of "The Stirlings of Craigbarnet," &c.

ut supra) to the house of Cadder"—denying, in fact, what the Keir, in 1818, *e converso*, held or supported—while it is added, that "the *Craigbernard* family *recognised* the Stirlings of *Keir* as *their chief;*" by which again, equally *e converso*, Glorat, who stands in the shoes of Craigbarnet, instead of being the conceived chief of the Stirlings as formerly, must be now degraded to a Keir vassal and subordinate. This, as too often happens in the work, is without a particle of evidence in its support, and, by some strange mode of ratiocination, is even made to infer an inferior Craigbernard and Glorat-*Cadder* descent from Keir, as if he actually was the Cadder heir!

We are above insensibly, if we may be pardoned, reminded of the noted Seville fruit, which, analogously, after ministering to our taste and refreshment, is at once discarded in the remnant, and abandoned to the lower *status* of the ground.

What has preceded is but a jet or outline of the merits of the case, the minute circumstances and evidences of which will be given in the subsequent chapters of the Exposition.

More than forty years have elapsed since these events affecting Drumpellier, Keir, and Glorat, during all which time, under competent legal sanction and authority, fortified, too, by the longest prescription that would validate *per se* even a doubtful right, Drumpellier has held his status of heir and representative of Cadder, and his *jus acquisitum* here, without the slightest legal challenge or opposition. And such being the fact, it is now impregnable and unassailable, beyond the reach of competition *a fortiori* by Keir, who never even, like Glorat, ventured to risk discussion, but always shrunk from and eluded it when challenged thereto, as may be concluded, from an innate sense of his own weakness and inability.

<small>Nevertheless, notwithstanding the foreclosure in favour of Drumpellier, the Keir Performance, of itself, without adopting any legal step, maintains the Keir-Cadder status;</small> But strangely indeed, in these circumstances, and without the least sanction of reason or evidence on their side, the Keir advisers or Triumvirate—irrespective of this legal foreclosure in favour of Drumpellier—and not daunted by the former Keir's disasters and abandonment of his pretensions, have boldly, in their own empty hall or *private* tribunal, where, like *Æolus*, they may of course blow, or rule as they choose, now actually arrogated to his representative—for the first time too—the principal status both of heir-male and even heir-general, it may be said, of the house of Cadder. And this in the face of Drumpellier's confessed right, while, moreover, no small uncertainty still even prevails in regard to the precise origin and descent of the Keir family,

which has never yet been properly sifted or established; at any rate, as may subsequently transpire, cannot be proved to be from Cadder. But even this is not all, as a culminating point, and in order to distinguish and decorate Keir with the gaudiest and most imposing trappings, the same notable advisers *proprio arbitrio* even beyond its utmost stretch, though at some risk and peril, as may also be seen, while actually usurping to themselves the power and authority of the Court of Arms, have liberally conferred upon him the ancient crest of Stirling of Cadder. *That* crest—the white swan issuing out of a coronet—is now, for the first time, conjoined with the Keir, upon the Keir shield of arms, made common to both, which, with its accessories, is engraved upon the second leaf of the Keir performance. And actually has made Keir assume the old Cadder crest, to which he is not entitled, while wholly ignoring the Drumpellier status and rights.

But still even this may not suffice. While the above was so *ingeniously* achieved—not only has the Drumpellier case been there misrepresented and prejudiced, but the work has further ignored and even expunged the family from the text of the Cadder history and pedigree, withholding from them the place they undoubtedly were entitled to occupy, and, as a clenching blow, doubtless, as devised, they have been precipitated even to the lowest grade of the *fibulati* Stirlings, in a meagre and imperfect account of them and some others, including strangers, in a kind of supplement.

Most certainly such *ex parte* puny attempts may only excite a smile: such flea-bites, in truth—the results apparently of petty rancour or spleen, owing to previous Keir mischances and defeats—against the Drumpellier-Cadder status, now hermetically sealed and secured.

But why or wherefore is Drumpellier to be so pointedly subjected, in the Keir performance, even though so secondary and insignificant, to such derogatory inflictions; to be degraded, in fact—ignored and expunged from the Cadder stock or pedigree—*cui bono* essentially? it may be asked. Merely for the sake of, and to clear the way there for, one who has truly been interpolated into the place which the former can alone occupy. The party whose family had dreaded and shrunk from a Cadder contest with his, legally abandoned its very idea, was fain, through an invariable enmity, to implore another hostilely to oppose and impede the then Drumpellier in the course of his successful career, actually has here not a leg to stand upon,[1] nor, it is believed, can possibly adduce a vestige of proper evidence in support of a Cadder descent. Yet, it seems, to the prejudice of the true party, he nevertheless must be held, through the *medium* of his work, to have one quite [1] Certainly, his Cadder claim—as based by the Triumvirate.

transcendant and irresistible. Such a consummation is indeed strange and unprecedented—not to add adverse to all reason and justice—only to be expected in the Keir performance.

Even in a lower view, supposing the Drumpellier case to be less cogent and conclusive, still, as having induced honourable controversy, which the Keir family were unable to meet, they on that account might have been more distrustful of theirs, whatever it may be, and through that delicacy, at least, that usually obtains, in such alternative, in enlightened and polished circles, towards an opponent, have forborne to strain matters against him; on the other hand, rather to have been lenient and indulgent, and given him the fairest advantage; but, at any rate, not at once *de plano*, without ground or apology, to ignore his pleas, and rudely and unduly, however impotently, expunge him, as has been done, from the very account of the Stirlings in question, in the text of their work.

On which above account, inter alia, Drumpellier is now forced, in self-defence, to the present Exposition of his already established and foreclosed Cadder status.

As, nevertheless, the preceding flagrant Keir attacks—this marked *expulsion* of Drumpellier, so wanton and reprehensible, together with his undoubted Cadder status and representation—may, in fact, be unknown to the public, he has unavoidably been compelled (and he perhaps may here meet with some sympathy) to come forward in self-defence, and vindicate them, placing things, as is conceived, in their true and unexceptionable light,—which is the main scope and object of the present Exposition.

This, accordingly, he will do in the ensuing chapters, which will comprise a due statement of the Drumpellier case, the peculiar *res gestae* in the matter, and the strange attempts and expedients of adversaries, as well as an inquiry into the origin and descent of Keir, after showing the untenability of his newly-assumed Cadder status and representation; besides answers to, and refutations of, assumptions, and violent or gratuitous conclusions, often hostile, in the Keir work, accompanied with comments and animadversions.

There is certainly another infliction by his assumed opponent upon Drumpellier, in his being forced in this way to submit private matters and complaints, however justified, to the public, whom they cannot be supposed much to interest, and for which every apology is tendered. The step, independently of the conceived right of every family to correct errors in the least compromising and prejudicing their interests, has been prompted, too, by the consideration that, were an opposite course and taciturnity to be preferred by the former, it might be construed into inability to meet the attacks in question, and thus consequent injury done to his heirs, who might complain of the omission, and whose claims and rights fall to be maintained and respected. At the same time, the personal feelings here of the present Drumpellier and his family may be poignant, and reasonably not to be disregarded. Coupling the strangely attempted recent abstraction from them of their appropriate chivalrous Cadder crest and status, that are identical, by their Keir adversaries, with the irretrievable loss since 1541 of valuable ancestral seignories and estates, through the questionable address and dexterity of a transaction between the Keir in that year and the unfortunate Cadder heiress—an original deed, embodying which, the same Keir adversaries, as if ashamed thereof, refrain from adducing, contenting themselves merely, notwithstanding the vaunted liberality of their respectable client in opening his charter-chest, with but a strange nondescript fragment, not equal to an imperfect copy happening to be with Drumpellier—he and the former alike may be admitted to have some ground of complaint. After such ruthless aggressions and deprivations, such contumely, continued injuries, and hostile acts, not often paralleled, both ancient and modern, may not Drumpellier, in the expressive and slightly *altered* words of Shakespeare (for which there must be apology), actually tax and upbraid the Keir family with having—

———— " *Fed* upon our seignories,
From our own window *torn* our *household coat*,
Razed out our *impress*, leaving us no sign,
Save men's opinion and our living blood,
To show the world that we are gentlemen !"

But it is not only the fine old chivalrous heraldic Cadder crest, the "white swan," the identical *impress*, too, of Edward III., if not also of his grandfather Edward I.,* issuing out of a coronet, identified with the Cadder representation, now proudly "set on high" above the Keir shield, on the Keir mural arch, engraved on the second leaf of the title-page of the extraordinary and reckless Keir performance ;—and thus, by the practice of chivalry, implying a *defiant* right and challenge to dispute its possession,† which Drum-

Further assumptions of armorial bearings by Keir.

---

* See Lord HAILES' *Annals*, edit. 1797, vol. ii. pp. 4, 5, note, with accompanying authorities.
† To quote Froissart somewhat here in illustration, as translated by Dugdale : " These fought hand to hand, the Earl of Douglas and Sir Henry Percy, and by force of arms the Earl won Sir Henry's pennon (on which was usually the family crest). Whereupon Sir Henry and the English were sore displeased, the Earl saying to him, ' Sir, I shall bear this

pellier, though not obliged, accepts and answers by the present Exposition,—to which exception may be made. The Keir ambition must not be stinted to such narrow limits; it seems all-grasping, and must include the arms and heraldic *insignia* of other families, who yet, it should be remembered, have their own descendants, and may not be inclined to favour the encroachment. It reaches and compromises the STELLULATOS *Strivelienses*, the great distinct baronial house of the Strivelins of Moray and Glenesk,* whose ancient arms and device of the stars are likewise assumed by the former. They are actually placed, together with the Stirling buckles, respectively, in two parallel rows,—the stars nearer even, and immediately above the Keir arms,—as conjoined heirlooms of one and the same stock, on the preceding Keir arch, evincing, in the plain language of heraldry, Keir's representation both of Keir and Glenesk, and further to redound to the fame and glory of his family.

It will not be pretended that *strangers* could, of their own accord, take, as in this instance, the arms or device of a great family; and what may render this assumption of the stars the more exceptionable, is the fact of their having been already forestalled, and quite justly sculptured (*semeè*, as styled in heraldry), with the exactly inferred purpose of the Keir advisers, on the walls of the ancient castle of the noble and distinguished descendants of the same Stirlings of Moray or Glenesk.

Lord Lindsay, in the *Lives of the Lindsays*, states that "Sir Alexander Lindsay married Catherine, daughter of Sir John de Striveling or Stirling,

token of your prowess into Scotland, and *set it on high* in my castle of *Alquest* (*Dalkeith*), that it may be seen far off,' obviously as a taunt to a challenge for its recovery."—*Baronage*, article "Percy, Earl of Northumberland," vol. i. p. 279.

* The two chief baronial houses of the Strivelins were the puissant *Vicecomites* of Strivelin or Stirling, and that of the Strivelins of Moray and Glenesk, as yet separate and distinct. The former bore three buckles as their arms, the latter stars 3, 2, and 1, that have, from their number, been represented smaller than usually. On this account the writer will take the liberty of styling the first, the *fibulati Strivilienses* (from their armorial buckles), and the last the *stellulati Strivelienses* (from their armorial stars), as a simple mode of particularising each. Curiously, these two eminent families were at one time also distinct in politics, the *fibulati* siding with Baliol on the competition for the Scotch crown, as direct representative of the royal line, as cannot now be disputed; the *stellulati* with Bruce no doubt from principle and independent motives.¹

The surname of Strivelin was numerous before, and still more after that epoch, and we must not suppose that every Stirling then was of the same stock or origin, or that certain south-country Stirlings actually were the ancestors of the far superior *Vicecomites* de Strivelin, as futilely and preposterously pretended in the Keir performance, though this is wholly *jus tertii* to Keir, he not being able (as will afterwards be shown), in the least, to connect himself, as his advisers would strangely inculcate, with such secondary Stirlings, whose arms, too, are yet unknown to us.

¹ See Rymer's Fœdera

and heiress of Glenesk and Edzell in Angus, and of other lands in Inverness-shire, by whom he had issue Sir David of Glenesk, the first Earl of Crauford" (so created in 1398[1])—" the cognisance of the Stirlings of Glenesk being three stars, in common with the house of de Moravia and other northern families[2] (the Stirlings being even sometimes designed territorially de Moravia). Sir Alexander differenced his paternal coat by placing a star in the dexter chief point, or upper corner of the shield. His son, Earl David, dropped it on becoming chief of the family, but the star was readopted by the Lindsays of Edzell, and *semée* on the bordure borne by those of Balcarres." It need hardly be added, that, in the latter noble stems, including the Lindsays of Edzell and the Earls of Balcarres—of whom, too, the present Earl of Crauford and Balcarres, father of the preceding noble and distinguished Lindsay historian, is the direct male representative—the right to the star, the armorial ensign of the Stirlings of Moray, rests, quite to the exclusion of Keir, to whom it is entirely *jus tertii*, and ought never, by correct heraldry, to have been placed *pari passu*, or conjoined, as above, with the Keir buckles.

Further still, it is stated in the case of James, Earl of Balcarres, claiming the Earldom of Crauford,[3]* that "David Lindsay of Edzell," in 1571, carried the *star* of Stirling of Glenesk " in the centre, by way of a family difference, in *right of*" his "*descent* from Catherine de Striveline, mother of David, first Earl of Crauford, the daughter and heiress of Sir John Striveline of Glenesk, head of an ancient and powerful family, whose arms consisted solely of stars. The stars, as a *cherished gentilitial* badge or emblem, *are still visibly sculptured* (together with the Crauford arms proper) *upon prominent parts of the old* CASTLE OF EDZELL, which lay within the barony of Glenesk." This last intimation fully bears us out in a previous important particular, while all besides is, *ut supra*, corroborative; and the Keir advisers, it may be added, should have first obtained permission before they so unauthorisedly and prejudicially conferred the stellular arms—so much cherished by their true possessors—in any way upon their principal or client.

Independently, too, over the gate or portal engraved on the first page of the Keir Performance, there are displayed five distinct shields—one of the

---

* And that was accordingly adjudged to the noble peer in 1848. The case was drawn up by the present writer, who may be relieved from some degree of delicacy in thus referring to it, from the subsequent passage being already quoted for another purpose in the Keir Performance (see p. 188). The facts in that passage, it may be safely added, are fully borne out by evidence.

[1] See Lord Lindsay's Lives of the Lindsays, vol. i. p. 51.
[2] Ibid, note.
[3] See, pp. 175-6.

COMMENTS ON KEIR PERFORMANCE.

[margin: Reiterated assumption by Keir of the Stirling of Moray arms in the Keir Performance, as also of those of Carse, and besides of Cadder.]

Stirlings of Moray, comprising again the stars ; and another of the Stirlings of Carse, the three buckles on a chief instead of a bend. This precisely quadrates with, and may have been adopted from, the corresponding practice of our families of old, thus heraldically to express on the gates or walls of their mansions their respective descents, alliances, and sometimes fiefs and seignories. And in this manner, in separate shields also, and with the same view, those so well known of the ancient Earls of Dunbar and March (including even the Isle of Man), were sculptured, and descriable not long ago, if not, too, partly still on the portal of their old Castle of Dunbar.* But as the Keir family are neither proved to be descended from, or to have had any main tie or connection with, the Stirlings of Glenesk or Carse, they were not entitled, on this occasion, after the above fashion, to sport or display their arms, no more than those of the Stirlings of Cadder, that may be said to occupy an additional shield on the preceding portal ; which, nevertheless, as they stand, must denote, by correct heraldic doctrine, that the former are represented by Keir ;—thus constituting, as may be maintained, another undue assumption, independently of that of the Cadder crest (as shown), to the prejudice and in disregard of Drumpellier. That this too, is so, may be inferred from the Keir motto, " *Gang forward*," being inserted *in extenso* on the gate or portal, immediately below the five shields, as alike applicable to the whole—thus evincing them to be within the same category, and hence of the same family, of which, again, as the arms of Keir occupy, in the same frontispiece, the fullest and most exalted position, he must be the chief. But what may be still further decisive is the fact of " The *Stirlings of Keir*, and their Family Papers "—the title of the work—being also prominently introduced in the large space below the portal. That must indicate them to be exclusively in view, no others being mentioned, and of course, by the true rules and doctrine of heraldry, which can alone apply, holders and possessors of the five superincumbent shields, with all their gentilitial honours and accessories, for whose behoof, and in whose right only, they could be displayed. Indeed, this even is sanctioned, in modern times, by similar frontispieces to

---

[1] See Lives of the Lindsays, vol. i. p. 51, note.

* Lord Lindsay, in his Lives,[1] here well remarks, in corroboration of what is thus stated (independently of the precedent of the old castle of Dunbar), that "in those days (*anciently*) families *exhibited* the arms of their different alliances in *separate* shields, instead of quartering them ;" and in proof of this, instances " four isolated shields of the fourteenth century," that were taken from the ancient castle, now in ruins, of Maxwell of Pollok, and placed elsewhere— all having the arms of Maxwell of Pollok and their alliances.

works decorated—and more justly—with gentilitial arms. As indicative of property, too, a party constantly, in like manner, puts his arms on a book along with his name and family. Why then should there not be the same indication or induction, from the parallel insertion of the five shields in question, in Keir's book, with the name of his family alone on the imposing portal in its frontispiece?

How the descendants and representatives of the ancient families above specified may brook or approve of this Keir use of their shields, it is not for the writer to predicate. Of these, as already obvious, the most distinguished is the noble house of Crauford, with their several cadets, lineal descendants of the preceding baronial Strivelins of Glenesk, and thus exclusively entitled to their stars; and next may be immediately in the same character innumerable Stirling of Carse descendants, claimants of the especial buckles on the chief on the Carse shield.

The Keir advisers might here perhaps recollect the fate of vaunting ambition, according to Shakespeare, and out of regard to their respected principal or client, been deterred from it on the present occasion. Besides, extreme and unwonted assumption, and the too open arrogating by a party of what he may even think himself entitled to, is rather against the known Chesterfield notion of its indicating or savouring somewhat of the *parvenu*, who, in his anxiety to make the world believe, contrary to fact, that he holds elevated birth and prerogatives, while dreading their disbelief, thus talks loudly, and indulges in undue and lofty aspirations. Among this class, we need not remark, the honourable Member for Perthshire does not come, and should not in the least inadvertently be confounded with it by the acts of others: while, from his noble and estimable sentiments, not to add admitted ancient descent and station, he may be the last to approve of what his too zealous partisans have above, as well as, moreover, elsewhere, in their performance, in a too sanguine or extravagant mood, been tempted to maintain—in truth, actually to misrepresent.

So deep was the delicate and refined feeling in such respects, with the known inference from an opposite conduct, among the old French *noblesse*—no bad precedent here—that though they thoroughly instilled their offspring with the full knowledge of their family claims and rights, and baronial or seignorial prerogatives, with which they behoved to be acquainted, they yet strictly enjoined them to be mute on the subject.

This we learn from one of Marmontel's works about the epoch of the first French Revolution, who being *de infima plebe*, and certainly one of its promoters, did not with sufficient coquetry approve of such elevated *retenue*, affecting, at one time, to ridicule it, though it was in truth his highest object and ambition to be honoured with the patronage and intimacy of the preceding, which enabled him so graphically, and with such zest, to delineate their leading and polished characteristics and manners (elsewhere subjects of study and imitation) in one of his most noted productions.

One word or two more on heraldic *insignia*, besides landed designation of the Strivelins of Cadder, and its orthography.

What is withal passing strange, the notable Keir Performance, apparently in a perverse or splenetic mood, either through blindness or caprice, has chosen not only to abjure the rights and interests of the Keir family, and, moreover, of all the *fibulati Strivelienses*, in so far as regards their armorial buckles, but also to sacrifice them to those of a distinct foreign race, for whom it seems to have an extraordinary *penchant* and predilection, even preferably to the Keir, though they never for a moment should have been brought into the discussion.

<small>Extraordinary attack by the Keir Performance upon the original and innate right of the Stirlings to the buckles in their arms, with a phantasy that they must have been derived from the Calders in the North.
¹ See Keir Performance, pp. 14, 15.</small>

The right of the *fibulati Strivelienses* to their three buckles, a distinguished chivalrous bearing, is proved to have dated, at least, from 1292, if not earlier, while antecedently they have not yet been shown to have been borne by another family. They hence may be said to be privative to, and indigenous in them; and such being the case, what could induce the Keir advisers to sport the notion,¹ that the arms in question were not so, but may have been derived from a *Calder race*, solely in the north, who thus, and not the former, were their ancient and original possessors? They expressly affirm that this *ancient* "*family* carried *buckles;*" to give some consistency to their conceived inference, while in support of this assertion, reference is merely made to one of their seals of arms, *so late* as 1431.* But even that seal, trivial at any rate, by no means bears out the above, as may be held unfair and untrue representation of the matter. It, on the other hand,

<small>See, too, in corroboration, p. 25 of this Exposition.</small>

distinctly proves that a STAG'S *head affronti*, or "caboshed" (*which the Keir work altogether* OMITS *or* WITHHOLDS!) was the *substantive* arms of these Calders,† as it in fact still continues, though a small *single* buckle,

<small>¹ See Keir work, p. 14.</small>

* As engraved in Laing's *Scotch Seals*, p. 31, No. 150 (the only authority quoted), who thus describes them as "*a stag's head*, and a chief charged on the dexter point with a buckle."

† See in corroboration also here, p. 25.

and not "buckles" in the plural number, as unwarrantably, too, stated in the Keir Performance, appears on the dexter side of the chief in the shield as an accidental accompaniment, in unison with a practice that may be explained hereafter. This solitary Calder buckle, with which we have alone to deal, independently of other reasons, may be as much the Calder *gentilitial* arms as the ancient Pelham buckle, whose history also will be unfolded; those of the English family of Pelham—and with what truth and reason will be seen.

From the far ancienter possession, certainly, of the three buckles as their exclusive appropriate arms—by the *fibulati Strivilienses* at least, as is proved in 1292, so long anterior to the slightest trace of the single buckle, an accidental device of the northern Calders, who, in 1511, bore it simply over the stag's head, as by an original seal the writer has seen—the legal presumption is, if there be borrowing in the matter, that the last borrowed or derived it from the *Strivelins*—not they their *three* buckles (which indeed they in no way could) from the Calders. Quite unwarranted.

It may be here observed that there is not a particle of proof in support of another hallucination of the Keir work, that the Strivelins may have acquired their buckles, and even further too, their estate of Cadder, by marriage of a Calder, or rather Cawder, heiress in the so favoured north,* from whom, of course, they must be sprung. This is one of the many visionary platitudes in which it abounds, and is, in fact, tantamount also, after the denounced example of Guthrie, to the *calling* "forth children from the barren stock."[1] While the Cadder or Calder of the Strivelins lay solely in Lanarkshire, quite remote from the former—and there are several Calders in Scotland, the name denoting a site near water—it thus need not, for partial opposite purposes, be feigned to have a northern connection. At the same time, too—which is not to be overlooked—when the Stirlings must have acquired their Lanarkshire Cadder, arms in Scotland were in their very infancy, if not wholly unborne by such families; so neither on this ground could they, as is preposterously inferred, have derived theirs from any of the name of Calder. As also strange hallucination of the Stirlings having acquired Cawder from the same Calders. [1] See p. 3.

---

[1] See Keir Performance, pp. 14, 15.

* "It is *possible* (so it prelects[1]) that Cawder in Lanarkshire *may* have belonged to a family of that name (Calder in the north, just previously mentioned there) *before* it was granted by William the Lion to the Bishop of Glasgow, *and that* Alexander Strivilin, *on* his acquiring the estate *through* an intermarriage with the family (*it may be equally added*, OR THROUGH ANY OTHER *reason why ?*), *may* have *adopted* the buckles." Still even here the indispensable identity of these *supposed* Lanarkshire Calders with those in the north is quite unsupported, and at this rate of imaginary *possibilities* or *perchances*—so alien to EXACT discussion—argument, or rather theories merely, would be infinite, without any rational or safe conclusion.

COMMENTS ON KEIR PERFORMANCE.

Remarkable absurdity of the Keir work as to the Cadder orthography.

But perhaps not the least absurdity in the Keir Performance may be, that, besides the imaginary humble adoption of their buckles from these comparatively secondary northern *Cawders*, the *fibulati Strivilienses* must also, out of apparent homage to such transcendent parties, though merely Thanes originally (the import of which is now well known), and not Barons, condescend to spell their Cader or Cadder after an identical subservient fashion. And hence we have it ludicrously and affectedly throughout printed "Cawder,"[1] quite unknown to the Cadder title-deeds during at least the fifteenth century (Cadare, Cader, and Cadder, too, being the appropriate wording); of course, as closely approximating to the "*Cawdor*" (now) of the north; but chiefly, as the work rather delectably enunciates, "because" *Cawder* "expresses the *pronunciation* of the word *which obtains in the district*, and which is *not* expressed *by any of the other spellings*" (*scripto* assuredly!) Was there ever such strange notion held before?—common slang thus to rule over written orthography—at least by antiquaries, who prefer the ancient to the modern in writs or matters like the present! And hence, forsooth, with equal reason, "Choholmondely" in England must be printed "Chumley;" "Somerville" in Scotland, "Somer'le," for that is the vulgar "pronunciation." or of "the district;"[2] "Pollok," in like manner, "Pook" or "Poog;" as also "Anstruther," there "Anster;" while "Hairstanes," still in the same country, *scripto* should be "Hastings," though sufficient to commove the choler of the Marquis of "Hastings," the Earl of Huntingdon, and Lord "Hastings;" not to add the strange change, according to the same fallacious test proposed, of "Saint John" in England, into "Sinjon," &c., &c. Such bizarre and new fashion, it need not be added, would only excite surprise or ridicule, or the wit and pertinent merriment of *Punch*.

[1] See Keir Performance, p. 6, note. It is even made to supplant "*Cadder*" in a *Drumpillier* writ!

[2] See Memorials of the Somervilles, edited by Sir Walter Scott, vol. ii. p. 482, through a quotation from Allan Ramsay.

Writer defends Keir against the unnatural attack even of his partisans.

Reverting, however, to the similar antecedent absurdity exposed, what will the *fibulati Strivilienses*, it may be asked, now say to the "*et tu Brute*" attack of the Keir editor or Performance upon their sacred and inherited armorial right to the buckles? Will they not, including Keir too, with the present writer, "haste to their rescue?" Meanwhile he is most happy to end this chapter with becoming unexpectedly the vindicator of Keir interests, though against their prior zealous defender and ally, who now, alas! sides with hostile strangers against them, and would fain preferably deck, to their injury and prejudice, after a jackdaw fashion, certain northern Cawdors—not even Stirlings—with plumage to which they have not the least right or claim.

One secondary though noticeable thing, too, has escaped the writer. A whole quarto page has been devoted in the Keir work[1] to the *edifying* and *needful* task of showing how the "surname of Stirling" has been "spelled" in no less than *sixty-four* instances, each minutely numbered and all imposingly arranged in two columns, with dates and references, embracing even the period antecedent to the Keir family—viz. " 1. Strevelyn ; 2. Strivelin ; 3. Striuelyne ; 4. Striveline ; 5. Striwelyne"—" 11. Strivelyne ; 12. Strenelyn," &c. &c., *et id genus omne*, &c. &c. &c.

To any who observe how slight and shadowy the differences (so unnecessarily, too, multiplied in the work, and of which this is but a slight sample) here undoubtedly are—like other examples of our old orthography that are respectively more or less so, and hence present nothing new or striking—the above may appear rather a make-weight in it, or something of a platitude, *quod tollere velles*. And it may be regretted that such elaborate, trivial industry, without a material result—less even than that of the complicated machine in Hogarth's picture to uncork a bottle—had not been employed in what was far more valuable, and preferably to be discussed in the wide range of subjects in the Keir compilation.

But be this as it may, another quarto page, most irrelevantly, is devoted to an obvious make-weight,[2] to the engraving of a shield of arms, from a stone at the Wrightshouses, near Edinburgh, impaling those of a Napier of Wrightshouse, on the right, with his wife's on the left—viz. a bend charged with three *rings*, each respectively, too, having an *addition* at its extremity not now exactly defined, as also a unicorn's head *erased* in chief. It need not be observed, that there is here no vestige of the arms of Stirling, notoriously composed but of three buckles, and not rings, that are sufficiently dissimilar, with no addition as above, and having neither the distinctive charge in chief of the unicorn's head, or the like. Yet—will it be believed ?—in this utter state of discrepancy between these bearings, the Keir work infers from that first mentioned—as of a Stirling—the marriage between a Napier and a Stirling, enhanced too, it seems, from being much earlier—as is also gratuitously assumed from an accompanying inapplicable date, to be noticed—than that between John Napier, the inventor of the logarithms, and Elizabeth Stirling, daughter of James of Keir, in the reign of James VI. The work must have been hard pressed for materials, indeed, to have had recourse to such make-weight to fill up a blank or deficiency. If, again, the least re-

---

Conceived inedifying platitude in the Keir Performance. [1] See p. 548.

Undoubted makeweight there, based upon gross error. [2] See Keir Performance, p. 44. The initials on the right are "J. N.," held there to be " for A. Napier of Wrychtishousis;" but in the reign of Robert III., the period in question —i.e., from 1390 to 1406— "William" can be proved the family representative.

search had been employed, it would have been found at once that the arms in question, so far from being in the least those of Stirling, were actually the heraldic insignia of "Denneston of Duntraith," who, as Nisbet, a very accessible authority, informs us,[1] carried "argent, on a *bend* azure, between two *unicorns'* heads sable *erased*, armed, or, THREE RINGS, with CARBUNCLES of the last;"—that is, a jewel or precious stone placed at the end of each ring, and obviously the precise addition noticed, and in the identical position with that to the three rings, also on the bend in the left impalement of the Wrighthouses' shield!

[1] First edition, p. 104.

The mutual identity is thus complete, proving both coats of arms one and the same; and the unicorn's head erased below the bend—while the upper one, in the above, still remains as in the Denneston of Duntraith arms—has been there obliterated either by weather or lapse of time.

It is almost superfluous to observe, that the form of the shield on the Wrighthouses' stone, is comparatively modern—not earlier, perhaps, than the seventeenth century—but not certainly coeval with the date "1399" (*literally*, as added to the accompanying motto), at a time when the husband's and wife's arms were not impaled, as in this instance, but given on separate shields. On what account such date may be there does not transpire, nor is it worth inquiring—no more than the initials I. S.—if they really be such—on the left of the shield in question. But, at any rate, the date "1399" is a manifest modern interpolation,—these *Arabic* numerals not having been then introduced or employed by us, so that no relevant antiquarian argument can be based thereupon.

On the whole, it must be confessed that the Keir Performance has been rather unhappy in its attempted armorial elucidations and conclusions: while even within the small compass of this *peccant* p. 14, there is more of error and hallucination to be exposed, besides the misrepresentations as to the origin of the Stirling buckles, and visionary Cawdor alliances, and subserviency.

Corroboration of the writer's impression as to the Calder arms in the north.

Yet the writer's sand-glass here is not yet run out. In corroboration, as has been remarked, of the stag's head *alone* having been the proper or substantive gentilitial arms of the Calders, or rather Cawdors, in the north, in exclusion of the buckles that have been substituted for them in the preceding work, so unfairly, upon a palpably misrepresented authority, the Exponent may appeal to the respectable evidence of Mr Thomas Crawford, professor of mathematics in the University of Edinburgh in 1646, and its known historian from 1580 to that year, who was, besides, a considerable antiquary and collector of ancient writs and muniments.

In his list of the arms of the principal families in Scotland, in a MS. in the Advocates' Library, he gives those indisputably of the above "Calders" (or Cawdors) "in Murrayland," or in Moray, where they certainly dwelt, and which he there states to be simply, " or, ane *Heart's* head sable." This is all, without any the slightest additional item, or charge, or even notice of the single buckle, which was thus held in the smallest account, certainly *not* as *gentilitial*, but insignificant, inasmuch as it was thus actually, at least more than two centuries ago—whatever its fate in modern times, not, after all, conceived to be different—disused or rejected by the family, whose proper exclusive bearing was a hart's or stag's head—pretty much identical. The former term "hart" is written *Scoticè* "hearts" in the manuscript, which affords a tempting occasion for competing with the Keir editor, in deference to him in the number of its orthographies—1. Heart ; 2. Heirt ; 3. Hairt ; 4. Hert, &c.—possibly as many as in his favourite Strivelin instance premised, and doubtless with as great results ; but he unfortunately is precluded by want of space.

ADDENDA TO CHAPTER I.

No. I.

(REFERRED TO AT PAGE 2, NOTE.)

(1.)—Proof (*inter alia*), in the Keir Performance, of carelessness, and a striking, almost unprecedented, omission with respect to announced desirable evidence.

The editor there remarks in his preface that, "not the least interesting part of the following narrative, is the story of the ill-fated heiress of Cawder ;"[1] that is, Janet Strivelin, the Lady of Cadder. We here cordially agree with him, though certainly his account of her is but slender and meagre, at least not so full or particular as might be expected, owing to his opportunities, and more direct sources of information. The history of

[1] See Keir Performance, p. x.

Janet is indeed striking, and the slightest additional notice of her acceptable. With this impression, we read the *new* intimation in the work of her having lived as far down as 1588,[1] for which reference is made, in its usual *peculiar* fashion, just commented upon, to No. 199, p. 425, of the relative vouchers and authorities; but upon a full examination, we, to our great surprise, neither found there, or elsewhere, anything of the kind, or in the least in support of the fact,—the reference here being, in truth, a mere nullity or vacuity, and inept. Why, it may be asked, baulk us so provokingly, and the framers of the Keir Performance write only to deceive? They must surely, at the time, have been somnolent; but though old Homer is occasionally excused in his writings for being so, owing to his *extra* merits, the same apology, perhaps (though we beg pardon for this liberty), may not be so confessed in their more juvenile case, owing, unfortunately, to their great deserts not being yet so apparent, or known to the world.

[1] See Keir Performance, p. 38.

But, be this as it may, to compensate somewhat for this disappointment and deficiency, the writer may adduce the following original, and, as it now proves, last notice of the ill-fated heiress of Cadder, who, it may be added, was only once legally married to the Thomas Bischop below, and never, as we might otherwise conclude from loose and unguarded statements in the Keir Performance, to any Keir. It is supplied to us by a letter of Queen Mary, under the Privy Seal, dated Edinburgh, October 8, "1551,"[2] to Matho Hamiltone of Mylburn, and his "airis and assignais . . . . of ye escheit of all gudis, soumes of money, actis, contractis,—jowellis, gold, silver, cunyeit and uncunyeit, &c., quhilk is partenit to * .... Striveling, sum tyme *Lady Caldoure*, and now ye *spous* of *Thomas Bischop*, and now partening, &c., to our soveraine lady, through being of ye saide † .... past in ye realme of Ingland, and yair remaining wyt ye said Thomas, hir spous, rebell and traitour to our soveraine lady, *helping and supporting him*, or throu her being, or quhen scho sall happin to be ordourlie denuncit rebel, put to ye horne, fugitivæ fra ye law, or convict for ye *foirsaidis crymes.*" Curiously, as might here follow, for *helping* and *supporting* her husband like a dutiful wife.

[2] Privy Seal Record.

The Keir Performance, therefore, may not be proficient in the "*exact* sciences."

(2.)—And proof, again, that it is careless in another particular, and ungrammatical too, besides what will elsewhere be exposed.

The above work at the outset, lamely indeed, attempts to establish that the person whom in part it improperly styles "Sir Alexander *de Striveling of Cauder*, Sheriff of Striveling[3] —(both the *surname* and *landed designation* here being unused by, and not given to, him, which constitutes another error and piece of carelessness, his style having been simply "Alexander, Vicecomes de Strivelin[4]")—was actually son of one Peter Stirling of Cambiesbarron, though no way related to such secondary a party; and even if so, this in no view would avail Keir, as his descent from the *Vicecomes* is untenable.

[3] See Keir Performance, p. 6.
[4] Ibid., pp. 5, 6.

* A blank is here in the Record, evidently to be filled up by "Janet," her Christian name.
† Another blank here, similarly to be filled up.

But, in support of such pretended filiation, however irrelevantly and inadequately, the work in question quotes a Latin grant to Soltray in 1225, witnessed by an "Alexander, son of Patrick de Strivelin,"[1] or by "*Alexandro filio Patricio* de Striveling,"[2] according to its version, as if from the original in Latin, never imagining, we may conclude, that the *genitive*, by the ordinary rules of grammar, comes into play in the last instance, and that it should be "*Patricii*" instead of the preceding "*Patricio*,"—this Christian name being here governed by "*filio*," and, moreover, as it is *actually* written in the original. Here is, then, not only a startling grammatical error, but no slight carelessness, again, in a point, the very *pivot* of the new filiation, and deemed of high importance in the work, from not properly quoting the original authority founded upon.

[1] In the Chartulary of Soltray, in the Advocates' Library.
[2] See Keir Performance, p. 5.

No. II.

(REFERRED TO AT PAGE 11, NOTE.)

THE STIRLINGS OF CRAIGBARNET OR CRAIGBARNARD; and evidence supplying a material deficiency at the outset of their pedigree in the Keir Performance, and substituting a true ancestor for the supposititious Duncan Stirling, foisted into the Glorat brief of service in 1818, to be afterwards noticed.

It was by erroneously holding that the said Duncan was (1) a younger son of a Stirling of Cadder early in the fifteenth century, and (2) the male Craigbarnet and Glorat ancestor—thus the putative connecting-link between the latter and the former—that Sir Samuel Stirling attempted his opposition to Drumpellier in 1818. No evidence, however, was condescended upon in support of such filiation and descent, while the Keir Performance now also repudiates Duncan, and states[3] that "the *first* Stirling of Craigbarnard, whose existence is proved by legal evidence, is JOHN *Striveling of Craigbarnard*, who is a witness to a deed in 1468," and "resigned in 1486" Craigbernard, &c., with other lands, "in favour of William Striveling, his eldest son, reserving his own liferent," from whom the subsequent lines of Craigbernard and Glorat are deduced. But the editor, in this material assertion of John, the father, being the first legally-proved Craigbernard ancestor, signally errs, and betrays great want of proper research; for if he had consulted an obvious and actually published record, he would have found there legal proof of a considerably earlier date, disclosing the true original ancestor of Craigbarnard as yet known, of whom he is unaware, but who must be substituted in the room of the supposititious Duncan Stirling.

[3] See Ibid., p. 127.

The record in question is no other than the "*Compota Camerariorum Scotie*," or of the regular public accounts and vouchers of the High Treasurer of Scotland, where, *inter alia*, the feudal casualties and crown-payments by subjects are registered, and which states,

COMMENTS ON KEIR PERFORMANCE, &c.

[1] See tom. iii. p. 280, under head *Ballivorum ad extra*.

under the year 1434, that the public officiary "*non onerat se de firmis terrarum tennandrie de* CRAIGBERNARDE *pertinentis ad heredem* GILBERTI *de Strivelyn in comitatu de Lennox, in* WARDA *existentis.*"[1] This must evidently have been through the nonage or minority of such heir, who may appositely be held to be the John Stirling of Craigbernard alluded to in the Keir Performance, who subsequently figured at the later period of 1468. It hence transpires—what is new in the pedigree—that, antecedently to 1434, there had existed a previous ancestor, *Gilbert* Stirling of Craigbernard, who must now be the patriarch of the family, but standing quite alone, and as yet unconnected with Cadder.

The writer is happy in affording this information, which, though presenting, it may be thought, a further obstacle in the way of their relationship, yet proves the family of Craigbarnet, or rather that of Glorat, now their male representative (allied to Drumpellier), to have independently figured, it may be said, for more than four centuries and a half. It of course enhances their antiquity; and it need not be added that they were both eminent, and of good repute and consideration. They occasionally held high offices in the State, and illustrate history, while in the present knightly Glorat heir is vested the representation of certain great and dignified houses, upon which, if there was room, we might enlarge, including the Stewarts of Coldingham, sprung from a natural son of James V., whose representative forfeited the Earldom of Bothwell; and through Jean, his mother, of the too-noted James Earl of Bothwell (husband of Queen Mary), her brother, as well as of the entire "House of Hailes." The latter were, indeed, of multiform celebrity—in the Church (conspicuously), war, and gallantry in every sense—being identified in history with two of our Queens; while Adam, second Earl of Bothwell, High Admiral of Scotland, was (as can be proved) solemnly betrothed to Margaret of England, as proxy for James IV.; and had it not been for his gallant charge at Flodden to retrieve the battle, where he unfortunately fell, might have attained even higher rank and influence in the State—perhaps, like his descendant, also to his loss. Truly, as to the Hepburns, we might say with Scott,—

> "'Twas a brave race, before the name
> Of hated Bothwell stained their fame!"

CHAPTER II.

STATE OF THE CADDER REPRESENTATION—THAT INVOLVES THE QUESTION AT ISSUE—ON THE DEATH OF ANDREW STIRLING OF CADDER, THE LAST DIRECT HEIR-MALE, IN 1522—PRIMARY STEPS OF THE DRUMPELLIER FAMILY IN 1817 AND 1818 TO ASSERT THEIR GENTILITIAL RIGHTS AND CADDER STATUS—RELATIVE CORRESPONDENCE BETWEEN THEM AND THAT OF KEIR IN THE ABOVE YEARS—ABSTRACT OF THEIR EVIDENCE THEN, WITH IMPORTANT CONCLUSIONS, AND ADDITIONAL CORROBORATIVE PROOF.

THE antiquity of the Strivelins or Stirlings of Cadder, whose old inheritance of Cadder had been in the Strivelin family as far back as the time of William the Lyon, who reigned from 1165 to 1213-14, together with their status of chiefs of the Stirlings, being so palpably stated and admitted in "*The Stirlings of Keir and their Family Papers*"—in other words, the recent Keir Performance—need not be dwelt or descanted upon.

From inadvertence, or want of due research, the compilers, as too often happens in that work, are unaware of the possession, from as old a period at least, by the Stirlings of Cadder, of their original patrimony likewise, of Ochiltree, in Linlithgowshire. Certainly the fact nowhere there transpires. But however interesting these topics, attention must now be directed, for due solution of the subsequent Cadder representation—the important Drumpellier point at issue—to the epoch immediately after the death of Andrew Stirling of Cadder in 1522, the last direct Cadder heir-male.

By an entail between William Stirling of Cadder and Luke Stirling of Rathenre in 1414, the Cadder patrimony had evidently, in the first instance, been settled on the heirs-male of William's body, without any female intervention.[1] These accordingly must have legally taken, and, so far as can be discovered, with the exception of Uchiltree, there was no resignation of any portion of the old family estate to alter its descent. In 1509 Uchiltree alone was re-granted to William Stirling of Cadder, his heirs and assigns, upon his express resignation.[2]

[1] See Keir Performance, p. 206, No. 10.
[2] See ibid. *passim*, including p. 291, No. 83.

During the entire period from 1414 till 1522 inclusive, when Andrew of Cadder died, the Cadder succession had invariably opened to parties who conjoined in themselves the status both of heirs-male and heirs-at-law of the body of the entailer in 1414, and who made up their titles to each other as "heirs,"—a term which, in our practice,* could, in these circumstances, alone denote heirs-male.

State of the Cadder representation at the death of Andrew of Cadder in 1522, and respective rights of the heirs-male and of line.

But, on Andrew's death in 1522, a disseveration of the former representation occurred, owing to his having left only one child, a daughter, Janet, his heiress, at least at common law; and the question then appositely occurred, Who, by that event, might legally be his heir? Indubitably Janet, direct heir of line of William of Cadder, in virtue of the re-grant of that property to him, his heirs and assigns, in 1509—to Uchiltree, and probably also some other family acquisitions since 1414. But again, it may be asked, *Who*, in 1522, was entitled to succeed to the bulk and remainder of the old patrimony entailed in 1414? From what we can discern, there having been no resignation of it since that year, it legally behoved *not to go to Janet*, the heir-female, but to the heir-male of Andrew of Cadder, provided he were of the body of the entailer, in terms of the entail; † and it is remarkable that some corroboration of it may perhaps be obtained from the grant of James V. to Sir John Stirling of Keir, of the marriage of Janet of Cadder in 1529, where, failing her, that of the "airis *maill* or *famel*" (*female*), also is conveyed, as sall "happin to succeid to the said umquhile Andro (of Cadder,) in his heiretage;"¹ preference being here given to his heirs-male. Sir John Stirling, however, a bold and unscrupulous character, had resolved to conjoin Cadder in its entirety with Keir, through a marriage between the said Janet and his son James; and with this view, he, soon after her father's death, contemplated obtaining a grant of her ward and marriage, which he ultimately effected, but with considerable difficulty and cost. It was not impracticable for such a man, in such an age, with the dexterity which marked his family—with the purchased concurrence of adverse interests, and with the connivance of others—to have the status of heir of Cadder (which she in some degree

¹ See Keir Performance, p. 332, No. 119.

---

* For full proof of this, by cogent precedents and authorities in the fifteenth and sixteenth centuries, see Supplemented Case, 1852, to claim of the Earl of Crawford for the Dukedom of Montrose, pp. 162-6.

† There may have been, as in all such cases, some subtleties and intervening incidents unknown, to give another aspect to the matter; but such seems the natural inference.

was), in the interim, specially imparted to her; and this may be kept in view in reference to what will follow. Intestine troubles subsequently occurred; Sir John, turbulent and intriguing by nature, and too often involved in feuds and sedition, was forfeited, and hence, for the time, out of the question; but immediately after the reversal of his attainder, May 10, 1527,[1] and actually on the 28th of the same month, he, wholly engrossed with his Cadder projects and exigencies, entered into solemn "*indentoures* in form of contract," with *rather* an *important* person, ROBERT STIRLING (simply so designed), no doubt for their material furtherance, wherein " ayir of ye saidis parteis band and oblisit yame and yair airis to observe keip and fulfill divers and sindry poyntis, articulis, and claussis as at mair lenth is contenit in ye saidis indentouris ;"[2] so they are respectively represented in the preamble of recorded transactions, to be subsequently adduced, the contract * itself not being recovered ; and from the same source we gather that the knight had then granted to Robert, in fulfilment of his engagement, the lands of Lettyr, Kirkmychel, and Blancrno, all parts of the Cadder property ; but owing to his only being wardator of Cadder, and obviously unable at that time validly to make such a concession, he further heritably gave the said Robert the lands of Auld Keir in warrandice of the same.

[1] Acts of Parliament, vol. ii, pp. 318-20.

[2] See Contract between James Stirling of Keir and John Stirling of Lettyr, March 1, 1553, in Drumpellier Case, Appendix, No. X.—a most weighty and striking evidence, only capable of one import, in favour of the concocted Cadder representative, *Robert Stirling*, a party.

This was the strongest security Sir John could give, and showed the magnitude, in his eyes, of the advantage he was to obtain, and, at the same time, the importance of the relative Cadder party with whom he dealt. Auld Keir was a xv pound land of old extent, and the original paramount Keir patrimony—his very heart's blood—and the last portion of his estate which one so imperious and overbearing would have thus disponed or conceded, excepting for a pressing necessity or object.

The preceding Robert Stirling, though thus great in his house or person, was small in his means,† and had but a slender provision as a cadet according to the practice of the time, through the title or interest of Bankeir, a

---

* Not an item of which is to be found in the *impartial* Keir work, nor aught relatively, though intimately affecting both families relatively.

† If Robert's mediocre or inferior condition here had been objected, he might have analogously retorted, in the noted apt reply of the Duke of Medina Celi, the preferable heir by its original descent to the Spanish crown, when affected to be despised by Charles IV. (that imbecile monarch) on account of the lowness of his stature—of a piece with Robert's lowness of means—" Yes, sir, it may be so ; but I am great in my house " (*grande in mia casa*) ; and so far by birth superior in regard to the Spanish succession, as explained here, to the King, who, on the other hand, was tall and portly.

portion of the Cadder estate. He was sometimes designed "in Cadder," from his dwelling in the family mansion, as might be expected in the case of a near, or perhaps the nearest, Stirling of Cadder relative, and who, from his restricted means, could not otherwise accommodate himself. Under all the circumstances, he must be inferred the Cadder heir-male, holding that identical status, and having, as premised, a claim to Cadder. It was incumbent on Keir, for the furtherance of his projects, to prevail upon Robert to forego this claim for an equivalent. Independently, too, he was entitled, in such character, to be tutor to the family, through the Act of Parliament in 1474;[*] but such claims or rights he must have forborne to assert, at the earnest entreaty of Sir John, who was wardator, and who, of course, was interested, and eager for the removal of the material bar in the way of his projects, both as regarded his own exclusive power and management of Cadder—so accordant with his character—and in order to secure to his own family the property, in the name of Janet, by subsequently marrying her to his son, and so uniting the two houses should they have issue. But then Robert must be fully compensated in return; and this accordingly originated the mutual indentures and contract between the parties in 1527, "quhairin" both "band and oblisit yame and yair airis to observe, keip, and fulfill divers and sundry poyntis, articulis, and claussis."[1] These must have involved the surrender by Robert of his claims to the Cadder estate at large; for what else had he to give in compensation for promised portions of the Cadder property, of such magnitude as to require the weighty guarantee of Auld Keir? Absolutely nothing. Robert being the only party thus dealt with, while a settlement accordingly was so incumbent, and indeed pressing, for the projects of Sir John, can anything more strongly evince or demonstrate the Cadder status in question, to have been in Robert, with its consequent rights and accessories?

It is impossible to give any other reasonable solution of the contract cited in 1527, and, at the same time, under the circumstances, one so natural and inevitable. In vain a different one has been requested of the Keir family, possessed, as they are, of all the Cadder writs and muniments, and doubtless

---

[*] May 9, in that year, which specially statutes and ordains, in respect of the "brief of tutorie" (the warrant for a service of a tutor), that "he yat is *nerrest* AGNET, and of xxv yeiris of age ... sall be lauchfull tutour." Aguet or agnate meant then an heir-*male exclusively*, in which sense it was used in the Roman law, from which we borrowed it.—For the above see *Scotch Acts of Parliament*, last edition, vol. ii. pp. 106, 107.

of this contract also, which, unfortunately, is not upon record—who have here raised no objection, and, as will be seen in the sequel, confess they have none to make.

It may also be material to observe that, if an heir-male could take, or had a claim to his estates, on the death of Andrew Stirling of Cadder in 1522, it must have been as heir-male of the body of William Stirling of Cadder, under his Cadder entail in 1414, the last and regulating one, it is conceived; which was thus accordingly limited, in the first instance; and if so, any compensation for the surrender of his rights—any *quid pro quo* in a landed shape—quadrating, as behoved, with the limitation, could only have been to him and such heirs of the entailer. And it so happens—remarkably and coincidentally again—that the actual portion of the Cadder estate, finally settled upon the family of Robert Stirling in 1553 (he having predeceased), in compensation, as may be inferred, for their Cadder claim and status, and based upon the solemn contract of 1527, was precisely so destined, exclusively to the heirs-male of the body. As any Cadder claim to descent behoved to be by an heir, so, in accordance, must be the compensation; and being hence so far in perfect conformity with the entail in 1414, it cannot but be admitted to have been, in part, in implement thereof, and for behoof of, and a requital to, the heirs thereby claiming—viz., Robert's children, who are thus evinced to be the Cadder heirs-male, indeed the only ones, as no other heirs-male or competitors, after every investigation, have been discovered. This necessarily exhausted the entail in their default, in the first instance, and accounts for the corresponding restrictive destination in the compensation in 1553 to heirs-male of the body.

The preceding Robert Stirling, "in Cadder," or "of Lettyr," as he was occasionally designed, is the undoubted direct Drumpellier male ancestor, through John of Lettyr, his eldest son and heir, who concluded the final Cadder settlement in that year with James Stirling of Keir. The same Robert Stirling, the undoubted Drumpellier ancestor, and family, to be proved the nearest Cadder

Even supposing we went no further, the question at issue, *identified* with the *Cadder representation*, might be held in favour of Drumpellier: but eventually proofs of their having been the *nearest* Cadder *heirs* after Janet and her issue in 1541, and, singularly again, entitled, as such, to portions of the Cadder estate, will be adduced in the sequel, and in (perhaps) a better place; while, indeed, more will transpire in the sequel of Robert being the male Cadder representative. laterally, which is, *per se* decisive, besides heir-male.

The latter evidence in 1541, somewhat resolving into the transaction of 1553—of which it may be deemed a part—is evidently *per se* here decisive. What, then, must it not be, taken with the remainder of the facts of the case, as will be seen, so perfectly in unison with, and corroborative of, the main conclusion?

<small>Andrew Stirling of Drumpellier, direct heir-male of the preceding Robert in 1818, takes steps for establishing his Cadder status and representation, *ut supra*.</small>

The direct representative and heir-male of Robert in 1817 and 1818—viz., Andrew Stirling, Esq. of Drumpellier—resolved to take legal steps to establish his Lettyr and Cadder status and descent, as transmitted to him through his ancestors, and duly to record the evidence in its support. The motive was justified by the parallel example of eminent and meritorious personages, and was in some degree analogous to what may have laudably prompted the honourable member for Perthshire to the Keir Performance; though he merely contented himself with an *ex parte* statement, through the medium of a private circulation, without going further, or adopting, as is conceived, the better and more satisfactory course of Mr Stirling of Drumpellier in 1818. The honourable member seems thus to have eschewed public and legal discussions, from which, however, he may have been deterred through obvious and prudential motives, as was the case with his ancestor in regard to his opposition of the Drumpellier service in 1818.

Mr Stirling of Drumpellier, being advanced in years in 1818, the task of establishing his rights legally by service devolved upon his eldest son and apparent heir, Mr William Stirling, than whom none could have more adequately discharged it. He was active and intelligent, and, independently of personal endowments and accomplishments which distinguished him in society, high-spirited, and in every way fitted to act up to his situation, and discharge the duties of the Stirling representative, as in fact he eventually was.

Mr William Stirling, younger of Drumpellier, acting under his father's instructions, and prompted by that courtesy and consideration for others which distinguished him through life, and at the same time by a sense of justice and high feeling, which made him scorn to possess that which he was not rightfully entitled to, thought it no more than due to Mr Stirling of Keir to inform him of his father's intentions, and, at the same time, to ask to be allowed to inspect the Cadder charter-chest, which, if granted, might either confirm the justice of his claims, or dispel the visions which tradition had raised. In either of these results he was ready to acquiesce, and would greatly have preferred this method of settling matters to the more public and disagreeable course which was the only alternative.

With this view, therefore, by letter he apprised Keir of the steps his father proposed taking, to establish his Cadder status by service, with a request that he might be favoured with an inspection of the Cadder writs. That application, so far, could in no way prejudice or affect his (Keir's) rights, because his family, for more than three centuries (*i.e.*, from 1541), had been infeft under a singular title in the estate of Cadder, that constituted, of course, the most indefeasible. While, however, respectably sprung, they never antecedently had claimed to be of Cadder, whose representation, on the other hand, maintained by Drumpellier, was *jus tertii* to them. If actually head or chief of the Stirlings, that status must have been otherwise based by Keir; and with the utmost deference thereto, Mr William Stirling merely restricted his application for the writs, without the least request for more, from the charter-chest of the Keir family. The application was refused by Mr Charles Stirling, Keir's younger brother, who generally acted for him, after referring the applicant to Mr Dundas, his agent, rather anomalously from what will afterwards be stated, and between whom there was much written communication regarding Keir and Drumpellier interests. *[Courteous communication of his purpose to Keir, though not descended of Cadder, yet owner by a singular title of their writs, with application for their inspection, that was unsuccessful.]*

So commenced the correspondence initiatory to legal procedure on the part of Drumpellier. It continued for some time previous to his service, under various phases, with all due explanations and insight into the merits of his case by Mr William Stirling to the Keir party, with, however, no return of the kind by the latter, who were entirely reticent—with what success and results will be seen. And the Drumpellier family have been induced to print this correspondence in the present Exposition, for the following reasons:— (1.) A deep regard and respect for a near and deceased relative, evincing that, whatever the conduct on the other side—which it is not intended unduly to assail—Mr William Stirling was open and candid in his bearing, without the least doubt or exception attaching thereto; (2.) That the whole jet or *parview* of the correspondence is favourable to Drumpellier, affording, from its tenor, a striking contrast to the other side,—for, while the former was consistent, and uniform, and, straightforward, as of a party alone influenced by the justice of his case, and honestly confident of it, the latter was dubious, vacillating, and incompetent, eliciting a different conclusion; and (3.) because, coupled, as will be seen, with the innate merits of the Drumpellier claim—which had been duly submitted to Mr Dundas—important, indeed clenching, conclusions, at the close of the correspondence must be drawn in its behalf.

COMMENTS ON KEIR PERFORMANCE,

Without further preamble, therefore, we may now produce the correspondence in question, which extended from the 28th July 1817 to 9th April following, interspersed too, as may be incumbent, with occasional, accompanying, and convenient explanations, in this order—viz.: *Firstly*, the said correspondence down to 6th March 1818. *Secondly*, a *verbatim* copy of the second branch of evidence contained in the statements of the Drumpellier merits and claims in 1818, which was then adduced and submitted to the examination of Mr Dundas, to which some confirmatory proofs and explanations will be added—in this way the public will be informed of its weight and import. The insertion of this document at this place may be somewhat awkward, it is admitted, but what follows requires it to be placed here. *Thirdly*, and *lastly*, will come the remainder of the correspondence, from 6th March to 9th April 1818, which may speak for itself, and which, taken with what precedes under the first and second heads, may warrant the important conclusion already alluded to.

The Correspondence that subsequently followed between the parties regarding their Cadder and family rights and interests, from 28th July 1817 to 6th March 1818.

I.—CORRESPONDENCE, from 28th July 1817 to 6th March 1818, between Mr WILLIAM STIRLING, Younger of Drumpellier, Mr CHARLES STIRLING, Younger Brother of the then Keir, and Mr JAMES DUNDAS, the Keir Law-Agent; together with allusion to a Letter, at the same time, from Mr SAMUEL STIRLING, Younger of Glorat, Advocate (afterwards Sir Samuel Stirling of Glorat, Baronet), whose concern and interest in the matter has been already shown.

[The following are all copied from the original letters, excepting Mr William Stirling's, which are, in most cases, taken from autograph copies, but, at other times, from copies made by near relatives.]

1.—EXCERPT LETTER, WILLIAM STIRLING to CHARLES STIRLING.

"LONDON, *July* 28, 1817.

"I had an interview, a few days ago, with the Duke of Montrose, previous to his leaving town, on the subject of an application my father had made for leave to inspect the papers of the ancient earldom of Lennox, now in his possession; which his grace seemed unwilling to comply with, on the ground of a possible interference with the interest or feelings of your family, to which he seems much and most properly attached. When he found, however, that the object in question was merely one of pedigree, and quite unconnected with anything like a claim to estates, as he had somehow taken into his head, he proposed, of himself, to speak with you in regard to it when he gets down, and to be guided by your answer, which, if favourable, will remove his objection.

"Such being the proposal, I could not well decline it, and therefore think it proper to acquaint you with what passed. And it having been found necessary to make out a sort of statement, in order to explain to him the exact nature of our investigation, I think it right to put you in possession of a copy of the same, whether right or wrong, which, if you are at the trouble of reading, and notice any errors, perhaps you will have the goodness to point out the same when we meet, which I hope will be in the course of a few weeks. Meantime, in case you see no fair ground of objection to the Duke's complying with our wishes, we shall feel obliged if you will say so when you see him on the subject. "W^M. S.

"(Y^r. of Drumpellier.)"

The Drumpellier family here acted in the fair and open way that distinguished them throughout, which never met with an adequate return, and even offered, as usual, to supply that of Keir with a statement of their case or evidence. What immediately ensued on the above letter between the parties (though they had Cadder communings between the letters) does not now appear; only this, that the former did not succeed in obtaining a sight of the Lennox writs, as may be inferred, owing to the invariably decided opposition, as will be seen, of Mr Charles Stirling to their main object. This seems supported by a passage in the next letter quoted. The Lennox papers might have been useful to Drumpellier, owing to Lettyr, one of their old Cadder patrimonies, having held of the house of Lennox; and in the hands of the superior, very often in Scotch charter-chests, there are deeds and muniments affecting the vassal.

2.—LETTER, WILLIAM STIRLING to CHARLES STIRLING.

"GLASGOW, 12*th January* 1818.

"I now beg leave, in pursuance of what has lately passed between us on this subject, to acquaint you, that I have this day sent orders to my father's agent (agreeable to my instructions from home to that effect), to obtain a brief from Chancery, in order to have him served heir to Robert Stirling, the first of Lettyr, who died in the year 1537; and also, if possible, to Andrew

Stirling, father of the heiress, and last of Cadder, who died about the year 1520, and to whom, there is every reason to believe, that Robert was, if not brother, at all events the nearest relative and rightful heir.

" In mentioning this, I hardly think it necessary to add, that there does not exist the most remote idea of claiming estates, or for anything whatever beyond the mere lower, and perhaps insignificant, pretension of representing, in point of blood, the long-decayed house of Cadder, from which, it has always been believed, among ourselves at least, that we are descended. Nor am I at all aware that, in the prosecution of this object—which to us is entirely one of some moment—there can be any possible interference with the interests of your family, whose possession of the Cadder estate, however acquired, is sufficiently fortified by the lapse of nearly three centuries without the slightest challenge, and a multiplication of most equitable, as well as most perfectly legal titles since that period, and whose descent we have always understood to be of an origin totally different, though perhaps neither less ancient nor less honourable than the one in question. Such at least, from the imperfect light we possess—having been debarred access by your friends, out of compliment to you, to some of the most natural and probable sources of information—in our view of the matter. But as it is very possible that we may be in some degree mistaken as to this, and, at all events, are desirous of acting in the most open and candid manner, I think it proper, by way of guarding against any misunderstanding on that subject, to give you the earliest and clearest notion of our intentions, that in case yourself or any of your family should be of a different opinion to ours, they may have the fullest opportunity of considering the bearings of the case, and of expressing their sentiments in consequence, which, if they will honour us so far as to communicate, shall meet with the most respectful deference and attention on our part, and every fair delay allowed for the purpose. On the other hand, should there be no indication of this sort, I would then endeavour, if possible, to put the Brief into execution before leaving the country, provided I hear from you in sufficient time to admit of my doing so.

" Submitting all this most respectfully to your and their consideration, on the part of my father, I beg to assure you that, in all events, and under all circumstances, I shall ever continue, with unfeigned regard, yours," &c.

" W_M. S.

" (Y^{r.} of Drumpellier.)"

The preceding letter is thus endorsed, autograph of W. S. :—" Copy letter to Charles Stirling, 12th January 1818, at his recommendation, and having been shown to, and approved of by him, at Cadder on the Saturday previous, delivered to him by me this morning in person."

If there apparently was some inclination here, on the part of Mr Charles Stirling, to listen to, and perhaps to forward the views of the writer, it will shortly be seen how little consistent this was with his future method of proceeding.

3.—LETTER, CHARLES STIRLING to WILLIAM STIRLING.

"GLASGOW, 14th January 1818.

" Enclosed you have a letter from Mr James Dundas, in answer to the one I wrote him enclosing yours to me regarding your father's claim for proving his descent from the family of Cadder. From what Mr Dundas says, it will be necessary that you are more explicit than you were in your former letter. Indeed, I think you had much better carry on the correspondence directly with Mr Dundas, as it will be a saving of trouble to all of us.
"C. S.
" (Brother of Keir.)"

In the foregoing letter appears that vacillation on the Keir side, which had shown itself somewhat on previous occasions, but is now to be made strikingly manifest in the correspondence that follows—so much in contrast with the Drumpellier conduct, which was invariably open, manly, and candid, frankly making everything in their possession patent to Keir.

4.—LETTER, JAMES DUNDAS to CHARLES STIRLING.

"EDINBURGH, 13th January 1818.

" I have received the favour of your letter of the 12th, enclosing a letter from Mr William Stirling to you. I really am so ignorant of the subject of Mr Stirling's letter, that it is altogether out of my power to form or communicate any opinion regarding it. I only see, from some memoranda of the late Mr Erskine, that, about the year 1540, James Stirling of Keir, son of Sir

John Stirling of Keir, had married Janet Stirling, heiress of Cadder. I would wish to know what Mr Stirling's object is by wishing to have his father served heir to Robert Stirling of Lettyr, or to Andrew Stirling, father of the heiress. Upon hearing from you I will again look into Mr Erskine's memoranda.

" J. D.
" (Keir's Agent.)"

5.—LETTER, WILLIAM STIRLING to CHARLES STIRLING.

" GLASGOW, 14*th January* 1818.

" However reluctant to trouble you further on this subject, I think it right to send you, in reply to your letter of this morning enclosing one from Mr Dundas, the annexed memorandum, and to add that, as my father's claim goes, certainly, on the one hand, to the establishment of a legal connection with the house of Cadder in point of blood, so, on the other, it is totally unconnected with anything like a claim to property of any kind. I am quite at a loss to know how I am to express myself stronger on this head than I have already done; but I can only add that, if it is possible to frame any legal obligation to that effect, I am sure my father will be ready and willing to subscribe it, along with his whole family, in any terms Mr Dundas may please to dictate.

" W$_M$. S.
" (Y^r. of Drumpellier.)"

The memorandum above referred to is proved, by a cotemporary copy, taken by Mr William Stirling, to have contained the material evidence in a statement of the merits of the Drumpellier case in 1818, and now given *verbatim* in the present Chapter, evincing that the Keir family, who saw the latter too, were, as speedily as possible, put into possession of everything on this subject.

In compliance with Mr Charles Stirling's wish, Mr William Stirling immediately put himself in communication with Mr Dundas, and held two conferences with him on the subject in question; after the first of these interviews, he wrote as follows:—

6.—EXCERPT LETTER, WILLIAM STIRLING to CHARLES STIRLING.

"EDINBURGH, *Monday, 19th January.*

"I have just parted with Mr Dundas, whom I waited on as you desired, and have had two long conferences with him on the subject offered to his decision, and am truly happy to find that he is perfectly satisfied, not only that your family have no such interest opposed to ours on the present occasion, but also that there is no fair reason why they should not grant us the fullest access to the papers relating to our own predecessors. He declines making use of the authority placed in his hands to say Aye or No of himself, but has promised, of his own accord, to write you on the subject what his sentiments are, and in the mean time he has given me the satisfaction of knowing that they are favourable to our request, to which he has no objection whatever, provided it is agreeable to you to comply with it otherwise. He was good enough to add that, in case you should wish it, he would have no objection to undertake a journey as far as Keir for that purpose himself, if it should be any satisfaction to you to have the sanction of his presence during the inspection, but that, in his opinion, this was otherwise unnecessary, as you had already a competent man of business in the neighbourhood, who was fully capable of attending on such occasions.

"All this, however, is a detail which it is unnecessary to enter into till the affair is approved of and sanctioned by your acquiescence.

"W. S.
"(Y^{r.} of Drumpellier.)"

Things would thus appear to have progressed favourably, and Mr William Stirling on the eve of obtaining his object, seeing that Mr Dundas, to whom Mr Charles Stirling had referred him—so naturally, one had thought, as a kind of umpire in the matter—entirely approved of it; but we now first find that the former had here actually reserved to himself a *liberum veto*, quite at variance with the professed sentiments of his law-agent; and the following letter most summarily and abruptly announces a determination on his part to refuse permission for the inspection of the Cadder writs, and a resolute opposition to the Drumpellier claims :—

7.—LETTER, CHARLES STIRLING (brother to Keir) to WILLIAM STIRLING.

"GLASGOW, 22d *January* 1818.

"I yesterday had the pleasure to receive your letter of the 19th, and the same post brought one from Mr Dundas.

"I think it right to be candid and explicit on the subject of your letter, by frankly communicating that your request for having permission to examine the papers in the Keir charter-chest cannot be gone into. However unpleasant it may be to my feelings, in the discharge of a duty I feel I owe to my two elder brothers and our family, yet, nevertheless, I deem it but fair to acquaint you that I have by this post instructed Mr Dundas, my brother's agent, to oppose in every fair way your father's claim for being second heir to the heiress of Cadder, or her uncle. I shall only add that no personal motive to yourself has induced me in adopting the measure to be pursued in this business; and I am persuaded that, when you coolly survey it in all its bearings, you will then be fully sensible that I could not have acted otherwise than I have done, notwithstanding how opposite that may be to your wishes.

"C. S.
"(Brother of Keir.)"

Without stopping to consider how Mr William Stirling would, as suggested, coolly acquiesce in the admonitory conclusion drawn for him by his correspondent at the end of the letter, there would seem to have been an undiscernible under-current in the business that may have regulated it. And the former unconsciously, owing to no fault or want of possible prevoyance of his, bandied from the one party mentioned to the other, who had a mutual correspondence—as Mr Charles Stirling to Mr Dundas, and Mr Dundas to Mr Charles Stirling—like a shuttlecock between two battledores. But be that as it may, he being so peremptorily and unexpectedly refused the inspection in question—the gauntlet having been thrown down, and war openly proclaimed by the last gentleman (with what prudence and success will afterwards be so plain)—Mr William Stirling could now only write the following appropriate and conciliatory letter in return :—

8.—EXCERPT LETTER, WILLIAM STIRLING to CHARLES STIRLING.

"EDINBURGH, 26th January 1818.

"I was favoured with your letter of the 22d on Friday, which, however contrary to my wishes and sentiments, as it certainly is, and perhaps to my expectations also, yet admits of no further argument; neither will I presume to trouble you with any expression of the regret it has occasioned me. You are most unquestionably right to discharge in the strictest manner that which you consider to be a duty to your own family; and if you seriously conceive, as you seem to do, that their interests are likely to be affected by our intended proceedings, are fully entitled to offer, without the least regard to us, every fair opposition.

"Of this there can be no doubt, nor shall there be any of the fairness of our conduct—having declared to Mr Dundas *our readiness to afford him every information, and to make him acquainted with any particulars that may be considered requisite for rendering that opposition effectual.*

"Let the result, therefore, be what it may, you at least will have no room for complaint. Should it prove unfavourable to us, which is very possible, we shall have nothing to say, unless perhaps to regret that the proofs by which we may be discomfited had not been brought forward at an earlier period, and in a less public manner. If, on the contrary, we succeed, I trust we may again be permitted to hold out the olive branch, and that you will have too much greatness of mind to allow anything that may pass on the present occasion to have the effect of shutting the door to any future overture of accommodation between the respective families, in which I cannot still help thinking that each might find their account upon principles equally honourable to both, and which, if it were by any means possible to effect, would be my highest pride to be instrumental in the accomplishment.

"W. S.
"(Yr. of Drumpellier.)"

The Keir and Drumpellier families being thus legally at issue on the subject of the prospective service by the latter—which the former was so resolutely and inexorably to oppose—there behoved to be communings between them, or their legal agents, in reference to their procedure; while Mr Charles Stirling, though still the Keir oracle in secret, and even adviser of the opposition, not appearing openly in the business, the different points were mainly mooted and discussed in the correspondence that follows between Mr William Stirling, acting for his father, and Mr James Dundas, acting for Keir.

There were, at the beginning of February 1818, no other avowed parties than Keir and Drumpellier. Samuel Stirling, younger of Glorat, Advocate, on the fourth of the same month, intimated by letter to Mr William Stirling that "*no* opposition will be made at present by my father" (viz., Sir John Stirling, Baronet, of Glorat) to the Drumpellier service.

Matters here, however, as will be shown very shortly, changed; and Keir, through his legal advisers, now finding to his cost that he had rashly—however boldly and confidently at first—by the urgency of his brother Charles, been precipitated into the contest, that legally was *jus tertii* to him, forthwith betook himself to the Glorat family as the only expedient for thus opposing Drumpellier—whom he prevailed upon so to act, and with whom, in the person of the preceding Mr Samuel Stirling, through Mr Dundas, he formed an alliance for the purpose. He then, though ostensibly only, quitted the field, leaving the chief management of the Drumpellier opposition to Samuel Stirling, assisted by Mr Dundas, who remained nearly *in statu quo*. And by this confederacy, which could not well be acceptable to Drumpellier, he had now virtually two instead of one to meet—viz., Glorat openly and Keir in secret, while the latter undertook to defray the expenses.

The above, which will be proved in the sequel, may be a necessary explanation in connection with the correspondence alluded to, which follows:—

9.—EXCERPT LETTER, WILLIAM STIRLING to JAMES DUNDAS, W.S.

"*Saturday, 7th February* 1818.

"I have now to acquaint you, according to my promise, that we intend to lay the *brieve for my father's service, of which I gave you a copy the middle of last week*, before a jury, in presence of the Sheriff of Edinburgh, on this day fortnight, Saturday the 21st instant, *provided that day should be perfectly agreeable to your friends in the west*. If not, I hope you will have the goodness to name any other, more so, and we will do all we can to meet their wishes. In the mean time, as I said before, *if there be any information in our power*, which you think can be of the slightest use to you in strengthening the present opposition, *it shall be heartily at your service*.

"W. S.
" (Yr. of Drumpellier.)"

10.—LETTER, WILLIAM STIRLING to JAMES DUNDAS, W.S.

" HOWE STREET, EDINBURGH, 19*th Feb.* 1818.

"Mr William Stirling presents his compliments to Mr Dundas, and requests to know if there be any answer to the letter he had the honour to send him on the 7th instant. "W. S.
" (Yr. of Drumpellier.)"

11.—LETTER, WILLIAM STIRLING to JAMES DUNDAS, W.S.

" 20*th February.*

" I had the honour of your note only late last night ; but, immediately on receipt of it, sent instructions to my father's agent to *postpone* the service for a fortnight, at all events, and as much longer as may, on further consideration, be thought convenient or agreeable to your friends.

"W. S.
" (Yr. of Drumpellier)."

It is evident from the above letter that *Mr Dundas had applied for a delay of the service*, in order, no doubt, that the Keir cause, by gaining time, might also acquire strength, and succeed in collecting evidence (however little) to justify an opposition to Drumpellier. The letter evinces Mr William Stirling's usual readiness to acquiesce in the wishes of his adversary.

12.—EXCERPTS from JOURNAL of WILLIAM STIRLING, proving what is premised.

"19*th February* 1818.

" Meantime it is proper to bear in mind the following particulars on the evening of the 19th. Previous to Mr Dundas writing me, as above, he and his partner Mr Wilson called and had a long conference with Samuel Stirling, at the lodgings of the latter, in which they insisted on *giving him a regular fee on the part of their clients*, and laid before him the statement of the grounds of their case.

"The conference concluded, however, by Dundas expressing himself much impressed with the *very open and handsome manner in which we had conducted ourselves*, and giving it as his decided opinion that the *Keir family had no ground to interfere upon the present occasion*, in which opinion Samuel Stirling concurred, and it was finally agreed to *write Charles Stirling* by next post, *acquainting* him with *their joint sentiments on this head*, and to *convince him of the same*. Meantime Dundas should write me asking delay, as he did the same night as above."

"*25th February, Wednesday.*—This day Riddell* saw Samuel Stirling for a long time in earnest conference with Wilson in the Advocates' Library, after which Samuel came up to Riddell and told him that *Wilson* had that morning *received a reply from Charles Stirling*, saying that, notwithstanding what had been said, he *was resolved upon an opposition*. The strain of the means he left to them, and desired *they would arrange to the best of their knowledge, and persevere*, and that, when they were able to determine upon anything, to let him know, and he would come into Edinburgh in aid, to give his sanction to whatever might be considered as the most advantageous plan : that after full consideration as to this, he (Samuel) and Wilson had agreed that the best way of proceeding would be for *the Keir family to withdraw their opposition*, and *that Sir John Stirling of Glorat*, Mr Samuel's father, should again come forward, as before thought of, *in whose name the proceedings should take place*, while *the expenses should be entirely defrayed by Keir;* and this scheme Samuel was to submit to his father, for his approbation, the same evening."

It hence is proved—in keeping with other corroborative evidence in the case—that Glorat originally, with just reason, declined to oppose Drumpellier ; that *Keir* avowedly *could not do so*, but had recourse to Glorat for that

---

* That is the present writer—he being chief counsel, and of course confidant, of Mr William Stirling in this case. He never saw or was aware of the above autograph journal, obviously written at the time, until last year ; and he has no hesitation now in concurring with what here follows in it as to himself. The information in question, which doubtless made an impression on him, certainly was derived from Sir Samuel Stirling, with whom he was for years on terms of the greatest intimacy.

purpose, whose learned heir-apparent at length agreed *to be retained*, and act as *their counsel against* Drumpellier,[1] and that even then, at a regular consultation, not only *he* (in fact a *second* time), but also the law-agents of Keir, came to the resolution that the *opposition* in question was *impracticable*, and that *Keir* especially had *no ground of action;* which opinion, it was agreed, should be formally reported to Mr Charles Stirling, whom they were to try to convince accordingly.

[1] See Letters of James Stirling early in the same month.

But here independently, and strangely enough, was *imperium in imperio*, and the same gentleman whose pursuits were merely mercantile, and who at the outset, as has been seen, had relinquished the business in question to Mr Dundas—in the face of law and the best advice—resolved again to exercise his *liberum veto*. He would listen to no remonstrances, but peremptorily—on the part of Keir—ordered the former to proceed, by hook or by crook, by every means and quirk in their power, to check and oppose Drumpellier in the pursuit of his legal object : the *finale* of which was, that they at length succumbed to him, and the opposition was now exclusively to be prosecuted in the name of the Knight of Glorat, Keir *ostensibly withdrawing*, but still *acting in secret*, defraying the incurred expenses, and aiding and abetting him in his hostile attempts against Drumpellier to the utmost of his power. And this, though Glorat had truly as little interest in the matter as himself, which will pointedly be shown in the sequel. So keen and inexcusable was their opposition.

Here, in conformity with the plan proposed, we shall intermit the correspondence for a space, to be subsequently continued under a third and final head, after the conclusion of what forms the subject of the next and second, to which we will proceed forthwith.

II.—PRINTED STATEMENT in 1818 of the *Merits* of the Drumpellier Case, with some Requisite Explanations and Correlative Additions.

Before giving the same, it may be premised that the family of Drumpellier are unquestionably direct heirs-male of Robert Stirling of Bankeir and Lettyr, (or "in Cadder,") formerly alluded to, who died in 1537. That status was fully vested in them, in the person of their representative, Andrew Stirling, Esq. of Drumpellier (father of Walter Stirling, Esq., the present

Drumpellier), by the service (previously contemplated and broached in the correspondence), 18th April 1818, after its proofs and merits had been keenly tested, and underwent the united scrutiny of Keir and Glorat, to whom they had previously, with that fairness and openness which characterised the whole conduct of the Drumpelliers, been duly disclosed and submitted. Yet in spite of their opponents—the one in secret, the other open—who here signally failed, the service of the above date, the merits of which had been subjected to the severest ordeal, passed without the least demur or challenge. Since then the status in question having been fortified by a double prescription of more than forty years, and admitted on all hands—which constituted of itself an indefeasible title—it may be unnecessary to recapitulate the evidence in its behalf. And with respect, again, to that grounded upon the "Indentouris" and contract between the same Robert of Lettyr and Sir John Stirling of Keir, in 1527, so much in favour of his important Cadder status and representation—indeed incapable of any other solution—it has been fully given at the beginning of this chapter; so what principally remains under this head is the proof to be adduced of the identity of Robert and his family, with the cotemporary Robert and his family, who legally in 1541 were declared, under judicial sanction of the supreme civil court, by Janet Stirling of Cadder—the direct Cadder representative—to be immediately to succeed to her, or, in other words, to be her nearest heirs, "failzeing airis," as she states, "of my awin body," of whom none now exist. This evidence is not only conclusive in itself, but it is also in perfect keeping with, and corroborative of, that just referred to from the contract in 1527.

<small>The "Indentouris" or contract in 1527, and identity of the two cotemporary Robert Stirlings and their families, before and after 1541, the material elements in the case.</small>

In this way, admitting the identity in particular, the nearest Cadder representation, and necessarily descent, will be fixed in Drumpellier exclusive of any competitor; and certainly Keir, who, independently of being wholly legally foreclosed and never once a party, is here in the far distance—even upon the flimsy footing of his pretended Cadder descent, anterior to 1300—though utterly unestablished, and unduly arrogated to him in the Keir Performance.

But in support of this remaining and conclusive fact of the identity, the matter being comparatively reduced to a short issue, though requiring due and apposite proof and illustrations, the statement of the merits of the Drumpellier claim printed in 1818, which was referred to, and that had previously been submitted to Mr Dundas, the Keir agent, shall next be adduced and reprinted here *verbatim* at full length—for the object noticed, and that will be fully obvious in the sequel—including its title, as follows :—*

"PROOFS that ROBERT STIRLING of Bankeyr and Lettyr, the Claimant's great, great, great, great, great grandfather, died in the year 1537, and is the same individual ROBERT STIRLING whose children, in a judicial procedure after his death, before the Lords of the Council and Session, were expressly declared to be next in succession to JANET STIRLING, only daughter and heiress of ANDREW STIRLING of Cadder, failing heirs of her own body.

It may be necessary to premise the *concluding head*, with stating that Andrew Stirling of Cadder, the last direct male representative of a series of Knights and Lairds of Cadder, died previous to the year 1522, leaving an only child—a daughter—a minor—of the name of Janet—who, by an alteration of the more ancient Investitures, from heirs male to heirs general,† in which manner they were limited as far down as the year 1509—became his heir and successor.

The grant of her ward, and marriage, was purchased from the different superiors, by Sir John Stirling of Keir, who strained every point to acquire the donation.‡

[*The proof of the Drumpellier descent from Robert having been here adduced beforehand under a first head, and being indisputable and admitted, as promised, we have only now to deal with this last and concluding one.*]

---

* The exponent has been induced to make occasional short additions thereto in the way of comments and references, to facilitate apprehension of certain points in the discussion and otherwise, but these will be at once perceptible, and distinguished from the text or reprint by being enclosed in brackets.

And there has also been inserted, with much the same view, at the *end* of the Performance, two pedigrees or genealogical tables, one marked No. I. of the Letter or Drumpellier family, and the other marked No. II. of that of Cadder and Keir, deduced from the text and contents of the Keir Performance, where unprecedentedly, as was stated, there is no such table. To the latter some short additions have been made by the exponent, also enclosed in brackets, but for the truth of the entirety of the statements so derived, i. e. from the above work, already, as may be obvious, partly demurred to and gainsaid, he is by no means answerable.

† [This only, however, from what is stated at the commencement of the chapter, involving more of importance on the point, applies to Uchiltree, that very ancient portion of the Cadder patrimony. Subsequent evidence derived from the Cadder writs in the Keir Performance, to which there was no access in 1818, evinces, so far as can be seen, that there was no such alteration upon a resignation as required for the purpose, in respect to the *remainder* of the estates.]

‡ 28th February 1522, Sir John Stirling of Keir paid 2500 markis to James, Archbishop of Glasgow, for the ward and marriage of Janet Stirling, daughter of Andrew Stirling, of Cadder. He also got the same grants from the King of her other lands.—

From *Extracts by the late Mr Ramsay of Ochtertyre from the Keir Charter-Chest*. See also the Gift to Sir John Stirling of Keir, Knight, of the marriage of Janet Stirling, daughter and heiress of the deceased Andrew Stirling of Cadder, 22d July 1529, *Privy Seal Book*, fol. 69. In a Deed made out under his son's inspection, to be immediately quoted (*Pub. Declaration and Procuratory of Janet Stirling*, 10th *December* 1541), it is stated, " Quod quondam Johannes Striveling de Keir, miles (the same as in the text), pro recuperatione Wardi, relevii, et non introitus (of Cadder), &c., *non minimam sui hereditatis et prediorum partem, ultra redemptionem, alienaverat.*"

In the character of her wardator, he treated her with the utmost rigour, detaining her in the closest captivity; and freely, as if he had been proprietor, disposed of portions of her estate. He next caused a pretended marriage, which was afterwards found null from the beginning, and dissolved by the Delegates of the Official of St Andrews, to be celebrated between her and his son James. And though she solemnly protested against this latter proceeding, and the whole of his unwarrantable conduct; yet, whether from the turbulence of the period, or from other causes, she never could obtain the smallest effectual redress.

Finally, after a struggle, and revoking a conveyance to the same effect, she was induced to resign her heritage in favour of her pretended husband, by an instrument of resignation, dated the 10th of December 1541.*

But immediately upon its execution, she expressly declared, in presence of the Lords of Council and Session—and the declaration is formally engrossed in their judicial acts recording the resignation—that a portion of that heritage, yielding a yearly rent of eighty merks—no small sum in those days—had been reserved for "THE BAIRNS OF UMQUHILE ROBERT STRIVELING, QUHILKIS ARE IMMEDIATLIE TO SUCCEID TO ME, FALZEING OF AIRIS OF MY AWIN BODY:"† certainly it will be allowed a fair and moderate bequest, in behalf of these

---

* "Anent our Soverane Lordis lettris purchest at ye instance of Janet Striveling, heretar of the landis and lordschip of Calder, agains Johne Striveling of ye Kere, knight, and James Striveling his sonne, That quhare ye saide Johne, havand her marriage, and ye dispositione of her warde landis, causit ane pretendit matrimony to be maid betuix ye said James and her, and sensyne ye saide Johnne hes halden, and as zit haldis her in subjectione, and will nocht suffer her to speik with hir friendis, and hes compellit her to mak diverse alienationnes and takkis of hir landis and hir heretage," &c.—Vide App. No. 3; [and also ADDENDA to this Chapter, No. 1.]

Decreet of Divorce, pronounced last day of January 1541, in Register of the Decreets of the Official of St Andrews, subjoined in the Appendix, No. 7.

† Publick Declaration and Procuratory by Janet Stirling Lady Calder, 10th December 1541. Acts of the Lords of Council and Session, Lib. 17, fol. 46, inserted in the Appendix. [See also as to this transaction, and the probability of her having been here concussed, with relative auspicious incidents and inferences, under No. 11. of the ADDENDA to the present Chapter.]

She was also, upon this occasion, prevailed upon to acknowledge the Family of Keir as Chief of the Stirlings; a procedure which, under all the circumstances, it is believed will, at the present day, have the effect rather of injuring their supposed right to that pre-eminence—thus so strangely grasped at—than of assisting it.

To comprehend the true nature of the transaction, it may be necessary to look "behind the scenes," and some light may be derived from a *secret* agreement, of a singular description, that then passed between Keir and a Thomas Bischop, his servitor, once a village attorney, who aspired to be a traitor and a foreign spy, and was at length, in his old age, a trader at Yarmouth, and an adulterer and burgess at Perth; who did not scruple to avow an act of adultery with the Heiress, who was afterwards bartered to him in marriage.

The deed is dated upon the 23d of February 1541, and states, "That for the 'HELP' and 'LABOUR' of Thomas Bischop, 'his SERVITOR, in SOLICITING and FURTHERING the conveyance made by her (Janet) of hir heritage' to Keir; he, therefore, assigns to the said Thomas a 'chalder of oats,' a 'tack of teindsheaves' (a considerable sum), the hand of the heiress, stript of her estate, &c.,—with the promise of a pardon from the King (nowhere to be found on record) 'for his ALLEGED lying with the said Janet whilst she was Sir James's wife!'"—App. No. 9. [See again, as to this matter, No. 11. of ADDENDA, just referred to.]

With regard to this unfortunate lady, little farther is known, than that she followed her husband to England, where she is believed to have died, shortly after, without issue.—App. *ibid.*

her nearest relatives, at a moment when, for no onerous consideration, she was making so large a sacrifice to an absolute stranger,—and likely to be recommended even by the *latter*, in order to purchase their connivance, or that of their curators, in such a transaction. [As to these nearest relatives too, it may be observed, that they were but pupils at the time, and therefore could neither move, nor be properly aware of what then occurred, for which see in the sequel.]

The Claimant proposes to show, that this umquhile ROBERT STRIVELING, AND HIS BAIRNS, were no other than his male ancestor ROBERT STIRLING OF BANKEYR, OR OF LETTYR, AND HIS CHILDREN, JOHN AND WILLIAM, above mentioned; and, consequently, that these individuals were the IMMEDIATE HEIRS OF THE HEIRESS OF CADDER, failing issue of her own body. In support of which position he offers the following proof. [There was also another child, *Janet*, recently discovered in with them, as will also be proved in the sequel.]

I.—The ROBERT STIRLING, in the instrument of 1541, is styled ROBERT STIRLING, simply, without any addition.—This was the ordinary appellation of ROBERT STIRLING of Lettyr, or Bankeir.

(1.) It may be here necessary to *remind the Inquest*,* that the latter, under the designation of Robert Stirling of Bankier, was married to Marion Fleming, daughter of William Fleming of Boghall (Ch. II. 1).

Among the Records of the Acta Dominorum Councilij et Sessionis, Lib. xliii. fol. 120, is a Decreet, of this date, of which the following is an excerpt, viz.:— 13. Dec. 1531.
" Decretis and deliveris yat *Marioun Fleming*, George Bog, Michael Gillespy, Johnne Striveling of ye Keir, knycht, ROBERT STRIVELING, James Brisbane, and Johnne Brisbane, hes done wrang in ye maisterful spoliation, ejectioun, and outputting of Robert Hereote forth of the hous, place, and landis of Gardarrouch, with the pertinentis, liand within ye regalitie of Glasgw, within ye scherefdome of Lanark," &c.

(2.) *Certified Extract from the same Record:*—Decreet of this date,—" Anent oure Soverane Lordis letres, purchest at ye instance of Dame Isabell Levingstoun, Lady Rosling, James Levingstoun hir bruyer, Maister Robert Hereote, and Gilbert Hereote, broyer to umquhile Allane Hereote—aganis William — 1533.

---

* [The present portion of the Drumpellier statement had been intended to be submitted to the Inquest who served the Claimant direct heir male of Robert Stirling of Lettyr in 1818, but was precluded by a mere preliminary objection in point of form, urged (as was shown) by Sir Samuel Stirling, the objector on the occasion, who wisely shunned the discussion it involved of the merits of the Cadder question, and thus contrived, backed by an interlocutor of the Sheriff-Substitute who presided, to have it momentarily staved off. In consequence of which, the portion alluded to was never submitted to the *jury*, though this was fully compensated *aliunde*, by the subsequent proceedings of Drumpellier, and his final success in the case. For an articulate statement of the matter, as well as inquiry into the ground and justice of the Sheriff-Substitute's interlocutor, the exponent may refer the reader to the next Chapter.]

52   COMMENTS ON KEIR PERFORMANCE,

26. Feb. 1538.
Fleyming of Boghall, and Marioun Fleyming, relict of umquhile Allane Hereote, and ROBERT STRIVELING, now hir spous, for his interes," &c.

(3.) *Act of Curatory, of this date, mentioned above,* in which "Johne Striveling, sone to UMQUHILE ROBERT STRIVELING, desirit Malcom Lord Fleming, and William Fleming of Boghall, curatoris to him."

24. Feb. 1542.
(4.) *Submission, of this date, mentioned above,* between certain parties therein specified, and "Johne Striveling, sone and air of UMQUHILE ROBERT STRIVELING," with consent of his curators, and Marion Fleming, relict of the said umquhile Robert, &c.

1. Nov. 1551.
(5.) *Instrument of Sasine, of this date,* in possession of Sir Charles Edmonstone of Duntreath, proceeding upon a precept by Archibald Earl of Argyll, in favour of William Livingston of Kilsyth, of the lands of Kirkmichael-Stirling, and Blairnerne, wherein John, son of ROBERT STRIVELING, is a witness.

2. March 1553.
(6.) *Certified Extract from the Register of Acts and Decreets, Book x. fol.* 127, *in his Majesty's General Register House at Edinburgh*—Contract, of this date, by which the lands of Lettyr and Balquharrage are destined to "Johne Striveling, sone and air of UMQUHILE ROBERT STRIVELING;" and failing heirs-male of his body, to William his brother.

II.—ROBERT STIRLING, the undoubted Heir of the Heiress, left Children, who are described as *Bairns,* in December 1541.—That ROBERT of Bankeyr or of Lettyr likewise left Children, who were Minors at this period—is apparent from the following Documents, viz.—

1533.
(1.) *Certified Extract from the Acts of the Lords of Council and Session, Book* xi. *fol.* 159, *extant in his Majesty's General Register House at Edinburgh*—Act of Curatory, of this date, of which the following is an extract, viz. : "In presence of the Lordis of Council, comperit JOHNE STRIVELING, SONE TO UMQUHILE ROBERT STRIVELING, and desirit Malcom Lord Fleming and William Fleming of Boghall *curatoris* to him *ad lites."—Appendix.*

21. Feb. 1542.
(2.) *Submission, of this date, above mentioned,* No. 4, between "James Striveling of ye Keir, sone and aire of umquhile John Striveling of ye Keir, knycht, his fader, on yat ane part; and JOHNE STRIVELING, SONE and AIR OF UMQUHILE ROBERT STRIVELING, with consent and assent of ane noblie and mychtie Lord, Malcolme Lord Fleming, Maister Hew Rig, *his curatoris,* and *Mairon Fleming,* ye relict of ye said umquhile Robert, on that oyer part.

1553.
(3.) *Contract, of this date, above mentioned,* No. 6, by which this John is proved to have had *a younger brother,* named William. [For more on this important subject, and pointedly corroborating the argument, reference may be made to what will be stated under an appropriate head.]

III.—The same ROBERT STIRLING must have died only a short time previous to the year 1541:—So, also, did ROBERT OF BANKEYR, OR LETTIR.

(1.) *Certified Extract from the Records of Adjournal in his Majesty's General Register House at Edinburgh*—" Colinus Campbell de Auchinhowye; convictus, de arte et parte, crudelium INTERFECTIONUM QUONDAM Alani Hammiltoun de Pardowy, ROBERTI STRIUELING DE LETTIR, et Andræ Strineling de Ballindroicht, ex precogitata fellonia commiss. in comitiua cum Colino Campbell juniore suo filio, Willielmo Campbell sua nepote et herede apparente, Johanne Roger eius seruo, et Karolo Campbell clauigero et decollatus." 15. Nov. 1537.

(2.) *Certified Extract from the Register of the Privy Seal in his Majesty's General Register House at Edinburgh*—" Ane respitt maid to Charlis Campbell of Skeringtoun, Coliu Campbell, sone of vmquhill Colin of Auchinhowye, Williame Campbell, and Johnne Roger, ffor yair tressonable biding and remanyng fra our Soverane Lordis army and raid of Sulway; and for ye art and part of ye SLAUCHTERIS OF VMQUHILL Alane Hammyltoun of Bardowe, ROBERT STRIUEING of BANKERE, and Andro Strineling in Ballingtrocht; and for all oyeris actionis tresoun in our Soverane Lordis persoun, fyre, murthur and thift being exceptit, and for xix zeris to indur.—At Striueling, ye ferd day of Junii, the zer of God ane thousand fyve hundreth xli zeiris." 3. June 1542.

IV.—In considering the different circumstances which may serve to ascertain the identity of such an individual, something would depend upon the place of his residence.—It might naturally be expected, that a person nearly connected with the Family of Cadder would have lived either at Cadder, or in its vicinity; at least, the actual residence there of a Stirling, in a feudal age, would go pretty far to infer a relationship. That ROBERT of Bankier or of Lettyr did actually reside at Cadder, and was occasionally thereby designed, is certain from the following Documents—viz.

(1.) *Dispensation, of this date, for the marriage of Robert Stirling and Marion Fleming, mentioned above;* by which it appears that the said Dispensation, as well as the banns for celebration of the said marriage, were published and proclaimed in the PARISH CHURCH OF CADDER.—This could hardly have taken place without a fixed residence within the parish. 11. June 1533.

(2.) It has been shown, that only three persons fell in the feud with the Campbells of Auchinhowie, viz. Allan Hamilton of Bardowie, Andrew Stirling, designed of Ballendrocht and Bankeir, and Robert Stirling, designed indifferently of Bankier and of Lettyr. In relation to that transaction, there is extant the following *Gift of Escheat, in the Register of the Privy Seal, Book xi. fol. 37, in his Majesty's General Register House at Edinburgh, of which the following is* *a certified copy*, viz.—"Ane letre maid to Archibald Erle of Ergile, his airis and assignais, ane or mai, of the gift of all gudis moveabile and unmoveabile, dettis, takkis, stedingis, obligationis, soumes of money, and utheris guidis quhatsumever, quhilkis pertenit to Charles Campbell of Bargour, and now pertenyng or ony wiss sal happen or may pertene to our Soucrane Lord, be resoun of eschete, throw being of the said Charles fugitive fra the law and at the horne, or convict for art and part of the slauchter of umquhile Alane Hamyltoun of Bardowie; Andro Striveling of Bankier;* and ROBERT STRIVELING IN CADDER, &c. Dated at Linlithgow ye xij day of November, ye zere of God ane thousand fyve hundred xxx vij zeris."

12. Nov. 1537.

From a previous entry in the Books of Adjournal, unnecessary to quote particularly, a violent feud appears to have existed between the Stirlings of Ballindrocht and the Campbells of Auchinhowie, both in the immediate vicinity of Cadder; in the course of which Colin Campbell of Auchinhowie had been slain by Andrew Stirling of Ballindrocht. In this feud Robert appears afterwards to have been implicated—which was probably the occasion of his and Andrew's death—an interference quite natural, upon the supposition of his being the male representative of the House of Cadder, and consequently obliged to espouse the interests of its members.

V.—The Claimant must remind *the Inquest*,† that, in terms of the Alienation of 1541, *a part of the Heritage of the Heiress of Cadder* was to be secured to the "BAIRNS" of an Umquhile "ROBERT STRIVELING." With this exception, the remainder was to be Keir's. He was to be Laird of Cadder, and would, necessarily, have the power of carrying into effect the anterior conditions connected with the property.

If, then, it can be proved that, immediately after the date of the transaction, JAMES STIRLING of Keir (for his Father, in consequence of his arbitrary and sanguinary proceedings towards *other* families, had before this been slain,‡) did enter into a Treaty with "the Bairns" of an "UMQUHILE ROBERT STRIVELING," *the undoubted Ancestor of the Claimant*, in order to secure to them certain parts of that estate;—and that the latter, by this and other arrangements, actually obtained several portions of that estate; and *farther*, if *none whatever* can be found to have been alienated to the "BAIRNS" of a separate "UMQUHILE ROBERT STRIVELING,"

---

* This Andrew Stirling of Bankeir was the same with Andrew Stirling of Ballindrocht. Both Robert Stirling and he had an interest in Bankier.

† [See again as to this, p. 51, note*.]

‡ He was murdered by Shaw of Cambusmore, near Stirling, in a fit of compunction for having been the unworthy instrument of Keir in assassinating Buchanan of Leny, whose daughters, coheiresses, he had *also* stript of a great part of their estate. To this act he was instigated by the widow of Leny, who, by Keir's machinations, had been reduced to the lowest distress.

can there exist the shadow of a doubt that the former were the identical persons there contemplated—those who were immediately to succeed to her, failing heirs of her body?

(1.) Her resignation is dated upon the 10th of December 1541; upon the 30th of January 1542, we find an indenture, in form of a submission to certain arbiters, between "*James Striveling of ye Keir, sone and aire of umquhile Johnne Striveling* of *ye Keir, knicht, his fader*, on yat ane part; and JOHNE STRIVILING, SONE AND AIRE OF UMQUHILE ROBERT STRIVILING, *with consent and assent of ane noble and michty Lord, Malcolme Lord Fleming, Maister Hew Rig, curators,* AND MARIOUNE FLEMING, RELICT OF YE SAIDE UMQUHILE ROBERT, on yat uyor pert,"—referring to the decision of the said arbiters, "all and sindrie actionis, debatis, pleyis, causis, questionis, and contraversies, or clames, yat ayer of ye saidis partyis hes to ask or clame at uyeris, or uyeris quhatsumevir, yat ony of ye saidis partyis hes or ony wise may haif, or muive agains uyeris, *in ony time before ye day of ye dait of yir presentis;* and speciallie anentis ye pley and questioune betuix ye saidis partyis, anent ye infefting of ye said Johne Striveling, as heir to his saide umquhile fader, in ye XV^{lib} landis of auld extent of Blauerne, Kirkmichael, and Lettir,"—" for relieving of ye saide Jameses landis and heritage of Keir, after ye forme of ane contract, and writingis maid betuix ye saide umquhile Johne Striviling of ye Keir, knicht, and ye said umquhile Robert," &c.—*App.* No. 8. 30. Jan. 1542.

(2.) And by a final contract between the same partis, of this date, there *expressly designed in the same manner*, it is fixed that the said John is to be infeft in the *lands of Balquharrage*, never previously, in any shape, held either by him or his father; a more valuable acquisition than Blauerne and Kirkmichael,* —and likewise in Lettir; which, failing the heirs-male of his body, were to descend to those of *his brother William;* after which the warrandice upon Keir was to be relieved.—*App.* No. 10. 2. March 1553.

These mutual agreements, no doubt, profess, *in part*, to proceed upon some clandestine, and *certainly illegal* transactions, that appear to have passed between Robert and Sir John, promising to the former these parts of the estate of Cadder.†

---

* The lands of Kirkmichael and Blanerne were held by the Family of Cadder of the Campbells of Auchinhowie, who held them of the Livingstons of Kilsyth, who held them of the Crown.

Now, Balquharrage held only of one subject superior (Keir) immediate tenant of the Crown. There would, then, here, be fewer feudal casualties exigible—a circumstance that could not fail of rendering it a more lucrative possession.

† [They were so far illegal, Sir John being only wardator, and not possessor of Cadder, and legally unable to intromit therewith, and hence, in warrandice for what he promised, was obliged heritably to infeft Robert even in his original family property of Old Keir, for which see full copies of the above deeds in 1542 and 1553 referred to in the Appendix, with more afterwards adduced in the text.]

This, *of itself*, would speak loudly in favour of the Claimant.* But these were only begun to be carried into effect *after the date of the alienation* in 1541;—*and immediately*, it will be perceived, *upon its execution*.—Instead of Blanerne and Kirkmichael, there is substituted Balquharrage, a more advantageous acquisition; *and it is extremely obvious, that even by their fulfilment Keir was* VIRTUALLY DISCHARGING THE STIPULATION OF THE HEIRESS.

It is in proof, that John ever afterwards possessed these lands in full property; as *also* his son Robert, until he disposed of them by sale. *Besides*, it can be proved that the *entire* estate of Bankeir, *another part of Cadder*, was, much about the same period, acquired by William, his younger brother.

As to the alienation even of an acre to the "*Bairns of an* UMQUHILE ROBERT STRIVELING," who was not his ancestor, THE CLAIMANT BELIEVES HE MAY SAFELY DEFY HIS OPPONENTS TO PRODUCE, TO THIS EFFECT, EVEN THE VESTIGE OF AN AUTHORITY.—On the other hand, independently of Balquharrage, a five-pound land of old extent—the ten-pound land of Lettir—Bankeir, Easter and Wester, all parts of the ancient inheritance of Cadder (to say nothing of the promise of Kirkmichael and Blanerne, also special portions of the same), were all, about the middle of the sixteenth century, acquired by the family of the Claimant; and to *these parts of the property of the Heiress, were* JOHN AND WILLIAM (*out of all question* "BAIRNS OF AN UMQUHILE ROBERT STRIVELING"), soon after the period of her resignation—duly "HELPIT AND PROVIDIT." †

From these single facts, the Claimant regards the Identity as fixed: what, then, must it be when combined with the other evidence?

But upon this point, and indeed the whole of the case, he cannot help remarking how extremely easy it would have been for the respectable person, who has declared himself so decided an opponent, to have advanced contrary evidence, if such had existed. Among other advantages, he is in possession of the ancient documents of the respective families of both Keir and Cadder, assuredly the most natural sources of information upon such a subject; but which, though freely imparted to others, have been carefully withheld from the Claimant. To them the latter presumes to think that he was peculiarly entitled, under the circumstances of the case, to have expected access;—and though he does in no shape presume to dispute the *legal right* which the individual in question has thought proper to exercise in withholding them, yet he considers it to be due to himself to record the *refusal* he

---

* [Certainly; and the agreement besides went partly upon the Cadder transaction in 1527, of a piece, it may be said, with Janet's stipulation about Cadder heritage in 1541, for which further see what is stated at the commencement of the present Chapter, and towards its close.]

† [Moreover, as was in part premised, it can be proved that there was another "bairn" of Robert Stirling's of Lettir, namely *Jane*, who was also provided by the Keir family, of course corroborating the argument; for which, as well as a minute statement of the ensuing important transactions—including their original groundwork—with some new evidence, see in the sequel.]

has experienced; and which, in balancing the general merits of his case, he trusts the Jury will not fail duly to appreciate.

In the mean time, one result of the opposition in question is, that it has produced a strict investigation of these important documents; and it is some satisfaction to the Claimant to be able to assure the Jury, from undoubted authority, that they *contain nothing whatever hostile to the present Claim.*

VI.—Upon the whole, the Claimant conceives he has satisfactorily established the point. Yet, in order to avail himself of every evidence, and to show the tradition and belief of his ancestors, he begs leave to adduce an additional authority of some antiquity, which, in similar questions, would be received even by the House of Lords,[*] though known to be scrupulous upon such occasions—and the more to be regarded on this account—that all the OTHER parts of it have already been legally substantiated.

It is the attestation of an old family Bible of Dr WILLIAM STIRLING, grand-uncle to the Claimant, who died in the year 1757, who, it is hardly to be supposed, could design to misrepresent a fact, which is evidently only introduced in reference to other matter, and upon which, from his professed religious principles and other causes, he does not appear to have set much estimation; and if erroneous from the quantity of evidence then in existence, independently of a fresher tradition, could at once have been so easily detected. By reference to the pedigree,[†] it will be seen that this individual was born in the year 1682, and was of course twenty-seven years of age when his father, the third John Stirling, died: *That* John was grandson to Walter, the son of John Stirling of Lettyr, and was actually fifteen or sixteen years of age when the said Walter died;—circumstances which cannot fail to give peculiar weight to the testimony of the author.—There, along with entries of the births and descents of several of his connections, all in his own handwriting, is the following statement of his pedigree, necessarily embracing that of the Claimant, with which he now terminates his Case :—

Cruise on Dignities, p. 239.

[*] Cruise, the latest and ablest writer upon Peerage Law, affirms—" *Hearsay* evidence, although not generally admitted in other cases, is received in cases of pedigree."—And then he refers to several great authorities; among the rest, to Lord Erskine, who gives it as his opinion, " that Courts of Law are obliged, in cases of pedigree, to depart from the ordinary rules of evidence, as it would be impossible to establish descents according to the strict rules by which contracts are established, &c. In cases of pedigree, therefore, recourse is had to a secondary sort of evidence, the best the nature of the subject will admit, establishing the descent from the only sources that can be had."—And to Lord Mansfield, who, in Buller's Reports, is stated to have declared, that " Tradition is sufficient, in point of pedigree ; AN ENTRY IN A FATHER'S FAMILY BIBLE, an inscription on a tombstone, &c., ARE ALL GOOD EVIDENCE."

— p. 240.

Cowper's Reports, p. 593

[†] [For which see the Drumpellier Lettyr Pedigree, No. I., at the close of the Performance.]

38   COMMENTS ON KEIR PERFORMANCE,

"XVIII. JUNII M.D.C.XL.
"NATUS FUIT PATER MEUS JOANNES STIRLING—
"CUJUS PATER FUIT JOANNES STIRLING—
"FILIUS WALTERI STIRLING—
"FILII JOANNIS STIRLING—
"QUI DESCENDERAT EX FAMILIA DE CADDER—
"ET CUJUS FUIT TERRA DE BALQUHARRAGE—
"ET TERRA DE LETTIR-STIRLING, PROPE DUNTRETH."

[For a further corroboratory statement of the argument here, see in the sequel.]

APPENDIX.

No. 1.—LETTER of GIFT to Sir JOHN STIRLING of Keir.
(Privy Seal Record, Book viii. fol. 69.)

1529. GIFT. Ane Letter of Gift maid to Johne Striuiling of Keir, knycht, his aires and assignais, ane or mair, of ye mariage of Jonet Striuiling, dochter and aire of umquhile Andro Striuiling of Cadder, &c. failzeing, &c. with all profittis, &c. Apud Edinburgh xxii day of Julii ye zer forsaid.

Per Signaturam manibus Serenissimi Domini Nostri Regis et sui
Thesaurarii subscriptam.

No. 2.—DISPENSATION in favour of ROBERT STIRLING and
MARION FLEMING.
(The Original produced from the Wigton Charter-Chest.)

1533. In Dei Nomine, Amen. Per hoc præsens publicum instrumentum cunctis pateat evidenter et sit notum, Quod anno Incarnationis Domini Millesimo quingentesimo trigesimo tertio, die vero mensis Junij xj°. Indictione quinta pontificatusque sanctissimi in Christo patris et Domini nostri Domini Clementis, divina providentia, Papæ Septimi anno xj°. In mei notorij publici et testium infra scriptorum præsentia personaliter constituti honorabilis vir, viz. Robertus Sterlyng de Ballinkeyr, et Mariota Flemyng, filia carnalis Gulielmi Flemyng de Boghall, comparuerunt in ecclesia parochiali de Caddar, Glasguensi diocesi, contrahentes se invicem pro matrimonio in facie ecclesiæ solemniter habentes et tenentes in eorum manibus quendam processum dispensationis in pergamino subscriptum sub sigillo pendente venerabilis viri magistri Gilberti Straichin, canonici Aberdonensis, ac commissarii sedis apostolicæ in hac parte una cum sua mannali subscriptione. Ac sub signo et subscriptione manualibus Joannis Guthrie, notarij publici, de data apud Oppidum Edinburgi viij°

die mensis Decembris, anno ab incarnatione Domini millesimo quingentesimo primo.—Quem vero processum dispensationis, dictus Robertus et Mariota, unanimi consensu tradiderunt mihi notario publico subscripto perlegendum et publicandum ; in quo vero processu mentio extat quod prædicti Robertus et Mariota, erant legitim dispensati auctoritate Sedis apostolicæ per dictum commissarium potestatem habentem in hac parte de tertio et quarto consanguinitatis gradibus—prout in eodem processu ad plenarium continetur.—Quo viso perlecto et publicato per me notarium subscriptum, discretus, vir Dominus Johannes Uther, presbyter et curatus dictæ ecclesiæ parochialis de Cadder, ante solemnizationem matrimonii inter prædictos Robertum et Mariotam, in sua conscientia exposuit et dixit se fecisse et proclamasse tria Banna in dicta ecclesia parochiali de Cadder tribus diebus dominicalibus festivis ad invicem succedentibus, et nullum invenisse impedimentum inter dictas partes præter impedimenta contenta in hujusmodi processu Dispensationis, quin dicti Robertus et Mariota poterant legitime procedere ad solemnizationem matrimonij in facie ecclesiæ—Et hoc omnibus et singulis voluit idem dominus curatus antedictus notum faceri per hoc præsens publicum instrumentum. Super quibus omnibus et singulis petierunt hinc inde dicti Robertus et Mariota, Instrumentum et instrumenta, publicum seu publica.—Acta erant hæc hora quinta ante meridiem aut eo circa sub anno, die, mense, indictione et pontificatu, prædictis præsentibus ibidem discretis virus Magistro Laurentio Leech, presbytero, Johanne Barbour, Roberto Boyle et Thoma Brown, cum diversis aliis Testibus, ad præmissa vocatis specialiter et rogatis.

 Et ego David Ingonis, clericus Glasguensis diocesis, publicus auctoritate apostolica notarius quia præmissis omnibus et singulis dum sic ut præmittitur, agerentur dirigentur, et fierent una cum prænominatis testibus præsens personaliter interfui ; Eaque omnia et singula præmissa sic fieri, vidi, scivi, et audivi, ac in notam capi—Ex qua, hoc præsens publicum instrumentum manu propria subscriptum confeci, et in hanc publicam formam Instrumenti redigi, signoque et nomine meis solitis et consuetis, signavi et publicavi in fidem omnium et singulorum rogatorum et requisitorum.

 No. 3.—DECREET in favour of JANET STIRLING, Heiress of Cadder.

 (Acts of the Lords of Council and Session, Book VI., folio 165.)

Octauo Julii, Anno MD.XXXV.

8. July 1535. Jonet Striueling.

Anent our Soueraine Lordis letres *purchest at ye instance of Jonet Striueling, heritar of ye landis and lardschip of Cadder,* aganis *Johnne Striueling* of ye Kerc, Knycht, and James Striueling his soun :—That quhare ye said Johnne havand hir marriage, and ye dispositioun of hir ward landis, causit ane *pretendit* matrimony to be maid betuix ye said James and her, and *sensyne* ye said Johnne hes *haldin,* and as zit haldis hir *in subiectioun*, and will *nocht suffer her to speik with her freiindis*, and hes *compellit hir* to mak diuerss *alienationis* and *takkis* of hir *landis* and *heretage*, and tendis to *gar hir analie ye remanent or maist part yairof;* and anent the charge gevin to ye said *Johnne and James*, to bring and produce ye said Jonet befor ye Lordis, yat scho may schaw hir mynd to yaim in ye premissis, with certificatioun and yai failzeit, yat ye Lordis wald decern all alienationnis to be maid be hir of nane avale, as at mair lenth is contenit in ye saidis letres ; ye saidis *Jonet comperand be Maister Henry Lauder, hir procuratour*, and ye said Johnne Striueling comperand for him and his soun. The *Lordis of Counsale decernis all alienationis to be maid be ye said Jonet off her landis and heretage, or ony part yairof*, to be of *nane avale*, and *interponis yir autorite yairto*, ay and *quhile scho brocht* before *ye* saidis Lordis, to *declare* hir *mynd* anent *ye* premissis, and yat lettres be direct herupoun, in forme as efferis.

[For observations upon the above, see ADDENDA, No. I.]

No. 4.—ACT OF CURATORY, for JOHN STIRLING, Son of Umquhile ROBERT STIRLING.

(Acts of the Lords of Council and Session, Book XI., folio 159.)

XXVI. *Februarii*, M.D.XXXVIII.

1538.
Jhone
Striueling.

In presens of ye Lordis of Counsale, comperit Jhone Striueling, sone to umquhile Robert Striueling, and desirit Malcome Lord Fleming, and William Fleming of Boghall, curatouris to him, *ad lites*, to persew and defend all actiounis concerning him, and to minister in ye said office of curatory as reasoun requirit. The quhilk desir ye saides Lordis thocht resonable, and yairfor hes gevin ye said Malcome Lord Fleming, and William Fleming of Boghall, curatouris to him, to perform and defend all his actiouns ; quhilkes personis hes tane and acceptit ye said office, in and apon yaim, and swor to lely and trewlie to minister in ye said office of curatory, *ad lites*, after yair understanding, for defence of ye said Johnne, in all his actiouns, as accordis of justice.

No. 5.—RESPITE to DAVID SHAW and GEORGE DREGHORN.

(Privy Seal Record, vol. 17. fol. 1.)

1541.

Respitt, of this date, to David Schaw and George Dreghorne, for the slauchter of umquhile Johnne Striveling of ye Kere, Knicht, &c.

No. 6.—PROCURATORY OF RESIGNATION by JANET STIRLING, Lady of Cadder, and Judicial Ratification thereof.

(Acta Dominorum Concilii et Sessionis, Lib. xvii. folio 46.)

xiij *Decembris*, *Anno* MD xlj°.

13. Dec.
1541.

MY LORDIS of Counsale, Forsameikle as I Jonet Striveling of Cadder, vpoun the vij day of December instant, come in presens of your Lordschipis, purposlie and of determit mynd to *haif ratefyt and apprevit ane letre of procuratore* maid vnder my sele and subscriptioun, with consent and assent of James Striueling of the Keir, now my spous, *makand certane personis mentionit thairintill my procuratoris coniunctlie and severalie to haif resignit in the handes of our Soucrane Lord, the Archebischop of Glasgow, and vtheris superiouris respectiue, my landis and heretage of* CADDER, VCHILTREIS, LETTER, BANKEIR, BRANZET, KIRKMICHELL, BLANERNE, *and* CHARGBRE, with the touris, fortalices, woddis, manor places, mylnis, tenentis, tenendries and seruice of free tenentis, aduocatioun, donatioun and rychtis of patronage of kirkis and cheplenriis of the samin, and all thair *pertinentis, for heretable infeftmentis and sesingis and sesing, to haif bene maid, and gevin thairof be my saidis superiouris, to the said James, and his airis quhatsumeuer*, offerand me to swer that I was vncompellit, or coactit to do the samin; and after that, it was inquirit at me be zour Lordschips, quhat profit I gatt thairfor, throw the terrowris gevin to me in zour presens, I tuk suspitioun that the sikernis maid to Thomas Bischope, in my name and at my command and desire, of the laudis of Vchiltreis, gevand now be zeir viii scoir of merkis, and act maid anent the pament to him in my name of ane thousand merkis, quhilkis I suld haif for my landis forsaidis, was insufficient and of nane avale; I THAIRFOR REVOIKT THE SADIS LETRES OF PROCURATORIE, WITH ALL THAT FOLLOWIT THAIRUPON, and revelit and schewin to zour Lordschipis *sum secret wourd* anent myself. And now, becaus I haif avisit and causit riplie avise with my said sikernes, and findis the samin sufficient and gude, and hes gottin the samin *ampleat* at my desire, and als be triing out of the verite perfitlie knawis the vther wourdis quhilkis I revelit to zour Lordschips war fals and vntreu, like as ony wiss man for diuerss caussis may consider and judge; I haif yerfore of new, of my awin free will, and certane science, vncompellit, coactit, circumvenit, dissauit, or deffraudit, in ony way bot of gude consideratioun, for the help and

and augmentatioun of the living of the houss of Keir, becaus It Is the principale and cheif houss of my said spousis and myne surnames, and that It was liklie to Dekyei throw alienatioun of the maist pairt of the auld heretage. And als for diuerss vtheris profittis geviu be my spous to me, and vtheris of my command and desire, and for utheris resonable causis, and consideratioinis moving me, *after I haif prouidit and helpit* THE BAIRNIS OF VMQUHILE ROBERT STRIUELING, QUHILKIS AR IMMEDIATLIE TO SUCCEID TO ME, FALZEING OF AIRIS OF MY AWIN BODY, TO *sume'kle of my heretage as geris now to be the zeir four scoir of merkis, maid vtheris letres of procuratorie;* quhilkis plesit zour Lordschipis to se and consider, makand James Hennersoun and vtheris, coniunctlie and seueralie, my procuratouris, to resigne all and sindre my landis aboue writtin in the handis of the superiouris thairof respectiue, ilk ane of them for thair awin partis, for heretable infeftmetis, and sasingis to be made and gevin of the samin be the saidis superiouris, to the said

James, his airis, and assignais quhatsumeuer : Quhilkis letres of procuratorie, I be the tennour of thir presentis, ratifeis, apprevis, and for me, and my airis, perpetualie, confermes, and sueris aud declaris to zour Lordschipis, be my grite aith, that I am nocht coactit, compellit, defraudit, circumvenit, or disavit, in making of the samin, bot maid the saidis letres of procuratorie, and now ratifeis and apprevis the samin of my awin fre will, and ardent desire for the causes abone writtin, and sall nouir revoik, nor cum in the contrar thairof in jugement nor outwith, be ony maner of way in tyme cuming, and that the saidis landis may be maid sicker to the said James and his airis, I desire the saidis letres of procuratorie, with this my writting and declaratioun, to be actit and registrat in the buckis of Counsale, and that zour Lordschipis wald geve actis, decretis, and interpone zour auctorite thairto, conform to zour practic obseruit in sic caisis ; and mair attour, becaus thir was ane resignatioun maid of the saidis landis of Vchiltreis be vertu of the saidis first letres of procuratorie, in the handis of William Menteith of West-cars, superiour thairof, and infeftment gevin thirthrow to the said James of the samin, quha, thairefter, at my command, and desire, disponit the saidis landis of Vchiltreis be charter of alienatioun to the said Thomas Bischope to my behuif, and the said Thomas obligatioun gevin to me that he sall resigne the samin in fauoris of me and my airis, howsone sentence of diuorse beis lede, and gevin simpliciter betuix me and the said James. Therefor, for my singuler wele and vtilite, I revoik, renunce, and dischargis the pretendit reuocatioun maid be me of the said first procuratorie in presens of zour Lordschipis, and will, consentis, and ordanis, that the said reuocatioun, actis and instrumentis, geve ony was maid thairupoune, sall be deleit and put furth of the bukis of Counsale, and to haif na strenth nor memorie in time cuming, and be thir presentis, ratifeis and apprevis the said first procuratorie togidder with the said resignatioun, charteris, evidentis, and all that follow it thairupon, in maner forsaid. In witness of the quhilk thing, I haif subscriuit thir presentis with my hand, the xi day of December, the zeir of God Ane thousand fyve hundreth and fourty-ane zeris ; Off the quhilk procuratorie the tenour followis :—" UNIVERSIS ET SINGULIS ad quorum notitias presentes litere peruenerint Joneta Striueling Domina de Cadder, salutem, quia, dum nuper recordarem quod quondam Johannes Striueling de Keir miles, pater Jacobi Strineling nunc de Keir mei sponsi pro recuperatione warde, releuii, et noneutroitus, mearum terrarum, et hereditatis, ac in protectione et defensione earundem non minimam sue hereditatis et prediorum partem vltra redemtionem alienauit in dicti mei sponsi grave dammum qui ad huiusmodi suas terras succedere debuerant, et quia idem meus sponsus et eius domus ceteris cognominis de Striueling ab antiquo perfuerant et principalis habebatur. Ne minorus gradus preeminentie fiat ob sue hereditatis diminutionem quam predecessores sue extiterunt sibi et sue domui auxiliari, suamque hereditatem augere animo deliberato mecum decreui, noueritis igitur me non vi aut metu ductam, nec errore lapsam, compulsam, nec coactam sed ex mea mera, pure ; libera et spontanea voluntate, pro Inuincibilibus amore, et fauore quos habeo et gero erga dictum meum sponsum, cum ipsius consensu et assensu fecisse, constituisse, et ordinasse, necnon tenore presentium facere, constituere, et ordinare, honorabiles viros Jacobum Henresoun   Ac eorum quemlibet coniunctim et diuisim meos veros legittimos et indubitatos procuratores, actores factores, et negotiorum meorum gestores, ac nuncios speciales dant et concedent dictis meis procuratoribus ac eorum cuilibet coniunctim et divisim meam plenariam et irreuocabilem potestatem, ac mandatum speciale ad pro me et nomine meo, in presentia dominorum meorum superiorum subscriptorum comparend. et ibidem sursum reddent ac in eorum manibus respective per fustem et baculum pure et simpliciter resignand. extradonand. et libere deliberand. a me et heredibus meis omnes et singulas terras meas infrascriptas, viz., in manibus cuiuslibet superiorvris illorum earundem tenendriam quam de ipso superiore in capite teneo prout particulariter subsecuntur ac totum Jus et clameum, que in huiusmodi terras habui, habeo, seu quouismodo habere vel clamare potero, pro me et heredibus meis omnino quieteclamand. in perpetuum, viz., omnes et singulas terras meas de LETTIR cum tenentibus, tenandriis, et libere tenentium seruitiis, earundem ac suis pertinentiis, Jacen. infra vicecomitatum de Striueling, in manibus excellentissimi principis et Domini nostri Domini Jacobi quinti Dei gratia Scotorum Regis illustrissimi, aut in manibus Mathei Comitis de Levenax, vel suorum commissariorum seu cuius-cunque alterius liberi superioris eorundem omnes et singulas terras meas de CADDER, cum turre fortalicio, pendiculis, et pertinentiis eorundem, Jacen. infra regalitatem Glasguensis, et vicecomitatum de Lanark, in manibus Reuerendissimi in Christo, patris et Domini Gawini Glasgwensis Archiepiscopi, tanquam in manibus Domini mei superioris eorundem, omnes et singulas terras meas de VCHILTRE cum molendino earundem, et suis pertin. Jacen. in baronia de Wast Carce, infra vicecomitatum de Striueling, in manibus Willielmi Monteith de West Kerss, tanquam in manibus Domini mei superioris earundem, omnes et singulas terras meas de BRANZET et BANKEIR Jacen. infra vicecomitatum de Striueling, Terras de KIRKMICHAELL et BLANERNE cum tenen. tenendriis et libere tenentium seruitijs, aduocatione et donatione, et jure patronatus capellaniarum earundem et suis pertinentiis, Jacen. infra vicecomitatum de Dumbartane, in manibus Willielmi Levingstoun de Kilsyth, aut in manibus   Campbell nepotis heredis et successoris quoudam Colini Campbell de Auchinhowy vel cuiusquam alterius liberi superiorum seu superioris earundem, et terras de CRAGBRE cum tenen. tenendriis et libere tenentium seruitiis earundem, Jacen. infra vicecomitatum de Linlithquhow, In manibus Roberti Mowbray, de Bernbowgall tanquam in manibus Domini mei superioris earundem, Quasquidem terras de LETTER, CADDER, VCHILTRIE, BRANZET, BANKEIR, KIRKMICHAELL, BLANERNE et CRAGBRE, cum turre, fortalicijs, teneu. tenendriis, libri tenentium, seruitiis, advocatione, donatione, et jure patronatus capellaniarum predict. ac suis pertinentiis. Ego dicta Joneta cum consensu et assensu prefati Jacobi mei spouse, In manibus dominorum meorum superiorum earundem antedict. per has meas literas procuratorii et resignationis respective modo prescript. sursum reddo pureque et simpliciter resigno, Ac totum jus titulum interesse et iuris clameum tam petitorium quam possessorium que in eisdem habui, habeo, seu quouismodo habere vel clamare potero, pro me et heredibus meis omnino quittecla. meo imperpetuum, pro certis sasinis et infeodationibus hereditariis de omnibus et singulis terris suprascript. cum turre fortalicio tenen. tenendriis libere tenentium seruitiis, pendiculis, pertinentiis, aduocatione, donatione, et jure patronatus capellaniarum earundem per ipsorum dominos superiores antedict. viz. per corum quemlibet in sua parte et tenendria earundem prout superius particulariter sunt diuise, memorato Jacobo Striueling de Keir meo spouso, suis heredibus et assignatis quibuscunque dandis et conficiendis, et generaliter omnia alia et singula faciend. gerend. et exercend. que in premissis et circa ea necessaria fuerint, seu quomodolibet opportuna ratum, gratum, firmum ac stabile habeu. et habiturum totum idem et quicquid dicti mei procuratores, aut corum aliquis coniunctim et diuisim meo nomine in premissis iuste uel rite duxerint seu duxerit faciend., volo insuper, ac pro me et heredibus meis decerno et ordino, quod si huiusmodi resignationes per procuratores meos antedictos de terris meis suprascript. ut premittitur fiend. aut eorum aliquo quouismodo imperfecta vel imperfecte fuerint facta vel facte in manibus cuiuscunque superiorum predict. aut aliorum qui prefat. resignationes protestatem recipere non habuerint vnde dictus Jacobus Striueling et heredes sui me moratis terris aut aliqua ipsarum parte gaudere non poterint, In hiis casibus quoties euenerint licebit dictis meis procuratoribus aut corum cuilibet coniunctim et diuisim ad quos meam potestatem irreuocabilem tenore presentium, do et committo, dict&s terras in manibus superioris vel superiorum legittimi vel legittimorum erunt. de nouo toties resignare semper et quousque huismodi resignatio vel resignationes valide fuerint et perfecti ; nec licebit mihi aut heredibus meis ob Inualidatem dict. resignationum seu resignationis fiend. ingressum aliquem aut regressum ad prefatas terras, seu aliquam ipsarum partem firmas proficua aut divorias earundem habere aut easdem quouismodo nobis vendicare uel acclamare, sed pro me et heredibus meis, exonero, renuncio, et quite clamo omnes et singulas prefatas terras cum suis pertinentiis, dicto Jacobo Striueling et suis heredibus quibuscunque, pro perpetuo in futurum. In cuius rei testimonium presentibus procuratorii literis, mea manu subscript. sigillum meum vuacum sigillo et subscriptione dicti mei, In signum sui consensus et assensus ad premissa sunt appensa, Apud Edinburgh decimo die mensis Decembris anno ane thousand fyve hundreth xli° coram his testibus Magistro Arthuro Tailzefeir rectore de creckmont, Thoma Dauidsoun burgen de Edinburgh, Willielmo Striueling, Johanne Patersoun, Willielmo Peirsonu, Jacobo Henrysoun, *Thoma Bischop*, Jacobo Bannatyne, et Nigello Layng, Notariis publiciis, cum diuersis aliis,

"JONET STRIUELING,
"*Lady of Cadder.*
"JAMES STRIUELING,
"*of ye Keir.*"

No. 7.—SENTENCE OF DIVORCE between JAMES STIRLING of Keir, and JANET STIRLING, Heiress of Cadder.

(Ex Libro Sententiarum Officialis Sancti Andreæ infra Laudoniam—in his Majesty's General Register House at Edinburgh.)

Ultimo Januarij anno I^m V^c xlj.

CHRISTI nomine Inuocato. Nos Audreas Myll prebendarius ecclesie collegiate nostre dioceseos de campis infra oppidum de Edinburgh, et Robertus Symsoun, Capellani Commissarii, in hac parte venerabilis et egregii viri magistri Abrahe Creichtoun, prepositide Dunglas, ac Officialis Sancti Andree infra Archiepiscopatum Laudonie cause, et partibus infra scriptis unacum, nonnullis aliis nostris in hac parte collegis sub illa clausula vobis aut duobus vestrum conjunctim, precedentibus specialiter deputati Judices pro tribunali sedentes, in quadam causa matrimoniali tendente ad divorcium simpliciter, coram nobis mota ed adhuc peudente indeciso inter honorabilem virum, Jacobum Striveling de Keir, filium et heredem Joannis Striveling de Keir, militis actorem, ab una, et providam domicellam Jonetam Striveling filiam et heredem quondam Andree Striveling de Cadder, ejus pretensam, et putativam sponsam, ream, partibus ab altera cognoscen juxta ea que vidimus, audivimus et cognovimus jurisperitorum communicato consilio, et secuto, quibus fidelem fieri fecimus relationem in eadem, solum Deum pre oculis habentes ejusque nomine sanctissimo primitus invocato, per hanc nostram sententiam definitivam quam ferimus in hiis scriptis, pronounciamus, decernimus, et declaramus, ex de dictis coram nobis in causa hujusmodi auditis, hinc inde, partium, petitionibus, responsionibus et allegationibus, pretensum matrimonium, et sponsalia, per verba de futuro carnali copula subsecuta inter prefatum Jacobum et Jonetam, contractum et solempnizatum in facie ecclesie, a principio, non tenuisse, nec viribus subsistere posse de jure. Eo quia, tempore ejusdem contractus, et solempnizationis de facto, licet *non de jure sibi invicem prefati Jacobus, et Joneta, actingebant, prout eciam de presenti actingunt in tertio, et quarto gradibus consanguinitatus* ignotum sibi Jacobo, tempore contractus et solempnizationis prefati matrimonii et sponsaliorum. Et propterea idem presens matrimonium et sponsalia annullanda, cassanda, et dirimenda fore, ac ipsos libellantem, et libellatam ab invicem divorciandos et separandos. Et quicquid alter, alteri, dotis causa, aut donationis propter nuptias dederit. Id alteri restituendum

31. Jan. 1541.

fore, licenciamque prefato, Jacobo alibi in domino contrahendi et ducendi concedendum fore, prout annullamus, cassamus, dirimus, divorciamus ac concedimus respective, quoa omnibus quorum interest notum facimus per presentes.

No. 8.—SUBMISSION between JAMES STIRLING of Keir, and John STIRLING, Son and Heir of Umquhile ROBERT STIRLING.

(Register of Acts and Decreets, Book I., fol. 194.)

Tertio Februarii, MD.xlii.

30. Jan. 1542.

JAMES STRIUE-LING.

In presens of ye Lordis of Counsale, comperit thir partyis underwritten, and geve in yis compromitt under specifeit, and desirit ye samin to be registred in the bukis of Counsale; the quhilk desire ye saidis Lordis thocht resonable, and yairfor ordanis ye samin to be registred in the saidis bukis, and to haif ye strenth of yair decrets in tyme to cum; off ye quhilk ye tenour follows:—'At Edinburgh, ye penult day of Januar, ye zeir of God ane thousand fyve hundreth xlii zeris, JAMES STRIUELING of ye KEIR, *sone and air of* UMQUHILE JOHNE STRIUELING of ye KEIR, knicht, his fader, on yat ane pert, and JOHNE STRIUELING, *sone and aire of* UMQUHILE ROBERT STRIUELING, with consent and assent of ane noble and mychtie Lord, Malcolme Lord Fleming, Maister Hew Rig, his curatouris, and Marioun Fleming, ye relict of ye said umquhile Robert, on yat vyer part, ar faithfullie compromit, bundin and obligit, and sworne to stand, abide, vnderly, and fulfill ye sentence, ordinance, decrete arbitrale, and deliverance of David Foster of Carden, and James Chesholme of Clessingaw, as jugis arbitratouris and amicable compositouris, chosin for ye part of ye said James, and Jhone Brisbane of Bischoptoun, and Thomas Kincaid of yat Ilk, chosin for ye part of ye remanent personis above writtin, as jugis, arbitratouris and amicable compositouris, equalie chosin betuix ye saidis partyis, in all and sindrie actionis, debatis, pleyis, caussis, questionis, and controverseis, or clames, yat ayer of the saidis partyis hes to ask or claime at vyeris, or vyeris quhatsumener, yat ony of ye saidis partyis hes, or ony viss may haif or move aganis vyeris in ony tyme bygane, before ye day of ye dait of yir presentis, and speciali anentis ye pley and questioun betuix ye saidis partyis *anent ye infefting of ye said Johne Striueling, as air to his said vmquhile fader,* in *ye xv. lib. landis of auld extent of Blanerne, Kirkmichall,* and *Letter,* liand within ye scherefdom of Dunbartan, for *relewing of ye said James landis and* HERETAGE *of* KEIR, *efter ye forme of ane* CONTRACT *and writtingis maid betwix ye said* VMQUHILE JOHNE STRIUELING of ye KEIR, knycht, and *ye said vmquhile* ROBERT *yairupoun.* And ye saidis partyis sall caus ye saidis judgis chosen for ayer of yame, to convine in ye paroch kirk of Glasgw, ye xv day of Februar nix to cum, at x houris before nvne, and yair accept ye saidis actionis, questionis, and debatis, in and upoun yame, and commoun yairintille, and to be sworne to deliuer yairon lelelie and trewlie, aftir yair vnderstanding, knawledge, and conscience, betuix yan and ye viii day of May nixt yaireftir at ye farrest; and in caiss of discord betuix ye saidis Jugis, ye saidis partyis hes chosen

Schir Jhone Morisoun ouirman and odman with yame in ye said mater, and quhat ye saidis Jugis and ouriman, or ye maist part of yem togidder, decernis and delineris yair In, baith ye saidis partyis sall vnderly and fulfill ye samin to vyeris In every poynt, but renocatioun, reclamatioun, or appelatioun; Prouiding yat ye said ouirman geve furth his decrete In ye said mater at ye day abone specifeit; and ordanis yis compromitt to be actit and registred in ye bukis of Counsale, and ye Lordis yairof to Interpone yair auctorite yairto, And haif ye strenth of yair decrete and letrez to be direct to compell ayer of ye saidis partyis to fulfill ye samin to vyeris in all poyntis. In witness of ye qubilk thing, ayer of ye saidis partyis hes subscriuit yis present compromitt with yair handis, day and zere for saidis, befor yir witness, *Richert Kincaid, Mathow Fleming, Robert Kincaid*, and *Jhone Young*, notar, with utheris diuerss.—JAMES STRIUELING of ye Keir—MARIOUN FLEMING, with my hand on ye pen, led be Jhone Zonng, notar publict.

[This important deed, though both concerning Keir and Cadder through the Robert Stirling mentioned, is quite omitted in the *impartial* Keir Performance.]

No. 9.— EXCERPTS from the KEIR INVENTORIES, in the handwriting of the late Mr RAMSAY of Ochtertyre, viz.

(1.) DISPOSITION by JAMES STIRLING of Keir, in favour of THOMAS BISHOP.

Disposition and Assignation by James Stirling of Keir, whereby, *for certain sums of money* paid him by *Thomas Bischop* his servitor, spouse affidat of the said Jonet Stirling (*i.e.* Jonet Stirling of Cadder, whose name occurs in a deed immediately preceding,) and *for his Help and Labour in solliciting and furthering the conveyanse made by her of her heritage to the said James.* He *therefore assigns* to the said *Thomas Bischop* the *marriage* of the said *Jonet Sterling*, as also *a chalder of oats*, and *two oxen* on the lands of Uchiltrees, near Linlithow (an ancient possession of the family of Cadder), and the said lands themselves, redeemable upon the death of the said Jonet, for 2000 merks ;—Likewise, *to pay the said Thomas Bischop* 250 *merks within a year after the date of the said disposition ;* and to free and relieve the said Jonet of all debts, claims, and demands against her, as heir to Andrew Stirling her father, or Margaret Cunningham her mother; and *also, to use his diligence for getting a remission from the King to the said Thomas, for his alledged lying with the said Jonet whilst she was the said James's wife*, &c. 23. Feb. 1541.

[For comments and remarks on this excerpt or version of a strange and suspicious document, concluded still to be in the Keir charter-chest, while the original is not produced in the Keir Performance, see ADDENDA, No. II.]

(2.) CONTRACT OF MARRIAGE between JAMES STIRLING of Keir and JEAN CHISHOLM.

Contract of Marriage between James Stirling of Keir to Jean Cheesholm, cousin (*i.e.* natural daughter) of William, Bishop of Dunblane, with consent of James 1543.

Cheesholm of Glassingall, her brother; whereby the said James obliges him to *cause* the Bishop sustain James and his Lady in all ordinary expenses for the space of five years; also to *cause* the Bishop, with consent of his Chapter, to grant a tack of the teind-sheaves of the lands of Keir, extending to 3 chalders of meal and a chalder of bear, for 19 years from 1544, at the rent of L.40. On the other hand, the said James, besides providing the Lady suitably, binds himself not to set, wadset, or set in tack, any of his lands without the council of the Bishop, and to take his advice in all things relative to his lands, person, or servants. The tocher of L.1000 to be employed in redeeming wadsets.

(Excerpt from the Keir Inventories above mentioned.)

(3.) LICENSE by QUEEN MARY in favour of JONET STIRLING, Wife of THOMAS BISHOP.

s. March 547.

License by Queen Mary, with consent of James Earl of Arran, her tutor, to Janet Stirling, wife of Thomas Bishop, to remain with her husband in England twenty days, and ratifying all deeds done by her in favour of Sir James Stirling.

No. 10.—CONTRACT between JAMES STIRLING of Keir, and JOHN STIRLING, Son and Heir of Umquhile ROBERT STIRLING.

(Register of Acts, Decrees, Book X., folio 127.)

"*Apud Edinburgh, primo Martii, Anno Domini Millesimo quingentesimo quinquagesimo tertio.*"

[1553.]

"In presens of ye Lordis of Counsale, comperit yir parteis vnderwrittine and gaif in yis contrak eftir following, subscrinit with yair handis, and desirit ye samyn to be insert and registrat in ye bukis of Counsall, and to haif ye strenth of ane act and decreit of ye lordis yairof in tyme to cum, and yai to interpone yair auctorite yairto: The quhilk desire ye saidis Lordis thocht reasonable, and ordainit and ordainis ye said contract to be insert and registrat in ye saidis bukis of Counsall, and to haif ye strenth of ane act and decreit of ye foirsaidis Lordis in tyme to cum, and hes interponit and interponis yair autorite to ye samyn, and decernis and ordanis letres to be direct to command and charge, compell, poynd, and distrenze ayir of ye saidis parteis, for fulfilling of ye said contract, Ilk ane to wyirris for yair awin parteis, eftir ye forme and tennour yairof, In forme as efferis; Off ye quhilk contract ye tennour followis. 'At Edinburgh ye secund day of Marche, The zeir of God Ane thousand fyve hundreth fyfty and thre zeris: It is appoyntit, aggreit, and finalie contractit, betuix honorabill partiis James Strineling, on yat vyir part, and Johnne Strineling, sone and heir of vmquhile Robert Strineling, on yat vyir part, in maner, forme, and effect as eftir followis: That is to say, *forasmekill as yair was indentouris, in forme of contract*, maid betuix the said *vmquhile* ROBERT

Contracting Strineling of Keir, and Streveling of Lottir.

STRIUELING and vmquhile JOHN STRIUELING of ye KEIR, knycht, quhairin ayir of ye saidis parteis band and oblisit yame and yair airis to obserue, keip, and fulfill diuerss and sindry poyntis, articulis, and claussis, as at mair lenth is conteutit in ye saidis indentouris of ye dait At Edinburgh ye xxviii day of Maii ye zeir of God A ne thousand fyre hundreth twenty sevin zeris; And now ye saidis parteis willand to renew ye samyn in forme subsequent, of new ye said James Striueling of Keir byndis and oblissis him and his airis to infeft ye said Johne Striueling, sone and aire foirsaid, and his airis maill lawchtfullie gottin or to be gottin of his body; quhilkis failzeing to Williame Striueling his bruder, and his airis maill lawchtfullie gottin or to be gottin of his body; and failzeing of yame all, to returne agane frelie to ye said James and his airis heretable, In all and haill ye ten puud land of ye landis of Lettir with yair pertinentis, and siclike in ye five puud land of Bochquharege, wyth ye pertinentis, lyand within ye schorefdome of Striueling, for ye landis of Blairerne and Kirkmichell, to be halden of ye said James and his airis, that ane half in blanche, yat vyer half in warde, and sall deliuer to him sufficient infeftment, charter, and siosing yairupon, made in competent and deu forme, contenand clauss of warrandice, as efferis : For the quhilkis, ye said Johnne Striueling, sone and aire foirsaid, sall resigne, renunce, and ouryiff, all and hale ye landis of AULDKEIR xv. lib. land, with yair pertinentis, quhairin he is presentlie vestit and seisit, as air to his said umquhile fader, In ye handis of ye said James Striueling, his superior yairof, ad perpetuam remanentiam, to remain with the said James and his airis in all tyme cuming, heretable, in propirte, wyth all rycht, titll, interes, and clame of rycht, propirte, and possessioun quhilkis he had, hes, or ony wyiss may clame haif yairto : And ye said resignatione being maid, ye said James sall incontinent yaireftir infeft ye said Johnne Striueling and his airis male foirsaidis ; quhilkis failzeing, ye said William his broder, and his airis male foersaidis ; and failzeing of yame, to returne heritable to ye said James and his airis as said is, in all and haile ye foirsaidis landis of ALDKEIR, quhilkis war resignit in maner foirsaid, in clauss of warrandice of ye principale landis abone writtin, viz. ye landis of Lettir and Balquharage, and to be haldin in ye samyn maner and forme yat yai ar haldin of befoir speceffit, and sall deliuer to ye saide Johnne sufficient infeftment, charter, and precept of warrandice yairvpone, in competent and deu forme. And forder, baith ye saidis parteis byndis and oblissis yame, yair airis, and assignais, to obserue, keip, and fulfill yis present contract ilkane, to vyirris, in all poyntis, for yair parte : And for mair suire obseruing and fulfilling yairof, ar content, and consentis yat yis present contract be actit and registrat in ye bukis of oure Soucrane Ladyis Counsale, and decernit to have ye strenth of ane decreit of ye Lordis yair of, and yair autorite to be interpouit yairto, with executoriallis to pas yairupono in forme as efferis. In witnes of ye quhilk thing, baith ye saidis parteis hes subscriuit yis present contract with yair handis, day, zeir, and place foirsaidis, befoir yir witnessis, George

Muschett of yat ilk, William Striueling, Andro Morton, Thomas Stevinson, William Patersone, and James Nicolsoun, notaris, with oyeris diuersis. Sic subscribitur,

"JAMES STRIUELING,
"*of Keir.*
"JHONE STRIUELING,
"*with my hand.*'"

[Neither is this deed—so important to Letter or Drumpellier, as well as to Keir—at all noticed in the Keir Performance.]

III.—REMAINDER of the CORRESPONDENCE already alluded to—viz., from March 6 to April 9, 1818.

Having thus fully given the Drumpellier statement at the intervening period, in, pursuance of the course that was proposed to be adopted, and with the particular view, it may now be, after a few remarks, proper to resume the correspondence partly adduced, and continue it from where it was intermitted.

It could not well be expected that the Drumpellier family would altogether brook or be pleased with a confederacy against them, of so strange and ambiguous a kind, as between Keir and Glorat, or could deal with any other than the Keir agent, with whom alone, according to the mandate of Mr Charles Stirling, the Keir umpire, they had originally communicated; as little with any one summarily thrust upon them in his stead. While, moreover, after the full and candid manner their evidence had been disclosed to the former, they were entitled, from just motives, to an equal return, and to be apprised of the grounds and proof on which an opposition to their projected Service was based—that Service, too, which had been so courteously postponed in accordance with the wishes and earnest desires of the Keir agent.

These incidents and considerations may be kept in view for reference, and for due apprehension of what follows of the correspondence in question, which shall next be taken up and concluded under this head.

13.—LETTER, WILLIAM STIRLING to JAMES DUNDAS, W.S.

" 18 HOWE STREET, EDINBURGH, *6th March* 1818.

" I rather expected to have heard from you before this, in reply to my last, but not having done so, suppose that you may probably stand in need of further time, and therefore have thought it best to *defer* our *proceeding* for another week, and have accordingly given instructions to my father's agent to postpone the *Service* till Saturday 14th.

" In the mean time, I request that, on receipt of this, you will have the goodness to acquaint me whether that day will suit you ? and if not, you will say pointedly what day will ? Also, that you will at the same time do me the favour to communicate the exact ground on which your friends at Keir found their opposition—viz., whether it rests exclusively upon any deficiency in our evidence ? or upon the existence of documents of an adverse tendency in their own possession ? If the latter, I entreat a communication of the same, in compliance with your promise to that effect the last time I had the honour of seeing you on this subject. W. S.

" (Y^r. of Drumpellier.)"

The request here of Mr Stirling was, in every view, just and well founded ; and we shall eventually see the answers he obtained. While he courteously made the time of his service suit the opposite party, they, by vacillation and repeated delays in procedure, evidently evinced their embarrassment and inability to meet or come to issue with Drumpellier.

As yet the mask had not been entirely thrown off, and Keir still appeared in person in the transaction, though it had been arranged that, when ground was legally to be broken, Glorat alone was to be the legal party, as he actually became in the sequel.

14.—LETTER, WILLIAM STIRLING to JAMES DUNDAS, W.S.

" HOWE STREET, EDINBURGH, 10*th March* 1818.

" My servant has just brought me your note, by which I learn that, in place of having lost my letter of the 6th, as you told me yesterday you had done, on the contrary, you have sent it *to Mr Samuel Stirling*, and that it is to him I am to look for an answer. The meaning of this I don't understand, but, to prevent any mistake on my part, I beg leave to inform you, that, with regard to the letter in question, I can accept of an answer from *no one but yourself.*

" You are the person to whom *I was expressly* and most particularly *referred* by *Mr Charles Stirling* when I came to town on the subject of the Keir papers, as being possessed of the entire confidence of himself and all his family. With you, accordingly I had the honour to confer so fully in regard to their papers, when you expressed your *acquiescence* in so *handsome a manner* in *our being allowed to see them*. When Mr Charles Stirling thought fit to alter his course, and declared so decided an opposition to our proceedings, you continued to be the person with whom I still communicated in regard to the new turn affairs had taken. It was to you that I delivered the *copy* of our *brieve* of Service, along with the frankest offer of our whole evidence. It was to you that I afterwards forwarded notice of the day fixed upon for our service; and finally, it was at your individual request that the Service has been, not only hitherto deferred, but *still* continues *in suspense*.

"Moreover, you are the person who gave me a solemn assurance, on the day on which I last saw you on this business, which I believe was the 28th January, that, in case the Keir family should, on investigation, be found to be possessed of any *documents hostile to our claims, that such documents* should be *formally communicated to us previous* to our intended *service*. To this courtesy you were pleased to say that we were particularly entitled, from our very handsome conduct hitherto in this business; that you had no doubt Mr Charles Stirling, to whom you would write the same evening, would cordially concur with you in opinion as to this; that I might set my mind entirely at ease on this head, and consider it *a settled point;* but, in case any accident should happen, or that Mr Charles Stirling should be capable of acting in so very ungentlemanlike a manner as to withhold such documents if they did exist, that he *must look about for another agent than yourself,* who in that case *would not act for him.**

"If I be correct in my recollection of the above circumstances—and if I am not, I shall be glad to be set right—you will see how utterly impossible it is for me to enter into these matters with any other than yourself, whose honour is bound for the due performance of what you have undertaken, and on which I now call for the *production* of the *documents in question, if any such exist;* and, on the other hand, continue willing to give you every fair accommodation in reason as to further time, or anything else in our power to grant with propriety. W. S.

"(Yr. of Drumpellier.)"

---

* So, it will be seen eventually, Mr Dundas quite consistently acted.

Mr Samuel Stirling now prominently figures for Keir, in terms of the Keir and Glorat confederacy; while Mr William Stirling, who was not thereby bound, and to whom it could not but be distasteful, declines, with very just reason, to act directly with any other than Mr Dundas, who was legally the Keir agent, to whom he had been specially recommended by that family, and who alone could discharge the promises made by himself. Mr Dundas, too, upon the whole, seems, in his unavoidable straits and exigencies—and they were not trifling—not to have been unfavourable to Drumpellier: and the requests by Mr William Stirling in the letter are important, backed by what will follow.

15.—EXCERPT LETTER, JAMES DUNDAS, W.S., to WILLIAM STIRLING.

"EDINBURGH, 11*th March* 1818.

"The greatest part of the conversation which you mention, in your letter of the 10th instant, to have had with me in the end of January last, I really cannot bring to my recollection, and therefore I presume there must be some mistake or misapprehension regarding it. But I have NO DIFFICULTY *in saying to you*, that, *so far as I am able to judge from* THE INVENTORY *of the* CADDER PAPERS in Mr Stirling of Keir's possession, *there are* NO *documents referred to* IN THAT INVENTORY *which are* HOSTILE *to your* CLAIM.

"J. D.
"(Keir's agent.)"

Mr Dundas admits there was nothing in the Cadder chartercheet against the Drumpellier claim.

16.—LETTER, WILLIAM STIRLING to JAMES DUNDAS, W.S.

"HOWE STREET, EDINBURGH, *Friday Evening*, 13*th March* 1818.

"I am sorry to find your memory so indifferent in regard to a circumstance which I should otherwise have thought likely to make an impression upon it. Far be it from me, however, to tax it further; whatever be the state of my own recollection, yet, if yours is doubtful, we will say no more on the subject.

"While I am willing, however, to waive my argument, you must excuse me for observing, that our case seems to me to lose little by the omission. To my mind, you are no less bound to afford one the satisfaction one seeks without a promise, than if you had given a thousand. For what is our demand? Simply, to be informed whether you have, or have not, in your possession any hostile documents, such as might have a chance, by being produced now, to save trouble to both parties hereafter. For the information afforded in your last, that there *is nothing hostile to us* in the *Cadder inventory*, I beg to thank you. But *why stop at the inventory*, when the *papers* themselves are in *your possession?* Why not give such a reply as shall preclude all doubt on the subject, by informing us in a distinct manner, either that you have such documents, or that you have not? This is a question on which you surely can entertain no doubt, after the investigation which has taken place ; and the satisfaction we require is of a nature which could not well be withheld from any adversary of a fair description, still less from us, whose conduct hitherto you have been pleased to express your approbation of, *whose whole evidence has been open to you from the beginning,* though *yours* has been *withheld,* and by whose acquiescence in your request for time, you have had the fullest opportunity to make the most of your case.

"For these reasons, I am under the necessity of persisting in my former demand on this head ; and I must likewise continue to insist upon a *specific* answer in regard to the *service*. This week is now lost to us by your delay, and next is Passion Week ; and for other reasons out of the question, of course nothing can now be done till the one following. When you first asked for delay, it was upon the ground of Mr Charles Stirling not having come to town. I am informed that he has since been here, or if not, you might have communicated with him otherwise. At all events, in taking advantage of the delay you have done—to which you are heartily welcome otherwise—there is certainly no reason why you should have involved *us* in the *studied uncertainty* we *now labour under* as to your *future intentions* on this head ; and I once more desire to know positively your wishes on this point, which, if in our power to accede to, we will.

"And here you must pardon me for saying, that I expect a direct and immediate answer from you to the foregoing, in satisfaction to yourself as well as to me. It was by Mr Charles Stirling's express desire that I have hitherto communicated with you on these subjects. If you are pleased to continue that communication, it is well ; if not, I trust you will at least have the complaisance to say so, that I may in that case be authorised to return to him who sent me to you. W. S.

"(Y^{r.} of Drumpellier.)"

Assuredly the vacillation, demur, and uncertainty in the Keir procedure, with the repeated entreaties for delay and postponement in regard to the Drumpellier service, are striking elements in the case, and while telling in favour of the latter—who, on the contrary, was prepared—seems adverse to his opponents, who must have found themselves in difficulty from the strength of his claim; not overlooking either, that while its evidence, hitherto unmet, was solely and articulately at the command of Keir, *not a single item* or scrap of paper was given by him in return, though possessor of the admitted full Cadder charter-chest, which, from what has transpired elsewhere, must have contained particulars more or less in point. Though often politely requested by Drumpellier, all writs and information were uniformly withheld from him by the Keir advisers. There was always here the utmost reticence by them, which may fairly be concluded to have been through the fear of such directly or indirectly corroborating a case of which they were already extremely apprehensive. Added to this, the said advisers would never apprise Drumpellier—as was befitting surely—of the evidence or grounds on which they intended to dispute his approaching service,—so opposite to *his* fair and open dealing with *them*, whereby they were, without scruple on his part, put in possession of all he meant to found upon in his own behalf, which they eagerly caught at, and sought to avail themselves of. Upon the whole, the writer can with difficulty see an apology for such strange untoward conduct in the circumstances, which he conceives, at least, would be the subject of marked comment and animadversion in a parallel ordinary transaction, only palliated, perhaps, by the evident irresolution of the Keir party, from the difficulty of their situation, and inability to take up a proper position and join argument; on which account they were ultimately forced *publicly* to quit the field, and act in secret, still with most hostile intents to Drumpellier, however truly unavailing.

17.—LETTER, JAMES DUNDAS, W.S., to WILLIAM STIRLING.

"EDINBURGH, 16*th March* 1818.

"Your letter of Friday evening, 13th instant, was not delivered at my house till very late in the evening of Saturday the 14th, which is the cause of this late answer.

"The reason for my stopping at the inventory of the Cadder papers is, that I have never seen one of these papers, *although they have been in my possession for ten days*. I am *perfectly satisfied* with the *correctness of that inventory;* and if you had been equally acquainted with the late Mr David Erskine as I was, who prepared it, you would have agreed with me. *I shall*, however, in the course of a few days, *take* an opportunity of *examining these papers*, and inform you *whether any documents such as you point at are among them*.

J. D.
" (Keir's agent.)"

18.—LETTER of WILLIAM STIRLING to JAMES DUNDAS, W.S.

" HOWE STREET, EDINBURGH, 17th *March* 1818.

" I beg leave to thank you for your obliging communication of last night in regard to the Cadder papers, and expect the favour of hearing from you on the subject as soon as possible, being particularly desirous, for reasons relating to myself personally, that our service shall not be delayed beyond the end of next week, or beginning of the following, which I trust will be perfectly convenient to Mr Charles Stirling and yourself.

" W. S.
" (Y^{r.} of Drumpellier.)"

19.—LETTER, JAMES DUNDAS, W.S., to WILLIAM STIRLING.

" EDINBURGH, 23d *March* 1818.

[Still more striking admission by Mr Dundas that there was nothing hostile to the Drumpellier claim in the old original Cadder writs.]

" *I have now examined the* OLD *writings of Cadder* in Mr Stirling of Keir's possession, and *have* NOT *found in them* ANYTHING HOSTILE TO YOUR CLAIM, *as* STATED *in your* BRIEVE. I have so far benefited by the examination, that I have, with the help of Mr Erskine's inventory, been enabled to read these writings, the contents of which have been most accurately and very *fully detailed* in that *inventory*.

J. D.
" (Keir's agent.)"

The important evidence here to the Drumpellier case is obviously given as scrimply and generally as possible, without any specification or *minutiæ* enlightening the question; prudentially it might seem avoided. There doubtless may be more to that effect, while in most of such repositories, it may especially be kept in view, several writs or papers do exist not of material value to the family, though often extremely valuable to others, which are not included in the inventory.

The brief or claim alluded to, seen or examined by Mr Dundas, as implied by him in the above letter, is specifically for the service of "Andrew Stirling, Esq., of Drumpellier," as lawful heir-male to Robert Stirling of Bankeir and Lettyr, through the respective links and generations it sets forth, "WHO DIED IN THE YEAR 1537, AND WHOSE CHILDREN," it states, "AFTER HIS DEATH, IN A JUDICIAL PROCEDURE BEFORE THE LORDS OF THE COUNCIL AND SESSION, WERE EXPRESSLY DECLARED TO BE NEXT IN SUCCESSION TO JANET STIRLING, ONLY DAUGHTER AND HEIRESS OF ANDREW STIRLING OF CADDER, FAILING HEIRS OF HER OWN BODY,"—thus comprising the very question of the identity, where no flaw could be picked by the rigid opponents.

This will also be adverted to in the sequel.

20.—LETTER, JAMES DUNDAS, W.S., to WILLIAM STIRLING.

"EDINBURGH, 7th April 1818.

"I have received the honour of your letter* of yesterday, and on all matters respecting the contest between you and Sir Samuel Stirling I beg to refer you to Mr Pearson (W.S.), his agent. J. D.

"(Keir's agent.)"

21.—LETTER, WILLIAM STIRLING to JAMES DUNDAS, W.S.

"HOWE STREET, EDINBURGH, 7th April 1818.

"You will permit me to observe, with regard to what you are pleased to term the contest between us and Sir Samuel Stirling, that I do not recollect the slightest mention of it in the conversation alluded to,† which related exclusively to the contest *between us and the family of Keir, by whose brother, Mr Charles Stirling, I was expressly referred to you, as the depository of Keir wishes*, on this occasion ; and from whom, therefore, and in relation to them only, I again *request an answer*. ‡ W. S.

"(Yr. of Drumpellier.)"

---

* No copy of this exists in the Drumpellier charter-chest.

† What this was does not transpire.

‡ Touching what does not transpire from any letter extant.

Mr William Stirling was here correct—the contest originally, and in the main, being solely between him and the Keir family, who evidently were now extremely happy to back out, and eventually quitted the business (that is, ostensibly), transferring the task of the contest in future, and throwing legal proceedings, which had not yet been instituted, upon Sir Samuel Stirling, baronet, their previous ally, though they secretly advised them, and paid the expenses.

22.—LAST and CONCLUDING LETTER in the matter, JAMES DUNDAS, W.S., to WILLIAM STIRLING.

"EDINBURGH, *9th April* 1818.

Immediate peremptory step next taken by Mr Dundas, almost unparalleled elsewhere, that speaks for itself— and so conclusive for Drumpellier!

"You really must excuse me from saying anything further regarding your contest, either with Sir Samuel Stirling or Mr Stirling of Keir. *I have told Mr Charles Stirling that I wished to have* NO FURTHER CONCERN IN THIS BUSINESS, and *he has freed me from it.* If, therefore, you wish for any further communication from him, you will have the goodness to apply to himself, *as I cannot say or write more on a subject of which* I HAVE TAKEN LEAVE. J. D.

"(Keir's agent.)"

In this manner Mr Dundas quitted and threw up the case, which he found himself—not, probably, from undiscoverable motives—unable to carry on ; and the contest was now between Drumpellier and Glorat, who bore the brunt of the action for Keir (who did not venture an appearance, or enter the field), ostensibly through his agent, Mr Pearson (W.S.), who has been already alluded to.

Conclusions from the Correspondence which has been adduced.

The whole of the preceding correspondence, together with the facts therein contained, is certainly in Drumpellier's favour, but *e converso* to Keir, and perhaps also to Glorat. This is shown by the following reasons :—

I. That the merits of the Drumpellier claim had been duly submitted, and through the *medium* of the reprinted statement given, besides other communications, to the Keir agent, who thereafter, in reference thereto, in its further elucidation, and to ascertain the facts and import of the same, had fully examined both the Cadder inventory and Cadder writs.

II. That owing to the Cadder writs being well preserved for centuries, and, it is believed, at the period, suited to the present discussion, while the transactions in part disclosing the proof in favour of the alleged Drumpellier status and representation affected the cotemporary Keir family also, no quarter better than the Cadder repositories could be figured for affording details and information in the matter in question.

III. That though the best means of knowledge, and testing and refuting the Drumpellier case, were thus on the Keir side, they, though so hostilely bent, after a full examination of the Cadder writs, were forced to admit that they contained nothing of a hostile nature, or that could impugn or traverse its facts and main conclusions—of themselves so decisive—and whose truth and soundness were thus fully admitted. Mr Dundas had especially examined the brief of service of Mr Stirling of Drumpellier in 1818[1], that truly comprised the essence of his case—the point of identity—there explicitly stated and founded upon, but to which he could not object; in other words, as may be inferred in the circumstances, which he fairly admitted and agreed to.

[1] See p. 76. Letter 19.

It is the latter portion of the correspondence cited that intimates this, which is the reason that has been adduced for its being inserted after the statement of the merits of the Drumpellier case—the *subjecta materies* here—enucleated into the middle of the former, to which it directly applies, and whereby we best elicit such evidence in favour of Drumpellier, however awkward the arrangement may be.

IV. But there remains more yet to be observed. Mr Dundas, the Keir agent, was notoriously one of the most able and experienced law-agents in Scotland, while at the same time intimately connected with, and an old friend of, the Keir family: he then, it may be concluded, could not but exert himself to the utmost, and neglect nothing to assist or advance their cause; yet it is conceived he latterly did not expedite it in the way to be expected from one ordinarily so active and acute. He was procrastinating—craved frequent delays, evidently, if possible, to obviate staggering difficulties, and make investigations to surmount them—which naturally annoyed Mr William Stirling, who was in no such predicament, and probably not quite aware of the motive—blame thus attaching to neither. Not only so, but Mr Dundas, as stated on 19th February 1818, in concurrence (as it must have been) with his counsel, Sir Samuel Stirling candidly and decidedly gave it as his opinion " that the Keir family had *no ground to interpose on the present occasion.*"

[1] See pp. 45-6.

But independently, also, after a full examination of the Cadder repositories, as premised, he having thus, as we may presume, obtained a complete insight into the question, and found the Keir case utterly desperate, while probably influenced, too, by discoveries of corroborative proof in favour of Drumpellier—on which, of course, he must be mute—he whom any further procedure displeased, immediately, like a just and honourable man as he was, emphatically told Mr Charles Stirling that he "wished to have no further concern in this business," of which being at length "freed," he immediately wrote Mr William Stirling "he had taken leave." What can be more striking or irresistibly decisive for Drumpellier?—the Keir family being the last whose case Mr Dundas would have thus deserted, but in an extreme emergency, unless for the motives assigned. This step, hardly paralleled by any other abandonment of an untenable case, may have disappointed that staunch Keir zealot, Mr Charles Stirling, to whom the converse would have been pleasing, influenced as he was by the excitement of family impulses, and who stood out to the last. But Mr Dundas was prompted by better dictates, and could not truly, just and prescient as he was, in reason and justice, act otherwise. In so far as he was enabled, he had written and exerted himself to the utmost for his client, whatever opposite scruples in his mind; but now, though rather unavailingly, there remained no other alternative than to adopt the conduct he did; and in the case of Mr Dundas, the eulogiatory lines of Lord Dirleton on the Earl of Cassilis in the seventeenth century may be partly applied—that he, in fact,

> "Scripsisse *manu*, NON *mente*—placebat
> Quodque aliis—*frustra* DISPLICUISSE SIBI!"

Further new evidence and corroborations in the Drumpellier case.

Having thus given an account of what occurred previous to the service in 1818, with the correspondence, and a statement of the merits of the case, exactly as it was laid before the Keir party and their law-agent at that time, it will be well now to adduce two or three other recorded facts and evidence, which bear strongly in favour of Drumpellier—and which were not then known—together with corroborations of the former.

Acts and Decreet, Register of the Supreme Civil Court, Nov.

1. Action by the Crown, September 5, 1553 (through the Lord Advocate), founding upon the *forfeiture** of Thomas Bischop, by which all the lands, goods, and evidents, instruments, and documents, &c., belonging to him, were escheated thereto, against David Watson, notary, to deliver to the Crown

* In the year 1545. See Acts of Parliament, vol. ii. p. 458-9.

" ane instrument takin in his handis of ye *sesing* gevin in coniunct fee to ye said Thomas and Janet Striveling, his spous, of all and haill ye landis of *Uchiltreis*, with ye pertinentis, lyand within ye scherifdome of *   ; and ane uther instrument of sesing,† takin in ye said Davidis handis, berand yat ye said Thomas revokit ye *pretendit procuratory*[1] and mandat maid be ye said Janet, his spous, for *renunciation, resigning,* and *overgering* of ye landis of *Kirkmychaell* and *Blairnerne,* with ye pertinentis ; togidder with ye instrument takin in his handis of ye intimation of ye said revocation " . . . . "and all utheris instrumentis takin in his handis quhilkis concernit ye said Thomas and his spous." David Watson, the defender, in consequence appeared, and being sworn, " declarit yat he hes na ma instrumentis, documentis, &c. &c., *except* ye saidis *twa instrumentis*, to ye quhilkis he confessis he was notar, and are contenit in his prothocoll." Therefore the Lords of Council order David " to extract and deliver " to the Lord Advocate, on the part of the Crown, " ye forsaidis instrumentis in competent, attentick, and dew forme."

[1] This evidently is her Procuratory of Resignation in 1541, so far as concerned these lands.

The latter, therefore, constituted the only title-deeds of the unfortunate Janet and her spouse, drawn up by the family agent, and evidently relating to the two conditions in her *procuratory in* 1541[2]—(1), the provision to herself and Bishop in *Uchiltree* ; and (2), the provision to the bairns of umquhile *Robert Stirling,* as concerning heritages she intended for them in implement of it. As must have been obvious from what has been stated, circumstances here prevented her from taking further steps, but as soon as possible thereafter, James Stirling of Keir, on whom the duty every way devolved, by the transaction of 1542, forwarded this business as to the engaging to infeft, under warrandice, John Stirling, eldest son of Robert of Lettyr, in the very preceding lands of *Blanerne* and *Kirkmichel,* besides Lettyr.[3]

[2] See pp. 61, 62.

[3] See Submission between Keir and said John, 30th Jan. 1542, p. 66.

This evidently, too, goes no small way in supporting the identity between *Robert of Lettyr* and his family with the Robert Stirling and his bairns in 1541, seeing, from what is thus stated, the implement of the provision to the latter was to be executed in the shape of one by the former.

Janet had evidently, it may be inferred, revoked these lands from her procuratory of resignation of the entire Cadder estate in 1541, the better to

---

* A blank here in the record.
† Sesing must be a mistake, there having been no sesing, but only a revocation, which must have been the subject of the instruments.

82   COMMENTS ON KEIR PERFORMANCE,

secure them, as then in fact substantially was stipulated—or at least some other portions of her heritages—to the bairns then of umquhile Robert Stirling ; but she certainly took no other steps than the above in the matter, or in respect to *any* DIFFERENT *Cadder heritages.*

Now, Recorded in the General Register of Deeds in Her Majesty's General Register House, Edinburgh.

[1] *Proving three of the oldest links in the exclusive Lettyr pedigree.*

[2] *Evidently the solemn and striking Contract in 1527. See pp. 68, 69.*

II. "Contract and appoyntment dated Edinburgh, April 5, 1606, between Robert Stirling of Letter, for himself, and Jean Guthrie, his spous,* and Johne Livingstoune of Balderane, on ye uther parte, as efter follows :—Fforsamekle as umquhile James Stirling of Keir, and laird of ye landis of Letter and Bochquharrage under written, for fulfilling of ane parte of ane *contract* and *appoyntment* maid, endit, and perfektit betuix *umquhile Robert Stirling of Letter, father to umquhile Johne Stirling of Letter* that last decessit, and *guidschire* to the said *Robert Stirling,* now of *Letter,*[1] on the ane parte, and umquhile Sir John Stirling of Keir, knyht, father to umquhile James Stirling of Keir that last decessit, on ye uther parte, quhilk contract[2] was thereafter of *new renewit* betuix the said umquhile James Stirling of Keir, and ye said umquhile Johne Stirling, eldest sone and air to the said umquhile Robert Stirling of Letter, on the ane and uther partis, registrat in ye buikes of Counsale and Session, for ye mair sure observing thairof be his charter, precept, and instrument of sesing, gave, grantit, &c., to ye said umquhile Johne Stirling, sone and air to ye said umquhile Robert Stirling of Letter, and his aires maill lachfullie gotten or to be gotten of his bodie, and all and haill the ten pund land of *Letter,* and all and haill the fyve pund land of Bochquharrage, &c., as for the principal, &c., as the said contract, charter, precept, and instrument of sesing following yerupon at mair lenth beares ; lyk as ye said James Stirling of Keir, be his uther charter, precept, and instrument of seising, gave, grantit, &c., to ye said umquhile Johne Stirling, son and air to ye said umquhile Robert Stirling of Letter, and his aires maill lauchfullie gotten, &c., heritablie, all and haill *fyfteene* pund land of ye said *umquhile* James his landis of KEIR of *auld extent,* with ye pertinentis within ye scheriffdome of Perthe, in *securitie* and special *warrandice* of ye foresaid *ten pund land of Letter,* and fyve pund land of Bockequharrage, so that, in caise it should happen the said umquhile Johne Stirling or his foresaidis to be troublet, molestit, &c., or removit fra the peaceable possession, &c., of the saidis landis of Letter and Bockquharrage, that then and in that caise it sould be lessum to ye said umquhile Johne Stirling and

* His second wife, after the death of his first, Jean Stirling, of the family of Glorat.

his foresaidis to have full and free ingress and access in and to the propertie and possession heretablie of all and haill ye foresaid *fyfteene* pund land of ye *saidis landis* of KEIR, with the pertinentis, and to the uplifting of the fruits, rentis, &c., as they micht have had of the foresaidis landis of Letter and Bockquharrage giff na sic impediment had intervenit, as the said charter of warrandice, precept, and instrument of seising following yerupon at mair lenth purportis; in ye quhilkis landis *respective* above written, as well principal as warrandice above specifiit, with yair pertinentis, the said *Robert Stirling*, now of Letter, was of lang tyme bygane dewlie and lawfullie *infeft* and *seisit* as *air* to the said umquhile *Johne of Letter his father*, as his infeftment and seising maid to him yerupon beers; thairforr, and for sowme of money underwritten, payit and to be payit be ye said Johne Livingstone of Balderain to the said Robert Stirling of Letter and Jean Guthrie, his spous, &c., the said Robert, &c., hes *sauld*, *annalleit*, and *disponit*, &c., in favouris of the said *Jonne Livingstone of Baldorane*, his airis and assigneyes quhatsomever, all and haill the *foresaid* ten pund land of *Letter*, and fyve pund land of *Bockquharrage*, &c., as for the principal, and alsua all and haill the foresaid fyfteene pund land of the said *landis of Keir* of auld extent, with the pertinentis,[1] and that in special claus of warrandice and securitie of the saidis landis of Letter and Bockquharrage—sall, with all diligence possible, dewlie and sufficientlie infeft the said Johne Levingstone of Balderane, his airis and assigneyes, in all and haill of the foresaid xvlb *of the foresaid landis of Keir*, of ald extent, with the pertinentis, in special claus of warrandice and securitie," &c.; and moreover, Robert assigns to Livingstone, "all uther actions and executions competent to the said Robert, his predecessors, airis, or successors, against Sir Archibald Stirling of Keir, knyt., his predecessors, airis, or successors, be vertew of quhatsomever contractis, bandis, or securities maid be the said Archibald or his predecessors to the said Robert or his predecessors, of or concerning the landis, principal and warrandice above written" (together with all relative writs and documents).

[1] Thus, when Lettyr was alienated by the family of Stirling of Lettyr, Old Keir, with the warrandice, went along with it to the purchaser—a striking circumstance.

The above fully proves what we have maintained, and establishes beyond a doubt that not only was Robert, who died in 1537, and afterwards his son John, infeft in *Auld Keir* in warrandice of the fulfilment of the contract in 1527, but also his grandson Robert; and that the said property remained in the family till 1606, when *it*—still unredeemed—was made over to the Livingstons. All feudal lawyers know that the principal house and demesne lands of a property constituted by far its most important portion, and were identified with the superiority and family representation, and, for the most part, were reserved and kept intact from other burdens and responsibilities. The principal messuage, too, when the family is represented by female heirs' portions, thus goes exclusively to the eldest; and far back, when peerages were territorial, whoever got the principal messuage, whatever became of the rest of the property, was *peer*. Now, it cannot be disputed that Old Keir must have comprised both the old family residence and demesne lands, hence it may be held or called the Keir paramount patrimony, than which Sir John of Keir, in 1527, could not have made a greater concession, excepting his own life,—strongly evincing the deep family rights and interests then in Robert Stirling, who, under the circumstances, it may be concluded, could thus be no other than the male Cadder heir.

Even the preceding, too, is not all, for antecedently a charter was granted by the same Robert Stirling of Lettyr, dated at Niddrie, 24th December 1599 (he appearing to have been embarrassed in his circumstances), to William Edmonstone of Duntreath, of "all and whole the ten pound land of *old* extent of KEIR, of the fifteen pound land of *old* extent *thereof*,"[1] in warrandice of the lands of Lettyr, in the same manner as they had been disponed in warrandice "by Sir *Archibald* Stirling of Keir to the said Robert Stirling."

[margin: Edmonstone of Duntreath charter-chest.]
[margin: [1] *Sic* (as to this description).]

Thus, independently of the grant to the same effect by Sir James Stirling of Keir to John Stirling of Lettyr (Robert's father) in 1553, there is proved to have been a new and later one by Sir Archibald, Sir James's son and heir, to Robert,—all evincing the weighty Cadder right and claim in the Lettyr family which required so strong and reiterated guaranteed compensation.

Having given these entirely new documents, each intimately connected with the condition in favour of the bairns of umquhile Robert Stirling, made by Janet of Cadder in her procuratory of resignation in 1541, we now proceed to show how, and in what way, the bairns of umquhile Robert Stirling of Lettyr were provided for, and with the greater reason, as, though plain enough in the Abstract of Evidence in 1818, it was not minutely gone into there.

As soon as practicable, James Stirling of Keir, who was accordingly so legally bound, and in order to purge the Cadder estate of all burdens, on 30th January 1542, entered into a formal submission [2] with

[margin: [2] See p. 66.]

I. "JOHNE STRIVELING, SONE an AIRE of *umquhile* ROBERT STRIVELING," undeniably of Lettyr, and the Drumpellier ancestor, whereby he actually bound himself, under clause of warrandice, to infeft John in the very lands promised of *Kirkmychel* and *Blancrne*, thus expressly implementing Janet of Cadder's important object in reference to them in his favour, already initiated by her, as we have seen, which identifies him as one of the bairns—and eldest of course—of the exactly corresponding Robert, her undoubted nearest heir collaterally in 1541.

And it is moreover proved, by the subsequent submission in 1553,[1] that these, together with Lettyr, had been promised to Robert by Sir John Stirling of Keir, the Cadder wardator, in the important indenture in 1527. Hence Janet, by her condition in 1541, and relative after-step, was, in the main, as was most natural, fulfilling Sir John's transactions, obviously touching a landed compensation for gentilitial claims, as formerly shown, or rights in Robert and his issue, who at the same time were thus, with certain accessories, as will be afterwards seen, to be alimented and provided in Cadder heritages, in pursuance of her condition.

The identity of the latter with Janet's heirs, independently of the other conclusive evidence to the same effect, is so transparent and self-evident as to require no comment.

Legal proceedings are proverbially tedious; but at length, on March 2, 1553[2]—a considerable interval no doubt—matters were fully settled by a "*contractus*" (as it is called) between "Striveling of Keir and Striveling of Lettir," showing Lettyr (or the Drumpellier family, in fact), beside Keir, to be here alone interested; and it thereby was "finalie contractit betuix honorabill partiis, James Striveling (of Keir),—and John Striveling, sone and aire of umquhile Robert Striveling," while summarily reciting the contract, May 28, 1527, betwixt "ye said umquhile Robert Striveling and umquhile Johne Striveling of ye Keir, kny^{ht}.," that the said "James Striveling of Keir" should infeft "ye said Johne Striveling—and his airis maill lauchfullie gotten or to be gotten of his body, quhilkis failzeing, to William Striveling, his bruder, and his airis maill lauchfullie gotten or to be gotten of his body," &c., in "ye fiue pund land of Bockquharrage" (Stirlingshire), "for ye landis of Blairerne and Kirkmichel, to be halden of ye said James and his airis, that ane half in blanche, yat uyer half in warde," "for ye quhilkis ye said Johne Striveling, sone and aire aforesaid, sall resign, &c., ye landis of *Auld Keir* xv pund land, &c., quhairin he is presentlie vestit and seisit as air to his said umquhile father, in ye handis of ye said James

Provisions to the bairns of umquhile Robert Stirling, 1537 and 1541, three in number, viz. JOHN, WILLIAM, and JANET, then pupils, and the former the Drumpellier ancestor, which could only be as next Cadder heirs, in terms of Janet of Cadder's stipulation in the latter year.

[1] See pp. 68, 69.

[2] See ibid.

Striveling, his superior yairof, *ad perpetuum remanentiam.*" So great was the guarantee to which Sir John of Keir, commonly the most arbitrary and impracticable of men, as fully proved, was compelled to effect his object; and what a weighty Cadder interest—*qua* heir-male unavoidably, as has been shown or inferred—must have vested in Robert Striveling and his family, to have rendered such a security for it, or a compensation in its stead, imperative! And it would be considered that the family of Keir had thus fully recovered *Auld Keir*, which was relieved out of the hands of Robert Striveling's family; but this, singularly, is not so clear, for there immediately follows this clause, that "ye said resignation being maid, ye said James sall incontinent yaireftir infeft ye said Johne Striveling and his airis maill," whom failing, his brother William, as before, in "ye foresaid landis of Ald Keir, &c., in clauss of warrandice of ye principale landis above written, viz. ye landis of Lettir and Balquharrage, &c., and sall deliver to ye said Johnne sufficient infeftment, charter, and precept of warrandice yairupone;"[1] and, moreover, as has been fully proved, this last clause of warrandice is inserted in future alienations and title-deeds of the property in favour of the disponees.

[1] See p. 69.

The terms of one-half of the property conceded being "blanche," was more favourable, and the substitution of Bochquharrage for Blairnerne and Kirkmichel preferable, and so far more advantageous,—the latter being held by the family of Cadder of the Campbells of Auchenbowie, who held them of the Livingstones of Kilsyth, who held them of the Crown, while Boquharrage held only of one subject-superior (Keir), immediate tenant of the Crown. There hence, in regard to it, would be fewer casualties or demands against the vassal, a most important consideration at that feudal period.

Hence James Striveling of Keir, by this advantageous access, in favour of John Striveling of Lettyr, as well as by obeying and implementing, in his behalf (as behoved), the proviso of Janet of Cadder in 1541, for the "bairns of umquhile Robert Striveling," her nearest heirs, with whom he and his family are thus identified, amplified by Boquharrage, fully, and perhaps more than was incumbent—John too, being only one of the three bairns who were to be provided—so far discharged his duty.

The preceding regards John Stirling of Lettyr, eldest son of umquhile Robert; and now we next come further, with the same view, to

II. WILLIAM STRIVELING, YOUNGER and only BROTHER through the same parents of the said JOHN.

WILLIAM, second son or bairn of umquhile Robert Stirling in 1541.

The evidence here (of which Nos. 2 and 3 are new) is extremely simple and conclusive.

1. Procuratory of Resignation,[1] 13th December 1541, by Janet Striveling, lady of Cadder, where she conveys heritably to James Striveling, of Keir, her Cadder patrimony, including the lands of "*Bankeir;*" directly establishing that Bankeir *generally* was a Cadder heritage or pertinent.

2. Action, 16th June 1591,[2] before the Supreme Civil Court by *Robert** Striveling of Lettyr, "broyer, *sone*, and *air maill* to umquhile WILLIAM Striveling of *Wester* BANKIER (who thus must have been younger brother of John of Lettyr),† against Sir Archibald Striveling of Keir, kny^t, sone and air of umquhile Sir James Striveling of Keir, kny^t;" wherein the pursuer charges the defender and a party with forging a pretended letter of reversion by William for redemption of the foresaid lands of Wester Bankier, to which otherwise Robert of Lettyr should have succeeded.

3. Previous litigation in 1590 at the instance of the *above Robert*,[3] also in reference to the said lands, who explicitly founds (without question) upon " ane *charter maid* to ye said umquhile *William* (his paternal uncle as before), BE *Schir James* Striveling of Kere, kny^t, of ye landis of *Wester Bankeir*, dated 20th November 1565."

This Sir James, the noted acquirer of Cadder, was of course bound to clear the estate of burdens, and the grant evidently must directly have been in implement of Janet of Cadder's *postulate* or *proviso* in 1541, in which the above William as one of the "bairns" there was included. No other claim or interest, after every investigation, has been discovered in him.

As to any reversion cited after being thus in possession, it is quite unimportant. The above grant to William[4] was even more favourable than of Uchiltree, settled upon Thomas Bishop and his spouse, which, as has been shown, was even originally under reversion, and subsequently redeemable by Keir.

And, finally, we come here to the only remaining *bairn* in question, offspring of "Umquhile Robert Stirling" premised.

III. *Jane*[5] by name, a daughter, and only sister of the preceding.

---

* Fully proved, by the evidence submitted to the jury on the occasion of the Drumpellier service in 1818, to have been eldest son and heir of the preceding John of Lettyr, and moreover explicitly by the new evidence cited in 1606.—See pp. 82-3.

† And that John had one only younger brother, *William*, his next collateral heir-male, is proved by the contract in 1553, formerly adduced.—See pp. 68-9.

88   COMMENTS ON KEIR PERFORMANCE,

¹ See ibid., p. 179, note 1.

With respect to her, the evidence is a single paragraph from the Keir Performance,¹ to which we are in consequence indebted, founded upon authentic Hamilton of Bardowie writs, viz. :—

"*Johne Strivling*, of Lettir, had a *sister*, '*Jane* Strivling,' in whose favour Sir Archibald Sterling of Keir" (son and heir of the preceding Sir James, acquirer of Cadder), and "Jane, Lady Keyr, granted a precept to their tenants in *Ballindrocht* (near *Cadder*) to pay her yearly 'three bollis ait meill,' which is said by a subsequent precept to be 'ane pension assignit to hir for supporting her honestlie :'" These precepts are dated "10th February 1589 and 1st May 1591."

The above John was incontestably the eldest son and heir of umquhile Robert Stirling, which makes this Jane daughter of the latter.

Being unmarried, this might, with obvious family aids, be a provision for her in that age, and otherwise than as a "bairn" of "umquhile Robert Strivling," she likewise could have had no claim thereto.

As an indispensable condition in his title to the Cadder estate, under Janet of Cadder's grant in 1541, it was, as before remarked, imperative on James Stirling of Keir, as standing in her shoes, and purging the burdens on the estate, to provide and secure the "bairns of *umquhile* Robert"—there specified as her nearest heirs—in parts of the Cadder patrimony or heritage. He did so provide the "bairns of umquhill Robert Stirling" of Lettyr, also *dead* in that year, who had been a contemporary of Janet, and who had, besides, been promised in 1527 parts of the estate of Cadder, as is to be presumed, in the same capacity ; while no others but the said Robert's heirs, after every investigation, and without the least contradiction, too, on the other side, though challenged to the opposite proof, received anything out of the Cadder estate under the above condition.

Conclusion from the preceding.

To stoop or attempt to refute a contrary hypothesis would be absolutely fighting with a mere shadow ; and can there then be a doubt that the said bairns of umquhile Robert Stirling of Lettyr—the undoubted Drumpellier ancestor—were the bairns specified by Janet of Cadder in 1541, and, consequently and indisputably, her nearest collateral heirs ? Upon the whole, never perhaps was a material fact, in *re tam antiquâ*, so well documented and established, including their having been so distinctly and fully shown to have been helped and provided in terms of her condition in that year.

The evidence of the family Bible.

The evidence from the Stirling family Bible may be here again appealed to, backed by further proof of its legal relevancy and admissibility ; while obviously in favour of the identity in question, it also corroborates the Drumpellier-Cadder descent, and necessarily Cadder representation.

In cases of pedigree, especially in peerage claims before the House of Lords, where stricter proof is exacted than in other courts, that of the impressions and traditions of members of a family—naturally very competent judges—either orally or *scripto*, as to matters of descent, and of gentilitial representation, is usually submitted, and duly weighed and considered. Thus the evidence in the recent claim to the Scotch earldom of Airth in 1839 of Mrs Margaret Gurney, sister of Captain Barclay of Urie, the claimant[1] was held relevant and allowed, though through mere hearsay, or what she only had heard an old relative affirm, in support of a cardinal point in the case, the *primogeniture* of Lady Mary Graham, their *ancestrix*—and identified with the Airth right of representation—who was born considerably before the middle of the seventeenth century, and married in 1662. Further, Lord Kenyon,[2] a high authority, said, " I admit that declarations of a *family*, and perhaps of others living in habits of intimacy with them, are received in evidence as to pedigrees." This exactly quadrates, as will be seen, with the point in question ; and he thus does not even reject what is less weighty, and thus telling *a fortiori* in its behalf; while English practice has now great weight in Scotch matters of pedigree, at least in peerage claims.

Then, again, as to proof *scripto*, or in a written shape, there are the autograph, historical, and family memoirs of James fifth Earl of Balcarres, that were adduced and relevantly admitted in the more recent and successful claim of his present noble representative to the earldom of Crawford, in 1848,[3] in order to fix points of extinction and family representation in respect to persons born before 1700.

The chief requisites exacted in law, to give effect to such family or historical proof, are: (1.) that it is the handwriting of the party ; (2.) that it comes from the proper custody—that is, from his charter-chest or family papers ; and (3.) that he had "*peculiar* knowledge of a fact (*mooted or in question*)," and "had not an assignable interest to falsify the matter."[4] In such cases it is both relevant and cogent ; all which elements, including peculiar knowledge, as is to be presumed, unite in the present instance. And what proof of the kind can be stronger or less questionable than the autograph entries of a father or relative in his family Bible, in respect to their births, marriages, and descents, so often attested, and thereby preserved as the best and

[1] See Minutes of Evidence in the Airth Peerage case, Aug. 6, 1839, pp. 76, 77.

[2] 3 Term. Rep. 719.

[3] See Minutes of Evidence in the claim, July 18, 1848, pp. 564-6.

[4] Tait on Evidence, p. 53.

COMMENTS ON KEIR PERFORMANCE.

[margin: ¹ Cowper's Reports, p. 593.]

[margin: ² [See p. 57, note.]]

most appropriate record for the purpose, out of pure natural affection, without any undue bias. And accordingly, as has been already shown,[1] Lord Mansfield, in Buller's Reports, declares, that an "entry in a father's family Bible, an inscription on a tombstone (certainly not superior to the former), are all good evidence;" while he says, too, that "tradition is sufficient in point of pedigree."[2]

Now, altogether, the above *dicta*, and legal postulates, over and above strikingly concur in the present evidence adduced in favour of the Drumpellier-Cadder descent.

It is the autograph attestation in the family Bible of Dr William Stirling, born in 1682, who had no earthly view to serve at the time, when neither he nor his family had contemplated legal steps to vindicate their Cadder status —indeed never questioned till this century, if even now—and who, from his known religious bias and sentiments, could have attached but little moment essentially to the fact, though falling to be noticed in this more genealogical age, and not be overlooked, with family incidents in the Bible, above all reserved for such reminiscences.

He had the circumstance, too, in his favour, it is believed, of other proof as to his descent, which, if mistaken, could thus have been easily rectified. The same gentleman, Dr William Stirling, was twenty-seven when his father, the third John Stirling in the pedigree, died ; and that John was no less than grandson of Walter, son of John Stirling of Lettyr and Bochquharrage (infeft in Auld Keir), whose actual Cadder descent (through Robert his father, so often noticed) is in question ; and in the family Bible of the said Dr William,[3] together with other autograph notices of births, marriages, and deaths, is the following express entry :—

[margin: ³ See Letter on Drumpellier Pedigree, No. 1., at the end of the Exposition.]

"XVIII. JUNII MDCXL.

[margin: ⁴ The exact locality of Lettyr or Letter-Stirling, by which both Robert Stirling and John his son were designated.]

"Natus fuit pater meus Joannes Stirling, cujus pater fuit Joannes Stirling, filius Walteri Stirling, filii Joannis Stirling, *qui descenderat ex familia de* CADDER" (of course in the male line, according to the usual understanding and acceptation), "et cujus fuit terra de Balquharrage et terra de Lettir Stirling prope Duntreth."[4] The last was clearly and correctly John Stirling alluded to, son of umquhile Robert Stirling of Lettyr, who has been proved Janet of Cadder's nearest collateral heir.

The above proof is in every view good ; and if mere hearsay, deponed to from a relative, proved a material fact, as shown in the Airth case in 1839, *a fortiori* must the direct evidence of Dr Stirling, an actual descendant, through his family Bible, tell, in the present one, of a Cadder origin or representation, not either of such antiquity as the former, being within the compass of two centuries, instead of what obtained there.

John Stirling of Lettyr, whose important Cadder descent is thereby proved, having lived to 1585, while the other links of the pedigree specified in the family Bible are *aliunde* proved correct, this creates a presumption in favour of that likewise from Cadder being so, upon the legal principle *rectum in uno rectum in omnibus*; so that, upon the whole, everything being thus uniform and corroborative, and flowing but in one current, the last piece of evidence, by established law, must be a strong auxiliary in the case.

The exponent has again stated the foregoing argument, though likewise adduced in the Abstract of Evidence in 1818, because he may be thus enabled more strongly to illustrate and corroborate it. And, for the same reason, he will next explain fully and articulately the important one from the exact state of minority, respectively, of the bairns of umquhile Robert Stirling of Lettyr, dead in 1537, and umquhile Robert Stirling, deceased in 1541, that was not so pointedly or expressly explained in the said Abstract. Not only now can it be proved that they were then certainly minors, but further still—which is new—in 1541, in the actual stage of *pupillarity*; which striking fact may *per se* fix and decide the question of the identity of their parents,—namely, the two preceding Roberts.

<small>Conclusive evidence of the identity in question from the pupillarity of the issue of both Robert Stirlings in 1541.</small>

I.—First here in respect to the "*bairns* of umquhile Robert Stirling," Janet of Cadder's *heirs*, in 1541, and that they were then *ex hac voce* pupil-offspring.

The epithet "bairns," even at present, as is notorious, denotes children; and, by Scotch language in the sixteenth century, technically defined pupil-offspring.

In support of which, it is only incumbent to quote as follows from the Law Glossary in the same century of the learned Sir John Skene, the Selden of Scotland, as he may be called, and Lord Clerk Register to James VI. before the union of the crowns.[1]

Under the head of the 'Custody of Children,' he inculcates that "The keiping of the BAIRNES pertenis to the mother"—"after the decease of the father, *until* the BAIRNE be of the age of *seven* yeres compleit, conform to the com-

<small>[1] See his Glossary prefixed to the old Scotch Acts of Parliament.</small>

moun practique of this realme, and the civil law." Then he adds, under the title of "Three Kindis of Age"—" For be the law of this realme, grounded upon the climacterick yeires of *Septinarius et Ternarius,* that is of sevin and three yeires, there is three kindes of age : the first is of *sevin* yeiris, during the *quhilk* tyme the BAIRNES are in *custodie of their parents;* the second is of fourteene yeiris, within the quhilk it is not leasum to marrie ; the third is of twentie-ane yeiris, after the quhilk tyme ane *aire* may enter to his landes."

Here it cannot escape notice, and confirms what is premised, that the term "*bairne*" is confined to tender issue, or pupils until the age of seven, or who had attained that age, without extending it further.

Elsewhere he uses "*bairne*" in the also appropriate and infantine sense of a child within seven years. Thus, in reference to a husband's having right, by the courtesy of Scotland, to the wife's heritages (as in England), he inculcates, "quhen onie man marries lauchfullie ane wife, and receive lande and heritage with her, and it happen that he begat with her ane *bairne,* quha being borne, is heard *cryand* betwixt four walles of ane house, and thereafter his wife deceasis before him, he sall bruik and possesse all the landes quhilkis perteineit to her,—albeit the *bairne* live or decease," "the *bairne* borne being soun or daughter." And it is added that "this law is never introduced in favour of the wife or BAIRNES, but is maid in favour of the husband allanarlie."

Hence the term "*bairne*" is above proved to denote an *infant* or *pupil,* within which category, therefore, the preceding "*bairnes*" of umquhile Robert Stirling, Janet of Cadder's heir in 1541, undoubtedly came.

Sub voce Curatius.

II.—And further, that the other cotemporary Robert Stirling, the Drumpellier ancestor, also dead in 1541, had likewise then left pupil-offspring or bairns—thus identical with the preceding.

[1] See p. 58. It has been legally established[1] that Robert of Bankeir or Letter had merely a dispensation for his marriage with Marian Fleming, his sole wife, dated 11th of June 1533. The actual solemnisation of marriage did not always immediately follow a dispensation ; and holding John, their eldest son, to have been born at the middle of 1534—and he may possibly have been produced later —that would simply make him a "bairne" or pupil of seven years, and William, his younger brother, if not Jane their sister (who might yet have been the *eldest,* her age being unknown), actually within that age *on the*

13th of December 1541, *when* the "BAIRNS" of the *other* Robert Stirling so precisely figure,* and who, from the proved sense of the term, must have been equally pupils. They thus all were appositely and exclusively comprised under the denomination of the "bairns of umquhile Robert Stirling," and hence clearly identical.

It is humbly submitted, then, that, by reiterated evidence, taken *semel et simul*, all to the same purport and effect, it has been proved that the bairns of Robert Stirling of Letter, the Drumpellier ancestor, were those declared by Janet of Cadder in 1541 to be her nearest heirs, failing herself and heirs of her body,—which indisputably fixes the identity.

The identity in question has never yet been attempted to be denied, except what is indeed most insignificant, and out of the pale of law, through mere assumptions, and gross misrepresentations so risked reprehensively in the Keir work, and to be exposed in the sequel. To stop to refute the negative, in the circumstances, would indeed be like fighting with a shadow. But in order merely to facilitate the better and more ready apprehension of the identity, it may be here expedient to conclude, under a comprehensive form, with giving the following TABULAR STATEMENT of the various uniform and irresistible points of coincidence and parallelisms, with the manifest RESULTS in its support :—

* The year then began on the 25th of March.

TABLE

COMMENTS ON KEIR PERFORMANCE,

TABLE OF THE IDENTITY AS PROVED, WITH RESULTS.

Two precise cotemporaries figured before 1541, having the closest connection with the Cadder Family as follows, respectively under Nos. I. and II., which also comprises their Issue—

I. ROBERT OF LETTER, also "umquhile" in 1541, Ancestor of the Drumpellier Family, and his Issue.		II. UMQUHILE ROBERT STIRLING in 1541, and his Issue.
No. I.		No. II.
1. The above had undoubtedly the Christian name of *Robert*.	Exact parallelism here.	1. So had the other individual here.
2. He was actually styled in *Cadder*, quite suiting a Cadder cadet, it being the family residence.		2. From his very near Cadder relationship—in fact, nearest—he may be presumed also, occasionally at least, to have resided at Cadder.
3. But his usual designation was simply "Robert Stirling," as under No. II. 3.	Exact parallelism here.	3. But his designation was Robert Stirling simply, as under No. I. 3.
4. This Robert had a most weighty claim upon *Cadder* in 1527, afterwards compensated for, that can only be accounted for by being the next Cadder heir-male (as the other Robert under No. II. 4.)	Parallelism here, nearly brought out, at least by presumption and extreme human probabilities.	4. He also peculiarly must have had such Cadder claim too, being certainly recognised as the nearest Cadder heir.
5. This Robert died in 1537, consistent enough with his counterpart under No. II. 5.	Very close parallelism here.	5. This Robert had predeceased 1541, consistent enough with his counterpart under No. I. 5.
6. This Robert had previously married, and left children.	Exact parallelism here.	6. This Robert had previously married, and left children.
7. This Robert's issue were clearly, in 1541, *bairns* or pupils, as in his counterpart's case under No. II. 7.	Exact parallelism here, and of itself, it may be said, fixing the identity.	7. This Robert's issue were clearly, in 1541, bairns or pupils, as in his counterpart's case under No. I. 7.
8. The bairns of this Robert, in the year 1542 and subsequently, were provided in, and obtained portions of, the Cadder heritage, that could only be, in the circumstances, according to what was shown as the nearest Cadder heir.	Complete parallelism here; indeed, the two families thereby proved ONE and THE SAME.	8. The bairns of this Robert were certainly, in 1541, as nearest Cadder heirs, to be secured a portion of the Cadder heritage.
9. This family provided, as stated, in a respectable portion of Cadder, while secured and infeft in Old Keir in warrandice for it, down to 1606, when they sold the same, are proved, by the family Bible of Dr William Stirling, born in 1682 (good evidence even in strict peerage law), to have been *descended of Cadder*, which further goes to identify them with umquhile Robert Stirling and his bairns, the Cadder collateral heirs in 1541, and they actually *continue* to the present moment.		9. After every investigation, this family, though well connected, and affording good means of proving the negative, if it obtained, *can no further* be traced down in a *separate capacity*.

RESULTS.—With all submission, it is really contended, from so many proved striking coincidences and parallelisms, that the respective families under No. I. and II. are *one* and *the same*. It is impossible, in the course of human events or human probabilities, that there could have existed at the same time two *separate ones*, in which so many palpable and unprecedented coincidents obtained. But, moreover—1. The Drumpellier opponents, after repeated challenges, have neither been able to meet or contradict the identity in question ; and, 2. Mr James Dundas, the Keir agent, after full examination of the Cadder charter-chest, the best source of knowledge, and Lettyr brief of service in 1818—which directly involves the identity—stated, he *had nothing to object to it*,—hence, in fact, it may be said, equivalent to its actual admission ; and lastly, 3. The striking fact under No. II. 9, that *nothing more* of the Robert and his bairns in 1541, in a *separate capacity*, can be discovered after that year, though certainly conspicuous and well allied, is additionally confirmatory,—it only being accounted for by the fact of *both families* under Nos. I. and II. resolving *into one and the same*—from whence they could not so separably figure—and the representation of the last of course being transmitted and continued by the first.

At any rate, in the lowest point of view, the *onus* or burden of disproving the main conclusions, it is apprehended, so relevantly drawn, must be thrown upon an objector, which, if he cannot do, they, by legal presumption, must be admitted, and, of course, the identity.

It being thus clenched and fixed, there only remains one other important conclusion in the case : that the Cadder compensation to be given to Robert of Letter, by the solemn indentures and contract between him and Sir John Stirling of Keir in 1527, repeatedly noticed, and that can solely be inferred to have rested upon Cadder gentilitial claims and rights in his person, must have been in his character of the male Cadder representative. It could not have been as the Cadder heir at common law, because he was there excluded at the time by Janet Stirling of Cadder, in whom such identical status, and all the property so descendable, then preferably vested, though, as now fixed through the question of identity, he and his family, as conjoining the latter with the former status, could have thus taken after Janet and her issue. But without being exclusively the Cadder heir-male in 1527, neither Robert nor his issue thereafter, so far, in his right, could have adduced a claim to the portion of the Cadder property then compromised or in view, which, on the other hand,

<small>The compensation in 1527 by Keir to Robert of Letter for gentilitial Cadder rights and claims, *ex necessitat.*, must have been as heir male.</small>

having been so fully admitted in their favour, and onerously acted upon and adequately discharged—while there was no other competitor—necessarily proves them such heirs.

And this argument evidently is in keeping and unison with that at the outset, on behalf of the male succession and representation, in terms of the Cadder settlement or entail in 1414, seeing they both mutually sustain and corroborate each other. They may even go further, and assist, in fact, in identifying Robert of Letter with another material party of the same Christian name, to be broached and canvassed in a subsequent chapter.

ADDENDA TO CHAPTER II.

No. I.

DECREET IN 1535 IN FAVOUR OF JANET STIRLING, HEIRESS OF CADDER.

(REFERRED TO AT PAGE 50, NOTE *).

See Abstract of Evidence in 1818. Also, Acts of Council and Session, Book vi. p. 165, July 8, 1535.

Looking with attention at the decreet referred to, we have there opened to our view an incident in a sad story, ending in the spoliation and degradation of Janet herself, and the severance of the Cadder property from the male branch of the ancient family.

We have seen with what eagerness, perseverance, and dexterity Sir John Stirling of Keir commenced and carried on his operations for making himself master of, or rather, getting into his power, Janet, only child and heiress at common law of Andrew Stirling, the last direct male heir of Cadder, who died in 1522, she being then merely a pupil, and who, most unfortunately for herself and for her future welfare, besides the premature bereavement of her father, lost her mother, Marjory Cunninghame, about two years afterwards.

After various vicissitudes, such as involving himself in treasonable plots, forfeitures, heavy costs in purchasing wardships, and by obtaining the concurrence of Robert Stirling (rather here an important personage) in his proceedings, by an arrangement with him as having hereditary rights to Cadder (afterwards anxiously compensated for, and who, had he chosen, might have been tutor of the family), Sir John at last, by a grant from the Crown in 1529 of her ward and marriage, succeeded in getting into his hands the sole and entire management of Janet and her property. So far Sir John's project had succeeded. Little or nothing else is known of Janet between this time and the year 1534, when she was duly infeft in her property, while Sir John afterwards *de facto* effected a marriage between her and his son James, which clearly was illegal, and but a pretended one, "*a principio, non tenuisse*," as the divorce in 1541 explicitly states, and certainly was against the lady's wish, though Sir John, to suit his views, assumed that it was all as it should be.[1]

If we had not suspected it before, we now have it brought before us, that the property, together with the Cadder influence and means, was the sole object Sir John had in view from the commencement. For what do we find? Not many months after the "pretendit" marriage, we see Janet appealing to the laws of her country for protection "aganis *Johne Strivelyn of ye Kere, knycht,* and *James Strivelyng, his soun*—that quhare ye said Johnne havand hir marriage and ye dispositioun of hir ward landis, causit *ane* PRETENDIT *matrimony* to be maid betuix ye said James and her, and sensyne ye said Johnne has haldin, and as zit haldis hir in subjectioun, and will nocht suffer her to speik with hir friendis, and hes compellit hir to mak divers alienationis and takkis of hir landis and heretage, and tendis to gar hir *analie (alienate)* ye remanent, or maist part yairof,"[2] &c.

[1] See p. 65.

[2] See Decreet, 8th July 1535, p. 59.

This ill-usage must have been indeed grievous, and probably of some standing; for it must be a rare case for a young *married* lady (as Janet *de facto* then was) thus to appear in a public court, claiming redress against her husband and father-in-law, unless her grievances had become aggravated and intolerable.

Janet, not unlikely, was advised to take this step by her nearest relatives ("friends," the term in the above decreet, expressing, in Scotland, the same thing), and, not improbably, Robert Stirling of Letter, who may have been disgusted at last by Sir John's extremely selfish and overbearing conduct. She may be concluded, naturally, to have had an attachment to him and his family, evinced, too, by her important stipulation in their favour when induced, or rather compelled, afterwards, in 1541, to alienate her entire heritage to his son. Robert, however, being unexpectedly cut off in 1537, she was left again exposed to the machinations of the Keirs, father and son. Who can wonder at what might appear to be exceptionable points in the unhappy Janet's career? Thrown upon the world an orphan at an early and tender age, under the guardianship and disposition in marriage of a "cruel" man (as he was actually styled in Sir David Lindsay's delectable Squire Meldrum), besides of most ambitious and aggrandising views, who, for the sole purpose of bringing her property (if not also representation) into his family, illegally married her to his son, against her will, and afterwards continued to treat her in a tyrannical and oppressive manner.

The preceding gives a sketch of Janet's position from the time she lost her parents till her putative marriage—at first a precarious, at last a distressing one. For the sequel of her story, let consideration be paid to the extraordinary fact of the resignation of her estates in 1541, after she actually had solemnly *recalled* a previous one, that, it may be well inferred, had been forced upon her; then Bischop's notable and peculiar transaction and inveiglement, as proved by the subsequent disposition of Keir to him in the same year, to be shortly touched upon. Whatever she may have then done, of a truth, unless expressly recalled by her—which she had scarce the means—may be attributed to them; and her conduct, in such striking circumstances, must be weighed with the extremest distrust and suspicion.

After the foregoing, can we arrive at any other conclusion than that, through her career, Janet was more sinned against than sinning? if, in fact, it may not be even added, at such a juncture, that she was the victim of a scheme originating with Sir John Stirling of Keir, but dexterously prosecuted to the utmost and most reprehensible extent by James his son, through means and subtle co-operation of Bischop,—a man of education, and no inferior law proficient, while the confidential family agent. The former accounts, it may be observed, of him are absurd and untenable ; he was, withal, a man of address and finesse, which enabled him afterwards conspicuously to figure in political life among the highest and ablest of the land, however unprincipled, and more swayed by his own peculiar interest than by those of others.

It was only subsequently, after making due inquiries and investigation, that the Exponent has been enabled to attain full knowledge of the parentage and history of this remarkable person, as to which he had been misled long ago, when the case was not so matured, by unsupported scandalous and depreciatory accounts, derived from partial quarters, which he now pointedly recalls.

No. II.

(REFERRED TO AT P. 67, UNDER No. 9.)

[1] See Keir's Disposition in favour of Thomas Bischop, 23d Feb. 1541—that in view in Abstract of Evidence in 1818, and present Exposition, p. 67, ut sup.

The notice in the Keir Performance of the final settlement made by James of Keir with Thomas Bischop, 23d February 1541, is incomplete, and not in the words of the original, existing in the Keir charter-chest. All we learn about it is through the medium of an autograph copy of the account of the deed in the Keir inventory, formerly taken by Mr Ramsay of Auchertyre,[1] and communicated by him to a brother antiquary, the celebrated Lord Hailes, from whose repositories we derived it.

The sums there at the outset to be paid by Bischop, appear odd, but may have been to give an air of onerosity to this strange transaction, while the term "*servitor*" applied to him, the same in a legal sense with *servant*, the meaning of which was plain and obvious,[*] confirms his continuance still as law or family agent of Keir, as he had formerly been of Sir John his father.

[2] See Keir Performance, p. 332.

The last grant of James V. of the marriage of Janet of Cadder, July 22, 1529, to Sir John and "his airis and assignais, ane or ma," not having been legally practicable in the case of James his son and Janet, owing to the legal bar to their union,[2] and only in 1541 first coming into play, could, plausibly at least, be conferred by James, now

---

[*] Thus, to quote from the Preface (p. 7) to Reports of Decisions of Court of Session by Lord President Gilmour—Edinburgh, 1701—the learned editor remarks "that the young men of this age, in point of painfulness, come far short of their ancestors : "—" the *candidats* of the *law were* clerks and *servants* to the experienced advocates, and had an opportunity of learning at the same time both the civil and the municipal laws," &c.

standing in his father's shoes, upon Thomas Bischop, the "spons affidat" or betrothed of Janet, and afterwards his actual wife. This special and aggrandising concession, together with the lands of Uchiltree, though redeemable upon the death of Janet by payment of 2000 merks,[1] were to be a reward and recompense, not inadequate, for Bischop's insidious and artful "help and labour in soliciting and furthering the conveyance made by her of her heritage" to Keir. [1] See p. 67. (under No. 9).

Further still, he was to be paid 250 merks, and this confirms his dexterous and advantageous settlement for himself, in the understood arrangement, as we may conclude, in respect to Cadder, with his interested principal or his advisers. They seem to have played into each other's hands, while Bischop here, instead of lowly truckling as a culprit, or as one who had injured or offended him, acts rather as a dexterous friend and benefactor to Keir, who again, so far from resenting the conceived affront offered by the former towards him, is to use his diligence to have it remitted by the king.[2] This is said to be Bischop's "alleged lying with the said Janet whilst she was the said James's wife." [2] See ibid.

But here, as must strike any calm inquirer, what need was there for such remission, even supposing Thomas and *necessarily* Janet were thus guilty of adultery? It was *not* then a *criminal* offence, and required no such royal intervention or condonation, not having been made so, as is notorious, until, by a special Act of Parliament, subsequently in 1563;[3] so that, after this, it need not surprise us that not a trace or inkling is to be found of such royal remission, so unduly contemplated. A charge or prosecution thus suspended over Janet (through Bischop) was but tantamount to an ideal threat, based upon ideal criminality. It might, however absurd and preposterous elsewhere, do well, and serve its purpose in this affair, which, it must be kept in view, was private, solely affecting her and the interested parties, who had all their own way, and who could play as they chose upon her legal ignorance, as they doubtless did, more or less ; while the remission promised to relieve the parties of the fancied prosecution with which she must have been terrified, was of course to be, in the event of her compliance with their objects, which it therefore tolerably accomplished. The preceding is upon the mere supposition of adultery, but in truth there was *none* in the case, Janet never, as has been proved, having been legally married to James Stirling of Keir, and hence neither she nor Bischop capable of such alleged offence against him ; while the proper steps actually were taken at the time for proving it illegal and null and void, as it truly was found *from* the *beginning*. Hence the charge of immorality, in their respect, only resolved into simple fornication—so frequent (as indeed even adultery) at that dissolute and profligate period, shortly before the Reformation in 1560, which it justly in the main elicited. Both then were highly countenanced by the example of the king, clergy, and the upper classes ; and it is a jest to suppose that this lesser offence or peccadillo would have attracted attention, or been for a moment thought worthy of a remission. [3] See Hume's Criminal Law Edit. 1797, vol. ii, pp. 303-4.

The implied charge, too, of immorality against Janet, *never proved*, without which, too, a remission that could neither in any view obtain, was useless—further evincing its ineptness —appears quite to be unsupported, and merely to resolve into simple allegation, that may be likened to that scandal of the present day, from which even the best families are not exempt, through the medium of servants and subordinates, who are not accustomed to speak too highly of their superiors. The truth may have been that, in her unfortunate, desolate situation, she may, at a period when little delicacy prevailed, even in the manners of the higher classes (and so exemplified in the case of Elizabeth of England, and certainly her inferiors), some indiscreet freedom may have been taken by Bischop, the family agent, then constantly with her, either casually or purposely, which most likely, under a false colour, with every aggravation, might have served and advanced their mutual designs; that of the one, to obtain her estate; of the other, her person, with necessary preferment in life—in both of which they lamentably succeeded.

This striking fact in the case, at any rate, cannot be denied, that *falsehood*, whose only object could be to inspire Janet with terror, and bind her to Keir's views, *was resorted to* by the interested parties in her instance, and but secondary immorality (if it obtained) exaggerated to her as heinous criminal guilt. There was here a direct perversion of truth and fact, only accountable for in one view, that creates the most unfavourable inferences against Keir; and if he thus erred in one respect, he may have in all, according to the legal brocard *falsum in uno falsum in omnibus*, which may not irrelevantly apply, and have actually perpetrated *in toto* that with which he has been charged.

[1] See pp.59, 61.

That Janet of Cadder had been the subject of undue coercion previously, and compelled, against her will, to alienate parts of her property by the deceased Keir, is proved by her own mouth in 1535;[1] and, according to her statement again in 1541, she even, at one time, had revoked the surrender of her estate to his son.

Upon the whole, we cannot abstain from concluding that Janet was more or less concussed, and that terror was used to elicit unjust results on the last distressing occasion, when fully stript of her heritage for the benefit of Keir.

We may not altogether, certainly, be able fully to penetrate the veil or cloud that may obscure this, at least, most startling and suspicious affair, not improbably promoted by the mystifications and address of Bischop (for which subsequently, in a grander and more public sphere, as may be seen, he was famous in history), by his profession, well up to the state of the law (however he might disguise it for a purpose), and not really apprehensive for himself; and who of course, as by the understanding with Keir, and also for his own advantage and reward, would "help and labour" to the utmost, by every seductive and plausible device, right or wrong, to attain the end with Janet, suitable to both their views.

[2] Preface, p. x.

But, at any rate, in the question at issue, for its due and possibly additional illustration, it would be desirable, besides what can be otherwise discovered, to obtain a full and literal copy of the original *self-inculpating* disposition (as it may be indeed styled), that has been referred to, by Keir to Bischop, *February* 20, 1541, of which we have only some imperfect abridged jottings, inasmuch, too, as it might likely disclose more both of Cadder or Keir at a critical moment. In these circumstances, the most natural source of information would be the Keir Performance, the framers of which had full access to the Cadder writs; while the editor remarks[2] that "not the least interesting parts of the following narrative is the story of the ill-fated heiress of Cawder." We then, certainly, would at once expect that, so far from suppressing, he would carefully be at pains to adduce all affecting her, directly or indirectly, in the fullest and most satisfactory way, in a matter so much exciting his interest and attention. But can it be conceived for a moment, that all he gives is but the following summary and imperfect fragment of the disposition of Keir to Bischop in 1541, which drops in upon us as from the clouds :—

"In the following month (February in that year) James Stirling granted a disposition and assignation, whereby, for certain sums of money paid to him by Thomas Bischop his servitor, and 'spous affidate' of the said Janet Striveling, and for his help and labour in soliciting and furthering the conveyance made by her of her heritage to the said James Striveling, he assigned to Bischop the marriage of the said Janet Striveling, and became bound to dispone redeemably the lands of Uchiltree to them in joint fee, with some smaller provisions, as also to do his diligence for getting a remission from the king for the said Thomas, for his 'alleged lying with the said Janet' while she was the said James's wife ;" but which assuredly she never was. [1]

[1] See Keir Perform- ance, p. 38.

And this without the editor adding a word more afterwards or explanatory on the subject, or his condescending to apprise us from what charter-chest or quarter the above is derived. Why this fragment, which does not further enlighten us in the least? It is even not so full or explicit as what has been here relatively adduced,[2] and it might even be figured that the former was taken from the latter. But be this as it may, from such strange unauthorised conduct, so contrary to the method observed in all proper and respectable histories and statements, where distinct accounts are ever given both of authorities cited and their references, only two conclusions can be drawn, both unfavourable to the Keir editor :—

[2] See p. 67, under No. IX.

I. Either that he has here, as elsewhere, been guilty of negligence and carelessness in such brief or imperfect adductions, and of palpable omissions ; or, II. That the grant of 1541 contains something that he rather disingenuously chooses to conceal—at variance with the rules of fair argument and discussion. He therefore, in this fragment, gives the smallest account of it he can, while he altogether withholds, or, it may even be said, he ignores, the original, which it is apprehended is quite within his reach ; at the same time that he refrains to state from whence he derives his fragment.

Such extraordinary retention may be inferred by some to be from their containing something especially hurtful and injurious to the Keir family and case—the best way of obviating which would be by fully adducing the original, together with what more may be in the Cadder charter-chest on the subject. And how can the Keir editor explain and account for it, after the intimation in his preface,[3] that, "Far from locking up his family muniments from the light of day, the present owner (Keir) has, with an enlightened liberality, opened them to his friends by *means of the present volume*." So far from seconding his distinguished client or principal in such meritorious conduct, he, in *that very volume*, as just proved, as instanced in the grant of 1541, as well as elsewhere, there thwarts and excludes it by an unaccountable withholding, in part, of the former ; and even if that grant is deeply injurious and suicidal to the Keir family, why allude to or adduce it at all?

[3] See Pre- face, p. xv.

CHAPTER III.

MINUTIÆ OF LEGAL PROCEDURE BY THE DRUMPELLIER FAMILY IN SUPPORT OF THEIR LETTYR AND CADDER RIGHTS AND STATUS — INCLUDING ESPECIALLY, AT THE OUTSET STRENUOUS EXERTIONS OF KEIR FOR HIMSELF, AND TO THWART AND OPPOSE THEM — BUT, AFTER MUCH FRUITLESS PAINFUL SCRUTINY AND RESEARCH, ONLY EVOKING AND CONJURING UP A GHASTLY AND MYSTERIOUS NEW PERSONAGE, JOHN STIRLING OF BANKEIR, THE TRUE (THOUGH LONG-SECRETED) KEIR REPRESENTATIVE, TO THE SURPRISE AND DISMAY OF THE KEIR CONCLAVE — AT LENGTH, AS HAS BEEN SEEN, DESISTED FROM — EXPLANATION AS TO THE SAID JOHN, HIS STATUS AND PECULIAR HISTORY — THE KEIR ADVISERS NEXT INDUCE GLORAT LEGALLY AND OPENLY TO OPPOSE DRUMPELLIER, THOUGH STILL ACTING CLANDESTINELY, AND SUPPLYING HIM WITH THE "SINEWS OF WAR" — DRUMPELLIER, HOWEVER, IN APRIL 1818, SUCCESSFULLY CARRIES HIS SERVICE UP TO LETTYR, THE MAIN AND MORE DIRECT OBJECT, IN THE FACE OF EVERY OPPOSING OBSTACLE, BUT PRECLUDED FROM GOING INTO THE MERITS OF THE CADDER QUESTION BY A MERE OBJECTION OF GLORAT IN POINT OF FORM, WHO, AS WELL AS KEIR, DREADED SUCH DISCUSSION — DRUMPELLIER, HOWEVER, HERE ALSO EVENTUALLY SUCCESSFUL, AND UNOPPOSED, GAINED THE FULL VICTORY, GLORAT, EVEN IN HIS TURN, HAVING ABANDONED THE FIELD — THE CASE NOW, AFTER THE EXPIRY, TOO, OF THE LONGEST PRESCRIPTION OF FORTY YEARS AND MORE, THUS FORECLOSED TO ALL AGAINST DRUMPELLIER — TOGETHER WITH SUBSTANTIATION OF OTHER MATERIAL FACTS FORMERLY STATED — INCLUDING GROSS MISREPRESENTATIONS IN THE KEIR WORK AGAINST HIM AND JANET OF CADDER — WITH GENERAL REMARKS, ETC.

THE intrinsic merits of the Drumpellier claim to represent the ancient Strivelins of Cadder, having, in the previous chapter, it is believed, been sufficiently unfolded to the public, we may next proceed to the legal steps and procedure taken, both by their adversaries and themselves, in the formal substantiation of their conceived gentilitial rights, after failure of negotiation, as has been seen, and a compromise between the parties.

¹ See p. 43, Excerpt Letter, No. 8.

The offer of the olive branch that had been made, in January 1818,¹ by Mr William Stirling, younger of Drumpellier, to the Keir authorities, resembles in some degree the courtesy of the Roman ambassadors on their mission to Carthage before the second Punic war, when they, with a similar object in view, offered the lappet of his toga; and the same result was met with on both occasions; for Mr Charles Stirling, the champion of the opposition, aiming at the part of Hannibal, haughtily declined the proffered civility, and put an end to all further negotiation by a declaration of war.[1] The din of arms was then heard in the enemy's camp, while triumphant preparations, under the direction of an able strategist, Mr James Dundas, were made to foil and vanquish the audacious and (as they deemed) too ambitious Drumpellier.

<small>Declaration of war by Keir against Drumpellier. [1] See his Letter, Jan. 22, 1818, p. 42, No. 7.</small>

The Keir party possessed the best and most fertile source of information in the matter, having (as we are apprised by the Keir Performance) an abundant supply of well-preserved writs in the Cadder charter-chest at Keir. But, independently of this great advantage, the keenest investigations were instituted by a staff of emissaries, despatched in every direction in search of information. The results of the endeavours disappointed expectations, and the Keir origin, descent, and claims refused further enlightenment, and obstinately and contumaciously persisted in remaining in a state of darkness and perplexity, which even to this day may be said to shroud and environ them.[2] But what caused still greater chagrin was, that not even sufficient evidence had been gleaned to enable them simply to oppose Drumpellier. At length, every iron having been in the fire, and the searches prosecuted with the utmost diligence, it was determined to avail themselves of the advice and co-operation of an able and eminent counsel. Accordingly a consultation was appointed to take place at Edinburgh, under the auspices of the late Lord Moncrieff (then at the bar), at which also Mr Samuel Stirling, younger of Glorat, advocate,* was to assist. And it was at this period that the offensive and defensive alliance was concluded between the houses of Keir and Glorat.[3]

<small>[2] The former disappointed in their expectations. [3] Offensive and defensive alliance in consequence with Glorat in the emergency.</small>

---

* Most of these (and many other) singular and amusing facts were communicated to the writer by the latter, afterwards Sir Samuel Stirling, Bart., in familiar intercourse, long subsequently, with much zest. The time having gone by when it was deemed they could be prejudicial to any one.

The writer had frequently, in those days, the pleasure of meeting the said baronet, Mr William Stirling (younger of Drumpellier), and Sir William Hamilton, an old and much esteemed acquaintance, with whom here he had the honour to be legally associated. They were all on terms of the greatest intimacy, and the Keir and Drumpellier contest, far from interrupting it, afforded an interesting subject for conversation and argument. John Lockhart was also of the party, and being anxious in all points of family history, and possessed of much ready wit, he was hailed as a welcome addition to their social circle. It is unnecessary to descant on the reputation and great merits of the last two gentlemen, for they are already patent to the world; but as not only the acts of great men, but also their words, thoughts, and feelings, are sources of interest to their admirers, the following scrap may be here given, as it affords a glimpse of the warm attachment

<small>[4] He wrote the amusing article on Heraldry, in the Encyclopædia, at the time.</small>

COMMENTS ON KEIR PERFORMANCE.

Keir conclave terrified by a sudden unexpected appearance.

The conclave had hardly commenced their deliberations, ere, like Canning's Brissot's ghost, a grim and grizzly phantom flitted before them, one which had long lurked concealed in the deepest Keir vaults and recesses, but whose being and identity had, after the lapse of centuries, quite faded out of memory, and might have remained for ever in oblivion, had it not been conjured up by the result of the assiduous efforts and investigations submitted to them, and thereby brought to light. They were now seized with fear and consternation.

[The iron mask, formerly so great a puzzle, was fully explained by the late Lord Dover.]

The spirit was that of John Stirling, "of Wester Bankeir" (as he was styled when in the flesh); and the horror which his mysterious appearance occasioned is accounted for by his wearing the semblance of a competitor of existing family rights, much in the situation of *Voltaire's* iron mask. He was no other than the Keir lawful heir-male, viz. son of James Stirling of Keir by the unfortunate Janet Stirling of Cadder, and thus conjoined in his person the male representation of Keir and female of Cadder!!

Had a bomb fallen into the meeting, it could not have produced a more startling effect. John, as an incumbrance in the way of the succession, had doubtless been kept concealed and *in retentis* for behoof of the reigning Keir family, who are only sprung from Archibald Stirling, his younger brother, by a different mother, upon whom *nominatim* and his heirs, both Keir and Cadder had been entailed—most arbitrarily and unjustly.

Consternation and dreaded results now by the former.

The search, therefore, so confidently set about to vanquish Drumpellier, was not only quite unsuccessful in its object, but (Balaam-like) it was also most injurious to Keir himself, who, to use rather a vulgar though significant expression, may be said to have "caught a Tartar," or to have raised a spirit from the dead, whose descendants and heirs (if any exist) would most certainly exclude the present proprietor from the chieftainship or representation of Keir—would deprive him of the high status which it has been the great object of the ambitious Keir Performance to support, and would degrade him to the rank of a cadet.

But, on yet further reflection, the matter bore a still worse aspect, and a more dreadful idea then struck the conclave—namely, that Robert Stirling,

which existed between them in the spring-time of life.

Mr Lockhart, in a letter to Mr William Stirling in 1816 (actually in reference to a point in the Drumpellier-Cadder claim), adds —" If Hamilton is still with you, tell him that the Chaldee MS. is still playing the devil here ; James Grahame has published two letters, and some anonymous minister a review against it. Leigh Hunt is also indicting Blackwood in London."

designed "of Bankeir," (the Drumpellier ancestor) who lived in the same century, might have been miscalled Robert instead of John, and might be the very John in question, in which case it would result the Drumpellier family would soar to a height never before contemplated, and actually prove to be male representative of Keir and the Cadder heir at law.

This appalling apprehension, involving the calamity of a double defeat, broke up the assembly. Immediate additional researches were ordered, and Drumpellier was to be skilfully and cautiously sounded, in the hope of effecting an *eclaircissement* of this anxious and most perplexing poin The latter gentleman and his counsel were forthwith questioned and cross-questioned thereupon. Bankeir and its incidents were continually rung in their ears, although what was the object of all these interrogations they could not well divine, not being then aware of the alarming discovery which their opponents had made, or that the Keir chieftainship was probably in store for them.

The said ghost-like John was indeed likely to be a most awkward legal bar in the way of the present Keir's representation of his family; for according to the practice of the House of Lords in peerage cases, proof would be required that John died childless, or else all his descendants extinguished, before a descendant from Archibald (Keir's ancestor) could prove his claim to such status.[1] And if John actually had left male descendants still extant, Drumpellier, the heir of the true Robert Stirling of Bankeir, though then obliged to yield up the representation of Cadder at common law, would still have been the Cadder heir-male, whereas the fate of Keir would have been far worse, for he would have been deprived *altogether* of family representation, and, moreover, he would have had the mortification to see an opponent declared not only female representative of Cadder, but chief of Keir by right both of male and female descent.

It may now be incumbent to go somewhat (*par parenthese*) into details as to the status and history of the said John—a remarkable person in the case, and peculiarly demanding our attention—as it may disclose, too, further explanations, and a substantiation of certain facts and conclusions which have either already been premised or will afterwards be stated.

There never was any proper or legal marriage between James Stirling of Keir and Janet of Cadder, notwithstanding the assertions of the Keir Performance. It suits the authors of the said work to give a fine colouring to

[1] See afterwards, and Pedigree No. II., subjoined to the Exposition.

Who precisely was this John of *Bankeir* or Wester Bankeir, so important, especially to Keir.

this indeed exceptionable transaction in order to favour the heart's desire of the present proprietor, or rather perhaps of his partisans, whose great aim seems to be to conjoin the two families of Keir and Cadder, and to establish a claim for him to the representation of the latter, than which it would be difficult to imagine a more preposterous and unfounded pretension.

Janet, from the beginning, held her supposed marriage with James to be compulsory and pretended[1]—in other words illegal—and on the last of January 1541 it was annulled by the Consistorial Court, on the ground of their being related within the forbidden fourth degrees of consanguinity;[2] the sentence expressly adjudicating that "*pretensum* matrimonium et sponsalia per verba de futuro, carnali copula subsecuta, inter prefatos Jacobum et Jonetam contractum et solemnizatum in facie ecclesie A PRINCIPIO non *tenuisse*, nec viribus subsistere posse *de jure*."[3] A curious specialty is next observable. Although there is good reason to believe that James was from the first as much aware of the ground of nullity as Janet was—indeed, it is difficult to believe that he, in the peculiar circumstances in which they were placed at the time, was ignorant on a point where she, a mere woman, was well informed—yet he did profess such ignorance. And the conclusion to be drawn from this seems to point at some sinister object which he must have had in view when he procured the insertion of the following clause in the decree of divorce of the forbidden *relationship* ("*consanguinitatis*" being) "IGNOTE SIBI *Jacobo tempore* contractus et solemnizationis pretensi matrimonii." Owing to this ignorance of one of the parties, specially by the consistorial law of Scotland, and indeed of every other European country, except perhaps England, the legitimacy of the offspring of such putative marriage was fully recognised,*

[1] See p. 59, No. 3.
[2] See decree in Keir Performance, p. 374.
[3] Ibid.

* The ignorance of *either* party alone, as regards any impediment to a marriage which has been contracted, certainly before, and even in Scotland after, the Reformation in 1560, if not also at present, as from a noted modern case,[4] makes the issue lawful, although it does not save the marriage from being rescinded, and declared void and null from the beginning.

In proof of what is thus stated, the writer may perhaps take the liberty to refer to one of his own works, entitled "Peerage and Consistorial Law," where the point in question is believed to be pretty well settled. (Pp. 446-476-527, 530.)

The important doctrine and exception in question, together with nearly all material of our Scotch code of marriage and legitimacy, we borrowed from the Canon Law, which inculcates that "sufficit *quoad hoc* (the object of the legitimacy of the offspring in the text, and in special reference thereto) *alterum* conjugugum fuisse *ignorantem*, et *bonæ fidei*," that is, of the impediment to lawful marriage, including the one affecting James Stirling of Keir, and Janet, Lady Cadder. (See *Struvius in jus canonicum*, pp. 323-4.)

A propos to a point in our consistorial law generally, it certainly was with surprise that we read the following passage by the Editor of the Keir Performance :—[5]

[4] Riddell against Brymer, in 1811.
[5] See Preface, p. xiv

although the union was at the same time nullified and declared to be void from the beginning, just as if it had never been.

It is admitted in the Keir Performance that John Stirling, afterwards of Wester Bankeir, was the sole issue of the above putative union; and therefore, through James's ignorance, whether real or pretended, he was undoubted lawful male heir of his father's house, although, at the same time, no legal marriage had taken place; a fact which will be still further corroborated and indisputably fixed by subsequent evidence. John's fortunes were singular. His father, who had been apparently anxious at the time of the divorce to secure his status and legitimacy, afterwards, from some caprice, in a great measure neglected him, and indeed almost ignored his existence, ultimately depriving him of his undoubted right of succession, both to Keir and Cadder, through the instrumentality of two royal charters in 1579,[1] whereby both properties were *nominatim* vested in *Archibald* (his *younger* son,* by a subsequent marriage with Jean Chisholm, natural daughter of William, Bishop of Dunblane), who is clearly proved to be the ancestor of the present proprietor of Keir. And it is even probable that, besides disinheriting his first-born in this cruel way, it was James, in the main, himself, who afterwards fixed upon him the stigma of illegitimacy which we find him bearing in legal trans-

Marginal note: The preceding John law-ful, by a specialty in Scotch consistorial law, though there was no legal marriage between his parents.

Marginal note: [1] See Keir Performance, pp. 39, 40, 45.

Marginal note: According to his not unfrequent carelessness, the Editor has no reference in the text to the Decree in the Chartu-lary of the work.

"The decree by the Bishop of Dunblane in 1539 is *not without value* in reference to the designations as applied to legitimate as distinguished from illegitimate children. Two ladies are there styled the *natural and lawful* heirs of their father, while other two are styled the *natural* daughters of the same parent, and are declared illegitimate." Not without value, indeed, it is effete, as it supplies nothing new or deserving attention, as may be obvious even to a consistorial *tiro!* The preceding were mere *voces signatæ*, of which there are myriads of instances of themselves respectively denoting legitimacy and illegitimacy; and we might as well cite, as peculiarly illustrative of their opposite import, the terms *lawful* and *unlawful* as the former. In the early part of the century at least, if not now also, in the Consistorial Court of London, a legitimate son and daughter were styled *natural* and *lawful*, while of course, *naturalis (tantum) per se*, indicated an illegitimate. Such obtained in most countries, and it can be fully proved in Scotland before the Reformation; and even Craig, our most obvious and hackneyed authority in such matters, uses and applies the epithets in the same senses.[2] If the Keir Compilers had previously initiated themselves in that work besides others, their value of the decree they adduced might have been much lowered. They are indeed thankful here for small mercies.

* This is further proved by the *testament* of James[3] (who deceased at his residence of Cadder in 1588, in which he constitutes, "of uew," his "sone *Archibald*" as his "assignay" to all reversions, contracts, and debts, "*as he were* my eldest sonne and air," and he "surrogatis him in his place in all things, as *if* he were *my (his)* verrie lauchfull air;" thus he clearly implies that identical status to vest in another, which other, in the circumstances, could alone be John, the disinherited eldest sou. No legitimacy is more clearly demonstrated in law—and especially by this admission of a father—than that of the latter.

Marginal note: [2] Vide De ford. Daillic, p. 311, § 13, and p. 312, § 16

Marginal note: [3] See Keir Compilation, p. 428-9.

108   COMMENTS ON KEIR PERFORMANCE,

[marginal note: ¹ See Keir Performance, p. 41, and what will be adduced hereafter.]

actions that took place subsequent to his father's death. The only possession that John seems to have derived from this unnatural parent was Wester Bankeir,¹ a property which had previously been held by Robert (Drumpellier's ancestor), and afterwards by his younger son, William (who had been designated thereby), and which was invariably the appanage of the nearest Cadder heir.

[marginal note: ² Ibid., p. 40.]
[marginal note: John on all hands held lawful.]

Sir James died in 1588,² and the above John, thus freed from an intolerable thraldom, was enabled to attend to and assert his remaining lawful rights ; and, "on 16th February 1592, a commission was granted under the quarter seal, for serving *John Stirling*, eldest son of the *deceased Sir James Stirling of Keir*, HEIR of his father in the lands belonging to him in Perthshire ;" and,

[marginal note: ³ See ibid., p. 41.]

"on 18th April 1593, John Stirling had sasine of the lands of Auchenbee in Stratherne, on a precept of Chancery, as *heir* of *Sir James his father*."³ For this information we are indebted to the Keir Performance, whose praise we are the last to withhold, when deserving it.

[marginal note: The strange unnatural conduct of John's father towards him attempted to be accounted for.]

John's legitimacy, therefore, which seemed quite clear from the beginning, is thus completely confirmed ; and we find him, in consequence of it, claiming whatever small remnants of property the spoiler had deemed too insignificant to deprive him of. At the same time our ideas of his father Sir James's unnatural conduct towards him are fully corroborated.

The probable reason of Sir James's anxiety to legitimise John, in the first instance, was, that without him he feared the possession of the Cadder property—the great object of his father's ambition and his own—not yet firmly secured, might slip from his grasp ;* but after having with much dexterity, aided by the artful intrigues and diplomatic address of his confederate, Thomas Bischop,† fully succeeded in stripping Janet of Cadder of her heritage, he found he had no longer any need of a lawful son, and having conceived

---

* This consideration might have occasioned the Royal confirmation *inter alia*, even as late as March 28, 1547, of Janet's "*rychtis*" and "*procuratouris* made to James Striveling of Keir," of course including the resignation of her estate to him, which might not have sufficed *alone*.⁴

[marginal note: ⁴ See Keir Work, pp. 395-6.]

† The notices of Bischop in the Keir Performance are extremely meagre, and those of Janet not so full as might be. The former was a most remarkable, though unprincipled character. He began life as a law-agent ; afterwards we hear of him moving in the highest diplomatic circles, and he was made a squire by an English monarch. There will hereafter be a biographical sketch of this worthy, omitting, as undeserving of notice, the wretched doggrel lines about him given as a makeweight in the Keir Performance. In an endeavour apparently to establish a charge against Bischop (whom he most improperly calls Janet's *second* husband)⁵ of ill-treatment towards his wife, the Keir editor adduces these lines ; but how they can bear upon the point, or how he can in any other way substantiate this charge, it beggars fancy to conceive.

[marginal note: ⁵ See Keir Work, p. 38, note 2.]

an unaccountable aversion to the unfortunate John, he spurned him as unworthy of the position he was born to fill.

"John Stirling of *Bankeir*," as he was styled, and other small unentailed Keir properties he is shown to have held, was, in 1597, provided by Sir Archibald, his highly favoured younger brother, with a sum of money, and also with a supply of coals, which were delivered at his lodgings in Glasgow, where he seems to have resided.[1] This gift, however, does not seem to be prompted by brotherly love, but was made on the express and very harsh condition of his disponing to Sir Archibald, in fee, his lands of Wester Bankeir, and renouncing an annuity of forty merks, which was payable to him out of Cadder.[2] This measure of fraternal liberality—amounting, in the main, to a new spoliation—stripping both the Keir and Cadder heir of the last portion of his small landed property, and only allowing him the common necessaries of life in a provincial town, where he was doomed to sojourn—is quite in unison with the treatment John had so long been accustomed to meet with at his parent's hands.

[1] See Keir Performance, p. 435-6.

[2] Ibid.

Another curious piece of information has come to the exponent's knowledge. The unfortunate John being possessed of feelings common to our nature, and no way disinclined to a matrimonial connection, proffered his heart and hand to the widow of one of his nearest Cadder relatives, viz., to Elizabeth Stewart, second wife of William Stirling of Wester Bankeir. In other words, the direct heir-male of Keir, and heir at common law of Cadder, deigned to solicit in marriage the relict of Robert of Lettyr's youngest son; and thus did the head of a house, which of late years has endeavoured to slight Drumpellier, at one time stoop to pay court to a mere connection of his ancestor. The Keir Performance can only specify John's second marriage to Margaret Colquhoun, the editor necessarily being quite ignorant of what has just been stated.

John of Bankeir, the undoubted male Keir representative, craves to be married to the widow of William, younger son of Robert, the Drumpellier ancestor, and is accepted by her.

In support of the above fact, viz., John's marriage to Elizabeth Stewart, and at the same time to prove that the former was occasionally styled *natural* son of Sir James Stirling of Keir, the exponent will here adduce these new pieces of evidence *verbatim*, that may speak for themselves.

1. Contract of marriage, January 2, 1572,[3] between "William Stirling of Bankeir,[4]   Stirling of Glorat, and John Stirling of Balquharage:" and John Stewart of Bowhouse and *Elizabeth Stewart* his daughter, whereby it is agreed that the said William shall marry the said Elizabeth, and that William shall infeft her "in liferent" in the lands of *Wester Bankeir*.

[3] Glasgow Commissary Records.

[4] *Sic*, it being so in the original.

2. Act of Court, 15th November 1575,[1] specifying "Elizabeth Stewart, *relict* of *umquhile* William *Stirling* of Bankeir," and "John Stirling of Lettyr, brother-german and nearest lawful air-maill of the said umquhile William."

[1] Glasgow Commissary Records.

3. Entry in the Records of the burgh of Glasgow, 8th February 1584,[2] to the effect that "JOHNNE *Striveling* of BANKEIR" (hence no other, by his description, than the preceding John,[3] the lawful Keir and Cadder heir, who was so styled), "and *Elizabeth Steward*, his SPOUSE, and Johne Striveling of Lettir," desired a contract, of the same date, to be registered between the said "*Elizabeth Steward*, relict of umquhile *William Striveling* of *Bankeir*,"[4] and the *said "Johnne Striveling,* now her *spous*," for his interest," for implementing the preceding contract in 1572, as to infefting the said Elizabeth in liferent in the lands of *Wester Bankeir*.

[2] Burgh Records of Glasgow.

[3] See Keir Work, p. 41.

[4] See No. 1., *ut supra*.

4. Term assigned by the Lords of Council and Session, 28th June 1590,[5] to "*Johnne Striveling, sone* NATURAL to umquhile Sir James Striveling of Keir, knicht, to exhibit" certain writs called for in an action against him by "Robert Striveling of Lettyr, brother sone and air-maill to umquhile William Striveling of Bankeir," which belonged to and "were in the keeping of *Elizabeth Stewart*," *his* (the *said* John's) *wife*, and intromitted with by him, and shown by another entry to have comprised a grant of the lands of *Wester Bankeir* to *William* in 1565, that was afterwards produced before the Lords by John. The latter, therefore, as the natural son of Sir James (who must have survived Elizabeth), is thus identified through her with John of Bankeir (under No. 3), whose wife, too, she was.

[5] Acts and Decreets of the Supreme Civil Court of Scotland.

5. Action before the same court, 16th June 1591,[6] at the instance of "Robert Striveling of Letter, broyer, sone, and air-maill to umquhile *William Striveling* of *Wester Bankeir*," against "Sir Archibald Striveling of Keir, kny[t], sone and air of umquhile *Sir James Striveling* of *Keir, kny[t]*, to *quhom*, his airis and assignees, ye pretendit lettres of reversion underwritten are allegit to be maid and grantit, and JOHNE *Striveling*, SONE NATURALL to ye said *umquhile* SIR JAMES, and *assignay* alledgit *constitute by him* to ye said pretendit reversion," of "all and haill" (as is further proved by the entry) the "forsaidis landis of *Wester Bankeir*." Nothing more transpires from the record than the above assignation by Sir James Stirling of Keir of the latter to John, his natural son (as he calls him). And it is quite clear that the above reversionary grant of Wester Bankeir by Sir James of Keir to John constituted the title to that *property* in his person, which the Keir Perform-

[6] Ibid.

ance[1] states John, Sir James's *lawful* son and *heir, received* from him, and hence identifying the latter with the former, which, indeed, is already done by the authorities under Nos. 3 and 4, *ut supra*.

It may be possible, too, that it was at the instance of John of Lettyr that John of Bankeir was here styled "natural son" in the litigations in 1590 and 1591: it is not improbable that a feeling of jealousy existed in his breast, inasmuch as if the latter had been out of the way, or illegitimate, he would himself have been heir-at-law as well as male representative of Cadder.

The writer is happy in being able to do some justice to one who suffered so much ill-treatment, not owing to any known fault on his part ; neither can his mother be in any way blamed for being the cause of it, for, whatever it may have pleased the Keir adherents scandalously to assert, no proper or truly admissible evidence has ever been adduced to sully Janet's character with a single stain. But if Sir James's caprice prompted him to act so unfeelingly towards his offspring—his undoubted eldest lawful son—is it likely that he would be very scrupulous in regard to Janet herself ? and does it not give colour to the dark suspicions that have been entertained and stated of his most cruel and unjustifiable spoliation of that ill-fated heiress ?

John Stirling of Bankeir does not seem to have left surviving issue by either wife, and his extinction may even be presumed by *Scotch* law ; but were this a peerage case, the House of Lords, who are favourable to the vitality and survival of heirs and their issue, might judge differently. This, however, is obviously a question which does not much affect Drumpellier. With the Keir family, in their *male* capacity, certainly (besides as the Keir representatives at common law)—they being descended but from a younger brother of the said John, who is thus rather an important person—it is otherwise.

We shall now return to the main deduction of the case. Still alarming perplexity in his regard haunted the minds of his *fortunate younger* brother's descendants, not perhaps even now altogether removed, but aggravated, of course, by the troublesome Drumpellier contention. A momentary gleam of hope here intervened by the discovery of a distinct family of Stirling of Balquharage, only afterwards acquired by that of Letter, inducing the idea of their being the same, and hence that the last mentioned had no case. But it was removed by, as usual, the full explanation of their opponents, restoring the gloom that had pervaded the scene, even deepened by the non-arrival and

[1] See Keir Performance, p. 41.

Baneful consequences to the present Keir family if John of Bankeir left male descendants existing.

Resumption of the main statement of the case, after the necessary episode of John.

momentary disappearance of the Cadder charter-chest that was despatched from Keir to aid the conclave in their Drumpellier attacks, and hence humorously said to be surprised and captured by the Drumpellier guerillas.

Keir researches against Drumpellier unsuccessful, and his counsel and agents advise him to abandon the case; but opposition secretly adjusted against the former through Glorat, who proceeds to act accordingly.
¹ See p. 46.
² See p. 78.

In the mean time, all the results of their researches tended rather to advance their adversaries' case than their own, and every fresh fact that was brought to light served only to increase their apprehensions. It has been seen that at a general consultation of the Keir party, at which Mr Samuel Stirling, advocate, younger of Glorat, was present, the unanimous decision was, that opposition to Drumpellier was impracticable,¹ and that this decision was to be reported to Mr Charles Stirling; also, that Mr Dundas, though an old friend and adherent of the Keir family, held the same opinion,² and afterwards declined to act more in the matter—which needs no comment; and it has been further shown that Mr Charles Stirling (on the part of his brother), contrary to the opinion of his legal advisers, and regardless of the advice of his best friends, obstinately determined, *coute qui coute*, to carry on the opposition.

³ See p. 44.

That, however, it was now agreed, could *not* be effected by Keir, he not being able, after every inquiry, to show any interest in the case, and therefore ostensibly quitted the field. But Mr Charles Stirling had recourse to Glorat for his inimical purposes, whom he actually succeeded in persuading (contrary to his prior expressed opinion and intention ³) to take up the gauntlet, and sist himself as a party against Drumpellier.

With this view, and legally to qualify an *ex facie* interest, Glorat took out a brief, in usual form, to be served heir of Cadder. It was not seriously to do battle with Drumpellier, or discuss the merits of the Cadder representation, which were truly barred to him—far less to dispute his male descent from Robert Stirling of Letter, who died in 1537, which was *at length* fully admitted—but merely, all that could be contemplated in the emergency, to put a spoke upon Drumpellier's wheel, and actually, what seemed strange enough, and in the very face of the brief, to stave off, for very prudential reasons, a Cadder discussion by his adversary.

A short account of this notable brief of service, also in 1818, may not here be irrelevant. The supposititious Cadder male descent or pedigree that it embodied was deduced in the person of Sir John Stirling of Glorat (father of the preceding Mr Samuel Stirling), through a remote ancestor, *Duncan Stirling of Craigbernard*, who was said to be second son of Sir John Stirling of Cadder (certainly a Cadder ancestor), who died in 1408. The Glorat family (now the male Craigbernard representatives) does not owe its origin to a Duncan Stirling ; and, indeed, his very existence is entirely fabulous, as has been fully shown in the *Addenda* to the first chapter.¹ And with regard to the alleged descent from the above Sir John Stirling of Cadder, not a particle of evidence has ever been whispered or heard in support of it, neither does the Keir Performance itself admit it.² But Glorat was not satisfied with one brief, but, as it were, to make assurance doubly sure, he also at the same time obtained another, to have himself served "the nearest and lawful heir of line of the said Janet Stirling of Cadder," previously represented as daughter of Andrew Stirling of Cadder, who died in or about the year 1522—the most visionary of all visionary conceits and ideas, and so ludicrous in contrast with the result. Yet in this the Keir party, having nothing better to offer or suggest, in secret warmly concurred. Both the Drumpellier and Glorat parties being thus in train, and the former having long before obtained his brief, repeatedly alluded to, his service, that had thus the priority of discussion, came to be broached, on 18th of April 1818, in the Sheriff-Court of Edinburgh.

¹ See p. 27, under No. 11.

² See ibid., p. 127.

Glorat takes out two pretended briefs as to Cadder, to oppose Drumpellier, under the secret auspices and backing of Keir.

It rather unfortunately happened that the Sheriff-Principal, an eminent counsel, and afterwards Lord Advocate, was unable to preside on the occasion ; and the duty accordingly devolved on his Substitute, who, in keeping with the custom of those days, was merely a writer or solicitor ; since which a change has taken place, and, happily, an advocate now usually fills the important post. The Substitute, however respectable, was more accustomed to common Edinburgh business than to feudal points of a delicate nature, such as services ; and therefore it may not occasion surprise to hear that (with the view, clearly, as premised, to bar a Cadder discussion), at the very outset of the proceedings, exception was taken, simply and exclusively on a point of form, on the part of Sir Samuel Stirling of Glorat, Bart. (*ci-devant* advocate, he having lately succeeded Sir John, his father, the expeder of their brief, in his title and estate), to the consideration of that part of the Drumpellier brief or claim which related to the declaration of Janet, heiress of Cadder, in favour of the children of Robert Stirling, as being next in succession to herself, failing heirs of her body.* This was the sole point touched in

---

* The literal words of the brief here are, " whose children, in a judicial procedure before the Lords of Council and Session, were expressly declared to be next in succession to

the discussion, the proof in support of which has already been fully given ; that of the Drumpellier male descent from Robert Stirling of Letter, dead in 1537, being admitted, as was premised—indeed, on all hands, and never then doubted or challenged for a moment—it is unnecessary to allude to.

<small>It is adduced at length in the first part of the Abstract of Evidence in 1818, not given in the present Exposition.</small>

The above exception rested substantially on the ground that such passage or adjunct was informal and unprecedented, and ought not to have been authorised by the Director of Chancery, from whom the brief emanated, and hence could not stand, but required to be expunged, and not submitted to the jury.

This, however, was peremptorily denied by Drumpellier, who, on the other hand, maintained that the brief was *perfectly valid*, and could, in this *very particular*, be supported by the practice of Chancery ; and while the present objector was but a "man of straw, set up by others behind the curtain, for the sole purpose of opposing and throwing difficulties in the claimants' way," the power of the Substitute was on this occasion purely ministerial, and it was imperative on him to remit the brief wholly to the inquest. Indeed, there would seem nothing informal or objectionable in the designation or description of Robert in the brief. It was for the express, equitable, and salutary purpose of fixing *designative* that he was the identical Robert, the heir of Janet of Cadder so circumstanced, and in view, irrespective of any other. No doubt it would also follow from thence, on the proof to be adduced, that he was the possessor of such Cadder status, of which, certainly, if possessing, he and his representatives were not to be deprived the benefit. On the contrary, it behoved to operate and tell in their favour, while, if any one deemed himself to be thereby in the least wronged or prejudiced, there was the fullest remedy and redress open to him in law, of which he might at once have availed himself.

Sir Samuel Stirling's counsel was Mr Robert Jamieson, who, being an able and experienced lawyer, was the more likely to have weight with the Substitute in any emergency or difficulty he might be placed in ; and, accordingly, he had the address to gain him to his side, and to expiscate a preliminary interlocutor from him in favour of his client—doubtless to his no small gratification,

---

<small>Janet Stirling, only daughter and heiress of Andrew Stirling of Cadder, failing heirs of her own body," which adjunct was attached *designative* to Robert of Lettyr in the brief, at the same time that in it the descent of Andrew Stirling of Drumpellier, as claimant, was articulately deduced from him as his direct male representative.</small>

and probably even surprise. We might naturally expect some reason or feasible ground, either from law or precedent, to be given to warrant such conduct; but, to our disappointment, the interlocutor was simply to the effect that,[1] " the Sheriff having considered the minute and answer, finds that the claim cannot go to the jury to any other effect than that of serving the claimant nearest and lawful heir-male general to Robert Stirling, who died in the year 1537, and remits to the jury to inquire into the heads of the brieve accordingly." It was thus quite oracular; the motives which led to the above interlocutor, or the process of reasoning by which it was arrived at, are not condescended upon; nothing could be more unsatisfactory. The finding was a mere *sic volo sic jubeo, stet pro ratione voluntas*—according to a careless, lukewarm, and much-deprecated practice at the time, happily now exchanged for a far better and more satisfactory one, which elicits the legal reasons and motives that rule and influence judges in their findings and decisions. In the present instance, the inferior judge possibly was incapacitated to act otherwise, not being a counsel, or legally very proficient in such feudal points, and hence he had recourse to such summary off-hand procedure.

[1] April 18, 1818.

Drumpellier at length carries his service unopposed as heir male of Robert of Lettyr, who died in 1537, but prevented from going into the merits of the Cadder representation by a quirk or objection in point of form by Glorat, who dreaded the discussion.

That it occasioned no small excitement among the members of inquest is indubitable, and in none more than in Mr Robert Hamilton, advocate, the learned Sheriff-Principal of Lanarkshire,[*] who had considerable practice in peerage and feudal points. His capacity of a member of inquest prevented his addressing the court, but he could not refrain from giving vent to his indignation, *viva voce*, reprobating the finding in question. A scene followed which is not easily forgotten.

In this way, and at such a juncture, Glorat, and his secret abettor Keir, momentarily eluded the danger of which they were so apprehensive—viz., that of a discussion of the merits of the Drumpellier-Cadder claim, on the other hand, so much courted by their opponent, and directly involved in the question of identity, so fully treated and fixed in the previous chapter, while they succeeded, through the instrumentality of the Substitute, in preventing its

[*] The writer, who of course attended as counsel, together with Sir William Hamilton, advocate (of European celebrity), can fully attest this. Than Sir William, he can positively add, none had a better opinion of the present case, and he was too shrewd and discerning a person to allow himself to be warped, or unduly biassed, on any subject. On no point was he more clear than on that in favour of the identity, as, it is apprehended, all must be who study its merits. Indeed, the writer never heard it fairly questioned.

being submitted to the inquest,—a fate, therefore, it did not experience,—and this through a mere objection or quirk in point of form, and only serving, as will be seen, the purpose of an instant. Nevertheless, the important, indeed, conclusive service, in the main, of Drumpellier—which his adversaries, after every exertion, could in no way assail—as direct heir-male of Robert Stirling of Lettyr, his remote ancestor, who died in 1537, proceeded, as a matter of course, and was then duly expede and obtained by him, in terms of his brief, under authority even of the Substitute's interlocutor.

Although the question of the identity of the same Robert Stirling of Lettyr, with Robert Stirling, the nearest collateral heir of Janet of Cadder in 1541, and cardinal groundwork of the Drumpellier-Cadder claim, has, as observed, been fully established in the previous chapter, and indeed, too, from what will follow, may be now held foreclosed, from whence its further discussion, or what obtained in relation thereto, becomes immaterial, and might be waived ; yet, in justification of the Drumpellier procedure in 1818, it may be incumbent to prove also that, by genuine Scotch legal practice, the Sheriff-Substitute signally erred in the interlocutor he delivered in that year, and that, with no small reason, commoved the choler of the Sheriff-Principal of Lanarkshire. On the other hand, so far from there being any such stinted rule or restriction as he then actually adopted—without, however, any authority or explanation—that identical practice authorised and warranted in retours the broadest descriptions and designations generally of individuals served to in the precise situation of Robert of Lettyr ; and hence, what was annexed to him *designative*, as shown in the Drumpellier brief of service (but so summarily repudiated and discarded by the Substitute), instead of being singular or unprecedented—as gratuitously, too, assumed by Glorat—was abundantly common, and quite regular and admissible. In support of this, the exponent will next appeal to relevant instances and authorities in the Table of Columns that follows—it being only proper to keep in view that Robert's designation or adjunct in the Drumpellier brief was simply in effect that he was Janet of Cadder's collateral heir.

<small>Interlocutor of the Sheriff-Substitute of Edinburgh in 1818 sustaining Glorat's objection not well-founded.</small>

WITH DRUMPELLIER'S EXPOSITION, &c. 117

INSTANCES AND AUTHORITIES selected out of many similar Services or Retours upon record on the point in question, mostly old, to show the practice denounced by the Sheriff-Substitute in 1818 to be fully warranted and deep-rooted with us.

Parties Served to by the Expeder of the subjoined Services or Retours.	Designations and Descriptions of those served to in pari casu with ROBERT OF LETTYR in 1818, in the aforesaid subjoined Retours.	
1st Retour, June 1, 1586, of Thomas Menzies, as heir of Margaret Ogilvie, his *mother*.	*Elder sister*, and *one of the three heirs* of the late *Alexander Ogilvie* of *Durne;* a more complicated description, and involving more points of relationship than in the Lettyr case.	Inquisitiones Generales, in Her Majesty's General Register-House, Edinburgh, No. 8363.
2d Retour, July 20, 1599, of James Polwarth of Caithlaw, as heir of Mr Andrew Polwarth, Sub-Dean of Glasgow, his uncle.	Brother of the late *Walter Polwarth*, father of the said James.	*Ib.* No. 14.
3d Retour, December 31, 1603, of John Weir, as heir of James Weir, the son of his paternal uncle.	"*Mercatoris in oppido de Barrie in patria de Rie extra mare.*" Here a foreign fact, necessary to the identity, was to be proved, and, though difficult, it was not to be excluded, as the Substitute of Edinburgh, in 1818, would certainly have done.	*Ib.* No. 220.
4th Retour, February 18, 1605, of Alexander M'Brek, burgess of the burgh of Perth, as heir of Robert Mercer of Balleif, his great-uncle.	That is (*sic,* as explained), *brother-german* of the late *Bessy Mercer, grand-mother*, on the side of the *father*, of *Alexander.* This throws Robert of Lettyr's description into the shade, through the more complicated relationships to be proved.	*Ib.* No. 226.
5th Retour, August 23, 1608, of William Weir, as heir of conquest of John Weir, his brother.	*Youngest* lawful son of the late *Quintus Weir, melter or founder*, and *burgess* of *Edinburgh:* thus a *collateral relative*, as Janet of Cadder was of Robert of Lettyr, with a particular description.	*Ib.* No. 380.
6th Retour, August 7, 1647, of Helen Keyth, as heir of John Keyth, her cousin on the father's side.	Son lawful of the late *Robert Keyth*, burgess of *Edinburgh*, "*qui vero Robertus fuit patruus dicte Helen.*"	*Ib.* No. 8645.
7th Retour, July 15, 1699, of Robert Marshall of Starrieshow, as heir of John Marshall, his brother-german.	Son of John Marshall of Starrieshow, "*qui abiit e regno Scotiæ ad Carolinam in America, A.D. 1684:*" a case, again, like 3d Retour.	*Ib.* No. 8115.
8th Retour, November 4, 1700, of Margaret Nisbet, as heir-portioner of conquest of James Cuningham, merchant in Edinburgh, the brother of her grandfather.	*Immediate* younger brother of Robert *Cuningham, provost* of the *burgh* of *Irvine, uncle*, by the *father's side*, of *Christian Cuningham*, wife of *James Nisbet, bailie* of the burgh of Irvine, and *mother* of the said *Margaret Nisbet:* a complexity, indeed, of collateral links and relationships!	*Ib.* No. 8256.

Hence the approved technical description, with such marked adjuncts, of persons served to in retours, and which elicited due proof, of course, was of a broad and collateral character; and this tells *a fortiori* in the instance of Robert of Lettyr in 1818, and shows how greatly the Substitute erred in so summarily and inadvertently quashing a designation which was simple and restricted when compared with such that have been cited; and if the Sheriff was deserving of blame, and here signally erred, so also did Glorat. Many more examples and precedents could be given of the confessed usage in question, which must duly rule, seeing *consuetudo vim legis habet*.

The exponent is not aware of any decision or authority to shake his conclusion, while the case of Casselis, in reference to retours, does not here apply.

<small>Keir in the mean time keeps in the background, and, though not a party, abetting and supporting Glorat.</small>

Keir confessedly was not in the field on this occasion: neither now nor at any other time has he been a party; and this makes his pretensions to the representation of Cadder—which, as well as his descent from that family, although so pompously and broadly set forth in the private Keir compilation, has never yet been attempted properly to be established—the more absurd and preposterous. His too zealous partisans have—perhaps inadvertently on his part—made him awkwardly figure somewhat in the guise of a pretender. And with respect to Glorat, had there been any ground for his plea against Drumpellier, it would have been far better for him to have joined issue on the merits of the question, than to evade it by mere preliminary objections: while it is notorious, as is most natural, that our law views those litigants with suspicion and discredit who adopt a dilatory and futile course, especially if it be to aid the secret views and interests of others—conduct which is at the same time reprehensible, and serves no good purpose, or elicits desirable results—and accordingly has been accustomed to subject such parties to expenses.

<small>But Glorat at length, after the above momentary success on a point of form, quits the field also, and does not prosecute his two briefs, as heir of Cadder in two capacities</small>

But Glorat only momentarily pursued this course; and after the sapient procedure before the acute and proficient Edinburgh Substitute, which only arrested Drumpellier, and staved off the question upon its merits for an instant, he immediately quitted the field, strangely for ever abjuring his own case, which he *might so easily* have prosecuted, if trustworthy, and, moreover, which he was *bound* to prosecute, in terms of his two proclaimed briefs of service. Like Keir, nevertheless, he now forbore to act, or even to trifle further in a concern of which he was heartily tired, and in which he had been instigated *sub rosa*, without having any fair or adequate motive, by the suggestions of Mr Charles Stirling, that energetic Keir zealot, whose feelings were so excitable. And thus the *two* notable Glorat briefs were consigned to "the tomb of all the Capulets," and allowed to become dead for ever.

But while such was the signal failure and utter prostration of his opponent, not so was it with Drumpellier. After this momentary *coup de main* against him, through the zeal and address of that able advocate, Mr Robert Jamieson, as soon as circumstances admitted (the summer vacation then intervening), he, in terms of his reservatory protest—viz. that it was still competent to him to prosecute his Cadder claim on a fitting opportunity and in another shape—brought his case fully and directly, upon the merits, before the Court of the Lord Lyon, the judge ordinary in matters of arms and pedigree,—a tribunal which may, in the circumstances, be deemed more relevant and appropriate than the former, and which is accustomed to decide matters beyond the "ken" and perceptions of the aforesaid *Leguleius*. And the Lyon Court, after due examination of the case, through the direct medium of, and identified with, the claim to the chief arms of the ancient Stirlings of Cadder, and consequent right to supporters, these going *semel et simul* together with their descent and representation, which both resolved into each other, and necessarily required to be discussed and proved—in the full exercise of its authority, on 18th August 1818, did thereupon " hereby certify and declare that the ensigns armorial pertaining and belonging to Andrew Stirling, Esq. of Drumpellier, seventh in legal descent, and by retour to Chancery, 18th April 1818, nearest and lawful heir-male of the body of Robert Stirling of Bankeyr and Lettyr, or Lettyr-Stirling, in the county of Stirling, who was killed in a feud in the year 1537, *and whose children, in a judicial procedure after his death, in presence of the Lords of Council and Session, were expressly declared, failing issue of her own body, which happened accordingly, to be next in succession to Janet Stirling, only daughter and heiress of Andrew Stirling of Cadder*, the last direct representative of the ancient house of Cadder, or of that ilk, which descended from the powerful barons of the Carse, whose paternal ancestor, *Willielmus filius Thoraldi, vicecomes de Strivelyn*, possessed the lands of Cadder,* among others, as early as the reign of King William the Lion, which commenced in the year 1165, are thus matriculated in the *public register* of arms in the Lyon Office ; " and

marginal: And then Drumpellier brings his Cadder case before the Lyon Court, and unopposed obtains a complete victory, having both the principal Cadder arms with supporters and representation formally awarded to him.

---

* Again, in this place, the Keir Performance,[1] according to a bigoted and absurd propensity, has here, when quoting the above, changed the orthography of "Cadder" into "*Cawder.*" Such practice is especially reprehensible in quotations on any occasion.

then they are specially stated to consist of the principal arms of Stirlings of Cadder, with supporters, as chiefs of the name, crest, motto, &c.

The above, like all the acts of Drumpellier, of course were carefully watched by his jealous opponents, who without doubt sifted and scrutinised them. It was a public procedure, before a regular competent court, open to all the world. The prize contended for was a high one, and had been the great object of both Keir's and Glorat's ambition; and, had they chosen, they might have at once accepted the gauntlet which, in the tone and spirit of law and chivalry, had been thrown down to all comers. This, however, they forbore to do; and their intelligible and sufficient reasons for not doing so are fairly construed into a deep sense of their utter inability to meet Drumpellier. It was quite consistent with their usual sagacious conduct, whereby they peremptorily eschewed all discussions in whatever savoured of the merits of the Cadder representation,—a representation which had now slipped from their grasp for ever, and which had been publicly recognised as Drumpellier's right, the court having in due form awarded to him the principal arms of Cadder and supporters, inseparable from that high gentilitial status, together also, explicitly, as proved, with the latter.

<small>Glorat, or any one conceiving himself entitled, might have opposed Drumpellier, rendering his success the greater and more striking.</small>

The diploma of the Lord Lyon, embodying the Drumpellier-Cadder descent, representation, and right to the principal arms and supporters, dated 18th August 1818, was formally recorded and matriculated in the public "register" of his court. Such register is expressly ordained, by an Act of Parliament of 1672, to be "true and *unrepealable*" "in all tyme comeing;" while, moreover, the statute empowers the court to have cognisance in matters of pedigree, and to determine whether applicants to them "be *descendants of any family*, the armes of which familie they bear, and of what brother of the familie they are descended;" with due attestation or proof "anent the verity of their having and useing those armes, and of their descent as aforesaid;" also to confer arms on those who are duly entitled to bear them.

<small>[1] Acts of Parliament, vol. viii. pp. 195, 196.</small>

The term "*unrepealable*," applied above to the register recording the *ultimatum* of the court, is very remarkable, and almost, it is believed, unprecedented. It has, like other points, given rise to discussions in relative questions, but never as yet has been fairly gainsaid, or shaken in its obvious meaning and import, by any judgment; so that the exponent is fully entitled to found upon it here as a conclusive argument on his behalf.

That the Court of the Lord Lyon was authorised and warranted to go into and discuss matters of pedigree, is supported by the broad admitted principle of the law of Scotland, that every tribunal must be vested with powers fully to "extricate its own jurisdiction." If this were not so, how could the Lyon Court properly decide almost all armorial questions so constantly before it, seeing that the descent and family representation of a party must, by the rules of heraldry, be the direct standard to be followed inevitably to fix and determine the right to his peculiar bearing. It is indispensable, therefore, that they should possess such special cognisance. And, upon this very principle, there is an instance of the Court of Session having even entertained and discussed a peerage question, to ascertain whether one who, at an election, was objected to as a peer, might or might not be duly elected a member of Parliament. This was considered to be quite within the said Court's jurisdiction and cognisance.*

The Lyon Court, which possesses judicial powers, quite cognisant to such a case.

In virtue, therefore, of the law of Scotland generally, and more particularly of the Act in 1672, as shown, the Lyon Court was competent to have judicial cognisance in questions of pedigree and descent, conjoined with the right to grant arms,—a power which it did not fail to exercise in the Drumpellier-Cadder instance. And if any doubt were entertained on this head, it would at once be removed by the precedents to the same effect which our legal practice affords.

Although proving a truism, the exponent, in corroboration of the above conclusion, will adduce the following instance that he has selected.

Sir Charles Forbes of New, Baronet, in like manner, in 1833, applied to or petitioned the Lyon Court for the principal arms and supporters of the noble family of Pitsligo, in character of heir-male ; when he was immediately opposed by another respectable party, Sir John Stuart Forbes of Pitsligo, Baronet, who, far from being recreant and passive, like Glorat in the parallel emergency in 1818, decidedly objected or opposed, in character of heir-female. Pedigree, status, and family representation became all involved, and were the groundwork in the matter ; whereupon there ensued a formal legal discussion between the litigants before the Lyon Depute, who was sitting in judgment, acting for the Lord Lyon, like any other in the supreme civil

Corroboration of this, inter alia, by that of Forbes of New v. Forbes of Pitsligo, 1833, besides the subsequent one of Smith Cuningham of Caprington v. Sir Robert Keith Cuningham, 1849.

---

* On 2d February 1790, the Court of Session thus discussed the right of Sir James Sinclair of Mey to the Earldom of Caithness, allowing the freeholders of Caithness (who had thereupon objected to his continuing on their rolls) to go into a peerage question, in order to determine whether or not Sir James was entitled to the dignity ; for if so, he must be expunged from them.¹

¹ See Faculty Reports of that date.

court, two counsel being employed and arguing on each side, which ended in a decision, pronounced in the same year, by the Court, in favour of Sir Charles Forbes, who obtained what he condescended on in his petition, according to the status and descent set forth there, thus duly and satisfactorily recognised.

We may here give a sample of part of the procedure in this case, evincing it was the same as in any other Scottish judicial court, and equally capable of regular argument and discussion, either *scripto* or orally.

From the writs and papers in the case.

On the 24th June in the above year (1833), the Lyon Depute pronounced an interlocutor or judgment whereby he there "*declines* receiving any *further written* pleadings" (for such, according to our old form, obtained in litigations), "but, in the event of the objector's" (Sir John Stuart Forbes) "being desirous of being further heard on the subject of this application" (by Sir Charles Forbes), "directs the Lyon Clerk to arrange with the agents of the parties a *hearing* in this case by counsel." And accordingly, on July 2, 1833, the same judge, by another interlocutor, "appoints the parties to be heard by their counsel within the Lyon Office on Friday, the 12th day of July current, at twelve o'clock, on the application of Sir Charles Forbes, Baronet." After which followed the full legal discussion, with the result and judgment alluded to.

Again, like the other tribunals in Scotland, with the exception of the supreme civil court, that of the Lord Lyon were judge ordinaries in questions of arms or pedigrees; and again, precisely like other judges in Scotland, the Lord Lyon was subject to a review of his interlocutors, upon advocation, by the supreme civil court. This is proved by the still later corresponding and reported case in 1849 stated below.*

It is very remarkable that the leading counsel for Sir John Stuart Forbes,

Thomas Smith Cuningham against Sir Robert Keith Cuningham, Baronet, June 15, 1849. Family Reports.

* Sir Robert Dick Cunynghame of Prestonfield presented a petition to the Lyon Court, praying permission, in character of heir-male of the family, to bear the arms of Cuningham of Lambrughton, with the arms and supporters of Dick of Prestonfield; but he was opposed by Thomas Smith Cuningham, who objected in the character of heir-female. Thus status and family representation again came into play. The Lord Lyon thereupon pronounced an interlocutor in favour of the petitioner, as "head and chief in the male line" of this branch of the Cuninghams, after a debate before him by the counsel of the respective parties.

The case was then advocated by the objector to the Lord Ordinary of the supreme civil court, or Court of Session, who, after due discussion, reversed the Lyon's interlocutor; which judgment, finally, upon appeal to them, was sustained and confirmed by the Court—of course in favour of the objector, who thus prevailed.

Hence, upon the whole, the cognisance and judicial authority of the Lord Lyon, as in any other civil court, in the first instance, and the objector or opposer in the preceding case of Sir Charles Forbes, the petitioner or applicant, was no other than *Mr Jamieson*, the *same* who acted for Glorat in the momentary *coup-de-main* against Drumpellier in 1818. The fortunes of war are mutable, as is proverbial; and Mr Jamieson, instead of succeeding, as on the former occasion, here met with a reverse. And the present writer, who happened to be counsel on the victorious side, can testify that Mr Jamieson—to whom he was thus again opposed—with the view of saving strife and discussion, if possible, between such respectable knightly parties, was warmly entreated to back or effect a compromise between them, but the attempt proved abortive. Mr Jamieson, on the part of his client, persisted in carrying on the plea, and the result was a failure, as above stated.

Now such being the fact, when Mr Jamieson was so strenuous and combative in a case which may have had some show of plausibility in its favour, can it be for a moment doubted that he would have recommended the same course to be adopted by Glorat, if he had thought there was any prospect of success?—would he not have advocated an immediate decided opposition to Drumpellier's claim in the Lyon Court, if it had been possible? The circumstances of both cases were exactly the same; yet in the Forbes case he advised an opposition—in Glorat's case he did not do so. The only relevant solution of this can be, that Glorat's opposing Cadder's claim on the merits was utterly—as one might see, too, at a first glance—hopeless and impracticable. Hence Drumpellier, though his claim was open to the severest scrutiny before the Lyon Court, was allowed unopposed to walk the course, and to obtain the most signal victory in the matter, both over his public pretended opponent Glorat, and over his secret adversary Keir, that can be imagined.

More than forty years have since elapsed, and as little without any challenge; and hence the Stirling of Cadder representation, conjoined with the

Remark able incident in the Forbes case, pointedly corroborating that of Drumpellier in its results.

finally, if not advocated or appealed from to the higher tribunal in the matters in question, was indisputable, and every way admitted. It afforded in 1818, under all its phases, full and ample means, both to Glorat and Keir, of opposing and joining issue with Drumpellier, if so inclined, on the merits of the Cadder representation, than which no case could have been submitted more broadly and comprehensively to the Lyon, or more relevantly and directly inviting discussion, without chance of the least cavil or *formal* objection thereto that could be pretended, as previously under its more limited guise before the Sheriff-Substitute of Edinburgh in the same year. But neither, for a plain reason—their incapacity legally to oppose him, as on every other occasion—would either of the above parties take such step, but allowed, as premised, Drumpellier to walk the course. So desperate was their case, that his could only be attempted to be met or rebutted by the gross misrepresentations of simple matter of fact, so discreditable in the Keir Performance, immediately to be exposed.

124   COMMENTS ON KEIR PERFORMANCE,

Case now completely foreclosed in favour of Drumpellier; and, further, the Keir triumvirate are peremptorily defied to prove the new descent they have arrogated to him.

inseparable right to their principal arms and supporters, quite identical therewith, and turning upon the same hinge, is now hermetically sealed upon an adequate, indeed "*unrepealable*" title, by a period exceeding the longest prescription, in favour of Drumpellier. Their Cadder status may indeed now be held absolute—indefeasible—and not to be controverted. But even independently of such irresistible facts, there is no party who, even supposing *res* to be *integræ*, could possibly qualify a Cadder interest against him. Keir has attempted it, irrelevantly enough, through his compilation, but the effort has been a signal failure, for it has not legally advanced an item, or the shadow of an item, in its support; and Drumpellier may safely *challenge* and *defy*, as *he now peremptorily does*, the whole of the Triumvirate to prove the descent of Keir—which they have so recklessly and futilely advanced for him—in the absence of all evidence, both legal and otherwise—from a very remote Cadder cadet, "Sir William de Stryvilyne," who figured so far back as 1292-3. It is, in truth, the greatest hallucination and error, not to add imposture, that has been introduced into any controversy; indeed, nothing else but to "give to airy *nothing a local habitation and a name.*"

Gross misrepresentations in the Keir Performance as to the proceedings before the Sheriff-Substitute on the occasion of Drumpellier's service in 1818, indispensable to refute, as prejudicing his case partly.

Before concluding here, it is with much regret that the exponent must advert to two gross misrepresentations—for he can use no other term—in the Keir Performance that were only summarily noticed in the outset.

It is so obvious throughout that it need hardly be repeated here, that though Drumpellier all along was most anxious to have the question of identity of the contemporary Robert of Lettyr with the Robert, Janet of Cadder's heir, discussed, he never could succeed in that object, owing to impediments thrown in his way by the other side—from very prudential motives, no doubt—and that the Sheriff-Substitute in 1818, at the persuasion of that skilful and experienced advocate, Mr Jamieson, would *not* permit his claim so far to be *submitted* to the jury, before whom, therefore, as has been shown, it never came.

[1] See p. 181.

Such being the fact, the exponent, on coming to that part of Keir's work appropriated to the Stirlings of Drumpellier,[1] was certainly not a little surprised at the sight of the following words: "Mr Stirling" (of Drumpellier in 1818, on the occasion of his service) "*failed* in establishing *before* the *Sheriff* and the *jury* TO WHOM HIS CLAIM WAS SUBMITTED, that the Robert Stirling to whom he was served heir-male was the *same* Robert Stirling who is referred to in the declaration by the heiress of Cawder,"—clearly the point of identity in question!!

What can be a greater perversion of fact than this? How could Drumpellier be said to have failed to establish his claim here before a Sheriff and a jury to whom he had *not* been allowed to submit it? This has been most clearly shown.[1] It is therefore contrary to all truth to assert that it was so submitted; on the other hand, it was still open, and as much uncompromised as ever, while the failure in the matter (eventually) was wholly on the other side.

[1] See Keir Performance, p. 179.

The Keir compilers cannot back out of this dilemma; for, independently of the plain unqualified import of the passage, which speaks for itself, while all ambiguity of expression should have been shunned, the term "claim" above occurring quite unrestrictedly, had been antecedently employed to comprise the question of identity, which was thus fairly in view,—the whole implying or denoting, so far as words go, that Mr Stirling had failed in establishing the identity upon the merits in a discussion actually before the Sheriff and jury to whom the claim in reference thereto had been submitted, which it never was.

But palpably erroneous and exceptionable as the point just discussed is, and the true construction being so obvious, what will be said of the next gross misrepresentation in the Keir Performance, that has been alluded to and complained of, even more glaringly and unrestrictedly so—viz., that Drumpellier "NEVER *followed* out his protest," which he had taken before the Sheriff-Substitute in 1818; viz., "that it was still competent to him to bring forward the *second branch* of his claim (*the identity*) in *another* shape," " or *carried* his case *further!!*"—When the direct contrary, again, has been so fully proved, and when, so far from being recreant and passive, as has been represented, Drumpellier, as soon as practicable, "followed out his protest," and did "carry his case further," precisely in "another shape," before a competent tribunal, as was so fully shown, and in a broader and more preferable form, where he strikingly succeeded, and walked the course unopposed in any way, even by his former bitter and pertinacious opponents, and had the question of the identity and the status as nearest Cadder representative *inter alia* formally recognised in his favour, and recorded, through the matriculation, in the unrepealable register of the tribunal. Thus the Keir Performance, most strangely and unduly, again here inverts the situation of parties; for by this it is evinced that Drumpellier did not cease to

Other, even grosser, misrepresentations in the Keir Performance, and here noticed for the same reason.

act, but, on the contrary, carried on his case most actively, while it was the Glorat and Keir party who did not carry their case further for a very sufficient reason—it being untenable.

What could have induced the Keir compiler to have had recourse to such perversion of facts, to such a false gloss, as the preceding? Was it with the view of assisting his case, and conferring a benefit upon his employer? Indeed, his employer would tender him small thanks for obtaining for him an advantage, even if he had succeeded in it, at so serious a cost—at the expense, it may be maintained, of truth and justice. And will he not indignantly reject it, when he arrives at the knowledge of the real state of the case? which it is to be hoped he may soon now do, and might perchance have done before he authorised the publication of portions of his book, had he bestowed somewhat of that acuteness of mind and that literary talent and shrewdness he has the credit of possessing on old historical subjects.

Utter oblivion and suppression of the Drumpellier family in the text of the work, where they were entitled, under the Cadder head, to a high and prominent place and notice, in connection, at least, with Janet of Cadder.

With all submission, it is apprehended the Drumpellier family, being legally proved the nearest heir of Cadder in the sixteenth century—including, too, their male representation, at any rate under the first alternative—their appropriate place in the history and pedigree of the Stirlings of Cadder, the admitted chiefs of the *fibulati Strivelienses*, and where they fell to be entered and discussed, should have been coeval with, and immediately after, the unfortunate and ill-fated Janet of Cadder, the heiress of line. To suppose them for a moment but mere cadets, or treat them as such, either at common law, or even in the male capacity, is quite out of the question.

Such being the case, we will next see how the matter is arranged and settled in the Keir Performance. However the discussion between Glorat and Drumpellier may have been known to the editor, which it assuredly was, as well as the important deeds in the Abstract of Evidence adduced in 1818, and to which he had full access, directly quoting and referring to it in his work, though sparingly enough, and only when it suited his purpose, the said most impartial writer has made his text of his full history of the Stirlings as he would represent it, and containing incidents of trivial and lesser weight, quite a *tabula rasa* as to the Drumpellier family. He has expunged them thoroughly therefrom—quite ignoring them, just as if they had never existed: while Keir, in his novel unsupported *status*, there reigns predominant, precisely as in the case of the usurped Strivelin armorial ensigns—in a great measure, it may be said, as has been shown—in the frontispiece of the work, and as chief and principal, forsooth, of all the Stirlings, especially including Cadder. How the editor can explain such procedure, on the ground of being a fair and candid writer, it is difficult to conceive.

If anything more especially demanded notice in the general history of the Stirlings, it was the imperilled state to which Auld Keir, the original predominant Keir patrimony, was subjected by Robert of Letter, the Drumpellier ancestor, in 1527, and his heirs being infeft therein in warrandice of their weighty Cadder claims by such a despot too as Sir John Stirling of Keir, as well as by his representatives. It was a most striking incident every way, and affecting Keir as much as Letter; but that also is withheld or suppressed, for which the editor has no apology, because both Auld Keir and Keir, when it suits his aims, form with him a favourite topic of discussion, and give scope in part to what some may call platitudes.[1] He devotes more than a quarto page to secondary minute particulars about them, mostly on secondary authorities, withal comprising Keirs *elsewhere*, Keir-hill, Keir-brae, Keir-know, &c., and not overlooking its various spellings in conformity with his addiction to the edifying subject of petty orthography, such as "Keyr, Keyre, Kere, Keer, Keire, and Keir;" and perhaps exceeding in the scale more *numero*, than relevantly *mensura*. But such course, it seems, might by no means be convenient in the preceding aspect and relations of the term, and therefore should be eluded, because it would bring forward rather an importunate and perplexing person to the *new* Keir-Cadder descent—namely, the aforesaid Robert Stirling, and necessarily his Drumpellier heirs—and have thrown Keir into the shade, who must be favoured to the utmost in all extremities; while the former, vetoed and cashiered, was not permitted to come between the wind of Keir and the supposititious ancestry given him. In such new pedigrees, new rules and expedients were fitting, and therefore the old hacknied impartial ones adopted by Lord Hailes, Lingward, and the like, must at the same time be ignored.

So much for the text of the book. It must, however, have been remarked, that in a kind of supplement or appendix the Drumpellier family suffer no small degree of wrong or diminution at the hands of the Keir compiler, resulting, no doubt, in him, from a palpable want of due research, or from ignorance, attended by a too free indulgence in bare assumptions, as exposed elsewhere, and making such a work as he has attempted indeed an easy matter. To him also, actuated by partial motives, may be attri-

[margin: This strikingly demonstrated, too, in the instance of Auld Keir, while secondary and lesser notices of it carefully introduced.]

[margin: [1] See Keir Performance, pp. 17, 18.]

[margin: Similar treatment of Drumpellier in a kind of supplement to the work.]

buted the position assigned to the Drumpellier family at the fag-end of the *fibulati Strivilienses* (mostly, too, only female representatives), with the last, who by any pretence or plausibility can be held to be comprised within such category, while *the whole*, moreover, are classed, it seems, as subordinates, or branches of Keir![1] Why, indeed, even viewing the former quite apart, and abstracting from their proved Cadder representation, they still were entitled, at least, to be deemed an old, respectable, and goodly stock of the *fibulati Strivilienses*, and accordingly so ranked—figuring as they have done, by undoubted evidence, for at least, it may be said, three hundred and sixty years, and forming, as has been fully established, noble and respectable alliances at the outset. More could be said on this head and others: to time, and to a juster appreciation of what is due to them and to their rights, the Drumpelliers may fairly leave such wrongs and insults to be redressed, however pressing motives and considerations, higher and more exacting, have rendered the present exposition—which, with all submission too, may be deemed rather clenching in the matter—imperative and indispensable.

And perhaps they may be pardoned for having felt deep sympathy with Janet of Cadder, on account of her harsh and cruel treatment, and actual spoliation by one no ways her heir, or who could legally claim authority over her,—but, in fact, truly an intruding stranger. Not only, too, may natural affection and relationship here concur, she having been the direct heir at common law of the Cadder family whom that of Drumpellier now represents, but also warm gratitude, owing to her kind and affectionate exertions in their behalf, in 1541, in her last extreme straits and difficulties—when forced to bid adieu to her former rank and status—by securing to them, so far as she could, a portion of her ancient and bereaved inheritance. On this ground they are peculiarly and indispensably bound to defend her cause as they have done, and protect it against these misrepresentatious and calumnies, originating from a selfish and ungrateful quarter, with which she has been assailed. On perusing the Keir Performance, there seems no end to misrepresentations; one connected directly with Janet, that has just struck the writer, besides, too, as will be seen, cruelly and gratuitously impeaching her honour, he cannot refrain from noticing at the close of these remarks. The editor coolly takes upon himself to assert, with the old view, doubtless, of enhancing the Keir glory and fictitious representation, that Sir James Stirling of Keir, the preceding Cadder spoliator, actually, *by his marriage* with the lady in question, "*acquired* the valuable estate of Cadder,"[1] in which, excepting the last notice of its value, there is not the slightest particle of truth or foundation. It is needless to repeat what has been so fully proved, that there never legally was a marriage between the parties, so that nothing earthly, either as to Cadder or otherwise, could have in such honourable way been acquired by Keir.

There *was only one way*, indeed—of a very different kind—by which that arbitrary and cruel acquisition, now plain enough to readers, could be, and really was, effected—and that the writer will refrain from further denouncing; while, in the main, it may also have been known to the editor, from what he himself states and sets forth in the Keir Performance.[2]

Not in any way to prejudice the editor, the entire passage above referred to, as to the acquisition of Cadder, as well as for another reason immediately to be seen, shall be here given:[3] "Janet Striviling" (of Cadder, from what precedes), "was infeft as heiress of her father in 1534, and soon married James Stirling, eldest son of Sir John Stirling" (of Keir also in like manner). "The marriage was a *favourable* one (?) for the Keir family, as *through it they acquired* the valuable *estate* of Cawder, which has ever since been united with Keir. But the parties seem to have been ill assorted, for soon after the marriage, questions arose in the civil court between the heiress and the father-in-law regarding the alienation of the estate; and at the *end of seven* years the *marriage was annulled*, CHIEFLY *through the dishonour of the heiress!!*"

Misrepresentations seem to crowd in upon us almost on the opening of the book. Here is another grossly and gratuitously calumniating the heiress, upon the erroneous footing of her having contracted a legal connection. There cannot be a question—at least, so far as words go—that the annulment of her putative marriage *ab initio* at the "end of seven years," as mentioned—that is, precisely in 1541, through the decreet of divorce which then passed at the instance of James Stirling of Keir against the said Janet,[4] the *only* way by which it "was annulled," and the *only* evidence for the fact cited in the above work—was here in view. And yet, so far from the marriage having been annulled, as thereby we must infer, "CHIEFLY *through the* DISHONOUR *of the* HEIRESS," there is not an item in the least savouring of the imputation within the four corners of the decreet. The annulment was solely, as thereby articulately proved, owing to the parties being related

R

within the fourth degrees of consanguinity, which, it may be observed by the way, did not imply, as is indeed admitted in the Keir work, the male descent or relationship of one of the families from the other,[1] or *vice versa*. Such casual connection could in no degree reflect dishonour on Janet,—which, indeed, is nowhere legally established in her instance. Whatever dishonour there might be in the case truly attached to Sir John Stirling of Keir, who forced the *de facto* and unhappy marriage upon her with James, his son, which she deprecated and abjured from the very first, and only accounted " pretended " or putative.

The editor is therefore not justified in the opprobrious allegation he has risked, and actual perversion of fact, and not only highly injurious to the lady, but, it may be said, derogatory to the credit and foundation of his statements. This is sufficient to add upon a subject that has already been duly canvassed, and whose discussion, like others in the Exposition, behoved to be regularly conducted, upon just and legal rules, through the medium of undoubted fact, irrespective of crude and scandalous unsupported imputations.

[1] See Keir Performance, p. 37.

CHAPTER IV.

IS NOT ROBERT STIRLING OF LETTER, THE DRUMPELLIER ANCESTOR, IDENTICAL WITH ROBERT STIRLING, PROVED YOUNGER BROTHER OF WILLIAM STIRLING OF CADDER IN 1492?—WHAT IS REQUIRED TO FIX THIS POINT!—THE INCONSISTENT, AND, AS MIGHT BE THOUGHT, SUSPICIOUS MODE OF GIVING THE CADDER WRITS AND EVIDENCE IN THE KEIR COMPILATION—THE TRANSCENDANT AND CHIVALROUS CADDER CREST IN THE ABOVE YEAR, NOW UNDULY CONJOINED WITH AN INFERIOR ONE OVER THE KEIR SHIELD OF ARMS—REFUTATION AGAIN OF THE ATTACK MADE IN THE SAME WORK UPON THE ORIGINAL AND EXCLUSIVE RIGHT OF THE *FIBULATI STRIVELIENSES* TO THEIR ARMORIAL BUCKLES—PALPABLE MISREPRESENTATION THERE OF THE ANTIQUITY OF THE KEIR ARMS, NOT YET PROVED TO HAVE BEEN BORNE PRIOR TO 1448—FURTHER REMARKS ON THE SUBJECT OF THOSE OF THE NORTHERN CAWDORS (INCLUDING ANOTHER MISREPRESENTATION THERE), WHO, IN RESPECT TO THEIR INCIDENTAL ARMORIAL DEVICE, MAY BE *IN PARI CASU* WITH THE PELHAMS IN ENGLAND—WITH ADDITIONAL ILLUSTRATIONS—AND WHAT MAY BE THE APPROPRIATE STIRLING OF CADDER AND KEIR BEARINGS—THAT OF THE FORMER PREFERABLE IN JUST HERALDRY—WHILE THEIR REPRESENTATIVE WAS STYLED STIRLING "OF THAT ILK," CONFIRMING THEIR BEING CHIEFS OF THE STIRLINGS, IN ACCORDANCE WITH THE KEIR PERFORMANCE, AND A STYLE NOW VESTED IN DRUMPELLIER AS THEIR HEIR.

THE Drumpellier case, far from being exhausted, is perhaps capable of probation still more articulate ; for, although Robert Stirling of Lettyr has been fully proved to have been *nearest Cadder heir*—a status which, from what has been proved, is certainly now vested in Drumpellier—it may yet be possible, by means of evidence supplied in the Keir Performance, to fix his *precise link of descent* from Cadder.

That work apprises us that,[1] " on 7th January 1492, William Strevelyne of Cawder granted a procuratory to *Robert* and Andrew Strevelyne, his *brothers*, for resigning his lands of Kirkmichael and Blarnarn in the hands of the superior, in favour of William Strevelyne, his son and heir-apparent, and Elizabeth Buchanan, his wife. There is still " (it adds) " appended to this

[1] See Keir Performance, p. 11.

procuratory the seal of the granter, which bears, on a bend engrailed, three buckles. The crest is a swan's head issuing out of a coronet, being the same as the original crest of the Earls of Crawford. David, the fifth earl, who was created Duke of Montrose in 1488, carried it on his ducal seal." An engraving of the seal appears in the Keir Performance, on the margin of the page.

<small>Is the Cadder Procuratory in 1492 otherwise useful besides apprising us of the old Cadder crest?</small>

We are thus supplied with original legal evidence that, in 1492, there existed two younger brothers of William Stirling of Cadder, the family representative—viz. Robert and Andrew. It is with the first-mentioned, Robert, that we have to deal; and, for the purpose in view in the present chapter, it is incumbent, in the first place, to ascertain his exact position; and for this we need only revert to Sir William Stirling of Cadder, father of the preceding William of Cadder, and the account given of him and his issue in the work already referred to. We there find, under that head, as follows—

<small>[1] See Keir Performance, p. 10.</small>

"SIR WILLIAM STRIVELING of Cadder and Regorton (1432-1487).[1]

"Sir William Strivelyne died on 6th May 1487. He had five sons—

"1. William, his successor (afterwards of Cadder in 1492);

"2. Humphrey, who was procurator for his father in a requisition concerning the lands of Easter Cawder, dated at Stirling, 10th May 1472.

"3. Robert, and } procurators for their eldest brother, William of Cadder, on 7th
"4. Andrew,   } January 1492;

"5. William, the second of the name," &c., &c.

The Robert Stirling in question was therefore third son of Sir William Stirling of Cadder, who died in 1487, and third brother of the William of Cadder in 1492. In the next place, it may be material to show that, in 1522, all the nearer heirs than he, with the sole exception of Janet of Cadder, had failed.

This appears sufficiently clear from the Keir compilation, where it is stated that the last-mentioned William of Cadder had but "one son," also named William, and of Cadder, who again was succeeded by an only son, Andrew of Cadder, who, dying in 1522, left but one child, Janet of Cadder.[2] This brings us to the outstanding heirs, as promised in the above pedigree. The first mentioned is "Humphrey" or "Umfridus," not a very common Scotch Christian name, second son of Sir William, who died in 1487, who, from his being styled "magister," was evidently a churchman, and thus legally extinguished, as he could have had no lawful issue.[3] Next in order is Robert, third son of

<small>[2] Ibid., pp. 12, 13.</small>

<small>[3] See Instrument in 1487, Keir Compilation, p. 202.</small>

the said Sir William; and of his extinction we have no proof. Not only may he have been alive in 1522, when Andrew of Cadder died, but for many years afterwards; and it is very remarkable that, if he had left surviving issue in 1541 (which may have been the case, the law, too, presuming in favour of longevity), they would have come within the exact category of "bairns of umquhile Robert Striveling," and the nearest collateral heirs of Janet of Cadder in that year; and thus he and his bairns would be thoroughly identified with Robert of Lettyr and his bairns, while the more inevitably, inasmuch as, although the latter was undoubtedly Janet's nearest collateral heir, and must very recently have sprung from Cadder, no other articulate way of connecting him (or indeed any other) with the main stock has transpired, than through this apposite and concurrent link. In these circumstances, it is apprehended that their identity is made out (and this is still further corroborated by what has, in another place, been advanced in favour of Robert of Lettyr being heir-*male* of Cadder), which legal presumption can only be refuted by explicit legal proof of the dis-identity of Robert of Lettyr with Robert mentioned in 1492, either through the predecease of the latter, or by some other equally cogent and irresistible argument.

After every research, the exponent has been unable to recover evidence to that effect, and the only remaining source which presents itself to his mind from whence information may be derived which possibly may here lead to an *eclaircissement*, is the Cadder charter-chest in Keir's possession; and if, upon due examination, it be found to contain conclusive legal proof against the presumption in question, then of course it must be discarded, and Robert of Lettyr's still indisputable status as nearest Cadder representative must be otherwise accounted for; but if, on the other hand, no such proof be discovered, then the presumption must stand, and the identity must be admitted. How this examination of the Cadder writs, for the purpose of fixing or corroborating a matter of fact, is to be accomplished, of course the exponent cannot take upon himself to say. It could only be through the medium and by the authority of their proprietor, the honourable Member for Perthshire, who, consistently with the liberality professed in the Keir Performance, might possibly be inclined to sanction it.[1] If, on the contrary, however, no notice be vouchsafed to this suggestion, and if taciturnity be preserved, then, after a reasonable interval has elapsed, the exponent will be emboldened to conclude that, as is ordinarily presumed on such occasions, silence may be implied to give consent in his favour, and that no evidence in point exists; and to this conclusion, directly in behalf of Drumpellier, the honourable Member for Perthshire may be necessarily held to assent.

At the same time it may be added, that due attention and consideration will always be paid by the exponent to evidence of an adverse nature—if fully relevant and legal—that may bodily be tendered and submitted to him, should such course be adopted or resolved on.

<small>Why not adduce the *original* Procuratory in 1492 as in all regular discussion?</small>
The exceptionable method pursued by the Keir Performance in adducing deeds in evidence has already been complained of, and a striking instance of it was pointed to in the case of a grant by Keir to Bischop in 1541, where the words of the original are not given, and the derivation of the document is actually suppressed.[1] The subject of the present chapter requires that attention should again be called to this most reprehensible conduct; and the question may naturally be asked, Why does the Keir editor give so summary and brief an account of the preceding Cadder procuratory in 1492?—so important as it is, from its legally fixing the status of Robert and Andrew, by grafting them on to the parent stem of Cadder, and also from the appension of the seal of their brother William of Cadder, thus for the first time disclosing the fine chivalrous old Cadder crest. Not a word of the original is supplied, and whether it be in Latin or in Scotch is difficult to be inferred from the meagre account that is given. This practice is most irregular, and quite alien at once to legal and to antiquarian discussions; and what makes it the more remarkable is, that in cases where the writs are less material, and sometimes where they are not even connected with the Stirlings, either *full copies* or *excerpts from the originals* are entered in the chartulary appended to the Stirling history, and reference is made to them on suitable occasions. One of this class of documents may be here instanced—viz. a notable grant by Bertram, the son of Henry de Ulvestoun to " Waldevo *Kokes*," his cousin, after a litigation between them about two bovates of land in the territory of Eyton,—of which document the editor is at pains to give an engraved *fac-simile!*[2] What this high and dignified family of *Kokes* have to do with the subject at large, is difficult to conceive. The grant does not contain the least mention of any Stirlings, nor has it the slightest connection with any family of that name. It embodies quite a commonplace transaction, is isolatedly introduced, and does not contain an item of information worthy of

<small>[1] See Chapter II., under Addenda, No. II.</small>

<small>[2] See Keir Performance, p. 197.</small>

notice, neither is reference made to it in the text, nor does the editor himself make any observations about it. It resolves, therefore, into another absolute make-weight.

Another irrelevant document, which is prominently brought forward in *fac-simile*, while the more material are withheld, is a precept of sasine by Walter Halyburton, 21st October 1437, to William Strivelyne, the Cadder[1] ancestor in the tennandry of Regorton, with his seal appended (but poorly executed),[2] and far inferior every way to that of Cadder, while of no importance or value to the work, rendering its addition the more irrelevant, if not unaccountable.

There may be greater reason for giving a *fac-simile* of a procuratory of resignation by Lucas de Strivelyne to George, Lord Leslie in 1448, of the lands of *Bouchquhumgre* (a designation well exchanged by his family for that of Keir), to which is appended a seal; and this is the *first* proved instance we have of the Keir family bearing arms. A *fac-simile* is here given both of the procuratory and of the seal, and very properly so, as the information conveyed is both new and interesting, but it also renders more striking the non-adduction in the text of the Cadder procuratory in 1492. It would almost seem as though the seal in the latter instance had been brought forward merely to afford Keir an opportunity of conjoining the Cadder crest with his own,[3]—a step not more irregular and indefensible than it may be hazardous and dangerous from what may be afterwards stated.

Moreover, in the Keir Performance, the Cadder writs and investitures, *ab initio*—besides corroborative ones of other properties to the same effect, with some quite foreign—are fully given in the said chartulary from an early period, viz.—from the demise of Sir John Stirling, "Domini de Caddare," in 1408, down to 1505 inclusive, in the persons of William of Cadder, his son; Sir William of Cadder, his grandson; William of Cadder, his great-grandson; and William of Cadder, his great-great-grandson, who respectively and successively were proved Sir John's heirs and representatives, the last of whom succeeded in 1505. After this date, the eligible practice of adducing a continuous chain of evidence strikingly ceases. Andrew Stirling of Cadder, who succeeded the last-mentioned William in the family property and representation, was, in his turn, succeeded by Janet, his only child and heiress at common law; but in neither of these cases are the titles and investitures produced, as had always been done antecedently in the most precise and regular way, and the main Cadder descent and pedigree is merely set forth in the following way :—

¹ See Keir Performance, pp. 12, 13.

"ANDREW STRIVELING of Cawder (1517-1522)."¹

"On 25 April 1517 he obtained a precept of *clare constat* from the said Sir William Menteith (of *West Kerse, previously mentioned*), for infefting him as heir of his father in the lands of Ochiltree.

"He married Marjory Cunyngham, who survived her husband, and died shortly before 16th February 1524.* Andrew died before 25th September 1522, leaving an only daughter,

"JANET STRIVELING, Heiress of Cawder (1522).

"She succeeded her father, Andrew Striveling, in 1522, in the estate of Cawder."

In this way Andrew and Janet are described as proprietors of Cadder,— which fact is undeniable ; yet they are not here shown to have been infefted in it, nor explicitly proved to be heirs of it. How totally unlike this is to the practice pursued with regard to their ancestry, as has already been premised ! Regarding Andrew, in the first place, the precept of *clare constat* in 1517 alone is *summarily noticed*, to prove the material fact of Andrew of Cadder being heir to his father ; while, in the exceptionable manner already exposed in the case of the Cadder procuratory in 1492, not a scrap of the document itself is given, nor is it in any other place referred to. Secondly, as to Janet, —in her case, if possible, still less evidence is given : there is not here—the preferable place—a single vestige of proof of her filiation, or of her being heir to her father.† And thus, so directly at variance with the practice in the previous links of descent, there is no reference to the chartulary or to any authority for the substantiation of the above facts.

What explanation can be assigned for so strange a deviation, and for such reticence ? The Cadder papers appear to have been well preserved at a very early period *ex abundanti*, so that there is no lack of evidence ; and every single link is established by articulate writs *in extenso* from the year 1408 downwards until about the beginning of the following century, when we find that they either disappear altogether, or are given in garbled extracts, or

---

* In proof of Marjory having survived her husband, reference is made to a single deed contained in the subjoined chartulary ; but no evidence whatever is adduced to prove any of the other facts here stated.

† The insertion of the grant of ward and marriage of Janet afterwards, does not come within this category.

merely summarily referred to. Is it likely that these later papers can have been lost or defaced, while the earlier have been so successfully preserved? Or, on the contrary, is it not more natural to suppose that the facts relating to Andrew and Janet should be more capable of being fully established than those of their forefathers, though so remote, by means of documents more abundant and in a more perfect state? How, it may be asked, does this suppression quadrate with the eulogium bestowed upon the Keir proprietor at the outset of the Performance,[1] when the editor speaks of his "enlightened liberality," and his having, so "far from locking up his family muniments from the light of day," actually disclosed and "opened them" to others? The reticence in question—the so strangely withholding the articulate evidence for substantiating the later Cadder links—really looks rather like a burlesque on the above, and makes it appear as if the praise had been bestowed in irony; it frustrates, in fact, what had been so liberally conceded in principle, and conceals, instead of fairly disclosing, the purport and contents of the Keir and Cadder muniments.

[1] See Preface, p. xv.

The exponent is far indeed from intending any undue reflection; but, with all submission, while he legally admits that *nemo tenetur edere munimenta contra se,* he is apprehensive that, in the minds of some, such peculiar conduct, otherwise seemingly unaccountable, may induce the suspicion that, both in 1492 and subsequently, there existed in the Cadder charter-chest that which expediency demanded to be withheld, lest it should compromise Keir interests and favour their opponents. This might very well be so, though the deeds thus shortly noticed, *in græmio,* incidentally, or by their testing or other clauses, &c. And it very remarkably happens that that is the very epoch—viz. from 1492 to 1527 inclusive—where additional and corroborative evidence might well be expected, most indubitably, it is conceived, in favour of Drumpellier.

Inference possibly to be drawn from such reticence.

It may, not improbably, have been some such evidence which prudentially induced Mr James Dundas—the able and devoted Keir agent—in 1818, after investigation of the Cadder charter-chest, suddenly and extraordinarily to throw up his agency in the case, and to dissuade and adjure as hopeless further proceedings against Drumpellier.

The exponent has been prompted to offer the preceding statement and comments, as possibly they may have influence on matters in question; on this ground they may be pardoned.

COMMENTS ON KEIR PERFORMANCE.

On referring, in the Keir Performance, to the notice of the procuratory of 1492, we there find, upon the margin of the page, an engraved *fac-simile* of a beautiful seal, appended by the granter, William Stirling of Cadder, disclosing the arms which that family then bore.[1] One feature of these arms is new to us, and very remarkable—viz. the crest; it is a white swan's head and neck, with expanded wings, issuing out of a coronet placed upon a helmet, with the lateral heraldic ornaments above the shield of arms. This crest, besides being quite in keeping with the rank and dignity of the Stirlings of Cadder, was a high and peculiarly chivalrous armorial *imprese* or device. The swan, of old, by its formal intervention, sanctioned and consecrated the most solemn observances and vows.[2] It was before "*duo cygni vel olores*,* allati—in pompatica gloria ante regem, phalerati retibus aureis *vel fibulis de auratis* † desiderabile spectaculum intuentibus," that Edward I., in 1306, at a royal feast, took a solemn vow of vengeance and retribution against Robert Bruce for his murder of Comyn, and insult offered thereby to God and the Church.

Spelman maintains[3] that *gloriæ studium ex eodem hoc symbolo*‡ *indicari multi asserunt*," while Ashmole observes[4] that "Edward III. had these words wrought upon his surcoat and shield, provided to be used at a tournament," viz. :—

"Hay, Hay, the *wythe* swan; §
By God's soul, I am thy man."

According to Lord Hailes[5]—from whose Annals the above is taken, and to whom we are indebted for this information, as also in sundry other antiquarian matters—this shows "that a *white swan* was the *imprese* ‖ of Edward III., and perhaps," he adds, "it was also used by his grandfather, Edward I."

It being thus in every view a high, kingly, and even a sacred emblem, no wonder the Drumpellier, as Cadder heirs, should be anxious to vindicate their right to the white swan and its accompanying coronet, with the due blazonry, as their crest; and they have just cause of complaint when the representative of another family, if he has done them a service by discovering to them what their original crest really was—a service which only consisted in his letting them have a peep into what may be considered the depositaries of

Sidenotes:
[1] See p. 11. Fine old chivalrous Cadder crest in 1492.
[2] Mathew Westm., p. 454.
[3] Aspilogia, p. 132.
[4] History of the Garter, cap. 5, sec. 2, p. 185.
[5] Annals of Scotland, edit. 1797, vol. ii. pp. 4, 5.
Drumpellier family naturally desirous to retain it.

* Both classically denoting swans.
† *i.e.* Golden buckles, thus enhancing the heraldic pre-eminence of the Stirling buckles, and making this a more suitable illustration; and, no doubt, their swan would occasionally be most appropriately so decked and adorned.
‡ A swan.
§ *white* swan.
‖ An "emblem or device," in Italian.

their own archives—has, at the same time, appropriated the said crest to himself, and conjoined it with his own ; and thus he, whose partisans have, in the Keir Performance, so unjustly accused the Lyon Court of want of scruple in granting Cadder arms to Drumpellier, although he had made good his undisputed claim to them, has himself had no scruple in *gratuitously* assuming a crest which he can show no right to, and without (as was imperative upon him) going through the legal process of submitting his claim to the Lord Lyon, and obtaining his formal sanction and approbation.

<small>But another spoliation here attempted by Keir or his advisers, after the fashion of his ancestors.</small>

The Keir crest, " a savage head couped " (or a negro's head, as it is sometimes represented), "having a ribbon gules or wreath about his head,"* is, in the Keir Performance,[1] only first proved to have been borne in 1662, on the knighting of Sir George Stirling of Keir, while no instance of its use previously has been there adduced. It may hence be inferred that, quite unlike Cadder, not very long before that year, the Keirs had no crest ; and, indeed, their seals of *arms*, carefully adduced in the work, from 1448—the earliest time they bore *such*—down to 1666, in the person of a cadet, exhibit none.[2]

<small>Keir crest has not been proved anterior to 1662.
[1] See pp. 49, 50.
[2] See ibid., p. 556, 557.</small>

The Germans are the great multipliers of crests, the princes having often seven, including that of the main stem in the centre ; and in conformity with the practice, two are now adopted in this country—the first, as in the Keir instance, in right of the paternal representation, and the other of the female, or in some other way, but not visionary, as in the Keir assumption of the Cadder crest. What with crests and redundant quarterings, the German coats are unmatched, including "arms of *pretension* ;" in which way the Queen of Spain takes also those of Portugal, to indicate her conceived right by descent to that kingdom. The Duke of Modena, whom it is the fashion to abuse in the public prints, is here well entitled to praise, on account of his moderation, for though the undoubted heir at common law (bating just opposing Acts of Parliament) to the kingdoms of England, Scotland, and Ireland, as well as of the House of Stuart, he has never taken their arms, which, in heraldry and by analogous practice, he might have done *a fortiori*, on the above pretended footing. Such claim is in him as elder Sardinian representative.

<small>Reduplication of crests with us.

Interesting case of Duke of Modena.</small>

Not the least curious and remarkable of the errors in the Keir Performance are the shadowy speculations about the derivation of the Stirling buckles. It is clearly proved that this family bore the buckles as far back as 1292—an

---

* See, as to this, the remarks on the Keir arms, afterwards.

early date in the history of Scotch heraldry—which gives them the *pas* and preference over every other Scotch bearers of the buckle; yet, notwithstanding this, the Keir partisans, who on most occasions support the claims and aspirations of their principal in the most gratuitous manner, and whose zeal and ardour frequently amount almost to bigotry, seem to think it impossible that this chivalrous emblem can really be indigenous to the Stirlings, and consequently feel themselves bound to discover from whence the exotic may have been transported. It has already been shown how futile was the attempt to bring forward the Cawdors of the north as competitors for the honour of having first borne the buckles; and now, lest the editor should fall back and seek support from his other equally hollow theory, we propose to examine it, and to deal with it according to its merits. The passage runs thus—

"Bunkle, of that Ilk, an old family in Berwickshire, carried on a bend three buckles.[1] Through intermarriage, the Darnley or Lennox Stuarts quartered those buckles with their own arms. It is *possible* that one of the early Stirlings who settled in the Border counties *may have intermarried* with the Bunkles, and thus acquired the buckles in the same manner as the Stewarts."

It is believed that this page in the Keir Performance contains within its limited compass more hallucination and error than is comprised in the same space, or greater, in any other work of the kind. To the paragraph just quoted we may reply, in the first place, that the Bunkles (rather Bonkills) did not bear the buckles on a *bend*, as the Stirlings did; they carried them of old 2 and 1, and afterwards with a *chevron between*,* as is proved by the subjoined evidence. Secondly, before we can admit that the Stirlings derived their arms from this family, it must be proved that the latter had the *prior* right to bear the buckles: this, however, the Keir work, according to its usual careless and reprehensible practice, does not condescend to do, but gratuitously and *de plano*, upon no discoverable ground at all, gives the Bonkills the preference. And thirdly, the Darnley or Lennox Stuarts *never did* either intermarry with the Bunkles or quarter their arms: the editor's statement is entirely fabulous. These Stuarts may be held to be sprung—contrary to the assertions of our older genealogists—from Sir Alan Stuart, first acquirer of

---

* And in an original index, autograph of "Robert Porteous Snaddon, herald, September 1661," to the then existing Lyon Records, subsequently burnt, the arms of "Bonkill" are thus given: "argent, a chiffron vert, betwixt three buckles azure."

Darnley (in whom that title originated), early in the fourteenth century, and whose direct representative, in 1429, was the gallant Sir John Stuart of Darnley, who, with his brother William, fell at the siege of Orleans. The earliest instance, it is believed, of the family arms, is supplied by his seal in 1426, which is appended to a deed in the *Tresor des Chartres* at Paris, engraved by Andrew Stuart in his *Genealogical History of the Stuarts*,[1] and which exclusively exhibits, as his bearing, a fess cheque of four tracts or lines (for Stuart), surmounted by a simple *uncharged bend dexter*. The latter was a distinguished and even a princely mark of cadency—being precisely what the Bourbons formerly took in their character of royal cadets, and placed over the French *fleur-de-lis*—while the additional tract or line in the Stuart arms, as borne in the Darnley coat in 1426 (they ordinarily consisting but of three), may serve as another difference. But neither there nor antecedently is there a trace of the Stuarts of Darnley having in any shape used the Bonkill insignia. It was subsequent to this, though in the same century, that they adopted the buckles, though not *quarterly*—as erroneously asserted in the Keir Performance—but placed, eight in number, on a border round their arms. This was proved by their family shield, tastefully sculptured, with due Gothic accompaniments,* on the front of their old mansion in the "Rottenrow" of Glasgow, on the eminence leading eastward to the Cathedral.†

This introduction of the buckles into the arms of Darnley or Lennox Stuart was not owing to any intermarriage between this family and the Bonkills, but was merely to indicate the original descent of the former as cadets from Sir John Stuart of Bonkill, younger brother of James, High Steward of Scotland (ancestor of the house of Stuart), who figured both before and after 1300.

Other Stuarts, said to be similarly descended, placed the buckles upon their *bend* of difference *peculiar* to themselves, but with which the Bonkills had nothing to do. There is no proof that the latter, when subsisting as a separate and detached family, took the bend.

But, independently of the above, what have the Stirlings to do with the

---

[1] In the Genealogical Table prefixed there.

* Of which, long ago, the writer took an etching.

† The above "Rottenrow"—corresponding with that in London—is a corruption of *Route de Roi* (and strangely Latinised with us, *via rattonum*—street of rats, as it may literally have been at one time), and was then the principal street of the city. Now, however, the mansion in question no longer exists, it having recently been razed to the ground in accordance with the prevalent and much-lamented disregard of old structures.

Bonkills, or the Bonkills with the Stirlings? The two families are quite distinct, alien in interests and alliances; nor, as things stand, can it be presumed they ever had any connection either by marriage or in any other way; nay more, it cannot properly be shown that any of the *Fibulati Strivelienses* were ever settled in the Border counties. The Keir editor,[1] after his sapient speculation on this head, has produced a repetition of the same twaddle upon the subject of the Cawdors of the north, which has been sufficiently spoken to and exposed. It is really quite inconsistent with the dignity due to such a discussion to indulge in so many wild possibilities and perchances.

[1] See Keir Performance, p. 14, and present Exposition, p. 21, note.

It is remarkable how ignorant the Keir editor is in all armorial and heraldic matters, as may further yet be shown.

The earliest instance of the buckles being borne by the Keir family is in 1448, on a seal of Luke Stirling; they are placed on a bend, as subsequently. It is impossible—at least, it has not yet been achieved—to produce an older coat-of-arms of himself or his ancestors. Yet the same work coolly, forsooth, observes here,[2] that "the buckles thus continued to be carried by Lukas Striveling in the 15th century, as they had been by *his ancestor*, William de Striveling, in the 13th, with this change, that they were borne by both the Cadder and Keir families on a bend instead of a chief." What a gross misrepresentation! This William de Striveling was obviously *no* such Keir ancestor, but the distinct eminent Guilielmus de Striveling who swore fealty to Edward I., and whose seal of arms, with the buckles so placed on a chief —however alien and irrelevant there—with another even still more so, are engraved in the Keir work.[3]

Other gross misrepresentation by the Keir work as to the antiquity of the Keir arms.

[2] Ibid., p. 17.

[3] Ibid., p. 14.

In this emergency, the Keir family are not entitled to found upon or draw any precedent whatever through his arms or otherwise, from this William, or rather Sir William, who is wholly *jus tertii* to them. Not a vestige of proof is adduced in the Keir work to show that he is their ancestor, though above so boldly and directly asserted, and inconsistently, too, seeing that elsewhere the fact is only "presumed"[4]—a word which, even in this instance, is most unduly used, as there is not the slightest ground for presumption. He was as much their ancestor as the celebrated Scoto-Anglo knight in the reign of Edward III., the English baron, who also, as will be proved in another chapter, bore the preceding identical arms of three buckles on a chief. This, again, serves to remind us (as before noticed) of the fictions of the denounced Douglas and the English Guthrie. Whilst reading the Keir Performance, we

[4] See Keir Performance, p. 15.

think we discern some resemblance to Churchill's portrait of the latter, when he says he

—— "Can call
All opposites to proof, and conquer all."

While, in the vain attempt to affiliate the Keir family on Sir William Stirling, the editor

"Calls forth living waters from the rock."
"Calls forth children from the barren stock."

We must turn our attention once more—partly to supply a deficiency—to the Cawders of the north, such extreme favourites of the Keir compiler, and whom, as has been shown, they so strangely and gratuitously seek to make paramount, in striking respects, to all the *Fibulati Strivelienses*, with whom, nevertheless, they had no earthly connection or relation. A word more as to absurd *Khular* conceit, grounded upon a device in the arms of the Northern Cawders.

There existed, and probably may still exist, at Cawdor Castle (belonging to the Earl of Cawdor, a female descendant) an original procuratory of resignation, dated at Campbell (Campbell Castle, a noted Argyle residence, her husband being of that house), 17th February 1511, by "Muriella Calder de Eodem" (his Lordship's ancestrix, and the direct Cawdor heir), styled, "Sponsa Johannes Campbell Militis," of the lands of Clunes and Boithe, in Nairn, within the county of Forres. It is witnessed by Hugh Ross of Kylravaik (representative of an ancient respectable family) and others, to which her seal, and her husband's, in her right, separately are appended, without being impaled, as by the modern fashion, which did not then hold; and that of the lady (as by a copy taken by the writer) contains her arms as Cawdor representative—viz. a hart's or stag's head, with but one small buckle placed above it. Formerly summarily noticed when there happened to be no room for more.

From the prominent charge of the head and antlers that engross the shield, with but the slight accessory of the buckle between the antlers, the former obviously constituted alone the family arms,—confirmed, too, by the Calders, as was shown, having ever subsequently discarded it, which also obtains in the case of the male Calders at present.* The buckle, therefore, is properly alien thereto, and may be otherwise accounted for by heraldic precedent and practice. It may be inferred, in its technical import, to be analogous to, or in *pari casu* with, the noted corresponding device of the single buckle also The Pelham buckle

---

* Such as the old knightly family of Calder of Muirtown, the most distinguished, according to the ordinary authorities.

taken by the English family of Pelham, quite distinct from their arms, alternately on each side of the shield, or as their crest (the position here being immaterial), to commemorate the capture by an ancestor of John, King of France, at the battle of Poitiers in 1356.

So stated in all the pedigrees of the family, who have been repeatedly ennobled.

Under the circumstances, it is submitted, the buckle, always a chivalrous and good heraldic *imprese* or device, may likewise have been adopted by the northern Calders in commemoration of an ancestral feat or achievement, though certainly of lesser importance;—a conclusion very natural, and not to their disparagement, but the contrary.

Abstracting from the special explanation of the Pelham buckle—while it is to be kept in view that the Pelham arms are quite distinct therefrom—it would be just as fair an argument, that the former originated the buckles borne by other English families, as that of Cadder those of Stirling—with what truth or foundation it need not be added. Conscious of the weakness of its argument here as it stands, the Keir Performance may be said

In its great straits, Keir work driven to a gross heraldic misrepresentation.

"Boldly to call *invention* to its aid,"

[1] See p. 14, including reference 3 in the note.

and reprehensibly, in support of its assertion that "the ancient family of Cadder" (in the north) "carried *buckles*,"[1]—thus in the *plural* number—in order to give some plausibility to what it maintains, from a visionary coincidence with the Stirling bearing, is forced to refer, as its *sole* authority for the fact, to a Cadder seal of arms in 1431, engraved in Laing's *Seals*.[2] But, instead of this, it only displays *one single buckle*, precisely as the Calder seal of arms, adduced by the writer, in 1511, and no more. Here, then, is another gross misrepresentation, and a *plurality* of buckles, gratuitously invented, or at least carelessly assumed, in the face of certain proof to the contrary before the author at the time, to eke out a miserable pretence or conceit, which already, it is submitted, has been sufficiently exposed and refuted.

[2] P. 31, No. 150.

The exponent, too, could further obviate or rebut any inimical inference that could be drawn from the single buckle formerly in the northern Calder shield. In old valid representations of the arms of Mackenzie, there is also the incidental device of a man's hand (that may extraneously be accounted for) to their exclusive *gentilitial bearing* of a stag's head caboshed.* Can

* Independently of other concurring authorities, in the index to or contents of the original register of arms in the Lyon Court (subsequently consumed by fire) autograph of Robert

any one pretend that it properly comes within *such category*, or really substantively constitutes their arms? And yet it equally might as the buckle in those of Cadder; and, what may be another illustration or rejoinder in point, this very accessory of the man's hand has likewise long been disused and ceased to be borne by the clan Mackenzie. Not only so, but likewise the parallel single star, actually placed, too, between the antlers of the equally caboshed Mackenzie stag's head, which Colin, the first Earl of Seaforth, their representative (raised to that dignity in 1623), is proved again, by a creditable MS. account of Scottish arms, to have substituted in his for the hand;—all which evinces that, in a gentilitial view, such casual accompaniments, however originating—whether in the shape of a single buckle, a single hand, or single star—were utterly inept and insignificant.

After the preceding, we may next advert to another notable dogma, *ex cathedra*, of the Keir Performance,[1] that "the origin of the buckles which have for *so long* a period been the chief Stirling arms has *not* been ascertained," though not quite in keeping with recent bold speculations to the contrary exposed. But no wonder, certainly, in the case of so minute and not unfrequent bearing; and when it would be also impossible to explain or account for innumerable others of much later adoption (always, however, excepting honourable armorial augmentations), as must be obvious to all who have sifted the subject, and know the deficiency of the requisite vouchers and authorities. To attempt it *positively* and *articulately* in such a microscopic instance as the Stirling buckles, which date at least from 1292, would be like seeking for a needle in a bundle of straw, and as difficult to ascertain as the origin of the Nile; indeed, that might be easier, from what has been lately wafted from Africa.

Important discovery in the Keir Performance.
[1] See p. 14.

We might only here land ourselves in fable and absurdities, and be obliged to repeat the twaddle of Douglas and such writers,[2] who derive the "*frases*," or "*strawberry leaves*," in the Fraser arms, as well as the surname, from a grant of an outlandish French king, at a most remote period, to "Julius de *Berry*," a supposititious ancestor, for "fine *strawberries*" (in keeping with his

Fabulous origin of some of our families.
[2] See Peerage, first edit., p. 427.

Porteous Suaddoun, herald, dated September 1661, those of *Mackenze* of *Kintail* (that is, of *Mackenzie*, chief of the family) are thus given—viz. "azure, a buk hcid caboshed or horned, argent, *wyt* a *hand* of the 2"—the second colour mentioned, and necessarily "or" or golden; while, in old illuminated heraldic MSS., the hand in question is represented as a man's hand, the "buk" or buck's head being of course a stag's or deer's head, as elsewhere given to Mackenzie.

name), "fully ripened before the ordinary time," that, with "other delicacies," he gave him at an entertainment;¹ or do what may be tantamount to converting (as again notoriously by the above) the three shields in the ancient arms of the Norman and baronial Hays of Errol,* the future hereditary Constables of Scotland, into heraldic and historical representations of the three fabulous rustics, from one of whom they are *made* to be descended, and who, forsooth, by their ox-yokes or plough-gear, retrieved the fortunes of the battle of Luncarty in 980. In reference to which and the exploit, Chalmers most justly says² that "tradition has here also transmitted what Scottish history has assumed as her own, the story of the *peasant Hay*, who, with his two sons and the *yokes* of his *oxen*, rallied the flying Scots, and regained the desperate battle. I *believe* the *whole story* is an *egregious fable*. I suspect the surname of Hay did not exist in that age, and the family of Hay came into Scotland *during the twelfth century*. I conjecture that such yokes of oxen were not then in use." Chalmers, in his latter remark, is again correct. The Hays only first figure in genuine Scottish writs in that century, which is as far back as any other Scottish families can well go, and an antiquity, as will be seen, futilely aspired to for Keir by his partisans. Nevertheless, for a considerable period, the noble house of Errol, in commemoration of the apocryphal Luncarty feat of an imaginary ancestor, have taken as supporters two men in country habits, or rustics, holding the oxen-yokes of a plough over their shoulders, to the utter exclusion of their original far preferable and appropriate ones—viz. two falcons proper, armed and belled, or†—a bird famed and prized in chivalry and heraldry, armorially befitting princes and nobles, and selected by Sir Walter Scott as the dignified bear-

---

¹ See ibid., p. 247, and Hector Boetius, commonly called the Father of Lies, &c.

² Caledonia, vol. i. p. 395, note (*).

Especially of the noble one of Errol, hereditary Constables of Scotland, and error as to their present supporters.

³ Errol Charter-chest.

Instance of a family baronial at the outset.

* Their original charter by William the Lion,³ who reigned from 1165 to 1214, grants the fief of Errol to Willielmo de Haia and his heirs, to be held of the Crown "*sicuti alii* BARONES *mei* liberius et quietius, &c., feuda sua de me tenent." Hence this is a fair instance of one of our most ancient *baronial* families, being *so ab initio*, and long before that of Keir, which was not, as will be seen, until 1473.

† Proved by MS. accounts of Scotch families and their arms in the British Museum, towards the latter part of the sixteenth century. The rustic supporters only fully figure at the beginning of the next.

If the writer is not mistaken, too, there was at Slains Castle—which he visited during the minority of the last Earl of Errol, when, by the kind permission of his guardians, he had full access to the fine family charter-chest there—an old stone preserved, on which the Errol arms were sculptured, with the original supporters stated in the text.

Dr Beattie's noted lines on the Errol family, stating (among just encomiums) that

"A *thousand* years have seen it shine,
With unabated flame"—

of course have kept alive the Luncarty delusion.

ing of the noble Marmion, in his noted poem.[1] With every submission, this is an unprecedented instance of a noble, constabular family withal—if we may use the term—unduly *rusticating* themselves at its outset, and erroneously making an ancestor or founder figure *en paysan*, or as a parvenu, instead of retaining the exalted and chivalrous rank inherent in him. It was elsewhere a Scottish boast not to know the *first* mean man in a family.

On the attempted corresponding origin of the Forbeses and the Guthries, &c., sufficiently puerile and ludicrous, we might especially expand—on the *alleged* ancestor of the former, from another *imposing* feat in slaying a "mighty *bear*," having first been named "*For beast*," subsequently corrupted into "Forbes;" and hence, too, the bears in their arms; or, by a different version, from despatching "a monstrous wild-boar," &c. &c.; and where Lord Hailes,[2] while noticing their descent, too, from "*Phorbas*," a Greek, observes, "there is a confusion here of *boars* and *bears* I will not attempt to unravel."

To such results, in the dearth of evidence, we might arrive, if we broached the *promising* subject above started in the Keir work; and no doubt there are many more such edifying illustrations—including the supposed origin of the crest and motto of the Hamiltons in the fourteenth century—in Scottish history and genealogy.[3]

Arms, in the main, originated with the Crusades, from the necessity of distinguishing by congruent marks and differences the parties who, from various quarters, participated in them. Every military sign and emblem, therefore, both then, and indeed afterwards, in a chivalrous and feudal age, would be preferred, and, when adopted, be transmitted to descendants—proud to take them in commemoration of their ancestors' valour—and thus form and constitute their family bearing.

Of course, buckles, so prominent and important in adjusting the coat armour, would especially come within such category, and be of very frequent use, which is the utmost we can safely say, or, it is conceived, ever can be said, as to their origin with the Stirlings. Their position originally, on a chief in the shield, as in the proved instance in 1292,* was peculiarly befitting a feudal chieftain or leader—the same in heraldry indicating a status of superiority and command. And curiously, under that technical acceptation, it was granted by Napoleon I.—who had his eye *on all—*

---

* As from the original seal of arms of Sir John Strivelin of Carse, appended to his deed of fealty to Edward I. in the Chapter-house in Westminster.

148   COMMENTS ON KEIR PERFORMANCE,

Curiously Napoleon, in public documents, called the English Lions Leopards to their prejudice, but quite according to Nisbet's doctrine.—(See his Essay on Armories, Edinburgh, 1718, pp. 159, 160, et seq.)

charged with stars, as an honourable distinctive augmentation to the arms of his marshals ;* while the bend dexter, again, charged with buckles, in those of the Stirlings of Cadder, was quite in keeping, in a warlike view, with the chief, it being but the military shoulder-belt under another appellation.

Almost the only instance of a due explanation of an ancient arms.

There is only one instance, at an ancient epoch, of the easy solution or explanation of old armorial bearings, through an ecclesiastical medium in the first instance, of which the writer is aware ; and it so happens in the identical case of the great episcopal and archiepiscopal see of Glasgow, the superiors of the *baronial* fief of the Stirlings of Cadder, as it will be afterwards proved. It is supplied to us by this accurate modern description in Latin of the original seal (then extant) of Robert, Bishop of Glasgow (installed in 1272), appended to a grant by him of the lands of Hauchiltree to Melrose,— a copy of which, as well as of writs connected with the see, in the Scottish College at Paris, was forwarded last century to the University of Glasgow, at their request, with whom they still are :—

" Huic cartæ appensum est sigillum . . . . ex una parte Episcopum veteri casula indutum cum baculo, et mitra hinc inde piscem et *arem* . . . . ex altera vero parte, triplici distincta segmine, in superiore, Episcopum sedentem, et coram eo *quemdam genuflexum pisciculum cum annulo in ore manu tenentem*, medio segmine REGEM *stantem* gladium strictum dextra tenentem, a sinistris REGINAM *coronatam* dextra *annulum* tenentem. In inferiore segmine Episcopum genuflexum supplicantem, et habitu pontificali indutum, inscriptum in circumferentia REX FURIT, HÆC PLORAT, PATET AURUM, DUM SACER ORAT," which we may render in English : " *The* KING *storms—she (the* QUEEN) *implores and beseeches ; and while the holy man* (SAINT MUNGO *or* KENTIGERN) *prays, the gold or golden ring appears or is recovered.*"

We have here graphically represented and explained the miracle which originated and constituted the arms of the archiepiscopal see, and next of the city of Glasgow, which in a great measure stepped into its shoes, and which Nisbet thus,[1] in the main, gives as borne by the latter—viz. " in base " (that is, of the shield), " a salmon fish, with a ring in its mouth, all proper, to perpetuate the story of a miracle said to be wrought by St Mungo, that

[1] Heraldry, first edit., vol. i. p. 365.

---

* See that rather rare work now, the *Armorial General de l'Empire Français*, by Simon, published at Paris in 1812, during the first Empire, vol. i., plates 5 and 6, and especially 12 and 13.

town's patron saint, in recovering by a salmon, in its mouth, the ring of a lady out of the water of Clyde, where she accidentally dropt it, which being got, prevented the jealousie of her husband."

But the preceding most ancient and more authentic version of the matter, exalts the parties thus miraculously accommodated and reconciled by the pious and good offices of Saint Mungo actually into a king and queen, hence making them the more remarkable and historical, though as yet we may be ignorant of their names.* The miracle of the Saint would in consequence be enhanced or perpetuated in a more exalted guise. As for the accompanying charges of the *bird* in the seal of Bishop Robert (as described), and still forming a part of the arms of the city of Glasgow, it seems not so easily explained.

We may conclude this chapter, so much devoted to heraldic *insignia*, with what may be deemed more immediately interesting—the due ascertaining what must be held the just and appropriate bearings respectively of the Stirlings of Cadder and of Keir.

Precise armorial bearings of the Stirlings of Cadder and Keir, and which preponderate in heraldry? and Sir David Lindsay's old register of arms. the regula regulans in the matter.

The relevant and legal groundwork here, or the *regula regulans* in the matter, must obviously, it is apprehended, be the original register or record of Scottish arms or matriculation-book of Sir David Lindsay of the Mount, a distinguished and accomplished person for his period,† and who actually discharged the important public duties, both at home and abroad, of Lord Lyon and principal herald of Scotland in the reign of James V.

Chalmers, in his well-known edition of Lindsay's works,[1] believes he was born in 1490, and in the service of James IV. and his Queen; but, at any rate, he was in that of James V., who succeeded in 1513, and by whom he was appointed to the preceding high office.

[1] See vol. i. pp. 3, 4, 6, and 11.

This register in question, to which we must here confine ourselves, is well authenticated,‡ and fortunately preserved. It is the only appropriate and legal voucher of the kind, and executed with taste and care,—the

---

* It might, in this new and preferable royal aspect, with the specific concomitants, form another eligible decoration of a window, according to the laudable method adopted in the cathedral church of Glasgow. The curious and eloquent seal in question, under the above description, seems unique, there being no notice or account of it elsewhere, even in Laing's *Seals*, though the latter excellent work contains other interesting ones of the see and chapter of Glasgow.

† He, accordingly, is thus apostrophised in these noted lines of Scott—

"Still is thy name in *high* account,
And still thy verse has charms,
Sir David Lindesay of the Mount,
Lord Lyon King at Arms."
Marmion, edit. 1808, p. 193.

‡ It belonged, of course, *virtute officii*, to Sir James Balfour of Kinnaird, Lord Lyon to Charles I., as is proved by this entry of his

arms entered, including those of successive Scottish monarchs and their connections, being finely painted or illuminated, for the publication of which, comprising *fac-similes*, too, of the same, in their due tinctures and colours, we were indebted, many years ago, to David Laing, Esq., the able and intelligent Secretary of the Society of Scottish Antiquaries, and who has done so much by his publications to advance the cause of Scottish history, besides illustrating other Scottish subjects of interest.

And therein, as might be expected, together with the bearings of the nobility and other barons, the coats respectively of the Stirlings of Cadder and Keir are entered and recorded—that of Cadder being argent, a *plain* bend sable, charged with three buckles or ; while that of Keir, on the other hand, has the bend *ingrailed* vert, the accompaniments being the same as the other.[1]

¹ See Keir Performance, following p. 12, where there is a coloured engraving of both arms, just as in the original.

There can be no reasonable doubt of their being accurately and correctly represented, having necessarily met the eye, and been subjected to the revision, scrutiny, and approbation, of the preceding able and accomplished Lord Lyon, the best conceivable authority in the case, and which we must admit and prefer to the exclusion of all others, whatever previous contrary notions or apprehensions, either in public or private, the presumed result of inadvertence or carelessness, may be entertained in the matter.

In the preceding matriculations there is obviously a material difference in the shape and figure of the bend—Cadder's being plain, while Keir's is ingrailed—to which attention is invited as the subject of after discussion. In the mean time, that they so far, in that cardinal point, were manifestly observed and adopted as the *regula regulans* in practice, will next be established.

Authorities and precedents in exact keeping and observance with Sir David's register in respect to the Cadder and Keir arms.

The writer may first here adduce a long extended parchment roll of arms, preserved in the Advocates' Library, Edinburgh, entitled, " Ye cotts of 267 name and title, autograph of Sir James, at the beginning—

"1630.

" Jacobus Balfourius, Kynardie, Miles Leo Armorum Rex."

And what is more important still, the MS. near the end has the following attestation, also autograph of Sir James, expressly and decidedly in its behalf:—" This booke and *registre* of arms *done* by Schir David Lindsay of the Mouth (Mount), Lyone King of Armes *regni Jac.* 5, conteines 106 leaves, which re-

gister was *approvin* be the *Lordes* of his majesties most honorable *Privee Counsal* at Halirud House, 9 December 1630." Such formal attestation brings the register still more home to Sir David as his proper official handiwork, besides showing that it was approved of, and had the regular sanction of, that high body, the Privy Council of Scotland. It only remains to be added, that the Cadder and Keir matriculations are included in the MS., within its 106 leaves mentioned, and thus form a valid and authentic portion of the record.

Knights,* .... landed gentlemen of ye Kingdome of Scotland as they *rer* (were) presented to our Soverane Lady Marie, by the grace of God, Queine of Scotland and Dowager of France, by Schir † .... Forman, Lyone King of Arms, in *anno* 1562." It proves to be a copy by Sir James Balfour, Lord Lyon to Charles I., formerly mentioned, from the original, that must have been made out under the auspices of Sir Robert Forman of Luthrie, the Lord Lyon, as stated,‡ the above year, and as will afterwards be proved. The arms of the respective parties are distinctly delineated with a pen on separate shields, with their names and titles above, the colours of the charges on the latter being indicated by initial letters: and those of "Striveling of Cadder" are represented as argent, a *plain* bend "black" or sable, charged with three buckles or; while those of "Streveling" (a blank here following in the title), argent, a bend ingrailed *vert* (or green), charged with three buckles or. Hence, the Cadder coat is thus precisely as depicted in Sir David Lindsay's register, as also the last mentioned, which could be no other than that of Keir, from its identity with the Keir matriculation there. But here the former directly and distinctly presents itself, the latter only anonymously. The male Cadder heirs and representatives certainly, then, came within the category of landed gentlemen or proprietors comprised in the roll, and therefore their arms (in other words, those of Cadder) would be included in the list, as they will also be proved to be in others to be adduced.

We have, therefore, the additional recognition and corroboration by another later (and also, as could be proved) noted Lord Lyon in 1562, of the plain bend being the indisputable right of the Stirlings of Cadder—precisely as entered in Sir David Lindsay's register, showing it to be the rule and standard in the case; while, on the other hand, the bend ingrailed as clearly Keir's, under an anonymous guise.

All writers agree that Queen Mary, then Dowager of France, returned to Scotland, after the death of her royal spouse, in August 1561, though the precise day be uncertain.

It was but natural, from every motive, that the *elite* of Scotland, embracing those in Forman the Lyon's roll, would be anxious to be presented to and greet their sovereign on her arrival, after so prolonged an absence from

---

* There is a blank here, from a small part of the parchment being torn away, on the parchment, or its age, precluding the deciphering of this blank.

† A dimness intervenes here, owing to a stain

‡ It is among his MSS. of a similar kind in the public repository mentioned.

it, since her very infancy. She was admitted at the time, even by her foes, to have been in the meridian of a beauty heightened, by inherent graces and endowments, beyond the power of a French education,—to such extent, to use the words of Buchanan, afterwards a bitter enemy, that (in her respect) "*natura rudis, ars videatur inops;*" and being naturally of a kind disposition, when not politically warped (and even then she could politely dissemble), could not but on this occasion be graciously disposed to receive the former. And how could the reception be more adequately and formally adjusted than by the above-mentioned Sir Robert Forman, the Lord Lyon (who certainly held that high and courtly office in 1561 and 1563, hence including 1562*), and by his preliminary announcement to the Queen, through the roll, of their respective names (*bating Keir's*) and arms, so much prized by their owners, and that were in part afterwards to be displayed before her on public festivals and at tournaments, which she gaily and warmly patronised. Pressing business, doubtless, and the perplexing cabals of the austere clergy, might have delayed the reception immediately upon her arrival in 1561 ; therefore 1562, the very next year, might have been more suitable, and, accordingly, was that of the presentment of the roll.

In perfect keeping, moreover, with the accounts of the Cadder and Keir arms in the Forman roll, as also, in the main, with Sir David Lindsay's register, as far back as James V.'s reign, both coats are, in like manner, represented in an old illuminated MS. of Scottish blazons and arms, also in the reign of Queen Mary, preserved in the Advocates' Library, to be more particularly adduced in the sequel, as it will likewise corroborate another important fact.

[1] Vol. 1. p 43

[2] Acts of Sederunt in 1700; p. 4.

[3] P. 77.

* Chalmers, in his notices of Sir David Lindsay, and edition of his works,[1] quotes a Commission by Queen Mary, upon record, 16th April 1561 (thus before her arrival in Scotland), to "our lovit Schir Robert Forman of Luthrie, Lyon King of Armes ;" and on March 10, 1561 (that is, at the end of the year, it then beginning on the 25th of March), "Mr Robert Forman, of ——, *Knycht, Lyoun King* of Arms,"[2] protested against the cognisance of the Supreme Civil Court in a question between him and their macers. And, lastly, we may here adduce this passage from the *Pollock Diurnal of Events :* "Upon the xxii, of September" (1563, from what precedes),[3] "Matho, sumtyme Erle of Levinax, wes, be oppin proclamatioun at the Mercat Croce of Edinburgh, relaxit fra the proces of our Soverane Ladie's horne be *Schir Robert Foirman* of *Luthrie, Knycht, Lyoun* King of Armes, and all the officiaris of armes, and deliverit the wand of peax to Johne Erle of Atholl, wha ressavit the samyn in the said Erlis name." This was the noted restoration of the Lennox family, after their forfeiture, that paved the way to the marriage of the Queen with Darnley. Sir Robert Forman must thus also have been Lord Lyon in the intervening year of 1562 ; and what might be more material about him could be adduced if required.

Not only in Scotland, but even in England too, as is remarkable, the peculiar Cadder and Keir armorial bearings, as above, were familiar and admitted, evincing them to be fixed and certain. In the British Museum there is an old manuscript, in 1580, entitled "Irish, *Scottish*, and Yorkshire coates, with other *outlandish* armes," where, under the head of "Scottish coates of their *gentilitie*"—that is, obviously, of the gentility and upper classes of Scotland—"*Streveling* of KEDAR" (clearly Cadder) is stated to bear "argent on a [bend] three buckles or," and "Strevyling of *Kert*" (as obviously Keir), "argent (a bend) *ingrailed three fermales*"* (buckles). Here the material distinction of the ingrailing in the Keir instance—while the *plain* bend, from the absence of any notice of it in the other, must be presumed—is as evident as ever; and the bend in both cases is above put within brackets, because it is in the MS. exclusively indicated by a slanting line, quite equivalent to the heraldic bend dexter in both the arms.

Even in England the technical distinction between the Cadder and Keir bends was well known in the 16th century.

And again, we may cite another MS. account still, in 1585, of the arms of the Scottish nobility and commoners, by the English Joseph Holland, in the same highly-prized and prolific repository, who quite corroboratively assigns to "Sterling of *Kert* (*Keir*), argent, a bend *ingrailed* blue, with three buckles or;" and to "Sterling of *Cadder*, argent, a bend *plain* blue, three buckles or."† Seldom, indeed, can such close uniformity in the main, with a cardinal standard like Sir David Lindsay's Register, in the present instance, be detected in *re tam antiqua*, removing any doubt on the point; and, if required, we might further appeal, so far as regards the Cadder arms, to Workman, the herald's, illuminated MS. book of the "Bearings of the Nobility and Barons," and higher landed proprietors of Scotland, in the reign of James VI., frequently referred to by Nisbet,[1] where the former, displaying the plain bend sable,

Workman's authority in support of the plain Cadder bend.

[1] See his Heraldry, first edit., Preface, p. iii.

---

* The same evidently as "Fermail," which is rendered a "*boucle, attache, fibula*," in supplement to Du Cange, *sub voce Fermalium*. Though the main features of the respective arms be preserved in the preceding and subsequent instances, there are occasional variations of the colours.

† There is a curious armorial device of the Earls of Lennox, after the middle of the same century, in these heraldic MSS.—nowhere noticed, so far as the writer knows—of the royal orb delineated after "The," and before the words "is to me," indicating, seemingly, that it or the crown was in "me," or their noble representative, or hoped to be so. This "poesy," as it was styled, and taken along with the orb occasionally as their crest by the earls in question, was similar to the motto of the Bourbons, "*Esperance*," assumed when cadets, and indicating the hope of succeeding also to the French crown, eventually realised. Want of room here alone prevents the writer explaining what he believes to have been the groundwork of the above striking Lennox device.

154   COMMENTS ON KEIR PERFORMANCE,

charged with three buckles or, are clearly included in the proper place, although it so happens that the names and titles of the parties are omitted, while, singularly, there is *no* mention of the Keir arms.

We next come, in further illustration in regard to Keir, to Nisbet's congruent intimation,[1] that "on the house of Falahall, where the arms of many of the barons of Scotland were illuminate in the year 1604," " are these of Stirling of Keir, argent, on a *bend* INGRAILED sable, three buckles or ;" and what is better still, and indeed best, to that expressly of the Keir Performance, June 2, 1662,[2] that Sir George Sterling of Keir, on the occasion of his being knighted, had " gott his armes extracted furth of the register on parchment by Thomas Drysdale" (a herald previously mentioned), "*quhilk* was, argent, a *bend* INGRAILED sable, three buckles or ; and for his crest, set on a wreath, ane savage head couped, having a ribbon, gules, or wreath about his head " (that has been partly already spoken to). The extract necessarily must have been from the Register of Arms in the Lyon Office,* in the main in keeping with that of Sir David Lindsay's, its proper authority, with the specialty of the bend being represented sable instead of vert as there ; to which the crest has, of course, been recently added. But, at any rate, it is now thereby—coupled with what was shown—proved conclusively, and *ex abundanti*, that the bend *ingrailed* was the true *distinctive* Keir bearing ; so much so, that it is hardly necessary to add, that such charge in 1700 is likewise ascribed by Father Hay,[3] a noted antiquary, to the Keir family—though *gules withal*, or *red* in its colour. This unfortunate Keir bend—

"*Camelcon*-like, that has so *many* hues !"

The cardinal point in question, therefore, as to Keir, is fixed ; while, on the other hand, it is as clear that the Stirlings of Cadder, uniformly since the time we can adequately and decisively pronounce on the subject, bore their bend (with the buckles, of course) quite plain, as is represented in Sir David Lindsay's, the Lord Lyon, Register, the ultimate authority, and clearly *regula regulans* in the matter.

To the last moment of their existence in *statu quo*, and even, as we have seen, long afterwards, the same arms have been ascribed to, and admitted in, the former ; and that the fact, never properly gainsaid or refuted subsequently,

[1] Heraldry, first edit., p. 410.
Further corroborations of the *ingrailed* Keir bend.
[2] Ibid., pp. 49, 50.

[3] To be afterwards referred to.

---

* It was subsequently burned by a noted fire in Edinburgh, together with many valuable heraldic writs and vouchers, so much to be regretted, in consequence of which we had afterwards what was styled the "*new*" Register of Arms in the Lyon Office.

has not the copious illustration of the differenced ingrailed Keir bend, is well accounted for by their ceasing so to figure, and the comparatively reduced means of the direct Cadder male representatives—a sore deprivation certainly, but for which we may leave the Keir family to answer.

Now, to elicit the necessary conclusion from the above, it is heraldically fixed that the simplest and plainest charges in coats-of-arms are the best and most pre-eminent, while any modification or alteration of them bespeaks the bearer to be of a subordinate distinct stock or race, though bearing the same surname.

Nisbet in effect inculcates this in principle, when he remarks,[1] that "the more the *bordures* (in arms) are *varied from plain ones*, by *accidental forms*, and charged with figures, they show the bearers to be *further removed* from the *principal* house;" indeed, he might have added, distinct from it: thus, *e converso*, clearly giving the preference to such as are plain, as peculiarly indicating and denoting its representation. "Bordures," or borders, in heraldry, are here in *pari casu* with the chief "chevron" and bend: and these all technically and equally fix and illustrate the present point.

[1] Heraldry, second edit., vol. ii. p. 10, under "Additional Figures in Heraldry."

Their modifications and differences consist, *inter alia*, in their being represented, instead of simply and plainly, peculiar, as premised, to the chiefs of a surname, on the other hand, embattled or *counter*-embattled—that is, embattled after a vandyke fashion, or *ingrailed*. In support of which we may select the following instances:—

The ancient and noble family of Keith, Earl Marischal, head of the Keiths, bore a *plain* chief, gules, charged with three pallets or;[2] and the Keiths of Craig,[3] who, whatever some of our genealogists may affirm, cannot connect themselves by proper or admissible evidence with that house, though, like Keir in respect to Cadder, of the same surname, took the above chief, but with the difference of its being *embattled*, besides a border.

Fully corroborated, too, by precedents and authorities.

[2] See Nisbet's Heraldry, first edit., vol. i. p. 70.

[3] See ibid., p. 75.

The noble family of Sandilands,[4] Lords Torphichen, bear, for Sandilands, a plain bend, precisely like that of Stirling of Cadder, but azure instead of sable. And Mr James Sandilands of Craibston, a Sandilands subordinate, who neither could connect by proper proof with the former, took the bend, as Nisbet informs us,[5] "*counter*-*embattled* the paternal coat of Sandilands (as) *differenced* from the *chief* bearing." Here he directly represents and admits the modification or alteration of the simple bend through the *counter-embattling*—corresponding precisely with its being ingrailed in heraldry—to be a difference applicable and suitable to an inferior of the same surname.

[4] See ibid., p. 94.

[5] See ibid., p. 95.

The knightly family of Riddell of Riddell, chiefs of the name, have uniformly borne "argent, a chevron, gules (quite *plain*), between three ears of rye, slipped and bladed, vert;" and Walter Riddell of Minto, as Nisbet intimates[1] in the "New Register of Arms" (in the Lyon Court), bore, "argent, a chevron, *ingrailed* gules (instead of plain, *ut supra*), betwixt three ears of rye, slipped and bladed, vert." Here the latter, like the Stirlings of Keir, exclusively differenced by *ingrailing* the charge of the chevron, as the former did the bend ; and yet the Riddells of Minto were quite unconnected with Riddell of Riddell, nor in any degree could prove a descent from them.*

[1] See Nisbet's Heraldry, first edit., vol. I. pp. 374, 375.

Law of Lawbridge in Galloway, according to Nisbet again,[2] "is the *principal* family of the name," and "carried, argent, a *bend* (quite *plain*), and cock in chief, gules ;" while Edward Law, the present Earl of Ellenborough, though quite a stranger, and unconnected with the former, yet bears corresponding arms—viz. two cocks and a bend, but *ingrailed*. Here the bend again, just as contended, comes appositely and directly into play.

[2] See ibid., p. 356.

To close with a higher and more distinguished precedent, at least equally in point. Sir John Stewart, ordinarily styled of Bonkill, younger brother of James, High Steward of Scotland, direct male ancestor of the royal house of Stewart, bore, as proved by his seal of arms appended to his bond of fealty to Edward I. in 1236, over the fess cheque,[3] for Stewart, and as the peculiar distinctive arms of his branch or house (of which they were male descendants), a simple plain bend, precisely like Stirling of Cadder.

[3] Original in Chapter-House of Westminster.

From Sir John, any one who now claims to be male representative of the Stewarts must deduce his descent, all previous heirs-male having failed ; so that both he and his arms, as a paramount *terminus a quo*, have been especial objects of care and attention. None as yet have accomplished the task.

The noble house of the Stewarts of Garlees, Earls of Galloway, towards the close of last century, indirectly unsuccessfully attempted it,† and though

---

* The writer can speak confidently on this head, being a cadet of the preceding knightly stem, and well versed, he believes, in the pedigrees and descents of all of the name.

† It was certainly a most impracticable effort, exclusively turning upon the suppositious identity of William Stewart, a simple *ecuyer*, who fell with his elder brother, Sir John Stewart of Darnley, at the siege of Or-

leans in 1429 (here the Bonkill link of connection), with Sir William Stewart of Jedworth, the Galloway ancestor, who publicly figured as a *knight* as far back as 1385, and who was proved (which the writer can further corroborate) to have *died* long antecedently, having been unjustly executed by the English either in 1402 or 1403.

It was, indeed, though strangely, keenly and

they established their male pedigree from Sir William Stewart of Jedworth, who figured towards the end of the fourteenth century, and died in 1404 —their most remote ancestor (precisely like John de Strivelin in that of Keir, 1338), beyond whom they could not go ; and though distinguished and highly connected, they yet, in reference to Sir John of Boukill—like Keir, as is conceived, to Cadder—must be deemed, if we may use the term, but abstract subordinates. They have, as appropriately, and like his family again, and indicative of the same genealogical rank and status, uniformly taken their corresponding bend, based upon Sir John's simple one (the Stirling of Cadder, we may hold, in their instance), over their fess cheque for Stewart, with the exact difference of its being *ingrailed*. No two cases can be conceived more parallel, or better exemplifying the bend in its two phases.

Their arms, too, are so precisely representing of in Forman's, the Lord Lyon, roll of arms in 1592, that was referred to. see pp. 150, 151.

Applying, therefore, the above relevant tests and precedents to the arms, as proved, of the Stirlings of Cadder and Stirlings of Keir, those of the former must designate in heraldry the chief and principal family of the name (indeed as concurrently represented in the Stirling pedigree in the Keir Performance), through their preferable and legally authorised plain and unmodified bend ; while that of the latter, being, on the other hand, modified or ingrailed, a subordinate one—not connected either with the other.

From the heraldic doctrine and precedents stated, the plain bend of the Stirlings of Cadder arms proves them the preferable family, and chiefs of the Stirlings.

And this finally receives direct confirmation from an old original illuminated book of blazons or arms of the nobility and barons of Scotland—formerly in part alluded to—in the time of Queen Mary, preserved in the Advocates' Library, Edinburgh. Under the category of the barons there (in the sense commonly used by us), we find a coat-of-arms exhibiting a bend *ingrailed* azure (instead, here, of vert), charged with three buckles or, on a field argent ; and another with a *plain* bend sable, also charged with three buckles or, on a field argent. The last, evidently, are the arms of Stirling of Cadder, just as represented in that decisive authority, Sir David Lindsay's Register, in the reign of James V., and hence alone evincing them—there being no other parallel of the kind—to be theirs.

publicly agitated at the time, between John, then Earl of Galloway, and the celebrated Audrew Stuart of Torrance and Castelmilk, his opponent, who stood on other ground—a very different case of identity from that of Robert Stirling of Letter with Robert, Janet of Cadder's heir, in 1541. The above leading and decisive facts will be obvious enough on a close perusal of the controversy.

But while the first-mentioned coat, that may be quite familiar and intelligible to us (though with the difference of the colour of the bend), has the appropriate title of "Stirling of the *Keyr*," thus disclosing the owner—and affording further proof, as was observed, of his apposite heraldic difference of the ingrailed bend—the other, *par excellence*, has actually, with the same view, the more significant and transcendent one of "*Skirmiling of* YAT ILK,"—that is clearly of "Stirling of that Ilk," for it could be nothing else (the orthography throughout not being—as indeed the Keir work informs us—in many such old instances, uniform or correct), and which, to all acquainted with Scottish language and epithets, inevitably proves the holder of the arms to be chief of the family and surname of Stirling, at the same time, from the latter, identified with Stirling of Cadder.

<small>Further points of corroboration here.</small>

It was clearly on this ground that Cadder, relevantly and conclusively, had the plain bend allowed him, and duly recorded in Sir David Lindsay's Register, while Keir only that ingrailed and subordinate,—the difference bespeaking, as was explained, their respective status and condition. The writer is thus happy in for once agreeing with the Keir Performance, and supplying a confirmation, *inter alia*, of their uniform recognition and admission—as so plainly inculcated there—of such chieftainship being in Cadder, besides, actually, a *new* spelling of Stirling, as above, to add to the felicitous list of sixty-four instances—whereunto, *mirabile dictu*, he may even further contribute in the sequel—with which the editor has so successfully and beneficially favoured the public, telling powerfully, at least *numero*, however some audacious and rash cavillers may perchance object to their *mensura* or intrinsic weight and importance.[1]

<small>Indeed, the Keir Performance admits Cadder to be chief of the Stirlings, or thus Stirling of that Ilk.

[1] See Keir Performance, p. 54s.</small>

It hence, now, is abundantly obvious what constituted the arms of Cadder, chief and principal of the Stirlings. They were most justly and competently, together with supporters as a due concomitant, formally confirmed by the Lyon Court, in 1818, to Andrew Stirling of Drumpellier, upon the express footing—*inter alia*, much more articulately and broadly set forth and stated than in his antecedent brief before the Sheriff-Substitute, that has been alluded to, in that year—of his being the nearest Cadder heir and representative, and who thereby alone would be entitled to them, notwithstanding the Keir work malignantly and most irrelevantly affects to scowl at the procedure,[2] under favour of a gross misrepresentation exposed,[3] and on the futility that the above court, duly vested with its own *peculiar* inherent

<small>The same principal Cadder arms, with identical status of chief of the Stirlings, or of Cadder, long and irretrievably vested in Drumpellier.

[2] See Keir Performance, p. 151.

[3] See p. 9 of Exposition.</small>

cognisance in such matters, were *de plano* forsooth to be barred and trammelled by the crude unauthorised finding, as proved and protested against, of an inferior *leguleius* and officiary, not possessing it, and in a case, too, of a different form and compass.

It would, of a truth, have been far better had the Keir of that day, in accordance with what is now ADVENTURED for his family in such lucubrations —though most gratuitously and preposterously—then fairly met and manfully opposed Drumpellier, if he conceived himself to have had a preferable right. But this neither he nor they ever ventured to do on one single occasion, when legal steps were taken by that of Drumpellier to vindicate their just gentilitial rights. They could only bark in secret, or attempt to move, as now for the first time, lamely and impotently enough, in a private character, under favour of the preceding.

The Keir family latterly contrived, last century, in the face of Sir David Lindsay's Register, to have their bend vert ingrailed, exalted then to a plain one azure, in which guise Nisbet, after noticing its being ingrailed on the house of Falahall in 1604, informs us it was entered in the "New Register" of the Lyon Court. In this, however (though it has evoked the criticism of Mylne, no secondary antiquary, and a great collector of old MSS., in one of his MS. in the Advocates' Library *), the Drumpellier family feel but little concern, nor are at all solicitous to know the ground of the alteration, to which, on the contrary, they heartily bid them welcome. They are quite content with their own regular unexceptionable matriculation adduced in 1818, which irrevocably or literally "*unrepealably*" secures to them what they humbly apprehend to be the far preferable *distinctive* charge in the Cadder arms, or those necessarily as shown by chief of the Stirlings—viz. the *plain* bend *sable* (instead of azure), just *precisely* as it is recorded in the authentic ruling Register of Sir David Lindsay, the celebrated Lord Lyon in the reign of James V., together with the due concomitant of supporters. The *sable*,

Vast absurdity of the Keir work that would trammel the Lyon Court by a Sheriff-Substitute's act, in a competent case before it, undiscussed before the latter, and to whom it was incompetent; while that work gives and takes arms ad libitum, proprio arbitrio, without control!

Keir family contrived last century to have their bend ingrailed, exalted to a simple one azure; but this is immaterial to Drumpellier, he holding the principal one in terms of Sir David Lindsay's Register.

---

* When actually stating this new matriculation (which he gives without mention, no more than Nisbet in his *Heraldry*, of its conveying any right to supporters), and where, after noticing the antecedent ingrailing of the Keir bend, he objects against its new form, that "if" thus "it be borne plain and azure, it's ye *same* wyt ye arms of Leslie." This is no doubt true, and a relevant objection, for it should always be remembered that, properly and in keeping with its origin at the Crusades, as well as its material bent and purport subsequently, heraldry is to difference, *not assimilate*—the result of this complete identity of the two arms in question, and that, if broadly admitted, would render it in a great measure nugatory and a dead letter. Happily the Cadder, now Drumpellier, plain bend sable is not obnoxious to the charge.

they may perhaps be permitted to say, here transcends the *azure*. They *alone* bear *such* bend, with the super-imposition of the Stirling buckles, to which they are thus exclusively entitled,—a right they honestly maintain, as they ever will do, in the face of the world,—and *guerre a qui le touche.*

There is, it may be observed, another piece of carelessness and negligence in the way, partly, in which the Keir arms are given in the Keir Performance, at the conclusion of the Keir pedigree.[1] It is *merely* stated, independently of the *arms* (using the term here in a *strict* sense), that the "*crest*" is "a *Moor's head in profile,*" and the "supporters two greyhounds." How unheraldic really, and unbefitting a true antiquary!—there being here no mention of their colours, so important in heraldry—whether the above should be "*proper*"—that is, in their natural guise, or otherwise depicted, as so often obtains there. And yet the editor had, in respect to the crest, data to direct him, which he has completely overlooked. On the occasion of the knighting of Sir George Stirling of Keir, June 2, 1662, it is mentioned in the work,[2] as was premised, that he then got for his crest (*inter alia*), by the extract "furth of the register," on a wreath, "ane savage head *couped*, having a ribbon *gules* (*red*) or wreath about his head;" while Nisbet,[3] quoting from the Keir matriculation in the "New Register" in the Lyon Court referred to, represents it as "a Moor's head *couped proper.*" Here both the *cut* and *position* of the head, with its colour, are pointedly and technically defined, yet without the editor, as was imperative, in the least availing himself of the information. As for the colour of the *supporters*, that is a point not so easily settled; for judging by Mylne's[4] and Nisbet's accounts of the matriculation (quite differently from the Drumpellier in 1818), none, so far as we can see, were thereby granted; and Nisbet only adds, that "the family had *been in use* to carry two greyhounds for supporters. But the editor might, it is thought, and ought to have been, apprised by them how they should be depicted, and stated it in the Performance, if the common method and regularity was to be adopted, as is notoriously elsewhere, and to which, in a work of such professed grandeur and scale, there should not have been an exception. Whether supporters thus assumed, but at what date seems uncertain (and of course they are not in Sir David Lindsay's matriculation), were actually otherwise granted, the writer cannot say, nor is it a point in which the Drumpellier family feel peculiarly interested.

But, on the head of the Keir arms, the work strangely exhibits a *re-*

Marginal notes:

Carelessness and want of precision in giving parts of the Keir arms in the Keir Performance, though possessing the best sources of information.

[1] See p. 82.

[2] See p. 50.

[3] See Heraldry, first edit., vol. i. p. 410.

[4] See p. 159, note.

duplication of carelessness and negligence, though not by any means there unprecedented. It professes to give them at the place cited as they were "engraved on the back of the title-page."[1] But this is quite erroneous. On that portion of the same *peccant* page at the outset, which, with the other, has been the subject of pointed comment, the arms have besides the addition of the *fillet*, wanting in the above to the Keir Moor's head, independently of the denounced interpolated old, and, it is conceived, usurped Cadder crest in 1492,—perhaps, after all, prudently or compunctiously omitted on the later occasion. But still there should be accuracy in plain matters of fact, which is here disregarded.

[1] See Keir Performance again, p. 82.

CHAPTER V.

PRELIMINARY REMARKS, AND EXPOSITION OF UNDUE ASSUMPTION OF THE STIRLING AND CADDER STATUS, AS CHIEF OF THE NAME, BY KEIR—WITH GROSS MISREPRESENTATIONS, ETC., IN THE KEIR PERFORMANCE—INCLUDING USURPATION THERE OF THE OLD CADDER CREST, THROUGH WHICH A FINE AND ESCHEAT OF THE WORK TO THE CROWN IS INCURRED BY AN ACT OF PARLIAMENT—THE KEIR ORIGIN AND DESCENT, THOUGH IMMATERIAL TO THE DRUMPELLIER FAMILY, WHOSE CADDER STATUS HAS BEEN FIXED AND RECOGNISED, NEVERTHELESS NEXT GONE INTO—THE SAME UNCERTAIN—NO CLUE THERETO SUPPLIED BY THEIR FIRST POSSESSIONS, AS IN THE CADDER AND DRUMPELLIER INSTANCES—JOHN DE STRIWELYNE, SO SIMPLY STYLED (AND NEVER OF RATHORAN) IN 1338, THEIR PRESUMED ANCESTOR—QUITE UNAPPANAGED, AND SOLELY INDEBTED TO HIS WIFE, A LADY OF FAMILY, FOR AN INTEREST IN ANY LANDS, RATHER STRANGELY SETTLED EXCLUSIVELY UPON HER AND HER HEIRS—THE SETTLEMENT INCIDENTALLY AFFORDS THE ONLY GLIMPSE OF JOHN, OF WHOSE FAMILY, TOO, NOTHING TRANSPIRES—A COMPLETE BLANK INTERVENES FROM THENCE DOWN TO 1414 AND 1423—REPUTATION OF ERRONEOUS REPRESENTATIONS AND BARE ASSUMPTIONS TO THE CONTRARY IN THE KEIR WORK—WITH IMPRESSIONS AND INFERENCES AS TO THE KEIR ORIGIN AND DESCENT *IN HOC STATU*—LUKE STIRLING OF WESTER RATHERNE (A SMALL PROPERTY, HOW ACQUIRED UNCERTAIN) AN ARMIGER OR SQUIRE, AND *ARTIFEX SUÆ FORTUNÆ*, PROPERLY THE KEIR FOUNDER, A MAN OF TALENT AND RESPECTABILITY, FROM WHOM THE KEIR DESCENT DOWNWARDS IS PLAIN—THE KEIR FAMILY FIRST BARONIAL IN 1473—CHARGE MOOTED AGAINST SIR WILLIAM STIRLING OF KEIR OF BEING PARTICIPANT IN THE MURDER OF JAMES V., WITH SOME NEW EVIDENCE—UPON THE WHOLE, NO PROPER PROOF YET OF A KEIR-CADDER DESCENT, FAR LESS REPRESENTATION, THAT OUGHT NEVER TO HAVE BEEN STARTED—KEIR ORIGIN STILL UNASCERTAINED, AND DEMANDING INVESTIGATION—NEW EVIDENCE MEANWHILE BY THE WRITER OF THE PRECEDING LUKE STIRLING OF RATHERNE IN 1414, AND A PROPERTY HELD BY HIM, FAVOURABLE TO HIS RANK AND CHARACTER.

THE exponent might here stop, and bid adieu to his readers, apologising for that tediousness and repetition of which he may have been guilty, and which is but too prevalent in antiquarian discussions,—the object of the exposition, so far as he can see, being fully compassed and attained. For more than forty years, without the least demur or challenge, the Drumpelliers, under proper authority, have held the proud status of representatives of the family of Cadder, who are admitted, even by that of Keir, to be the principal stock and chiefs of the Stirlings,—while the latter aspire only to be but distant Cadder cadets. Indeed, the Drumpelliers never have had a competitor on the merits of the question; for although Keir once came forward with the intention of advancing his claims, he quickly withdrew and left the field, as if scared by his own footsteps. Drumpellier thus standing on impregnable legal ground, and it being evident, by his pedigree or descent, when justly viewed, that Keir, independently of other striking objections, has no interest or concern in the matter, it may be asked by some, why the former should even go into the present discussion? For whatever the bent and import of the Keir Performance, it is quite without the pale of law, and is so far in its unauthorised and irregular shape—its groundworks, too, being but *petitiones principii*—no more to be feared and valued than the mere blusterings of Æolus in his empty hall, or the vague and wild ruminations of one in his private study.

<small>The Drumpellier-Cadder right being legally fixed, properly supersedes the necessity of more.</small>

Nevertheless, still holding to the ascertained position of Drumpellier, and the inviolability of his legally foreclosed status, the writer, in order to preclude the *manifest misrepresentations* of the Keir Performance *ex facie* from misleading, or any way compromising and *injuring* the exponent's *interests*, as also with that love of fairness which urges him to justify his views of certain portions of the work, and finally to exhaust the whole of an antiquarian subject, will again direct attention to the said Performance, especially to that part of it which contains what is to form the principal topic of the present chapter—viz. the pedigree and descent of the Stirlings of Keir.

<small>Nevertheless, though the Keir origin and descent he now im-material, the Keir work shall be further canvassed, chiefly to refute gross injurious misrepresentations that *ex facie* might mislead.</small>

And he will first commence with the subject of the asserted Keir-Cadder origin.

The gradations in the varied assumptions of the Keir Performance, in this instance, are indeed notable and curious. It is first only "*presumed*" by the editor[1] (gratuitously of course) that Sir William Stirling (a very remote putative ancestor), repeatedly alluded to, who figured before and after 1300, and who is represented there as third and youngest son of John Stirling of Ochiltrie (and third and youngest brother of Alexander Stirling of Cadder), was "*ancestor* of the *Keir* line." But gathering courage, he next, at the actual outset of "the Keir line" and pedigree,[2] by boldly placing the said Sir William as the first, and at its head, announces as an undoubted fact what before was only presumed. This is pretty well for a beginning! And

<small>[1] See Keir Performance, pp. 7, 8.</small>

<small>[2] Ibid., p. 13.</small>

moreover, under the "Contents,"[1] the knight is inserted as the connecting link, and as one of the "*generations*" between the subsequent Keir line and the antecedent pedigree stated, through John, his father, from Sir Alexander, father of the latter again (in 1180-1245), and a motley anterior class up to 1130! The entire generations in question are *seriatim* numbered, *as if actually obtaining* through father and son from that very distant epoch downward;[2] and the present Keir is in this way made the *twentieth* by lineal descent from the first Walter Stirling, the alleged original ancestor represented to have figured in the above year. Such a pedigree, not easily established ordinarily—not some even of far less compass—is yet gravely given to us as a reality, though resting on mere assumption and fable. What apology can there be for it, considering the readers the editor has to deal with, and whose judgment and intelligence he must estimate very lowly, if he thinks for a moment they can thereby be deceived?

And of a piece and in keeping with this pleasing delusion so set forth, he as gratuitously and unscrupulously holds and styles the preceding Sir William, before and after 1300, "ANCESTOR" of Luke Stirling of Ratherne in 1448,[3]—giving them mutually the same arms, to the identification of their common origin,—the family of Keir, it seems, being directly descended of the former, which clenches the matter to his own satisfaction.

But we have not yet reached the climax of such castle-building, for finally, as a corollary to the whole—quite ignoring Drumpellier and every other competitor—Keir, in virtue of the above, is made to soar to the utmost gentilitial heights, and not only in the work to be made heir and chief of Cadder, but of all other Stirlings, even from the most remote and distant period.[4] We are here insensibly reminded of Bunbury's caricature of the progress of *error* (which we would kindly substitute for the mendacious term), or more pertinently remark, in reference to such vain editorial attempts, that "what was but a *presumption* in one page was in the next *positive* evidence, and then rose to a *demonstration*"[5]—to use the actual words of Lord Alemore in his exposure of another faulty argument so constructed, in his speech in the celebrated Douglas Cause in 1767.

So far as to the Keir descent from a putative ancestor in the shape of a most remote Cadder cadet; but what shall we say, again, to these palpable untruths and misrepresentations which the Performance risks?[6]—viz. (1.) That "the Cawder estate in the sixteenth century descended to an heiress" (Janet, of Cadder), "who married her kinsman, Sir James Stirling of Keir, *and* THUS the *Cawder* and *Keir* families *became* UNITED;"[1] and (2.) That "Sir James Striveling married the heiress of Cawder in 1534, and THUS *united* the families of *Keir* and *Cawder*;" while, after discussing the same Janet, it announces that it had "now traced the main or *Cawder line till its* JUNC-TION with the Keir branch,"[2] the descent of which branch, it adds, "will next be shown;" which accordingly follows, under the title of "the Keir line," with Sir William Stirling, their supposititious ancestor, as its patriarch!

<small>Gross misrepresentations in Keir work as to Keir representing Cadder.

[1] Keir Performance, under the "Origin of the Stirlings," p. 3.

[2] See p. 13.</small>

The above is bad and faulty enough, yet the editor, according to his fashion, must soar still higher in error; and, moreover, asserts (1.) That the Cawder line "terminated in an heiress, who was married to James Stirling of Keir, and *thus* AGAIN *united* both families;"[3] and (2.) That "Sir James Striveling married the heiress of Cawder in 1534, and thus RE-*united* the families of Keir and Cawder,"—hence preposterously exaggerating, and even doubling, such putative union!

<small>Two even more exaggerated and preposterous untruths.

[3] Text History of the Stirlings, p. 8.; Contents, p. iv.</small>

With respect to the above marrying, or rather *giving* in marriage (*by* the EDITOR), it has yet been shown that there was no marriage at all between the above parties—that *de facto* celebrated against Janet of Cadder's will having, by the decreet of divorce in 1541, been declared null and void;[4] it further bearing that the same "*a* PRINCIPIO NON *tenuisse, nec viribus subsistere posse de* JURE." Such illegal connection could never constitute a union, as is thus asserted, nor could the before-mentioned *assumed* and visionary descent from Sir William Stirling tie the present Keirs to the Cadder family, as is implied by the most reprehensible words "again united" and "*reunited*,"—the supposititious results of both fictions in the passages cited.

<small>No legal marriage here between Keir and Cadder.

[4] See Exposition, p. 65.</small>

There was no union, reunion, nor proper junction between the families. There never had been, there was not then, and has not been still—however certainly a peculiar legal specialty operates, as was shown, in favour of the legitimacy of the issue of Janet of Cadder by Keir,[5] but within which category the present family of Keir do not come. The preceding passages are not the less obviously calculated to lead casual readers into glaring error. They convey the impression that the present Keir may represent Cadder in both the male and female lines, than which nothing can be more contrary to truth. The fact of his possessing the property of Cadder proves nothing, because the original cardinal right merely through a *singular* title by which he holds it, is well known. The representation of a family, of a

<small>[5] See here, p. 106 of the Exposition, including the note, ibid.</small>

truth, does not go with the property into the hands of a purchaser, the former being here exactly in *pari casu*. Of a piece, again, with the foregoing, is the following account, which certainly is out-heroding Herod :—

"The Stirlings" (evidently meaning the Keirs from the context) " first appear as owners of land in the twelfth century. After possessing lands in different counties, they acquired, in the reign of William the Lion, the estate of Cawder, which has continued in the family without interruption to the present time, a period of nearly seven centuries. Few families can boast an inheritance which has descended through so long a line of ancestors."[1]

Keir's right to Cawder estate only through a singular title as late as 1541, not by any relationship.

[1] Keir Performance, Preface, p. x.

This embodies glaring errors. It assumes that there was only one family of Stirlings. There is no doubt of the fact that a family of the name and same stock—viz. the *Vicecomites* de Strivelin, and their descendants—were possessors of lands in several counties from the twelfth century downwards; also that they acquired, *inter alia*, Cadder and Uchiltrie,[2] which remained with them and their heirs; and that Janet Striveling, the admitted Cadder heiress, and proprietrix of both, and of other estates, was in 1541 (as was shown), cruelly and dexterously, deprived of her entire possessions by James Stirling of Keir, by whom or his family previously, contrary to what is represented in the passage cited, they were never held. There thus, too, at complete variance with it, was a marked interruption in the lawful succession formerly alone vested in the Stirlings of Cadder, chiefs of the name—quite to the exclusion of the Keirs, whatever futilely may be now pretended, and from whom descendants exist, though deprived of the ancient patrimony.

[2] See, for this, next chapter.

We need not here recur to the other gross misrepresentation, though not to be overlooked, that the Keir family acquired Cadder by marriage,[3] than which nothing can be more reprehensible, it having been already discussed.

[3] See pp. 128, 129.

What a strange attempted spoliation of antecedent *status* has been disclosed, and cool appropriation in the Keir Performance (including gross misrepresentations) in behalf of its cherished client, of what belongs to others— at least not to him, though, it may be said, not so cruel and flagrant as the spoliation and self-appropriation, also to the prejudice of Cadder heirs and the Drumpelliers, of the estates by Sir James of Keir. But why in the least make the honourable Member for Perthshire, who perhaps is unaware of such arrogations, walk in the shoes of the latter? And there is besides, it may be added, the rehearsal of such acts in both their phases in the case of the

Keir-Cadder spoliation, both ancient and modern, in the Keir Performance.

old Cadder crest (not alluding to other armorial assumptions), as was formerly shown, to which we must once more advert.

At an early stage of the Exposition, the writer maintained that its usurpation for Keir "*proprio arbitrio*" by his partisans was "beyond *its* utmost stretch," and may have been at "some risk and peril," further still, afterwards "hazardous and dangerous."[1] It may be therefore requisite for him to prove these allegations. The crest has been thus quite irregularly appropriated, without the countenance of law or authority. And the important Act of Parliament in 1672 that has been already cited,[2] the admitted basis or rule of all armorial rights and procedure, expressly ordains *the escheating* of "all such *goods* and *geir* as shall have *unwarrantable* armes *ingraven* on them" (the penalty also by an antecedent Act in 1592); while it specially statutes, that "*whosoever* shall" (one year or day after its passing) "use *any other* armes *any manner* of way" than in virtue of a matriculation in the Lyon Register,—which is previously enforced—"shall pay one hundred pounds money *toties quoties* to the Lyon, and *shall likewayes escheat* to his *Maiestie all* the *moveable goods* and *geir* upon which the saids armes are *engraven* or otherwise represented." It cannot be denied that the Keir Performance, printed under the auspices and authority of the honourable Member for Perthshire, and his own property, he having been, and still is, its distributor, falls within the category of his "moveable goods and geir;" and hence, as it has unwarrantable and unmatriculated arms (which, by Exchequer practice, includes crests) engraven upon it, comes within the very class of denounced subjects in the Act, and is thus not only subject to the penalty of a fine, but actually to be escheated *in toto* to Her Majesty. This certainly follows *ex terminis* of the Act, that has not yet been superseded, on the contrary, it at least is still in part enforced.

The writer will forbear adding more on such grievous visitation and infliction on an assumed right, that the exponent cannot be supposed favourably to view, and which he is legally entitled to object to, and question in any way in his power, it not being, as above, duly sanctioned or authorised.

We may perhaps have dwelt rather long upon the preceding ungrateful topics. To complete, however, the present investigation, although clearly not descended from Sir William Stirling, the Cadder cadet, before and after 1300 —no doubt a very convenient and eligible person for a complimentary and unrestrained genealogist to pitch upon as an ancestor to a visionary pedigree

Dangerous dilemma to which Keir has been exposed by assumption of certain armorial insignia in the Keir Performance, including both a fine and actual escheat of it to the Crown.

[1] See p. 13, and see also p. 135.
[2] See Acts of Parliament, vol. viii., pp. 95, 98.

COMMENTS ON KEIR PERFORMANCE,

Fully to refute any Keir claim to a Cadder descent, inquiry next mooted into the true Keir origin and descent.

in behalf of a favoured party—it may still be asked, is there any other way or means, even by hook or crook, to connect the Keir family with the Stirlings of Cadder? Properly to answer this, it may necessarily be incumbent to go into the question of the Keir pedigree or descent, and fully to broach and sift it; which accordingly we will now endeavour to do, subsequently drawing from the investigation requisite and relevant results and conclusions. In this way especially, to use the words partly in the decreet of the original nullity of Janet of Cadder's marriage in 1541, we may be able to see how it "*a principio tenuisse*" et "*viribus subsistere posse de jure.*"

Quite uncertain.

No small uncertainty prevails as to the origin of the Keir family, which is involved in obscurity, nor have any fair or authorised attempts been yet made to fix it to an individual Strivilin stem. The Keir Performance has been shown to be completely unsuccessful in the endeavour to make them remote cadets of the admitted chief and principal Cadder stock; and even Father Hay, who figured before and after 1700, an eminent antiquary in his day, and a great collector of family gleanings, writs, and muniments, is here at fault, and, in absence of aught else, is driven to infer that the Stirlings of Keir are descended from "Henry, third son of the Earl of Huntingdon,"—a notion apparently untenable.[*] And the difficulty is rendered manifest by the deep unavailing researches which were instituted by the Keirs in the hope

---

[*] The former, too, was the well-known author of an essay on the origin of the royal family of Stuart, and of a *Vindication of Elizabeth Mure from the Imputation of being a Concubine*, published respectively in 1722 and 1723; and in a volume of MS. and genealogical collections by the said Mr Richard Aug. Hay, Canon Regular of Saint Genovefs of Paris, Prior of the Pieremont, which was his full style and description, we have as follows, under date 1700 (in the matter in question), that—"Stirling beareth, argent, on a bend *ingrailed*, three buckles or" (indisputably, as was seen, the Keir arms). "In some heralds' books the bend is gules" (this is an instance moreover of the bend being of a SANGUINARY tint, the family being here truly of the cameleon kind). Then he adds: "The first that had this name is said to have been Henry, sone to David, Earle of Huntingdone, brother to King William, because he was borne in the toune of Strivelyne, as another of the same Earle's sones was named Brechin, be- cause borne there." Then he explicitly gives his authorities for the latter facts, and adds, that of "this Henry, third sone to the Earle of Huntingdone, descend the *Stirlings* of Glenesk, who failed in ane heir female" (directly certainly), "married upon the Lindsay *and* the *Sterlings of Keir.*" There is nothing further worth noticing in the accounts or traditions of the Keir origin. The Keir editor is here so far pressed as to be obliged (in his usual predilection for perchances and empty possibilities)[1] to have recourse to a mere "*perhaps*" of Sir James Dalrymple, who figured as late as last century, that a Walter de Striveling in the reign of David I. "was the predecessor of *Stirling* of Keir," which unsupported idea, as it truly is, even if well founded, would not connect the latter with Cadder. As to Nisbet's concurrent notion, the former also quotes,[2] probably derived from Sir James, as above, it is but of a little moment, and he was more of a herald than genealogist.

[1] See p. 21, note; and for this reference to Sir James, see Keir Performance, p. 4.

[2] See Ibid.

of discovering even an interest in the question sufficient to enable them to oppose Drumpellier in 1818.

All we here find material in the Keir work at the earliest date, resolves into one abstract writ or grant in 1338,[1] that introduces us to a "*Johannis de Strivelyne*," simply so styled, and therein proved the husband of Mary, aunt of "Johannes de Ergadia, Dominus de Lorne," whereby he conveys the lands of Rathorane and others, in Lorne, exclusively to *her*, "*et heredibus suis*,"* strangely without any mention of her husband as a party, or in the least of his heirs, he figuring but as an appendage to the lady. The Keir compiler chooses to omit, in his account of the grant, in this certainly the appropriate place, the destination of the lands, so important, as will be seen, to the *subsequent* pedigree, and necessarily to his client. He assumes merely that the grant was to her, "on the occasion of her marriage;" but as she is styled there the *wife* ("*uxori*"), "Johannis de Strivelyne," she must have been previously married to him, perhaps long before; while, as is notorious, in such settlements there is always allusion to the actual matrimonial connection, as their basis, or, in other words, the occasion of them—here wanting—or mention of the *dos*, or dowry. This holds in the present day, and antecedently in the same century, in 1363-4, David II. (as superior) confirms the grant and concession which Sir Roger de Mortimer made to Margaret de Meneteth, "*spouse sue*" (not *uxori*, as in the prior instance, and here denoting his betrothed), of the lands of Foulis, Perthshire, "in liberam *dotem*, antequam *matrimonium* inter eosdem in facie ecclesie celebratum fuerat."[2] Something of the kind, though certainly not to such excess, for the credit of the Stirlings, might be thought to have intervened on the part of John, on the occasion of his marriage to Mary, the Lorn lady; although from whence it or the *dos* could come, as things stand, and as will immediately be seen, it might beggar fancy to imagine. All he could offer to her, as she deserved, was the homage of his heart, or "*stark* love and kindness," as was

^{margin notes:} The isolated John de Strivelin in 1338, the presumed Keir ancestor, whose existence then is only proved by an unique grant of lands to his wife, he having none. [1] See Keir Performance, p. 198. [2] Regist. David II., p. 33, No. 80.

---

* This is indisputable. Rathorane is first, in the dispositive clause, given unrestrictedly to Mary, "et heredibus suis," and in the *Tenendas*, "dicte *Marie* et heredibus suis," while the clause of warrandice, that so far exhausts the grant, is still "*sibi*" (*undoubtedly Mary alone* by the context) "et heredibus *suis*." John nowhere appears, but incidentally on one occasion as a sequence to Mary, as her husband, in the dispositive clause. This would seem singular, the husband being, in our law at least, ordinarily held no secondary, but rather a prominent party—indeed, there accounted "*dignior persona*," and requiring full and explicit mention. But for a full copy in all essentials of this rather *unique* charter, both to modern and antiquarian apprehension, with some further remarks, see ADDENDA, p. 187, &c., No. I.

long ago graphically tendered by another male party of old, precisely in the situation contemplated. The *aunt* of the Lord of Lorn,* as we may conclude, not a chicken in 1338, and her admirer might have been but poor when they married, especially the latter, so that the *subsequent* kind grant by the head of her house may have been in part to supply the deficiency; and as men's affections are *sometimes* fickle and changeable, added to Mary not being in the meridian of life, it was as well, under the *peculiar* circumstances, that he should secure her independently in the property conveyed.

<small>Complete blank in original Keir pedigree, from previous date in 1338, down to 1414, as far as records are concerned.</small>

With the above information we must content ourselves for a long space, there being nothing more about this John Stirling, while there is utter silence as to his issue. From 1338, the date of the above solitary grant, down to 1414, it is but a *tabula rasa*, and an extraordinary blank in the descent. John thus presents himself, both in regard to the past and future, as a naked rock springing up in the middle of the ocean. Like Adam, legally he has neither father or mother, nor, indeed, any connection save his wife, to whose side he is tied, though no blood relative. He in law stands quite isolatedly, owing his name and existence alone, we may say, incidentally to *her* grant, without the designation gratuitously given him in the Keir Performance, and more preposterously still, empty *superincumbence* of a fictitious ancestry with which he has been there saddled.

<small>Desperate expedient in the Keir work to supply the deficiency, by poaching upon other families.</small>

The expedient of the Keir editor in this emergency is quite what might be expected from him. In order to fill up such a palpable *vacuum*, or in some degree to compensate for it, and make the Keir family tree less naked and more efflorescent, he has recourse to his old *petitiones principii* and gratuitous assumptions.

<small>[1] See Keir Performance, p. 15, and authorities quoted there.</small>

Because a John de Strivelin—who at the same time is contradictorily represented as "Jocus de *Sherlynghong*"[1] (a strange designation seemingly, indeed, a jocose hit, and perhaps quite alien to Strivelin, so making the party thoroughly different), is stated, in a historical account, to have been taken prisoner at Halidon in 1333, thus antecedent to 1338, when we have the first and only genuine notice of the John Stirling in question, therefore the latter must be *presumed* to have been the former, and entitled to his military

---

* She is called *Amita* of John de Ergadia, in 1338, a classical term, explained as *Patris soror*—that is, here, sister of Alexander de Ergadia, who had considerably predeceased John de Ergadia, his son and heir, figuring, as proved by the *Rotuli Scotiæ*, as far back as 1311.—See *ibid.*, vol. i. p. 101, &c.

valour, for the illustration and aggrandisement of the Keir pedigree! In support of which borrowing of foreign plumage, there is not a shadow of proof; and the editor is still more reprehensible in unqualifiedly and gratuitously here styling another John Strivelin, stated to have fallen in the same battle, "his cousin."

Moreover, it being historically transmitted that, in 1339, a John de Strivelin, a valiant squire, fell at the siege of Perth, the editor, with his usual assurance, immediately identifies him with the husband of the lady of Rathorane; and also, without the least vestige of proof, says,[1] "he was *father*" of the next in the order of succession of the Keir ancestry. He here again

[1] See Keir Performance, p. 15.

> "Calls forth *living* waters from the rock,
> He calls forth children from the barren stock,"[2]

[2] See p. 3.

after the fashion of Guthrie so denounced by Churchill.

But notwithstanding these shifts and desperate resources, to which he has been reduced in order to add decoration and efflorescence then to the untractable Keir stem, it is still a branchless trunk, bare and naked as ever.

It should be borne in mind that the Strivelins were a numerous race, even before 1300, and much more afterwards, and that in the 14th century the Christian name of John was held in especial favour in the two principal families of the name,—*i. e.*, the *Fibulati*, and the *Stellulati*. In the first place, there was *Sir John de Strivelin*, a military character in the reign of David II., who, espousing Baliol's cause (*i. e.*, turning renegado), eventually became an English knight and baron; of whom more hereafter. Then there was a *John Strivelin*, who obtained the lands of Kinnedy from Robert Bruce.[3] And Lord Hailes,[4] quoting from Knighton, apprises us of *two John Strivelins* being at the battle of Halidon in 1333, one of whom was killed, and the other made prisoner. Then there was a great knight, *Sir John de Strivelin*, "Dominus de Glencsk,"[5] who cannot be proved dead till 1357; and though his chief succession devolved upon Catherine, his daughter and heiress, and Alexander Lindsay, her husband, father of David first Earl of Crawford, be yet, it is believed, had collateral male relatives. And, moreover, may be noticed "Johannes de Strivelyn, *Dominus* de *Kader*," head of the great house of Cadder, admitted by the Keir Performance to be chief of the Stirlings (and distinguished by the peculiar uniformity and import of their possessions inherited from the *Vicecomites de Strivelin*), who, in 1368, under

[3] See Robertson's Index, p. 19, No. 97.
[4] See Lord Hailes's Annals, edit. 1797, vol. iii. p. 92.
[5] As by writs in the Crauford Charter-chest.

Original Wigton or Cumbernauld Charter-chest.

172   COMMENTS ON KEIR PERFORMANCE,

that description witnessed an obligation by Malcolm Fleming, "*Dominus de Biger*," as tutor to his son Patrick, in favour of Robert Erskine of Erskine, in reference to the lands of Dalnoter.

<small>Quite futile and irrelevant the attempt.</small> And such being the case (while these may be far from being the only instances of the kind), it would be idle and preposterous to hold that the preceding John Stirlings, for the glory of Keir, resolved into, and lost their identity, but in one *John Stirling*—namely, the Keir ancestor, rather an abstract personage, to whom, like the queen-bee, in status and importance, all must be tributary and subservient, as would obtain, in no small degree, if we adopted what is stated and concluded by the Keir editor in regard to the latter; while, on the other hand, *a fortiori*, some of the preceding John Stirlings, including him of the *Stellulati* tribe, far more famous and influential, might better claim the same as a cadet or *subordinate*, and require him to follow in *their* wake—*they* then holding, by the way, the very *status*, as has been shown, most lamely and impotently, arrogated by the editor to the Keir family, as supreme over the other Stirlings.

<small>Misrepresentation here of Keir work. William Stirling, infeft in Rathoran, who is retrospectively proved to have died in 1393, may be presumed heir of John de Strivelin (never otherwise so described) in 1338, but whether as son or grandson is uncertain.

1 See Keir Performance, pp. 15, 16.</small>
The Keir Performance next explicitly states that John Strivelin[1] "of Rathoran," who never is proved so styled, and through his wife alone had an interest in any lands, he being otherwise unprovided, "was *father* of William of Strivelyn of Rathoran." This is truly unauthorised, there being *no* evidence of such filiation. It is only proved, retrospectively, by a document as late as 1423, to be shortly adduced, that a "William Stirling" had died, infeft, in 1393, in the lands of Rathoran; which, coupled with the destination in the original Rathoran grant in 1338 (and we now see its importance, though so strangely at first omitted or disregarded by the Keir editor) to the heirs-general of Mary, the disponee, wife of "John de Strivelin"—while there appears to have been *no* other intervening title-deed or right—may induce the legal presumption that he, William, was her heir. And as the doctrine, *pater est quem nuptiæ demonstrant*, will here apply necessarily, at the same time, his also, but in what degree it is impossible to say. As their marriage had been at least in 1338, or even earlier, he may have been as much their grandson as son. Indeed, as Rathoran was granted to *Mary's* heirs-general, quite irrespective of John, it might have been taken by a different heir, of a subsequent marriage by her with another Stirling. But it is admitted that this is an unlikely alternative, and the antecedent one is far more probable and to be presumed—only the Keir editor should not, after his occa-

sional careless fashion, without evidence, have explicitly assumed the filiation in question, for precision is *something* in genealogy.

On 11th January 1423, *Luke* Stirling (to give him properly his English or Scottish name, he being affectedly styled *Lukas* in the Keir Performance¹),* was by a retour served heir of the above William Stirling, his father, in the preceding lands of Rathorane, which supplies the sole evidence of the existence of William, merely retrospective, and all that is known of him, as the next or second link in the Keir pedigree.²

So far the fact in part stands as to the Keir origin and early descent—as yet known—but, in another view, necessary fairly to complete the subject, it has not a little in its favour.

By the alliance of John de Strivelin, their presumed patriarch, with Mary, aunt of John, Lord of Lorne, before 1338 (certainly at a remote epoch), who, it is admitted, was the heir of a northern princely house, at least not inferior

---

Side notes:

Luke Stirling of Rathorne (in 1414 and 1423), the son and heir of the previous William, the next link in the Keir pedigree.

¹ See Keir Performance, pp. 16, 17.

² See ibid., Chartulary, p. 209.

Valuable information about the names Luke and Peter.

³ See Keir Performance, p. 16, note.

⁴ Ibid., p. 4, including note 6.

---

* The Keir editor also is at pains to show³ that "the Christian name of Luke is of great antiquity in the earldom of Stratherne," where he of Ratherne first figures. This is rather an insignificant matter, like others on which he lays stress—not overlooking his edifying topic of redundant petty orthographies. The Christian names of the Evangelists were in great request from the earliest times, and appropriated by families generally throughout Europe. Thus John predominates everywhere; and Matthew is a kind of heir-loom in the great house of Montmorency in France, and was also used by that of Lennox in Scotland; while Mark was cherished by the Ker family on the Borders. And into this category we may, *de plano*, admit Luke, without being obliged to resort, like the Keir editor, to the cumbersome and inferior instance he quotes, of "*Luke*, son of Theobald, son of William, the son of Clement, Lord of Pethlandy, in the middle of the 13th century," from the Chartulary of Inchaffray, which he seems sapiently to cite as a recondite and decisive one in so critical a point.

Again, the *rare* and *unknown* name of *Peter* peculiarly requires illustration;⁴ and first, a "*Peter*, son of Walter de Strevelyne," *circa* 1160, is prominently introduced as the second Keir ancestor, though in reality as much so as of the present writer; and then, in a copious note, comes the *mirabile dictu*, that "*Peter* continued to be used by the Angus branch of the Stirlings," for "in a charter by Hugh de Fraser, Lord of Kynnell, to William de Camero," &c., "*Peter* de Strevelyne," &c., actually is a witness, with the valuable information of its being still extant in the Southesk charterchest—though strangely the date, however not unprecedentedly in the work, be withheld. But this is not all; we further learn there was another charter by "Hugh Fraser, Lord of Lovat," &c., "to *Peter* de Strevelyne and John his eldest son" in 1407, and so on, &c. &c. 'Tis a pity, indeed, the editor had not been as express and communicative in his other authorities, at least as *important*, in respect to whose special contents, and even custody, we have seen, he is so capriciously mute. The Irishman said,

" He swore by St Peter
To make out the metre;"

and similarly we might hold the former strives with his Peter for a make-weight to his work, though, alas! less effectually, and, it may be said, without rhyme or reason. The better or more adequately to illustrate the vocable in question, we might have suggested Peter the Great of Russia, Patrick the Irish saint, or, grander still, St Peter at Rome, whose beloved *sons* (putting aside the Angus Peters) are so known, and daily vociferating in the Cowgate of Edinburgh.

to the Lords of the Isles (and not improbably their head), we may conclude him to have been a man of rank and condition; though the Keir editor, as usual, overshoots the mark in styling the above potentate the "*last* of the male line of the ancient Lords of Lorne," as it were to make it appear that Keir is their nearer descendant, which is contrary to fact.[1] And William de Strivelin, John's heir, whether son or grandson, must have been a person of still higher rank, in right of his ancestrix Mary, whom we may hold to have been a daughter of Lorn. And the exponent can also prove—by new evidence, which is not in the Keir Performance, but which will here be introduced in the sequel—that Luke de Strivelin, in 1393, who, as son and heir of William, will come next in the succession, was explicitly styled, in 1425, "noble," with other creditable epithets, from whom the main descent of Keir, through good and eligible alliances, can be legally traced down to the present moment.

Hence, in the first place, he may indulge in the proud vaunt—at which some of our great families aim, and on which they even plume themselves—that it is impossible to prove the first *mean man* of his race, it having been well allied and noble at the outset. And, secondly, that it is ancient, having actually existed, as must be evident, for considerably more than five centuries; which—to all who are acquainted with the state of our records and narrowed means of probation—it is not so easy to establish, even in the case of some of our noble and historical families, who are not a little proud of their pedigree.

There is, therefore, in the case of the Keir Stirlings, a good *terminus a quo* to start from, and a reasonable hope that, by future recontinued researches, which are still demanded, they may succeed in attaching themselves, at a remote period, to a dignified appropriate Stirling stem. And even if unsuccessful, we may yet complimentarily admit in their instance—

"Certa retro series gentis, sed cujus origo,
Ut fons oceani latet!"

Luke Stirling, on the death of William his father in 1393, appears to have been slender in his means—in fact, to have had no lands—for neither he or his descendants are proved actually to have possessed Rathorane, or drawn the rents, whatever their right; he not till 1423 at least—if even then; and he is only stated in the Keir Performance, which must have had access to the best information, to have "*acquired*" Ratherne or Wester Ratherne; but this may not have been till considerably after 1393. No evidence either is adduced in support of this assertion, far less of the date of the acquisition, as so often happens in the above work. It was by this comparatively small property that Luke was first known, and always afterwards styled.

In such circumstances, the family would seem—by those mischances and alternations not uncommon in life—to have retrograded in the world. Luke Stirling was, we may conclude, a man of spirit and address, *artifex suæ fortunæ*, it may be said, founder of the Keir family; and, being also of rank and condition, an heir worthy of any. In 1414 he obtained,[1] upon his resignation, a regrant of the lands of Wester Ratherne, howsoever acquired, from Euphemia, Countess of Stratherne, the superior, with limitation to him—styled "*dilecto armigero nostro*"—and the heirs-male of his body; whom failing, to "*Willielmo de Strevelyne Domino de Cadare*," with remainder to his; by reason, it is said, of an entail to be made between them, which will elicit future comment. The Keir editor, according to his fashion, represents these parties here as "*cousins*"—an interpolation for which there is no excuse. There is no proof either here or elsewhere of their being respectively so styled, or of such relationship between them, the more remarkable, owing to the known import of a "Scotch cousin," and its being rather lavishly bestowed.*

Countess Euphemia may especially attract our regard. She was daughter and heiress of David, Earl of Stratherne, eldest son of the marriage of Robert

---

* While "cousin" always and literally denoted *blood*-relatives, so broad was its import as occasionally to comprise such as were even illegitimate as well as legitimate, which, *inter alia*, is proved by these instances:—[2]

In Lord Hailes' Annals there is the following passage:—[2]

In the year 1186, William the Lion, of Scotland, "married Ermengarde, daughter of Richard, Viscount of Beaumont. Her grandmother was a bastard of Henry I. Hence, according to the language of those times, she was styled the *cousin* of Henry II."

Even comparatively in modern times, Mr Hume, in his *Criminal Law*, notices a case in 1621, where a pursuer declares he "is *cousing-german*" to a party, though it transpires from the process he was a bastard.[3]

The above *a fortiori* supports the remark in the text; and, owing to this broad application of "*cousin*," to all blood-relatives, its absence in the case of Keir in reference to Cadder, or indeed *vice versa*, is the more striking. Even by the sovereign (who would have more reserve in this respect) it was applied to commoners not in a near degree of relationship. Thus, in 1340, there is a pension by David II. of five merks sterling,[4] "Roberto de Auandia *consanguineo nostro*;" and another by the same prince of the fee of the Thanedoms of Kincardine and others, "dilecto consanguineo nostro Waltero de Lesley militi."[5]

If there had been an actual relationship between the parties, the settlement by Luke de Strivelin of Wester Ratherne, in 1414, might have been first to himself and the heirs-male of his body, whom failing, "dilecto *consanguineo nostro* (*i.e.*, Luke's) Willielmo de Strevelyne, Domino de Cadare," and the heirs-male of his body.

II. with Euphemia Rose, hence lawful from his very birth. He is distinguished from the issue of that prince by his first connection with Elizabeth Mure, owing to a speciality or demur in their case, according to some (not altogether grounded upon the naked question of legitimation by subsequent marriage), and on such footing, at common law, might have been preferred to the latter in the royal succession. This, however, was precluded by the express entail of the Crown, by Act of Parliament in 1373 ; but as Euphemia may be viewed as a princess of the blood, Luke Stirling, like many of as high rank in our day, might also well attend upon her as above, especially in a feudal age, in the capacity of an "*armiger*" or *squire*.[1]

[1] See here, p. 185.

Striking difference at this moment between Countess Euphemia's heirs and representatives and Luke's.

But how strikingly are the vicissitudes of life exemplified in the heirs respectively of the Countess, and of Luke her squire, at the present day. Her direct heir of line, and standing in her shoes exactly as she did in those of Earl David, her father, in reference to the Earldom of Strathearn, was Mr Barclay Allardice of Urie (through his *Allardice* descent), so well known in certain circles, and recently deceased, who in such character claimed the identical Earldom of Strathearn, as well as those of Menteith and Airth ; and what followed we may narrate in the words of Sir Bernard Burke in his work entitled *Vicissitudes of Families* :[2]

[2] Page 111.

"It is painful to allude to a *mésalliance* of one nobly and even royally descended, and that, too, in our own day. But it is a fact too well known to render it indelicate to make mention of it, that the only *daughter* and heir of Mr Barclay Allardice united herself in marriage with a man of low degree of the name of Ritchie. However lamentable this degradation of ancient blood may be, the heir of this marriage has the singular advantage of possessing what is believed to be a well-founded claim to one of the oldest and greatest of the earldoms of Scotland, and to the honour of being representative of one of the princes of the blood-royal of that country."

Such is now the direct heir of Euphemia, Countess Palatine of Strathearn, Luke's superior and mistress in 1414 ; while his representative is the honourable Member for Perthshire, Laird of Keir. A prior Strathearn or Allardice heir here might cast the same anxious melancholy glance upon the incident, as the captive prince did upon the revolving wheel of the car of Sesostris to which he was bound, so figurative of the revolutions of fortune.

Luke, progressing in life, came to acquire, in 1433, a wadset of the half of Keir, from Norman Leslie of Rothes, while he had held lands in the barony of Leslie, of which George, Lord Leslie, was superior; and at length, in 1448, an absolute and full right to the former.¹ To one of the transactions in that year his seal of arms is appended, being the same as Leslie's, three buckles on a bend dexter, also corresponding with the Stirlings'.² This, as formerly stated, is the *first* instance of the armorial insignia of Keir. There is none earlier, that can be only met by a gross misrepresentation³ (of which there may be too many) of the Keir editor, already exposed, of Luke having inherited them—and his family having thus a prior right thereto—from that true bugbear and visionary ancestor, Sir William Stirling in 1292; who, however, bore the buckles on a chief, and, as is unquestionable, may be as much the ancestor of any *parvenu* as of Keir. It is really surprising how the editor can, as he coolly does, descend to such vain misrepresentations and mere assumptions.

    Luke does not appear to have attained a higher dignity than *armiger* or *squire* (being so far unlike Sir John, the Cadder representative in the previous century, who then held the superior title of knight), of which an additional notice will be given in the sequel. According to the Keir Performance, he "died" between 10th December 1449 and 13th April 1452,⁴ and was succeeded by his oldest son and heir, Sir William Stirling, the first knight of the family, styled of Ratherne and Keir,⁵ he having acquired the other half of Keir, and hence consolidated the whole of that property in his person; who again was succeeded by his son and heir, Sir William Stirling of Keir, who is stated in the Keir work to have obtained a royal letter in 1473, uniting and annexing all his lands into "a barony," to be "callit perpetually the barony of the Keire."⁶ This, it is believed, is the first mention of such barony, and *extunc* the family may be styled baronial—that is, obviously, as of the lesser barons, and not of the greater or hereditary barons, or lords of Parliament, as they were designated. The editor calls that of Keir an old baronial family. No doubt, as being so since 1473, nearly four centuries ago, they may be so viewed, especially in contrast with many of a later date; but they cannot be classed with those who had their lands erected into baronies much earlier, and have transmitted the honour to existing descendants, or with such, of which we have instances, who obtained grants from the monarch of their fiefs as far back as the twelfth century, to be held "*sicut unus baronum meorum.*" Unduly to eke out the Keir family to that epoch, and thus exaggerate the importance of Keir, has been reserved for the notable Keir Performance, and secondary or subordinate writers.

178   COMMENTS ON KEIR PERFORMANCE,

Sir William of Keir charged with the murder of James III.

The most remarkable feature in the preceding Sir William of Keir's life, is his having been of the party opposed to his sovereign James III.; and he has even been charged with his murder. However general the *clamosa fama* has been against him, it may be said mainly to rest on historical authority.

His exculpation here in the Keir work.

[1] *See Exposition, p. 4.*

[2] *See Keir work, p. 25.*

The Keir Performance (throwing out of the question Ferrerius, who has already been spoken to[1]) brings forward as its *cheval de guerre*, to "exculpate the Laird of Keir of any part in the assassination of James III.," an Act of Parliament, which it asserts to be "*almost cotemporary* with the event,"[2] and "which provides, 'be the command and advertisement of our sovereign lord the King,' that 'for the eschewing and ceasing of the heavy murmurs and noise of the people of the deid' (death) 'and slaughter of our sovereign lord's father .... that the person or persons that put violent hands on his person, and slew him, are nocht punished,' a reward should be given to 'any who should make known those that were the overthrowers of the late King with their hands,' James IV. being 'maist desirous' that the 'perpetrators be known and punished after their demerits,' calling the murder an 'odious and cruel deed,' and a reward of one hundred merks' worth of land is offered for the discovery."

Acts of Parliament, vol. ii. p. 230.

[3] *See Lord Lindsay's Lives of the Lindsays, vol. i. p. 160.*

[4] *See p. 191.*

This is all it literally gives or says of the Act, without condescending to add its date, or where it may be entered in the Acts of Parliament—contrary again to the mode adopted in all regular discussion—so we must supply the deficiency. We find that it actually passed February 20, 1491-2—that is, at the very end of 1491, the year then beginning on the 25th of March—while the *assassination* of James III. occurred as far back as the 9th of *June* 1488.[3] Thus, instead of the Act being, as the work asserts, "*almost cotemporary* with the *event*," it was certainly more than three years and a half after. It hence is flagrantly wrong in the assertion; and we here again, as elsewhere, are disagreeably forced to subject it to the alternatives,[4] each self-inculpating,—first, of either being guilty of extreme carelessness or inadvertence; or, secondly, of undue concealment of dates for the purposes of the argument, which may be served better by the Act being immediately on the death of the monarch, than, as was the fact, long subsequently.

From the passage quoted, however, just as it stands, the Keir Performance draws its grand argument in the matter, and contends that "if at the DATE" (thus curiously, though erroneously, founded upon, though not given) "of this Act, and previous to it, rumour had pointed to the Laird of Keir as the guilty person, the King would have been *obliged* to *take cognisance* of him, to satisfy the heavy murmurs and noise of the people"—*ergo*, the Laird was innocent.

This is indeed a futile plea or defence. Is it not obvious that while James III. actually was assassinated, and there *were* perpetrators of the crime, as little, in consequence, were criminal prosecutions instituted against such or indeed any; *or* "the King .... obliged to take cognisance of them," as urged? There was a golden bridge thus made for the guilty as for the accused; which equally, in the discussion, favours the former as the latter. To have made the argument tell, there should have been a specification of accused parties in the Act, with silence observed as to Sir William Stirling, from which an exception might be construed to his advantage—as contrasted with the others—and the object of the Keir Performance in some degree attained. But the Act inculpates none *nominatim*, and it just resolves into such a case as the recent Bull of Excommunication by the Pope of those concerned in the unnatural attempt (as it was deemed) to deprive him of the Romagna, which has been likened to *firing* a "blank cartridge." "*Nobody*," to quote the words of an able cotemporary print,[*] which equally apply in the present instance, "is there *named*, and *therefore nobody* need care. The document may be held as referring to the northern Italians generally : but as it refers to no person in particular, nobody will say that he is one of the persons meant, and nobody, lay or clerical, can offer practically to apply it to any person more than another."

Such attempted exculpation futile and indecisive.

And of course both being identical, the same result obtained on the one occasion as on the other. As premised, nothing followed on the Scottish Act, 20th February 1491. The suspected royal parricides were never criminally prosecuted. They all remained quiet and unconcerned by their native hearths, inhaling their native air, under protection of their *lares*. All! did we say—*no*, it was *not* so : there was a *solitary* exception. Notwithstanding the Act proved thus harmless and "scaithless," there was *one* individual who may be said to have taken guilt to himself ; and public attention, after the interval of more than three years and a half, being thereby recalled to the crime, he, it would appear, as the most guilty party, if not its actual perpetrator, dreading, as we might conclude, on his special account, more direct procedure, the very next year *absconded* from Scotland. He was no

[*] *The Scotsman*, April 2, 1860.

180   COMMENTS ON KEIR PERFORMANCE,

See here Lord Lindsay's Lives of the Lindsays, vol. i. p. 166, where it is proved that the Pope had condemned the murder of James III., and acted accordingly, June 27, 1491.

Striking and new incident in the matter stated by Crauford, an approved authority of the Keir work.

1 See ibid., pp. 5, 6, 8, 9.

other, though this fact hitherto be unknown, than the *Sir William Stirling of Keir* in question. He found the means then to betake himself to Rome—to the head of the Church, "the common parent," as it was then styled, "and protector of Christendom;" the very place where, by the indulgence of the Holy Father, parties were pardoned for atrocious crimes, and absolution granted—which, it may be inferred, was the object of his journey. The fact is stated by Mr George Crauford—historiographer of Scotland, author of the "History of the Stewarts, and of Renfrewshire," the "Peerage of Scotland," with other antiquarian works, who figured before and after 1700, and an approved and material authority of the Keir Performance,[1]—in an MS. pedigree or account by him of the Stirlings of Keir, preserved in a private charter-chest. After deducing the descent down to Sir William of Keir, in the reign of James II. inclusive, he next comes to his heir, in whom we are interested, "Sir William, the gentleman" (he affirms) "*branded* with being accessory to the horrid murder of King James III., to *expiate* which" (he adds), "I suppose, he went in *pilgrimage to Rome in* 1492, AS *from his* LICENSE for THAT EFFECT." Such is the natural inference or conclusion drawn by Crauford; but, at any rate, we have the new striking fact, nowhere else stated, of Sir William having gone to Rome at a critical moment, which, in the peculiar circumstances, it seems difficult otherwise to explain. It is singular, too, that in the Keir Performance there is a blank as to the knight from 1492 to May 18, 1495, nothing there being disclosed about him during that interval, which is rather confirmative of the above, while it is an exaggeration, as usual, on its part, that after the murder of James III., his son—who, however, was the head of the same party to which Sir William was attached—"conferred upon him repeated favours," &c.

The writer does not intend to scan the knight's case too rigorously. We may make allowance for the age in which he lived, and his deep feelings of rancour for the destruction of his fortalice and devastation of his property, antecedent to James III.'s murder, by the royal forces—which, if guilty, may have instigated him thereto, although no real exculpation—and some Scottish families would seem rather to prefer a historical ancestry, though questionable in their acts, to one passive or recreant, whom they would deem *ignavum pecus*.

It may be unnecessary to carry the Keir descent from this epoch downward, it being so notorious and well documented. The above Sir William was father of Sir John of Keir, that severe and despotic character, who has figured so prominently in this Exposition, and of whom further striking traits and characteristics will be given in another chapter. It would not be edifying to rehearse again here the episode of Janet of Cadder, or Sir James of Keir's treatment of her, and still more unnatural and cruel treatment of John, his eldest son, who found his principal comfort in his alliance with the family of Lettyr or Drumpellier, through marriage with the widow of a younger member. To this, and much more indeed, we may bid adieu for the present.

Having progressed so far, we now come to the main point—viz. the results and conclusions for which this statement and inquiry were undertaken.

In the *first place*, in what has been submitted, and after every inquiry, there is not the least trace of relationship between the houses of Cadder and Keir, not the least tangible connection; no proof even of their having been styled consins, notwithstanding the Keir editor's gratuitous assumptions— though it is a term of rather loose acceptation with us, and not withheld where there was any pretence for it. And this is the more striking, as both families were noted and distinguished, and figured on many occasions in a prominent manner; so that, if they had been related, it is difficult to see how it did not transpire in some shape or other. On the contrary, it may be said to have been ignored by the Keirs—while equally by the Cadders—who never till the present day sported such a notion; and even now it is only done by the Keir Performance (that wholesale dealer in gratuitous assumptions), which is equivalent to nothing. Again, if Keir had been, what his work decidedly assumes, a cadet of Cadder, a junior branch of a family which the editor admits to be chief of all the Stirlings, then we might have expected to find him holding some Cadder property, given them in appanage, according to the usual practice at the time, and so well exemplified in the case of Robert of *Bankeir* (afterwards of Lettyr), the Drumpellier ancestor, thus actually *portioner* of *Cadder;* but there is not a vestige of it. John Strivelin, the first presumed Keir ancestor in 1338, stands quite isolated and without property; and, what is very remarkable, only sharing what he might have by favour of his wife, and to which *her* heir (through the cardinal title in that year[1]) alone succeeded, while all the property of the descendants were "*conquest*" in them, and first acquired under a singular title by their efforts and address.

Margin notes: No proper proof of relationship between the houses of Cadder and Keir. — [1] See Keir Performance, pp. 15, 16.

How opposite the case of the Stirlings of Cadder, who uniformly held Cadder and Uchiltree, which were both traced to the great *Vicecomites* de Strivelin—the chiefs of all the *Fibulati Strivelienses*—as far back as the time of William the Lion, who reigned from 1165. Indeed, these estates formed the old exclusive patrimony of the *Vicecomites*; the main inheritance, though accompanied by latter accessories or acquisitions, which yet did not, as in the Keir instance, constitute their chief property. Secondly, the fact, again, of the Keir family having taken as their arms three buckles on a bend in 1448, about the time when they held of the great and paramount house of Leslie, who had the same bearing, might be accounted for by the peculiar practice whereby an inferior tribe or vassal was accustomed to carry what, strictly speaking, belonged only to the superior. Indeed, as we have seen, the identity of the Keir arms with those of Leslie forcibly struck Milne the antiquary. Of the practice in question, we have many examples, of which a few will now be given.

<small>The Stirlings of Cadder here stand in the shoes of the ancient Vicecomites de Strivelin, the chief and main stock.</small>

The ancient and once numerous house of Innes in Moray did not scruple to take as their arms the stars of the paramount Morays or de Moravia there, as they were then called; and the Strivelins of the north, as we have seen. Again, many of the families in Stirlingshire and Dunbartonshire took the saltier and cinquefoils of the old Earls of Lennox, while on this head Nisbet remarks,[1] that "in many shires of our kingdom, where our ancient earls, lords, and great men had been patrons and superiors, there we find *their* armorial figures more frequent than others in the bearings of many of the present nobility and gentry, which show their progeniture to have been *clients* and *vassals* to them." In support of which he instances the families of Murrays, Johnstones, Jardanes, Kilpatricks, and others in Annandale, who bear, with different tinctures, the saltier and chief, the noted arms of the Bruces, lords of the district; and he adds that, "in Fifeshire, lions are carried upon account the lion was the armorial figure of M'Duff's earls and over-lords of Fife," together with other precedents of the kind.

<small>The fact of the Stirlings of Keir, in the circumstances, bearing the buckle, indecisive, and immaterial.

[1] Vol. ii., second edit., under "Marshalling Arms," p. 58.</small>

Independently, too, it has been proved that families of the same surname,[2] though of distinct lineage and unconnected, took the arms of what was deemed the principal house, with a mark of difference, *ingrailing* the chief heraldic charge, precisely as in the Keir case. Hence, coupling this with what is premised, the Keir arms can supply no satisfactory proof of a Cadder descent. They may have been taken either as vassals and dependants of the Leslies, or subordinates to the head and principal stock of the *Fibulati Strivelienses*, through merely having the same name, while aliens from them in blood. But, even supposing the Keirs to be inherently Strivelin, that could

<small>[2] See pp. 156, 157.</small>

not benefit them, for they would then only be in the same situation as the Stirlings of Cragbarnet, Glorat, Ballaga, Law, &c., who likewise bore the buckles, although evidence is as yet wanting to prove them to be connected with Cadder. Indeed, the Keir Performance[1] is at pains to inculcate that "no evidence has been found of the exact relationship of the first Stirling of Craigbernard to the house of Cawder."

[1] See p. 127.

Thirdly and *lastly*, as little good can result to Keir from the entail in 1414, where it may be inferred that Luke Stirling of Ratherne, his ancestor, was to take (though this be not explicitly proved) as a substitute of the Cadder succession, in the event of the failure of the male issue of William, Laird of Cadder, and where nothing transpires of their being cousins or relatives, which would bear out the gratuitous assumption of the Keir editor.

The Ratherne grant or entail in 1414 also immaterial.

An entail notoriously implies a deviation from the regular order of succession. And there was in Scotland, according to a peculiar bent or usage, a preference often given on these occasions as substitutes, to parties who happened to be of the same surname, though not blood relations; and this, no doubt, was somewhat akin to clannish feelings, which in these early times existed so strongly in the breasts of our countrymen, or rather, perhaps, to the law of Thanistry that also ruled in Scotland—as it must in all rude and turbulent states—and which, without reference to lawful family representation—talents not always being hereditary—preferred, in the succession, the stronger or most powerful of the name, to the weaker.

Such was most probably the case in the Cadder and Keir entail, since no proof of relationship exists; and, from the same marked predilection, if any one now ventured to question or derogate from Keir's rights or literary merits, the exponent is persuaded there is not a single Drumpellier but who would be ready to exclaim with Churchill, nearly in his words:—

> "The praise be Stirling's, freely let him bear
> The wreath which genius wove and planted there;
> Foe as I am, should envy tear it down,
> Myself would labour to replace the crown!"

The word "foe" must be here taken *cum grano salis*, and only to denote one opposed in an antiquarian discussion like the present; while, on any other point than the mere Cadder representation, the Drumpelliers would be happy that the cause of the honourable Member should succeed, and should be elevated to even higher rank and pre-eminence than what he at present either possesses or aims at.

All that has been above said might also hold, *a fortiori*, with regard to Luke, whose acuteness, ability, provident propensity, and, above all, the fact of his being styled "nobill" (as will be proved), combined to render him a very desirable collateral taker in the Cadder entail in 1414, failing the direct lawful heirs.

<small>Entails often formerly in favour of parties not lawful blood relatives.</small>

<small>¹ Great Seal Register.</small>

<small>² Ibid.</small>

<small>As also to strangers, by descent.</small>

Of such peculiar family arrangements or settlements, apposite instances are by no means wanting. Indeed, antecedently to 19th January 1512-13, there is an entail of the Hamilton estates by James, Earl of Arran,[1] and the heirs-male of his body, whom failing, even to certain *spurious* offspring (quite strangers at common law), including Sir James Hamilton of Finnart, his natural son, to the exclusion of several lawful heirs-male. This may not improbably have been owing to the talents and energy of Sir James, so well known in history as the *Bastard* of Arran. Then again, by a royal patent, June 1, 1677,[2] the old barony of Sinclair was settled or entailed, with the original precedence, after the direct issue of John, Lord Sinclair, upon certain Sinclairs of *Herdmanston* and their heirs-male; and yet the latter, though of ancient descent and the same surname, were of quite a *different stock* of Sinclairs to the former: however, they might just as much be deemed of the same race as Keir and Cadder, so far at least as entails may go in proving relationship. But still further do these cases resemble one another, for the Sinclairs of Herdmanston bore the same arms as their noble namesake. After a corresponding fashion, also, David Ross of Balnagowan, the head of the ancient Rosses in the north, heirs-male of the original Earls of Ross, in 1711 entailed his large estates upon a General Ross, and after him upon a younger son of the Lord Ross in Renfrewshire, although his lordship was of quite a distinct family, being of the Norman Rosses, while they most truly are stated, in a Balnagowan process in 1760,[3] to have been all "utter strangers to the family of Balnagowan, to whom they have no manner of affinity other than the sound of a surname." And to give one other instance, of an older date, supplied to us through the regulating Errol grants, in the discussion before the House of Lords in 1797, upon the question of the right to the Errol dignity. The ancient earldom of Errol, with the high and transcendent hereditary office of Constable of Scotland, and the estate, was duly settled and entailed by powers obtained from the crown, the 16th February 1674,

<small>³ Before the Supreme Civil Court; Minutes of Evidence in the case.</small>

failing certain immediate heirs, upon William Hay of Drumelzier, and the heirs-male of his body. Some would hence suppose that the latter were Errol collateral heirs-male; but no such thing. The Hays of Drumelzier were only cadets of the Tweeddale family, who, although from an old and baronial stock, and bearing the same arms and surname (the arms having the addition of female quarterings), are as yet in no way shown connected with Errol.

The above instances are given, as showing how it frequently happened that descent was postponed to other considerations, such as name, favour, or talents; and this may have happened in the Cadder and Keir entail in 1414, which hence need not further demand any attention in the present question. Were it necessary, numerous other illustrations in point might be adduced from our settlements and entails of landed estates.

There is hardly any more now to be offered on this head. The original descent of the Keir family may hence be viewed as unascertained, yet affording scope for the talents and research of the Keir Triumvirate, in whose hands the question may at present rest. At the same time the exponent will be happy to communicate to the proper party, with the same spirit of liberality that has invariably influenced the Drumpelliers, what may further transpire or occur to him in elucidation of the Keir pedigree and descent at that distant period. <small>Upon the whole, the original descent of the Keir family unascertained, and requiring further investigation.</small>

In the meanwhile, the writer has lighted upon some new evidence touching Luke Stirling of Ratherne, in a private charter-chest. It is an instrument, 17th April 1425, exemplifying a decreet of perambulation on a disputed right of property, where "*providus et discretus* vir Lucas STERVYLYN* de *Ratherne*," also therein described as "ane *nobill worthy* man and *squear*," or "*armiger*," as he had been styled in 1414[1] (thus combining in him rank, nobility, chivalry, and nearly all human excellence), on the one side, and "ane worthy man, Johne ye Bruce of Gyrsmeston," on the other, are litigants; and whereby the inquest adjudged "yat ye landis yat were in debat" (between those described) "suld remain wyt ye land of *Camlyn*" (*Lucas' property*, as its pertinent), "for quhy?"—as the decreet graphically asks, to elicit the *rationem* decidendi—"yat ye said Lucas allegit yat he held ye saidis landis <small>In the mean time, the following new evidence, in 1425, in favour of Luke Stirling of Ratherne, the Keir founder, is submitted by the writer.</small>

<small>[1] See Keir Performance, pp. 206, 207.</small>

<small>* This is indeed a discovery, being a new orthography of Stirling (besides a previous one contributed by the writer), casting others into the shade, to add to the felicitous list of sixty-four instances with which the editor has so successfully and beneficially favoured the public.[2]</small>

<small>[2] See Keir Performance, p. 548.</small>

of ye *Camlyn* of ye *King William*, and so was fundin of before tyme be his charteris, and yair upon he schowit fair evidentis selyt in ye court."

Here then is a new possession of Luke—*i. e.* the Camlyn—which, with its adjuncts or pertinents, lay, as is stated, in Clackmannan. It is a respectable one, and quite unknown to the Keir Performance, and the writer cannot but confess he felt an interest in it. From the notice above, that Lucas held the above lands of King William (who succeeded in 1165), by his evidents, which, by some latitude of expression, might import that he stood in the shoes of a predecessor, who held them at so remote a period, it was inferred—(1), That Luke, so far, was here a crown vassal, instead of a subject superior merely, as in right of certain other estates; and (2), That the evidence might connect him with a long line of ancestry, as owners of Camlyn up to the time of King William, and enhancing the antiquity of his descent far beyond his present state, besides fixing and illustrating it. But unfortunately more evidence was discovered in the same quarter, in a certain measure baffling these hopes and expectations, it being found by an earlier judicial award in 1330, that one John de Fethellis was then proprietor of the property, and who, in proof of his title "duas cartas cum una confirmatione ibidem demonstravit videlicit *unam* regis *Willielmi* libere donationis *Thome medico* et heredibus suis. Et aliam cartam dicti Thome medici de resignatione terrarum de Camelinge alano filio Walteri filii *Swyni* cui idem Johannes Fythellis hereditarie successit." Here, then, we have the succession to Camlyn minutely traced through Thomas, probably the King's physician, the first owner, and John Fythellis, his heir, down to 1330—rather an old date—some time after which only the Stirlings must have acquired it, though whether first only in the person of Luke, or by him as heir of a predecessor, is uncertain. But this perhaps, as material to the Keir genealogy, may be left to the Triumvirate to investigate.

ADDENDA TO CHAPTER V.

No. I.

FULL COPY in essentials of GRANT by JOHN DE ERGADIA, Lord of Lorn, to MARY, his Father's Sister, or paternal Aunt, of Lands of RATHORANE, &c., in 1338.

(REFERRED TO AT PAGE 169.)

"Omnibus has literas visuris vel audituris Johannes de Ergadia, Dominus de Lorne, salutem in domino. Universitati vestre notum facciumus per *presentes*, nos dedisse, concessesse, et hac presenti carte nostra confirmasse MARIE *amite nostre* UXORI *Johannis de Striuelyne, et heredibus* SUIS, quinque *deniaratas* terre de RATHORANE et unam *denariatam* que vocatur Garwpennynge [and a few others of but small valuation, one only a halfpennyland, &c.], in *Lorne*, constitutas, *Tenendas* et habendas predictas terras, a nobis et heredibus nostris DICTE MARIE et HEREDIBUS SUIS, per omnes suas rectas metas antiquas, libere et plenarie, cum omnibus suis pertenentiis libertatibus et aysiamentis. *Reddendo* nobis annuatim unum par calcarium ad festum Pentecostes vel valorem ipsorum si reperiri venalia non poterint pro omni servitio et demanda. Quas quidem terras nos et heredes nostri SIBI [*clearly* MARY] et HEREDIBUS SUIS contra omnes viros et mulieres warantiz abimus et defendemus. Datum apud Perth in nativitate Sancte Marie, anno Domini millesimo ccc° tricesimo octavo. In cujus rei, &c. His testibus Domino Malcolmo Kenedy Camerario Scocie, Domino Michaele Scote Milite, Michaele Fisser, constabulario de Perth, et multis aliis."

For full copy see Chartulary to Keir work, p. 198, No. 2.

Independently of the husband being accounted *dignior persona* in law, owing to the admission of females into fiefs (previously only descendible to male heirs) in the thirteenth century and afterwards, it became incumbent, with the view of obviating the inconveniences and difficulties that might arise therefrom, and still preserve the feudal system intact in the main, to vest those duties that a wife, when an heiress, could not discharge, in the husband, who was quite adequate for the purpose. On this ground, too, as can be fully proved, when she was a Countess in her own right, he sat in Parliament as an Earl, just precisely as if he had been personally vested in the dignity, besides discharging on her behalf feudal services and duties.

All this could not but raise the husband to a greater position than before in 1338, the date of the preceding Lorn charter, and makes the palpable disregard—nay, almost ignoring —of John Strivelin, the husband of Mary, the grantee there, the more strange and unaccountable.

With submission, according to regular practice, John de Strivelin, as well as his heirs, actually should have been included, instead of quite omitted, in the *tenendas* and subsequent clause, with Mary and hers, in virtue of their common tie and union. Indeed, this is evinced by the very next grant in the Keir Chartulary,[1] it being a royal confirmation in 1357—thus in the same reign—to Marjory de Strivelin, proved *wife*, too, of John de Menteith (and so far standing in Mary's shoes), the noted Carse heiress, of her estates, "TENENDAS et *habendas*," &c., "JOHANNI DE MENTEITH et Marjorie SPOUSE *sue*" (the former the husband, again, and standing so far in the place of John de Strivelin) "et *heredibus unter ipsos legitime procreatis seu procreandis* quibus forte deficientibus, heredibus dicte Marjorie legitime." .... "*Faciendo* inde annuatim nobis et heredibus nostris predicti JOANNES et Marjoria sponsa sua et heredes sui ac ipsius heredibus deficientibus, heredes ipsius Marjorie predicte servitia de predictis terris," &c., "debita et consueta."

[1] See Chartulary to Keir work, pp. 198, 199.

What a contrast between this case and the former, though between parties similarly placed—both the females being the heirs in the properties (though that of Rathorane, consisting only of penny and halfpenny lands, was but secondary indeed compared to the ample and rich lands of Carse), and the husbands so far strangers; yet the husband, in the last instance, most prominently figures just in a manner as the heir, though he in the previous one be absolutely *nil*. How is this to be solved?

In the mean time, we may add one or two more cases.

William, Earl of Ross, having no male issue naturally, in 1370 obtained a regrant of his Comitatus de Ross to his eldest daughter, Euphemia, who was married to Sir Walter Lesly; and though she exclusively was heiress to this noble fief, it was conceived to the said[2] "*Waltero de Lesley militi* et Euphamie spouse *sue*, ac eorum alteri diutius viventi, et heredibus de ipsa Euphamia legitime procreatis seu procreandis .... et ipsis WALTERO et Euphamia sponsa sua et heredibus de ipsa Euphamia legitime procreandis fortasse deficientibus," then "Joanna junior filia dicti comitis, et heredes sui," were then to succeed.

[2] Great Seal Register.

Here Sir Walter, the husband, precisely in the same situation again with the preceding John de Strivelin and John de Menteith, and equally a stranger to the family, is yet mentioned and introduced repeatedly in a pointed and prominent way, while he afterwards took the title of Earl in right of his wife.

One instance more, if that be requisite, showing, too, that husbands, so far from being ignored, like John de Strivelin, were in a great measure well remembered, and even explicitly mentioned, after their deaths, in deeds.

Mariot Chene, an heiress in her own right, in 1364-5, in half of the barony of Strabrock and others in Caithness, obtained a royal confirmation of them[3] "dicte Mariote et *heredibus inter ipsam* et JOHANNEM *de Douglas* procreatis masculis seu femellis" (of whom she is previously styled "*sponse* QUONDAM," thus proving he had predeceased) "quibus forte deficientibus heredibus predicte Mariote legitimis quibuscumque."

[3] Regist. David II., No. 132; and for another instance, see p. 197, note.

Upon the whole, the Lorn charter in 1338 must be deemed anomalous and *unique*. How it may, in the point at issue, be otherwise accounted for, remains to be seen. Meanwhile the writer can only attempt to explain it as he has done in the text.

No. II.

PROOF refuting the Statement in the Keir Performance[1] that JOHN, Lord of Lorn, in 1338, Nephew of Mary, Wife of JOHN DE STRIVELIN, was "the last of the male line of the ancient Lords of Lorn."

(REFERRED TO AT PAGE 174).

[1] See p. 15.

1. Charter by David II.[2] (who reigned from 1329 to 1370), without date, "to John Lorn of all his lands in Lorn, quhilks were Alexander of Lorns, within Lorn."

[2] Robertson's Index, p. 30, No. 2.

2. The charter in 1338,[3] adduced by "*Johannes* de Ergadia, Dominus de Lorn," of lands of Rathorane and others in Lorn, " Marie amite nostre uxori Johannæ de Striwelyne, that has been sufficiently spoken to.

[3] See p. 187.

3. Statement by Fordun,[4] that Matilda de Bruce, sister of David II., died at Aberdeen in 1353, and had married an Esquire, Thomas Isaac, by whom she had two daughters, the eldest of whom was married " nobili et potenti viro *Johanni de Lorn, domino ejusdem* qui procreavit ex ea *filios* et filias."

[4] Scottish Chronicon, edit. 1759, vol. ii. p. 348.

4. Antecedent entry in an Exchequer Roll of David II.,[5] that in 1328 the Thanedom of Formartin was in the hands "Comitis de Sotherland, et Matilde de Bruce, spouse Thome Isaac ; " thus confirming Fordun's account of the marriage.

[5] In Her Majesty's General Register-House.

5. Other entry in an Exchequer Roll of David II.,[6] bearing payment " Johanne de Lorne *nepte domini nostri regis* de mandato." This evidently was the wife of the preceding John, Lord of Lorn (in the Keir Performance), daughter of Matilda de Bruce by Thomas Isaac, and necessarily niece of the monarch.

[6] Ibid.

6. Winton, one of our most authentic historians or chroniclers, born about the middle of the fourteenth century, and who figured towards the close, and thereafter gives this account of the descendants of Alexander of Argyle or Lorn (see under No. I.) by Red Comyn's daughter, who figured before and after 1300 :—[7]

[7] See Macpherson's edit., vol. ii. p. 57.

> "The thryd *douchter* of Red Comyn,
> Alexander of Argayl [*ut sup.*] syne
> Tuk and weddyt til his wyfe,
> And on her he gat intil his lyf
> John of Lorn [see No. 2], ye quhilk yat
> EWYN *of Lorn* AFTER THAT."

7. Attestation,[8] 14th of October 1371, by the Rector of Kellen, that the widow of Eugenius Macyvar "impignoravit" part of her lands in the barony of Glasbrack "JOHANNI

[8] Transcript of old evidents in the Advocates' Library, among sundry others of authentic writs.

Alani DOMINO DE LORN,"—that is, to *John*, the son of *Alan* (possibly here a casual mistake for Ewyn), Lord of Lorn.

From the preceding authorities, then, the Lorn pedigree, within the period stated, may stand as follows :—

I. ALEXANDER OF ARGYLE or LORN, by a daughter of the Red Comyn, *had*—   *Had* a sister, MARY, proved, in 1338, wife of John de Strivelin.

II. JOHN DE ERGADIA, DOMINUS DE LORN, in 1338. He married Johanna, daughter of Thomas Isaac by Matilda, sister of David II., by whom he had—

III. EWYNE OF LORN, who possibly may have been the same with *Alan*, proved father of John, "LORD OF LORN" in 1371 (see No. 7), and *who* thus had issue—

IV. JOHN, LORD of LORN, then—in 1371— existing.

Thus, quite in refutation of the Keir Performance, John de Ergadia, Lord of Lorn (under No. 2), was not, as it asserts, the last heir-male of the house, he having had issue (with other sons and daughters, see under No. 3) *Ewyne*, besides the presumed continuation of the male line, down at least till 1372 (see under No. 7), backed with the striking circumstance of the *new* dynasty of the STEWARTS, Lords of Lorn, not appearing upon Record till the next century.

There is often no small intricacy and disceptation in respect even to the higher Highland pedigrees, that certainly are the better of scrutiny, and not unfrequently more or less *in dubio*. In the mean time the writer offers what may be essential in regard to the above point in the Keir Performance, all that he is at present interested in, and which it may settle as contended.

CHAPTER VI.

FUTILE ATTEMPTS AGAIN OF THE KEIR PERFORMANCE, THROUGH THEIR VISIONARY ANCESTOR, SIR WILLIAM STIRLING, BEFORE AND AFTER 1300—WHO, THOUGH A BROKEN REED, IS UNSUCCESSFULLY RESORTED TO BY THE FORMER IN EVERY EMERGENCY TO CONNECT THE KEIRS WITH THE GREAT *VICECOMITES DE STRIVELIN*—TRUE DEDUCTION OF THE ORIGINAL ANCESTRY AND DESCENT OF THE LATTER, THE FOUNDERS OF THE *FIDULATI STRIVELIENSES*—THEIR ANCIENT PATRIMONIES, UCHILTRIE AND CADDER, SO LONG IN THEIR LINE—REFUTATION OF THE PREPOSTEROUS EFFORTS LIKEWISE OF THE KEIR WORK TO CASTRATE OR IGNORE AS ANCESTORS THE EARLIEST OF THE ABOVE *VICECOMITES DE STRIVELIN*, AND TO PLANT IN THEIR ROOM CERTAIN MOTLEY NONDESCRIPT STIRLINGS, AND FURTHER STILL, TO MAKE THE KEIRS, STILL THROUGH THEIR VISIONARY ANCESTOR, SIR WILLIAM STIRLING, THEIR DESCENDANTS AND REPRESENTATIVES, BY A FABULOUS PEDIGREE, EKED BACK TO 1130, THE MORE TO REDOUND TO THE KEIR ANTIQUITY AND GLORY—ALL LITTLE WORTHY OF SERIOUS DISCUSSION—CHURCH TENURE—THE FIEF OF CADDER, SO LONG THE HEIRLOOM OF THE *FIDULATI STRIVELIENSES*, SINGULARLY A BARONY HELD OF A BISHOP AND ARCHBISHOP, VESTED WITH THE HIGH POWERS OF A REGALITY OR PALATINATE, OF WHICH THERE ARE A FEW PARALLEL INSTANCES IN ENGLAND AND SCOTLAND—SIR JOHN DE STRIVELIN, THE SCOTTISH RENEGADO AND ENGLISH KNIGHT AND BARON, WHO FIGURED BEFORE THE MIDDLE OF THE FOURTEENTH CENTURY AND AFTERWARDS—CRUDE AND ABSURD NOTION, IF INTELLIGIBLE, OF HIS ORIGIN IN THE KEIR WORK—WITH GENERAL REMARKS AND CONCLUSION.

ALTHOUGH quite *jus tertii* to Keir, and a signal or rather outrageous interpolation, as it may be styled, in the Keir pedigree, it is singular to how many accounts the Keir Performance strives to turn the Sir William Stirling before and after 1300, in consequence of which he has been so often needlessly brought upon the carpet, and the exponent thus forced to notice and drive away this "will of the wisp."

And now especially it seems he must be made a bridge to connect the isolated John Stirling, the first presumed Keir ancestor in 1338 (whose whole interest in land consisted in what his wife exclusively possessed in the shape of Rathoran), with the great *Vicecomites de Strivelin*, the chiefs and

The ubiquitous Sir William Stirling, in 1292, again vainly attempted, by the Keir

by the Keir work, to be made the link of connection between Keir and the *Vicecomites* of Stirling.

principals of the *fibulati Strivelienses*; but the bridge is impassable, and no way round has as yet been discovered, so that the said John Stirling must remain a scarecrow in the mist, and genealogically in his prior state of single exclusiveness, irrespective either of a descent from Cadder or from the *Vicecomites de Strivelin*, or indeed from any Stirlings.

Original ancestry of the *fibulati Strivelienses* deduced through the Cadder.

But to preclude further attempts at such invasion of Cadder and Drumpellier rights, it may be proper here, as far as is practicable, to give a full statement of the original and early ancestry of the *fibulati Strivelienses* in the persons of the ancient and distinguished *Vicecomites de Strivelin*, from whom (like the Stewarts) the former derived their descent and their surname.

[1] See his "Genealogical History of the Stewarts;" London, 1798, pp. 3, 8, 10, *et seq.*

And in doing so, the eligible plan and method of the celebrated Andrew Stuart,[1] in adducing the proofs of the early ancestry and descent of the Stewarts, shall be here adopted, by stating the respective links and generations *seriatim* under distinct heads, with the evidence and conclusions relative in like manner in their behalf.

I.—TORALDUS or THORALDUS, VICECOMES (*the first generation*), *and conceived ancestor, from what will transpire, of the* STRIVELINS *in question.*

PROOFS.

[2] Chartulary of Kelso.

Charter by David I.[2] (without date), but who reigned from 1125 to 1153, to the Abbey of Kelso, of a saltpit in Carsaak, dated "apud *Strivelin*," which is witnessed " Roberto, Sancti Andree Episcopo ; Johanne, Glasguensi Episcopo ; Edwardo, Cancellario ; Duncano, comiti ; Herberto, Camerario ; TORALDO, VICECOMITE ; Alwino MacArchile, Uctredo filio Fergusii." All the above witnesses were persons of the highest rank and consideration, holding great public offices ; and, besides the two first Bishops of the kingdom, the Chancellor, and Chamberlain, there is Duncan, Earl of Fife, Alwin MacArchile, held by antiquaries to be ancestor of the Earls of Lennox, and Uctred son of Fergus, the Lord of Galloway. Thoraldus is held to have been a Saxon chief or leader, whom, with various Saxons, Normans, and strangers, David I., during what Chalmers styles the *Scoto-Saxon* period, imported into Scotland to colonise and civilise it.

From the date of the above charter at Stirling, taken with what will follow, we may conclude that the Sheriffdom he undoubtedly held was that of

Stirling. This charter must have been signed in or before 1147, that being the year when, according to the "Chronicles of Melrose and Holyrood," John, Bishop of Glasgow, a witness thereto, died.*

II.—WILLIELMUS, FILIUS THORALDI, VICECOMES de *Strivelyn*, son and heir of the preceding THORALDUS.

PROOFS.

1. Charter by William the Lion (without date, but who reigned from 1165 to 1214) to the Abbey of Arbroath, of a *salina* or *saltpit* in the Kars, which is witnessed by "Andrea, Episcopo Cathanensi," and, *inter alios*, by "WILLIELMO, FILIO THORALDI." Chartulary of Arbroath.

He also attests other charters of the time.

2. Charter (without date) by the same King William to the Abbey of Dunfermline, of Gillandreas Macfathen and his children (actual slaves), witnessed by "Waltero de Bedun, Cancellario; *Waltero, filio Alani*" (the *High Steward of Scotland*); and by "WILLIELMO, THORALDI FILIO," dated apud Strivelyn. Chartulary of Dunfermline.

3. Charter (without date), by "WILLIELMUS, FILIUS THORALDI, VICECOMES DE STRIVELYN," to the Church of Saint Mary of Stirling and Abbot thereof (the same as of Cambuskenneth), of the Church of Kirkintulloch, "cum dimidia carrucata terre pro anima mea et animis patris mei et matris mee," and which is witnessed "ALANO FILIO *ejus*," and others. Chartulary of Cambuskenneth.

4. Papal bull by Pope Celestine, addressed to Nicolas, Abbot of Cambuskenneth, confirming several grants in their favour, dated at Rome on the Ides of May 1195, including the grant of a carrucate of land "in villa de Bynnyn, ex concessione et confirmatione Jocelyni, Episcopi Glasguensis, et Ibid.

<small>Chartulary of Dunfermline.

* There is a grant by David I. to the Abbey of Dunfermling "*de rectitudine Navium de Inverese*," which is witnessed by "Herberto, Camerario," and "Thoro, *filio Swani*,"—"Thoro," it is concluded, being a contraction for *Thoraldo*. It is *very likely*—these Christian names being then exotics in Scotland, shared at least by very few there, while Saxon, too—that the preceding is the Thoraldus in the text. And Sir David Dalrymple, in his Collections,[1] notices a confirmation[2] by "*Thoraldus (sic) filius Swani*" to the Abbey of Holyroodhouse of the claim he had to the church of Travernent.

Admitting the identity, we would have, then, an older ancestor still, and, as may be inferred, of repute and condition, to the *Vicecomites de Striveline*, in the person of Swane, making the pedigree even more ancient than the visionary Keir one, while more distinguished. But in case of any doubts, and the writer inclining to a *strict* and correct genealogy, and certainly not desirous to imitate the extreme laxity and gratuitous assumptions of the Keir Performance in such respects, has preferred giving the above here in a kind of *suspense* state, rather than formally and unqualifiedly in the text.

[1] P. 429.
[2] Also in the reign of David I.</small>

WILLIELMI FILII THORALDI, et ex regia confirmatione ecclesie de Kirkintulloch cum dimidia carrucata terre," that had been granted by William's antecedent charter. Jocelin was Bishop of Glasgow in 1174.[1]

_{1 See Keith's Bishops, p. 139.}

_{Cumbernauld Charterchest.}

5. Mortification by David Fleming, Lord of Biggar, to the Church of Kirkintulloch, in the reign of Robert III., 1399, in which he confirms the former grants to the said church by his predecessors, and wherein is contained a literal transcript of the original donation by "WILLIELMUS, *filius* THORALDI, VICECOMES *de Strivelyn*," as specified above, together with a confirmation of the same by his successors, the Cummins, Earls of Buchan, upon whose forfeiture in the reign of David II. (who succeeded in 1329) the barony of Kirkintulloch was granted to the Flemings.

This Willielmus filius Thoraldi, *Vicecomes de Strivelyn*, had issue :—

1. *Alexander*, his *successor*, styled "*Alexander filius Willielmi filii Thoraldi*," and afterwards simply "Alexander, *Vicecomes de Strivelyn*."

2. JOHN, proved *brother* of the latter, under his description of "Alexander filius Willielmi filii Thoraldi" (see next generation, No. 2); as also under his later style simply of "Alexander, *Vicecomes de Strivelyn*" (see ibid., No. 4). He eventually succeeded the said Alexander his brother.

3. *Alan*, who, as son of the preceding Willielmus filius Thoraldi, Vicecomes de Strivelyn, witnessed his grant of the church of Kirkintulloch to the Abbey of Cambuskenneth (see previously, No. 3). The seniority of John to Alan may be held from what will follow, though not precisely proved.

III.—ALEXANDER FILIUS WILLIELMI FILII THORALDI, or simply, as he came to be styled, "*Alexander*, VICECOMES DE STRIVELYN," and *Justiciary* of *Lothian*, son and heir of the preceding William; also Sheriff of Stirling, and *proprietor* both of OCHILTREE and CADDER, the original *patrimonies* of the *fibulati Strivelienses*, down to 1541.

PROOFS.

_{Chartulary of Dunfermline.}

1. Charter of William the Lion (without date, but who reigned from 1165 to 1214), confirming a grant by Malcom, Earl of Athol, of the Church of Molin to the Abbey of Dumfermling, which is witnessed by "ALEXANDRO FILIO *Willielmi* FILII *Thoraldi*."

2. Charter by "ALEXANDER *filius Willielmi filii Thoraldi*" (without date),

to the Church of St Michael of Linlithgow of *two carrucates* "in *villa mea* de *Okiltree*;" there particularly described, and witnessed by "JOHANNE FRATRE *Alexandri*" (that is clearly of the granter), Okaltrie, or Uchiltree, of which important Strivelyn possession we have thus the first intimation, appears to be fully as old a Stirling patrimony as that of Cadder. *(Chartulary of the Priory of St Andrews.)*

3. Formal agreement and convention (without date) between the Church of Linlithgow and "*Alexandrum* filium Willielmi filii Thoraldi," to the effect that Alexander, by permission of the Church of Linlithgow, " habebit capellam et cantariam in *curia sua* de *Okiltree* et ad opus suum et familie domus sue, et hospitum suorum, salvo jure matris ecclesie, et decimis et oblationibus, &c., ad ecclesiam pertenentibus; ita tamen, quod capellanus qui ibidem serviet, per ecclesiam eligatur, et instituetur, in capelano (while) Alexander "de suis sumptibus inveniet necessaria in victu et vestitu et laboris mercede." And in return, too, Alexander is to give to the Church of Linlithgow "duas bovatas terre in perpetuam elymosinam in VILLA SUA de sua OCHILTREE, et unum toftum ibidem, et decimam *Molendini sui.*" *(Ibid. This and previous number proves the first possession of Uchiltree by the Vicecomites, though unknown to the Keir work.)*

"*Alexander* filius Willielmi filii Thoraldi," by this interesting feudal and ecclesiastical document, is proved to have lived in baronial state in his domain of Ochiltree, having his court and separate chaplain, by agreement with the above church, for behoof of his family and guests; nor is the mill of Ochiltree to be overlooked, always a high feudal perquisite and accompaniment. Ochiltree thus appears to have been as considerable a property as Cadder (perhaps then even more so), while both remained *pari passu* with the Stirlings of Cadder until the *denounced* 1541, quite irrespective of Keir. What shall we think of the research of the Keir Performance, which does not contain a particle of the above valuable information as to Uchiltree,—certainly so far back,—nor the least glimpse of Alexander having had an interest in it?

4. Charter by William de Lamberton to the Priory of St Andrews, of the Church of Bowerden (without date), witnessed "*Alexandro, Vicecomite de Strivelyn*," and "*Johanne fratre Vicecomitis de Strivelin.*" Alexander here appears in his now exclusive style of Sheriff of Stirling, while his having thus had a brother *John*, identifies him, if that were requisite, with "Alexander filius Willielmi filii Thoraldi," who is explicitly proved to have had such too (see under No. 2), and who, it will be seen, succeeded to Uchiltree. *(Register of the Priory of St Andrews.)*

5. Quit claim by Simon de Preston (without date), "*coram Alexandro, Vicecomite de Strivelin*, et Waltero de Lyndsay, Vicecomite de Berwick, *tunc* *(Chartulary of Newbottle.)*

196   COMMENTS ON KEIR PERFORMANCE,

Justiciariis de *Laudonia*," of the lands of Lenots in Berwick to the Abbey of Newbattle, bearing to have their seals appended.

<small>Records in the Tower of London.</small>
6. Inspeximus by Henry III. of England, dated 20th September 1260, of a confirmation by William the Lion, who reigned from 1166 to 1214, of an agreement between Maurice, Earl of Maneth (Menteith), and Maurice the younger, his brother, in regard to the right to the earldom of Menteith, which last is witnessed, " Alexandro filio meo, Comite Malcolmo de Fife, Willielmo de Boscho, Cancellario, Comite Gilberto de Stradherne, Philippo de Mubray, Rogero de Mortemer, ALEXANDRO, VICECOMITE de *Strivelyn*, Waltero de Lindescia, Harveio de Kinros, Harveio Marescallo," all men of high rank and consideration in Scotland. The agreement is extant, and bears to be dated in 1213, so *that* probably may be the date of the latter.

<small>Original Chartulary of Glasgow, when in the late Bishop Cameron's hands.</small>
7. Charter by "Alexander, Vicecomes, domini Regis de *Strivelin*," whereby he grants "pro anima Regis Willielmi domini mei—et pro salute Regis Alexandri domini mei et successorum," to the See of Glasgow, "tres marcas annuatim in pura et perpetua elemosina de *Molendino meo de* CADDER."

This charter, thus proving the family then possessors of Cadder, as they already have been of *Uchiltree*, through the medium of the mill, which was dominant over the rest of a fief in the person of the same Alexander, was confirmed by Walter, Bishop of Glasgow, who figured from 1207 to 1232. The Keir Performance thinks it may have been about 1221.[1]

<small>[1] See ibid., p. 6.</small>

<small>Chartulary of Coldingham.</small>
8. Charter by Alexander II., eighth year of his reign (1221-2), to the Priory of Coldingham, of an exemption "ab omni teloneo," which is witnessed by "*Alexandro, Vicecomite* de *Strivelin.*"

<small>Original Chartulary of Glasgow, when in the hands of the late Bishop Cameron.</small>
9. Charter by the same monarch, ninth year of his reign (1223), confirming an agreement between Walter, Bishop of Glasgow, and Jordan de Carrockis, in relation to the lands of Stobo, which is witnessed by "Alexandro, Vicecomite de Strivelyn."

<small>This Alexander, a high magnate, simply styled *Vicecomes de Strivelyn.*</small>
This Alexander may be styled the great *Vicecomes par excellence* in the family, being evidently among the *magnates* of the country. His invariable style, since disusing the patronymical (after the practice, as will be seen, that obtained also in the case of the Stewarts), was simply "Alexander, Vicecomes de Strivelyn;" and under this description, without any adjunct, he thereby was exclusively known, and figures on numerous public occasions—testing royal charters, with courtiers, dignified churchmen, officers of state, &c. From what transpires in the Keir Compilation,[2] owing to the insertion of a Sir Alexander de Strivelin, Constable of Rokesburgh in 1241, under the head

<small>[2] See p. 6.</small>

of the Vicecomes, one might infer (although not directly stated there) that these were identical ; but this could not be, both on account of his distinct designation, *in toto*, from that of the Vicecomes, and the latter, as we may presume, having then predeceased.

The Vicecomites of Stirling had not yet, in the time of Alexander, adopted the surname of Strivelin, which they came afterwards to take, just like the cotemporary Stewarts, from the high office they so uniformly held.

In illustration and in support of this last concurring fact, we may next give, duly established by evidence, the specific designations and styles of the heads and leading members of the Stewarts—every way a parallel case during the period in question—and, further still, embracing that also, when they had relinquished their original coinciding patronymics, and assumed their well-known surname—quite *ex-officio*—of Stewart.

The family had not then taken the surname of Strivelin, but only afterwards, precisely as the Stewarts did theirs.

I.—"WALTERUS FILIUS ALANI *Dapifer Regis Scotiæ*" (the same with *Steward* or *Senescallus* at the period), founder of the House of Stewart, who eventually took that surname solely from their high office. He figured principally from 1165 to 1177.[1]

II.—"ALANUS FILIUS *Walteri Dapiferi*," the son and heir of the preceding, figured from 1177 to 1204.[2]

III.—"WALTERUS FILIUS ALANI SENESCALLUS," the son and heir of the preceding, also styled "DAPIFER *Regis Scotiæ*," hence further proving these two terms to be synonymous. He figured from 1204 to 1246.[3]

IV.—"ALEXANDER SENESCALLUS SCOTIÆ," *proved son and heir of the preceding Walter Fitz-Alan*, and so designated in 1256-60, and thereafter. Hence, precisely like "Alexander, Vicecomes de Strivelin," in 1221 and 1223, &c., instead of patronymically, as had before obtained in both families.[4]

[1] For legal evidence of this, see Andrew Stuart's History of the Stewarts, p. 3-7 inclusive.

[2] Ibid., pp. 8, 9.

[3] Ibid., pp. 10, 11, 12.

[4] Ibid., p. 12-14; and also Rymer's Fœdera, vol. i. pp. 558, 715, and vol. ii. p. 1082.

But subsequently it is established by a Chamberlain Roll in 1289,[5] that the two sons of this last "Alexander, Steward of Scotland," James, his eldest and successor,* and John of Bonkill, as he has been called, were, respectively, merely styled "Jacobus *Senescallus*," and "Johannes *Senescallus*," the high hereditary office now, *per se*, constituting the family surname, while an exact

[5] In Her Majesty's General Register-House, Edinburgh.

---

* As every valid evidence regarding the Stewarts, whose connections and alliances have been often mistaken and misrepresented, are valuable to antiquaries, the writer has ventured to adduce here a charter from the English Patent Rolls, confirmed by Edward I, in 1296, by no inferior person, Richard de Burgh, Earl of Ulster and Lord of Connaught ; granting " Domino *Jacobo Senescallo* Scotie" (mentioned above in the text), " et Egidie sorori mee Castrum meum del Ros, et Burgum at totum dominium pertinens ad dictum castrum," with

In the Tower of London.

parallelism will be proved in the *Vicecomites* we are discussing in the next link of connection.

<small>Cases of the Stewarts and Strivelins mutually illustrative.</small>

In these circumstances what must we again think (and it really gives us too much to think about) of the *precision* and *accuracy* of the Keir Performance, which, in the face of these undoubted facts, takes it upon itself literally to misrepresent the preceding Alexander the Vicecomes as "*Sir Alexander de Striveling* of Cawder"¹—*perchance* for a purpose—though with the adjunct, "Sheriff of Stirling," he never figuring as in the first instance, and to the suppression of his true established description.

<small>¹ See p. 6.</small>

Alexander the *Vicecomes* does not appear to have married or left issue. Certainly there is no trace of either fact; and he evidently was succeeded, as is to be presumed in the circumstances, by John his younger brother, so fully proved, to whom we next come. And here again, too, the Keir Performance flagrantly errs, as usual, in gratuitously representing John as the *son* (*not* brother) of the above *Vicecomes*, and continuing the line accordingly.

In the precise words of Churchill's philippic against Guthrie,² by the former giving a putative son to the unprolific Alexander, he also

<small>² See p. 3.</small>

"Calls forth *living* waters from the *rock;*"

nay,

"Calls forth *children* from the *barren* stock;"

thus identifying itself with such writers, not overlooking, either, the *immaculate* Douglas, in whose footsteps it thus follows.

IV.—*Johannes* de STRIVELYN, afterwards *Dominus Johannes* de STRIVELYN, proprietor of the family property of *Ochiltree*, and also *Vicecomes* of Strivelyn, *younger brother* and heir of the preceding Alexander the great *Vicecomes*.

PROOFS.

<small>Chartulary of Soltray.</small>

1. Charter by JOHANNES de *Stryvelin* to the House of the Holy Trinity of Soltra (Soltray), of a toft and croft "in villa *mea* de *Oucheltree*, et cum services of his English vassals, to be held by the said James, "et Egidia *uxori sua* in liberum *maritagium* et in liberam *Baroniam* de me et heredibus meis et eorum heredibus de corporibus eorum procreatis." It is witnessed, *inter alios*, "Domino Johanne de Soules, Domino Waltero de Lindeseye," and "Domino *Nichalaio* de *Chambell*"—which last notice is interesting. The writer can nowhere find a trace of this marriage, or Irish connection, in any pedigree or history of the Stewarts, even Andrew Stuart's.

<small>This is another instance at variance with the Ratheran grant in 1368, see p. 187.</small>

communi pastura *eiusdem ville*," &c. "Volo preterea (it is added), ut predicti fratres (the religious house of Soltra as above), habeant annuatim unam tronam bladi de singulis carrucis meis et hominum meorum ubicunque existentium *ex parte australi* aque de *Forth* in autumno." It is without date, but witnessed by "Domino Gilberto, *Capellano*" (the family chaplain, as may be presumed by the antecedent evidence as to Uchiltree in regard to his brother *Alexander the Vicecomes*),[1] and by "Galfrido preposito de Ouchiltric."

[1] See p. 195, No. 3.

He was thus, like his elder brother the *Vicecomes*, in full possession of Ochiltree, besides, as here intimated, other possessions on the south side of the Forth, and coupling this grant with what will follow, the family (precisely as in the Stewart instance), in his person, must now have taken the surname of Stirling.

2. Charter by Nicholas de Soules, Pincerna (Butler) Domini Regis Scotie, to the Abbey of Newbottle, of a saltpit in the Carse of Kalender "secundum recognitionem factam per *Johannem Vicecomitem* de *Strivelyn*, ex precepto Domini Regis."—(Without date.)

Chartulary of Newbottle.

3. Confirmation by Alexander II. to the See of Glasgow, of certain lands specified in a perambulation taken the 28th year of the King's reign (1242)—namely, Conclud and others, which is witnessed, "JOHANNE, VICECOMITE de *Strivelyn*," who thus had fully succeeded Alexander his brother in that sheriffdom that he is proved to have held also by the previous authority.

Chartulary of Glasgow.

4. Charter by Maldowen, Earl of Lennox, to Stephen of Balantyre, of half a carrucate "terre de Kynerine," which is witnessed "Domino Waltero, Senescallo Scotie, DOMINO *Johanne tunc Vicecomite de Strivelyn*, Domino Johanne de Vallibus." It has no date; but as the learned editor shows that Earl Maldowen succeeded in 1225, and is supposed to have lived till about 1270, it may have been between those years.

Chartulary of Lennox, edited by James Dennistoun, Esq., Advocate, pp. 35, 36.

5. Grant of the lands of Dunipace by Adam de Norham to the Abbey of Cambuskenneth (without date), which is witnessed "Domino Daniel de Graham, Domino *Johanne de Strivelyn*."

Chartulary of Cambuskenneth.

6. Grant by Adam de Norham of the mill of Stonehouse to the Abbey of Newbottle, which is witnessed "DOMINO JOHANNE, *Vicecomite de Strivelyn*." It has no date, but immediately following there is a supplication to Alexander II. to confirm it, which is done, accordingly, under the titles thereof

Chartulary of Newbottle.

"Confirmatio Alexandri Regis," dated thirty-second year of his reign—viz., 1246, about which time, therefore, the preceding must have passed.

<small>Original ancestry of the *Fibulati Strivelienses* thus established.</small>
In the above way the original ancestry and descent of the *fibulati Strivelienses* have been deduced, through their representatives the *Vicecomites* of Strivelyn (then as much the capital of Scotland as Edinburgh), which high office was in a manner hereditary in the family, and from which they derived their surname. With it they conjoined their noted patrimonies of Ochiltree and Cadder, besides, as elsewhere transpires, other valuable domains and *fiefs*.

<small>Unnecessary, from what is admitted in the Keir work, to deduce it further down than the above John, the *Vicecomes*; but different original ancestry, interpolated in the room of the preceding, falls now to be refuted.</small>
It is unnecessary for present purposes to carry their descent and representation further down than the preceding Sir John de Strivelyn, the first of those who took the surname, proprietor, *inter alia*, of Ochiltree, and Sheriff of Stirling, especially as he is admitted by the Keir Performance—however mistaken in his filiation—both to have been heir and successor of Alexander the great *Vicecomes*, and ancestor of the subsequent chief and paramount line of the Stirlings of Cadder, whose direct descendant and representative was Janet of Cadder in 1541—in whom it admits that status.

The preceding Sir William Stirling (namely, of 1292), so often mentioned, may be accounted a cadet, or younger male descendant, of the preceding Sir John the *Vicecomes*, though not in the way represented in the above work, and certainly not, at any rate, as the Keir ancestor.

But there still remains what the exponent cannot permit to pass without comment and refutation. The same notable Performance has actually taken upon itself *de facto* to suppress or ignore the line of the *Vicecomites of Strivelyn anterior* to Alexander the *Vicecomes* mentioned (who nevertheless is admitted into its pedigree), deprived him and his successors of their true ancestry, as proved—of whom not unlikely it might be ignorant—and interpolated in their room as such certain new and nondescript Stirlings, as they may be <small>New pedigree here untenable, because Keir must first connect himself with it, again, through his visionary ancestor, Sir William Stirling, in 1292.</small> styled, quite foreign to the Cadder pedigree, but yet of whom the Keir Editor is so fond as to give them Keir, moreover, as their direct descendant and representative.

This is obviously an utter absurdity, because with this view he is, by his own showing, forced first again to connect him with Alexander the *Vicecomes*, through that ever insurmountable barrier the so often cited Sir William Stirling, in 1292—whom further, in his exigencies, he preposterously fabricates into a descendant of the same *Vicecomes*, though he died without issue—and hence, on all hands, the indisputable bridge of communication being thus broken down between Keir and these *parvenus*, the matter might be at once safely dismissed without the least additional comment. But, further still, as the exponent must be jealous of any such attempt, however futile, to deprive the *Vicecomes*, or his family, of their true ancestry —wherein he also has an interest—he will next proceed to show its innate nullity, and hence the impossibility of attaching them to any other stem than that which has been established.

As already observed, Alexander the *Vicecomes* was a high magnate—perhaps more so than any of his race—an official and leading public character, who figured about Court, and attested various public grants of importance under his fixed Vicecomital title, and never otherwise, except at the outset, when as "*filius Willielmi filii Thoraldi*," he is proved proprietor of the Cadder patrimony of Uchiltree, where he had his chapel and court.

<small>New ancestry with whom the Keir work has honoured Alexander, the great Vicecomes de Strivelin.</small>

Keeping this in view, we come to a "charter" (it should be a confirmation[1]) by Alexander II. to the Hospital of Soltre, in 1225, pointedly founded upon in the Keir Performance[2] (but carelessly and imperfectly as usual), without giving its import (in which, too, the grammatical error formerly noticed in an ADDENDA, I. p. 27, was perpetrated), whose testing clause in the original, though not in the work, is precisely as follows:—"Testibus Thoma de Strivelyng, Archidiacono Glasguensi; Roberto, *capellano*; Gilberto de Strivelyn, *clerico*; Waltero, et Willielmo Beset; *Alexandro, filio Patricii de Strivelyn*" (*the last mentioned, and with whom the clause ends*).

<small>[1] Namely, of a grant by Duncan de Swaynstone to Soltra, therein stated *in gremio*.
[2] P. Sou Ibid., p. 5</small>

Now, can any one suppose for a moment, after reading the preceding clause with attention, that the Keir Performance could have assumed and concluded *that this* last Alexander, son of Patrick de Strivelin, thus so humbly figuring at the close of the list, was actually Alexander, the great *Vicecomes*, who was so differently designated—while never surnamed *de Strivelyn*— which alone disproves the identity. Nevertheless, the work does so, and founds upon this witness, *so appearing* with his patronymic, as the connecting link to his anterior denounced pedigree, when he is but an isolated obscure person, who cannot be affixed to a Stirling stem, and must be classed with those of unknown origin, not uncommon at the time.

<small>The first—preposterously and futilely—is attempted to be identified with a humble "Alexander, son of Patrick," in 1225, an unknown stranger.</small>

In the parallel question of the origin of the Stewarts, especially discussed early last century, in further exposition of the present subject, a putative ancestor in like manner was started—one "Alden, or Aldan Dapifer"— whose Christian name, with the usual liberty of former genealogists, was transmuted into Alan Stewart, and, with a little more fancy and imagination, into no less than the Stewart of Scotland, son of an asserted Walter Stewart in the reign of Malcolm III. This was obviously to enhance and corroborate, as was deemed by some (after the fashion of the Keir Performance), the antiquity of the Stewarts, as Stewarts of Scotland.

<small>Fallacy exposed by a similar misconception at the outset of the Stewart pedigree, here again illustrative.</small>

The same "Aldan Dapifer," like Alexander, son of Patrick de Strivelyn, figures in the testing clauses of two charters, respectively by Earl Gospatrick and Waldeve, Earl of March, his son (here quoting from Lord Hailes, as we are always happy to do, who supplies the particulars in question). To the "charter by Earl Gospatrick (he says) there are eight witnesses—'Andrew, the archdeacon; Adam, his brother; Nigel, the chaplain; Ketel, the son of Dolphin; Ernold; *Alden the Steward (Dapifer)*; Adan, the son of Alden; Adan, the son of Gospatrick." And "to the charter granted by Earl Waldeve, there are nine witnesses; *Alden Dapifer* is the seventh in order. There are only three among them (he adds) who seem to have been landed gentlemen; all the three are placed *before* Alden Dapifer."[1]

<small>[1] See his Essay on the Origin of the House of Stewart, Annals of Scotland, edit. 1797, vol. iii. pp. 55, 66.</small>

Now, upon the first of these two charters Lord Hailes remarks—"Is it possible for credulity itself to believe that the Alden, placed so low in such company, was the High Steward of Scotland, a man at least as honourable as Gospatrick himself?"

"I have no doubt (he concludes) that the witnesses to this charter were the dependants or household servants of Earl Gospatrick, and that if we interpret *Nigellus Capellanus* to be Nigel, the Earl's chaplain, we must interpret *Aldenus* or *Aldanus Dapifer* to be Alden, the Earl's steward." "I persuade myself that Alden *Dapifer*, and Alan the father of Walter, Steward of Scotland in the reign of Malcolm IV., were different persons."[2]

<small>[2] Ibid., p. 57.</small>

With all submission, then, applying this precedent, which tells in many respects, and is so mainly illustrative, to our question, we may equally ask, if not *a fortiori*, is it possible for credulity itself to believe that the previous "Alexander, the son of Patrick de Strivelin," not merely following (like Alden) in the testing clause quoted, an archdeacon, and chaplain, but also a common churchman, and two obscure and nondescript Besets, while even the individual last mentioned there—that a man so differently described, and so postponed to such inferior people, could have been the high

Alexander, *Vicecomes* de Strivelin? On the contrary, as he thus figures, he can only be held a humble individual or retainer, and upon parallel grounds—independently of what otherwise *per se*, as shown, fixes the point —if Alden Dapifer was not High Steward of Scotland, no more can the said Alexander be deemed the great *Vicecomes*. The last, in striking contrast, has always the precedence befitting his manifest rank—while never surnamed Stirling—besides publicly and officially figuring on the most exalted occasions; and therefore we may safely consign this humble Alexander, the son of Patrick de Strivelin, who is equally a stranger with his son, so preposterously adduced by the Keir Performance, to that obscurity and oblivion from which he should not have been dragged.

But even this is not all. The Keir Performance,[1] after some irrelevant remarks touching "Thomas de Strivelyn, Archdeacon of Glasgow,"[*] who so much precedes this secondary and unknown Alexander in the foregoing testing clause in 1225, actually styles him, without the least ground for such inference, "the *supposed brother*" of that very individual, after he had been metamorphosed into the great *Vicecomes*, that he might be made as dignified as possible, while it adds that another equally, in truth, obscure "Gilbert de Striveling," also mentioned there, "*may have been* a brother or *other* relative of (the above) *Alexander* and *Thomas*." {*Other incidental and preposterous anomalies here in the Keir work.* [1] *See pp. 5, 6.*}

True genealogy is not a thing thus casually or carelessly to rest upon such loose ruminations. "*May* have beens," perchances, empty suppositions, and suchlike, in which the Keir Performance indulges, are repudiated, and excluded from regular discussion and argument. And it was long ago sagaciously rejoined by an antiquary, when it was said one, after such fashion, *may* have been either brother or cousin of a party, that in truth he was "neither"— which may relevantly here apply. In quitting this, after all, insignificant topic —though intended to be of high consequence to Keir—we must advert to {*Apprehended nature of true genealogy.*}

---

[*] We really, it is to be regretted, are constantly stumbling upon some piece of carelessness and unprecision in the Keir Performance.[2] It gives us a full excerpt from Crawford's *Lives of the Officers of State* relative to the above Thomas's family and history, but without the least reference to the page. Hence we are necessitated to find it out ourselves; while he states the fact so as to lead one to believe that Crawford actually had said that Thomas "was a younger brother of Alexander" —that is, from the context, of the humble, obscure Alexander, last in the testing clause in 1225—when, on the other hand, he had quite a different Alexander in view, whom he directly specifies,—viz., "Alexander Strivelyn, *miles*—a donator to the Abbacy of Arbroath *pro anima Emergerdæ filiæ Regis Scotiæ*"—hence a *knight*, quite distinct and of far greater note and importance.—(See Crawford's *Lives*, who quotes here from the Chartulary of Cambuskenneth. p. 12.) {*This proves indeed a flagrant misrepresentation in the Keir text.*}

[2] See p. 5.

another reprehensible omission of the Performance.[1] It twice adduces the preceding Gilbert de Striveling in the testing clause in 1225,* simply as a laick, to make him apparently more fitting company for his imaginary brother, the too favoured Alexander, transmuted into the pseudo *Vicecomes*, when he is explicitly described and defined there by the adjunct *clerico*, clearly fixing him, on the contrary, to be only a humble monk or ecclesiastic, but which material adjunct it chooses twice to withhold and suppress! Is not this just repeating or playing off the same prank (for we can use no other term) with Douglas, already exposed curiously in reference to another *Gilbert* in the same century—a Christian name that seems subject to strange liberties— viz., to him of "*Hameldon*,"[2] who, though likewise identically testing a clause as a *clericus* in a deed in 1272, is yet made too a *laick* by the former, and the actual ancestor and founder of the house of Hamilton. Much, indeed, may be expected from the Keir editor, when so closely tracing the footsteps of such a bright exemplar and pattern!

It is ludicrous enough, but, seriously speaking, profitless, to follow out the subject. The Keir Performance, yet holding, against all truth and likelihood, that Patrick, father of Alexander de Strivelin, in the Soltray testing clause, in 1225, was likewise so of Alexander the *Vicecomes*, further to *extend* this *new* baseless ancestry, represents him, without the slightest proof of such identity, to be Patrick Strivelyn of CAMBUSBARRON, in Stirlingshire; which last he *supposes* again to have been father of the preceding Thomas, Archdeacon of Glasgow; thus stringing all these nondescripts and before unknown relatives together. The supposition is just as tenable as the above identity; while it seems about this irrelevant Peter of *Cambusbarron* and his property minute and, of course, useless researches have been made.[3]

But now comes the grand *finale* and crowning conclusion for the transcendent antiquity of the Keir family: no less than cruelly—by means of the Keir editor's fairy wand alone—transplanting the said Peter, the *ci-devant* father of Alexander the Vicecomes, and, as erroneously, the *ci-devant* of Cambusbarron, far from his domestic hearth and household gods, and fixing him, in the utter dearth, as usual, of testimony, in the alien district of Teviotdale! What preceded being now disregarded and fairly out of view, he is converted into Peter Stirling, possessor of *Edinham* there; and,

* For a full and accurate copy of it from the Chartulary of Soltray, Advocates' Library, see present Exposition, p. 201, where it is given.

moreover, no doubt to his vast surprise had he learned it, eldest son of Walterus de Strivelyng, having an interest in the same quarter, who figures about 1150, and is one of the witnesses to a charter of confirmation to the church of Kelso, by Henry, Prince of Scotland, son of David I.!

To such great results, from little, or rather void causes, indeed, can *skilful* artificers and partisans arrive. It was thought fitting by the Keir compilers that Keir should be the representative of as old a family as any in Scotland, while, however extraordinary and grotesque these unstable flights and divergences of his alleged ancestry, they nevertheless behoved to be carried out, in order that at the outset of the Keir pedigree there might be something peculiarly grandiose and ancient. And accordingly we have there "I. WALTER DE STRIVELYNG," their announced patriarch or ancestor in "1130-1160,"[1] to catch the eye of casual and *ex facie* readers, who, contented with what they see on the surface, might be disinclined to penetrate further into the details and mysteries of the subject, which, though flimsy and shadowy when sifted, yet might be to them uninviting and abstruse. The Keir editor might be now thought to have gone far enough, but still he is not yet satisfied, and more strikingly *ad captandum vulgus* (and, as some would say, to throw dust in their eyes), he, at the beginning of his work, under the special head of the "CONTENTS,"[2] strings all the foregoing motley, nondescript Strivelings together, and however, in the leading members, mostly unconnected, and strangers to each other, gravely metamorphoses them *seriatim* into father and son. By this notable device the entire putative pedigree collectively is made to form no less than twenty articulate and successive "generations"—all *numerically* specified, as if actually fixed and coherent, commencing, as the first, with the "Walter de Strivelyng," already mentioned, in 1130, and ending, as the twentieth and last, with the honourable Member for Perthshire!

This really, it may be said, is—

——— "imponere Pelio Ossam;"

even as difficult, if not more so, and boldly attempting a thing that hardly would have gone down last century, when, through the auspices of Douglas and other *Empirics*, such strange and unaccountable liberties were taken with pedigree and genealogy.

But, seriously speaking, when we recollect, too, over and above, that the

Summation in said secondary and ridiculous matter.

proof of the cardinal link connecting "John de Strivelyn," in 1338, who may be styled, as things stand, both "*lack*-land and *lack*-parent,"—the first only admissible Keir ancestor, with John and Alexander, the respective *Vicecomites de Strivelin*, before and after 1266; the latter of whom, be it remembered, has been shown to have died without issue,—is utterly wanting; and it would be a jest to hold it in the least assisted as so futilely pretended, by means of Sir William de Strivelin, in 1292, who is here an absolute stranger; while intervening links, also interpolated, are—as could be shown too—quite unauthenticated, and incoherent—the entire *superficies* of the preceding supposititious Keir-Cadder descent, as well as of the putative southern, in all its phases, must at once collapse, and, brittle as ice, at the first touch of inquiry be shivered into atoms.

[1] *See Keir Performance, Preface, p. x., and work, p. 3.*

We cannot but be amazed that such an unprecedented pedigree should be coolly palmed off upon the public, that the Keir family, through such a *medium*, should be maintained to have flourished for more than SEVEN CENTURIES, while " few families[1] (it is at the same time announced) can boast of an INHERITANCE which has *descended* through so long a line of ancestors;" and will it be believed that *this* actually *alludes* to *Cadder*, which the Keirs only first acquired in the *peculiar* way shown by a singular title in 1541? Not to misrepresent the case, the precise words of the original may be here given.[2]

[2] *Ibid.*

Triumphant Keir results, however, arrogated by the Keir editor to the Keir family.

"The Stirlings (of Keir, by the work) first appear as owners of land in the twelfth century. After possessing lands in different counties, they acquired, in the reign of William the Lyon (who reigned from 1166 to 1214) the estate of *Cawder*, which has *continued* in the family *without interruption* to the present time, a period of nearly *seven* centuries." And then follows what has just been quoted, the whole *semel et simul*, inculcating that from the reign of the above prince down to Keir, the present possessor, it had invariably continued in his family. What a perversion of fact, and capable of such manifest refutation !—the family, forsooth, to have flourished for *seven* centuries, when it only dates from the isolated and *unattached* (that is to say, to any other stock at present) John *de* Strivelin in 1338—a descent, however, more than five centuries back, with which, it is apprehended, if the Keir family could have been content, they would have stood on far higher ground, than by grasping at that to which they can properly establish no right.

Having discussed the ancient possessors of Cadder, a subject of such high ambition, and, it is believed, all new material on that head, we may next, perhaps, be excused for giving some account of the fief that may be remarkable, and in a certain respect deserving our attention. It held of the Episcopal, subsequently the Metropolitan See of Glasgow, when it became an Archbishopric, and such tenure was next highest to that immediately under the Crown, and even a more favoured one, because exempt from the oppressive drawbacks of minority and non-entry, &c., on a *civil* superior, while also pressing upon the vassal, and detracting from the profits and emoluments of the *dominium utile*.

Chalmers justly remarks that "the tenure of lands under the Church was very mild, and very liberal, as (he adds) we may learn from the chartularies;"[1] and, moreover, refers "to the custom of St Mungo" (the patron saint) in the bishopric of Glasgow, whereby "the widow of a tenant on the *bishop's rental* was entitled, while she remained single, to hold her husband's lands for life." This custom was sustained by the Court of Session as late as 1633[2] (it should have been 1533). These tenants were a sort of copyholders, whose right to their lands might be considered absolute; and it is incontestable that many proprietors and leading lairds in the Barony of Glasgow came within such category, and held portions of their property under such a title—among whom we must include Alan Heriot, whose widow was Marion Fleming of Boghall, the subsequent wife of Robert Stirling of Letter in 1533,[3] and which lady actually, as by the regular account of it in the ADDENDA,[4] was the party in whose favour the above legal plea or exception was so sustained by the Court of Session.

But what may be still more remarkable and striking at first sight even under such mild dispensation, the Stirlings of Cadder held their ancient fief as a *barony* of the great See and Regality of Glasgow, as was legally maintained and proved before the Supreme Civil Court by their successors in 1552, 1576, and 1586, by evidence adduced in the ADDENDA.[5]

The licnt practice and prepossessions of the Church were pretty much the same over Europe before the Reformation, and that of England quite quadrates with the fact or notion then of such a barony within such a See. There were, it seems, of old, in the sister kingdom, two kinds of baronies, the *majores* and *minores;* the owners of the first of which Spelman styles "REGIOS BARONES;"[6] to distinguish them he adds, "*a Baronibus* EPISCOPORUM *Comituum* ABBATUM," and (which last also may be kept in view) thus including those with whom we are concerned.

Fief of Cadder held under a favourable tenure, with curious custom of St Mungo, and Cadder a Barony held of Glasgow.
[1] Caledonia, vol. I. p. 735, note (p).
[2] See under Addenda, No. I.
[3] See Ex. p. 58.
[4] See again Addenda, No. I., *ut supra*.

[5] See Addenda, No. II.

[6] Glossary, *sub voce* Baro and Baronia.

And Cruise,[1] the best and latest writer on dignities in England, concurrently states that "the great lords, particularly those who were earls *palatine*, called their immediate tenants or vassals *barons*. Thus (he adds) the Earls of Chester and the *Bishops* of Durham had their *barons*."[2] With respect to the Bishopric of Durham, that See, it is well known, had the high rights and privileges of a palatinate, or *jura regalia*, according to Hutchinson, which were identical with the former, or a regality; so that the bishop, being thus a kind of independent potentate or prince, could on principle both claim and exercise the privilege of including barons among his higher vassals, and designating them and their fiefs accordingly. And if so, certainly the Bishop or Archbishop of Glasgow too, as he must have done, who not only was lord paramount of an extended district with large fiefs, but whose See likewise had been constituted into a regality by a special grant of James II. in 1450.[3]

Nor is Cadder the only instance of a Scotch fief holding as a barony of an archbishopric in such circumstances. The distinguished family of Dunbar of Kilconquhar, direct heirs of the ancient though forfeited Earls of March, held their large and valuable fief of Kilconquhar as a *barony* of the Metropolitan See or Archbishopric of Saint Andrews,* which had been duly invested with a regality, while certain abbacies even with us, also possessing a regality, extended the same privilege to their vassals, who duly enjoyed it. The Lords Hay of Yester held their fief of Atheotmore as a barony of the Abbot of Arbroath,† and the old family of Edmonstone their fief of Edmonstone‡ of the Abbot of Dunfermling, thus quite in unison again with the identical practice in England as stated by Spelman.[4]

There are still several points upon which the writer might dilate, connected with the discussion, from which he is at present barred by want of

---

* The family ended in heirs portioner, when, February 5, 1568, a grant passed the Privy Seal to Arthur Wod, of the non-entry and mails of the fourth part of the "*Barony* of KINNEWCHAR (the noted corruption of *Kilconquhar*), in the *Regality* of *Saint Andrews*, of which barony the Archbishop of Saint Andrews is there stated to be superior," and of whom, of course, it held as a baronial fief.

† Supplication in 1542 by John Lord Hay of Yester, stating "he had ye landis of Aitheatmure (in Lanarkshire) in heritage, halden be him immediatelee of ye abbot and convent of Arbroath," while it is proved by their chartulary in the Advocates' Library, that the latter were invested with a regality.

Summondes again in 1550 by William Hay of Yester against certain tenants, stating that he has "ye landis and *barronie* of Atheatmure wyt ye pertinentis."

‡ Proved by authentic Edmondstone documents which the writer has seen, while the Chartulary of Dunfermline also establishes that that religious house had the rights and privileges of a *regality*.

room. He can only further discuss, with the view of concluding in the main the subject of the *fibulati Strivelienses*, a remaining and outstanding party of that class, sufficiently warlike and distinguished in his day, but flourishing at a distracted and turbulent period, when there was no small vacillation and uncertainty in the political horizon.

He is no other than Sir John de Strivelin, styled also "Baron Strivelyn," the noted Scotch renegado—"Scoto-Anglo," as he was styled—who figured much in history during the reign of Edward III., with whom he hostilely sided against his own country, holding high commands and offices under that monarch, who largely requited his services, and by whom he was summoned to Parliament, from 1342 to 1370 inclusive.[1] Sir John de Strivelin, Baron Strivelin in England, the Scottish renegado, or Scoto-Anglo, Knight (temp. Ed. III.) [1] See Dugdale's Baronage, vol. ii. p. 143.

He strangely has been confounded with Sir John Stirling of the Carse by our Scotch writers, including Crawford, who adds that he "was a mighty great complier with the English in favour of Edward Baliol, and is the same John Stirling whom Sir William Dugdale mentions was a peer of England, and called by a writ of summons to the Parliament there,"[2] thus unquestionably the preceding, though here mistaken for him of Carse. The immaculate Nimmo, who was the subject of special comment at the outset, and his later editor, retail the same error, but the two knights in question are entirely distinct. The last mentioned, Edward Baliol's and Edward III.'s adherent, subsequently, as might be expected, made England his domicile, being conspicuously engaged in their warlike expeditions against Scotland; and by his marriage with Barbara, eldest daughter of Sir Adam Swynburn, Lord Swynburn, he left only female descendants who continued his line. [2] See his Remarks on the Ragman Roll, Nisbet's Heraldry, last edit., vol. ix. p. 30. And as to the Ragman Roll, see too Addenda, No. III. Mistaken for Sir John of Carse.

On the contrary, Sir John Stirling of Carse still remained, like his ancestors, in Scotland, and was succeeded in his large Scotch estates by Marjory, his only child and heiress, who married John de Menteith, by whom she was the ancestrix of the distinguished family of the Menteiths of Carse or Kerse, who still flourished in the reign of Charles I. See partly here Keir work, Chartulary, p. 198-200.

These Menteiths were therefore the heirs-general, or of line, of the ancient Strivelins of Carse; and it is remarkable that the bold and ambitious Sir John Stirling of Keir, dead in 1539 (so well known to us), with the object, doubtless, of engrossing in his family the entirety of Stirling interests and representations, both directly and indirectly, obtained from the crown, March 16, 1524[3] (not long after one of his Cadder grants), that of the ward and marriage of the tenandries and baronies of West Carse and Alveth unto (it is added) [3] Privy Seal Register.

the "lauchfull age of twenty-one years of William Menteith of West Carse." He probably destined William for one of his daughters, but fate (perhaps fortunately) ordered it otherwise, and he did not succeed here in his objects, whatever they were.

As to anything materially illustrative of the Scoto-Anglo knight, Sir John Stirling, of his origin or status, it was but little to be expected from the Keir Performance, nor certainly are we here undeceived by the result. What the editor has attempted on this head will be next given.

<small>Nothing to be gleaned about the Knight in the Keir work. His origin and descent there unintelligible, and a verbal jumble of the oddest kind. See Keir Performance, p. 195.</small>

He sets out with remarking that "it is *probable* that branches of those early Stirlings (in the south formerly noticed, and whom he vainly strives to make the Keir ancestors) had *crossed* the border and settled on the *English side*,"—a fact, as will be seen, even if established, which it is not—and thus amounting to another of his gratuitous assumptions—here of the purest insignificance. Next he starts away with the abrupt intimation that "among the burgesses of Berwick who swore fealty to Edward I. in 1291, were Adam de Strivelin and *Johannes de Strivelin*." But what, again, has this to do with the subject? The act of fealty by these isolated and obscure Stirling burgesses, which no one denies, is quite a *non sequitur*, unless we were to suppose—and it is all we can make of it—that their residence *at Berwick* was confirmatory of the preceding assumption of the early Stirlings (among whom they are to be comprised) having crossed the border, and "settled on the ENGLISH SIDE," in which event, however, there would be a piece of ignorance, for Berwick properly continued to be Scotch, and altogether Scotland, till the reign of Robert Bruce inclusive,* and even later, so that the burgesses in question could never have made an English "flitting," but just remained on their own soil at Berwick, following out their occupations as before. And, lastly, coming apparently to the point (which exhausts all about the origin of the Scoto-Anglo knight in the Keir Performance), the editor thereupon states that "THIS SIR JOHN DE STRIVELING was connected with the county of Northumberland. He rose to great importance by adhering to the English side during the disturbed reign of David II."—here clearly introducing and discussing the knight. What the *ci-devant* "*Johannes*, the burgess," was, *must* thus follow from the context, he being *the John* immediately before mentioned, and hence must have been *identical* with him,

---

* Though as notoriously, like some other Scotch towns, in part occasionally seized and held by the English.

and quitted his shop and *toga* for armour,—much, doubtless, to the honour and exaltation of his chivalrous counterpart! Such a *raffacciamento* in genealogy! It seems an anomalous and unintelligible jumble of the oddest kind!* Neither is the English knight proved to have been originally settled in Northumberland. The contrary must be inferred from what will be stated;[1] adventitious circumstances alone connected with his interests and professions, it must be concluded, had fixed him in that quarter. The only way we can, and in part merely, rescue the Keir editor from the absurdity (letting the other fallacies alone) to which he, as above, may be amenable, is by holding that he had the English knight exclusively in view in the passage quoted, beginning with the words, "*this* Sir John de Striveling;" but in order to make such excuse available, we are forced, rather awkwardly, to travel backwards beyond an intervening detached paragraph to the very title of the article, announcing "Notices of Sir John de Striveling, who was summoned to the Parliament of England," &c., which is at variance with the rules of correct writing, and that perspicuity and precision indispensable to an historian, within which category, doubtless, the Keir editor would like to be included.

[1] See next page.

It is obvious from what Fordun, in 1335, and others, state about the Sir John de Strivelyn in question, that he was a renegade Scotsman, who had adopted the English party and interests. In that year, he informs us that there came to the siege of Lochleven " dominus Johannes de Strivelyn, *miles Regis Angliæ*, cum magna multitudine tam Anglicorum quam *Scoto-Anglicorum*, inter quos erant Michael de Arnot," &c., " cum *aliis* pluribus *ad pacem Regis Angliæ* conversis." Sir John, in the above capacity, heading them, as, from his admitted military talents, he did upon other occasions.

Edit. Gooali, vol. ii. p. 313.

That he was forfeited in Scotland must have followed in consequence; and precisely in the reign of David II., which was from 1329 to 1370, thus including 1335, there is in the index of missing charters, by that monarch,

---

* That justice be done to the Keir editor, the passages discussed, forming the outset of the article, shall be here fully and collectively given, without any interruption, as in the text.

" The earliest notice of the Stirlings is in the reign of David I., as proprietors of lands on the Borders; and it is probable that branches of these early Stirlings had crossed the Border, and settled on the English side. Among the burgesses of Berwick who swore fealty to Edward I., in 1291, were Adam de Strivelin and *Johannes* de Strivelin.

" This *Sir John de Striveling* (hence the latter!) was connected with the county of Northumberland. He rose to great importance by adhering to the English side during the disturbed reign of David II. In 1335 he directed the siege of Lochleven, in the service of Baliol,"[2] &c.

[2] Keir Performance, p. 195.

published by Robertson, Deputy Clerk Register, one entered to "Adam Ereskine of Barrowchan, of the *forfaultrie* of JOHN STRIVELING *in general*," which seems a striking coincidence, and points pretty distinctly at the preceding, who thus must have been a Scotch proprietor, probably of substance and condition. Coupling this important fact with his being included (as may be held) by Fordun with Scoto-Anglicani, and the next argument from his armorial bearing, he could not, in refutation of the Keir work, have been originally a Northumbrian, but of pure Scotch growth.

It is especially established by Dugdale, that Sir John the knight was repeatedly summoned to Parliament,[1] and figured as an English baron; and it so happens that in a fine copy of his Baronage, in the library of Caius College, Cambridge, in which the arms of the old barons there are accurately delineated in their proper colours, those of Strivelyn are specially included, that could be no other than the knight's, he being the only Strivelin who came within such category, and are described as "argent on a chief gules, three round buckles or," which being as clearly the peculiar armorial charges of the Strivelyns of Carse,[2] obviously so far as such arguments from arms may go, would indicate him to have been of that distinguished stock, and necessarily a Scotsman, though *not*, as premised, Sir John *of Carse*.

No burgess, at that feudal and chivalrous epoch, could have aspired to or sported a coat of arms, so the Keir editor's hallucination *ex facie* of the Berwick burgess having been the knight—or, forsooth, of their blood or family, as may follow from the language he uses—is refuted.

The same Sir John Strivelyn, the baronial knight, is stated to have married "Barbara, the eldest daughter" of Sir Adam of Swynburne, Knight, Lord Swynburne, "who, in her right, was Lord of Swynburne."[3]

But by the following new evidence it may be proved that he had formed another matrimonial alliance, there being an authentic precept by Edward III. in 1364, to the "Eschætori Regis in Comitatu Northumbrie," as to taking the fealty, "*Johannis de Strivelyn, chivaler qui duxit in uxorem* Jacobam tertiam filiarum Ricardi de Emeldoun, defuncti de proparte sua manerii de Jernuth, qui de rege tenet in capite, per servitium *militare*."[4] Hence, apparently, a good and suitable match. He besides, as proved by the same record, obtained in 1366 "custodiam manerii de Camboys" and others in Northumberland, "que fuerunt Isabelle que fuit uxor Willielmi Devonii defuncti."[5] Upon the whole, Sir John appears to have been a great favourite of Edward III., whom at least he faithfully served, and by whom, in return, he was largely and honourably remunerated.

He is styled "Baron Strivelyn" by a well-known and eminent writer in the reign of James I.,[1] who, in reference to Bewcastle, in the vicinity of the rivers of Lod and Leven, that run into the Esk, states, "that in Edward III.'s reign it belonged to *John, Baron Strivelyn*, who married the daughter and co-heir of Adam de Swinborne" (see p. 212). Thus he was the possessor of another important fief or property.

If what has now been adduced may lead to more of importance in the matter, the writer, who can supply nothing additionally at present, will, of course, be well pleased.

[1] Camden, p. 1027.

Upon another point mooted in a previous chapter[2] the writer has one more observation to make, to elude the chance of any doubt or misconception. Though he had apprehended or inferred there a settlement or entail also of Cadder upon direct heirs-male in 1414, from the intimation at the outset of the Ratherne regrant in that year, and scope or bent of the procedure, especially as to Ratherne, still he has not due means of establishing the fact. Indeed, the entire withholding of the Cadder writs—the natural source of requisite information—by the Keir family, coupled with their marked silence and abstinence from explanation on such occasions to the Drumpelliers, so constantly maintained, while the opposite conduct was always pursued by the latter, may bar apposite probation both here and in certain Cadder *minutiæ*. Upon this account, perhaps, they may claim from the public some indulgence and forbearance in what they offer on such points.

Independently, however, of such Cadder settlement or entail, as well as of Ratherne, as would seem to have been intended from the outset of the regrant in 1414—and to the arguments based on which the writer still holds[3]—the conceived *status* of Robert Stirling of Bankeir, the Drumpellier ancestor, entitling him to have been served tutor to Janet of Cadder during her minority, with his great family weight as next Cadder heir in a feudal age, could not but make him of weight and importance. It alone might have elicited the striking transaction between him and Sir John Stirling of Keir in 1527 for renouncing, it may be concluded, and not insisting upon, such gentilitial rights and authority in favour of the Knight, the Cadder wardator, to whom their non-claim

[2] See pp. 29, 30. Qualification of what the writer has said about the inferred Cadder Settlement in 1414 to heirs-male.

[3] See pp. 30, 31.

or relinquishment was advantageous; and who, therefore, so far as he could, compensated Robert and his heirs in return in parts of Cadder, under the remarkable warranty of his old Keir patrimony. This transaction, unless upon a gentilitial footing—not unlikely including claims upon Cadder—so decisive for Drumpellier, it seems impossible to explain. The respectable Keir agent in 1818 could offer no different solution, while he so distinctly admitted he could not disprove the arguments and conclusions on the opposite side that were specially submitted to him. And taken with what otherwise so forcibly obtains for Drumpellier—even bating the import of any Cadder entail in 1414—more especially the fact proved of the same Robert of Bankeir and Letter and his heirs being next collateral heirs of Janet of Cadder, while backed with the remaining concurrent features and incidents of the Drumpellier case—ancient and modern—it may be held to be fully substantiated.

The preceding is stated by the exponent from mere motives of openness and candour, though strictly not required, the general or material question confessedly being, as shown, long legally foreclosed in his favour.

Having now brought to a conclusion, without any recapitulation, which indeed would be supererogatory, and perhaps annoying to the reader, a case requiring exposition, it may be admitted, on the other hand, that a *status* and descent have been unduly arrogated for the first time by the Keir Performance to the Keir family without a vestige of evidence—nothing of the kind, independently of its refutation, being condescended upon—to the manifest prejudice and injury of a party, the true force of whose claims and gentilitial rights has been unduly ignored and misrepresented.

Remarks on the conduct of the Keir claim and pretensions. Ignorance of the now long undenied and formally recognised Drumpellier status cannot be pleaded in excuse by their opponents, after the remarkable collision between them and the late Keir in 1818, with the determined opposition then threatened and attempted, but afterwards so inconsistently abandoned by him and his partisans. The memory of these events, they having been of so singular a character, with the mutual correspondence—already given in the Exposition—must naturally be presumed to be in the Keir charter-chest, as well as the printed abstract of evidence for Drumpellier in 1818, quoted partially in the Keir work to serve a purpose, but when inimical no doubt prudently withheld. Besides ignorance in law, even though it could be pleaded, *neminem excusat*, and due previous investigation, that neither obtained in the present instance, is always expected of an assailant. .

The case now for Keir in its recent irregular or subaltern shape—not legal, like that of Drumpellier in 1818, as would have been far preferable—seems to have been carelessly and inadequately managed; and had the honourable Member for Perthshire, instead of being controlled by the imprudent counsels and suggestions, as is apprehended, of his partisans, directed his well-stored mind to bear upon the subject, he might perhaps have piloted his crew so as to have saved them from shoals and rocks upon which they may have lamentably struck.

The writer has been informed that proof-sheets of articles in the Keir Performance were sent to parties for their consideration and revision prior to its distribution ; and if so, why, it may be asked, was not the same eligible plan observed in respect to Drumpellier ? Common delicacy, owing to the remarkable collision between Keir and Drumpellier in 1818, might properly have prompted the step in ingenuous minds, so that no unfair or undue advantage, as might have inadvertently happened, should be taken, owing to former enmities, by the first one over the latter—at least, that those points might be mutually understood and kept open upon which they disagreed. This, it is believed, is the conduct of fair disputants even in ordinary society, and if adopted on the present occasion, through the explanations that had ensued, might have precluded untoward consequences, not only to Keir, but to Drumpellier, in being thus unavoidably compelled, as he so much regrets, to appear in print *pro aris et focis*, and defend his family rights and interests against manifest invasion and misrepresentations.

<small>A more eligible mode of procedure might have been adopted.</small>

But at once recklessly, without caution, *de plano*, for the Keir editor, of his own accord, as he has done, and for the *first* time, roundly to inculcate that Keir was not only descended of Cadder, but, moreover, its chief and direct representative, as well as of all the Stirlings, as if a fact quite certain and undoubted, only tends to make the inevitable contrast, when tested, as it has been, by truth, to its utter abnegation, through the printed correspondence, unfolding the prostration of the late Keir, with his forced abandonment openly of such pretensions, after so arrogantly advancing them, as well as his opposition to Drumpellier in 1818, the more ludicrous and striking. Independently of their refutation by other irresistible evidence to the same purport, the absurdity of the attempt is thus shown in the most glaring colours, to the undoubted prejudice and injury of the honourable Member for Perthshire.

Necessary origin of the present Exposition in March 1859.
After a protracted interval (more than forty years since 1818, the date of the last Drumpellier legal occurrences), the writer was again "summoned to arms" by the present worthy Drumpellier representative in March 1859. He had the honour then of being requested to undertake the duties of his counsel, as upon the former remote occasion, and to defend his gentilitial rights, including the Cadder representation, so unduly assailed, and bestowed upon another by the Keir Performance. Although the writer has not for long laid himself out for much practice, and, somewhat like Horace's gladiator, unwilling again to encounter legal turmoil and contention, had rather put his arms aside—after being engaged in analogous antiquarian combats, certainly of no small account—he yet, in the peculiar circumstances of the case, and out of regard to old estimable clients, could not resist the appeal, and has accordingly complied therewith, though considerably off the irons, as may be apparent by the Exposition, for which he duly apologises.

He hence bent his attention to the subject with renewed care and investigations; and he is happy to state that, good and valid as the Drumpellier case was in 1818, it has thereby, in his mind, been strengthened and corroborated, through further material facts and conclusions (independently of what may even transpire and result from those in the Keir Performance), and which correct impressions on some secondary points he had entertained, but now recalls. At the same time, they can be backed, he conceives, by legal doctrine and apposite and relevant illustrations—the whole to the advantage of Drumpellier, and humbly submitted in the Exposition.

Other considerations, too, and impressions, naturally present themselves to the writer. If he may be pardoned for alluding to private incidents—to use Buchanan's words,

"Si mihi privato fas indulgere dolori"—

he cannot but recur, as not wholly foreign either to the case, but rather irradiating it, to the happy days he formerly spent in the society of talented individuals so intimately connected, and who were then more or less interested in its phases and progress, as the facts gradually developed themselves. These were Mr William Stirling, younger of Drumpellier (who has well figured in the controversy), Sir William Hamilton, and John Gibson

Lockhart—all long since gone and departed; including, too, it is believed, the whole of the *dramatis personæ* in 1818, Sir Samuel Stirling, another common intimate, though on the opposite side, among the number.

The writer, who must also soon follow, thus remains a forlorn secondary wreck amidst the loss of such remarkable genius and talent.* He was occupied in these melancholy though pleasurable reflections this very day, 18th of April 1818, when it so happened he had finished this Exposition, when all at once it occurred to him, though not thought of before, that it was the anniversary also of that on which Andrew Stirling, Esq. of Drumpellier (father of the present Drumpellier), obtained his signal victory over the united forces of Glorat and Keir—the first actually in the field, the other not, but his determined enemy in *secret*—by successfully carrying his service, notwithstanding every possible opposition by them, as heir-male of Robert Stirling of Bankeir and Letter, who died in 1537. This was the main hinge and pivot in the case, while almost immediately thereafter, as a necessary sequence, he had his status formally and strikingly recognised and admitted, without even the least challenge of the preceding, who, utterly discomfited, had left the field, or of any remaining party, as nearest heir and representative of the ancient Stirlings of Cadder. When it is added that those opposed to him were Mr Robert Jameson, Advocate—a name at our bar speaking for itself—and who could leave no stone unturned legally to foil an opponent,[1] and Mr James Dundas, W.S., at the head, too, of his legal body (both likewise long ago deceased), it must be admitted, without disparagement to any others, that Drumpellier successfully passed the severest ordeal in his case that can possibly be figured.

[1] See Exposition, p. 122-3.

EDINBURGH, 18*th April* 1860.

---

* To these also may be added the late estimable Lord Anderson, snatched away still more prematurely; and with respect to whom, an incident, also *in re antiqua*, affecting him, the writer, and the Keir editor withal, in analagous keeping, it may be said, with the *penchant* of the latter, as in the instance of the leading merits of the Drumpellier claim, to ignore true leading facts, and third parties in a case, will be found in the ADDENDA, under No. IV.

ADDENDA TO CHAPTER VI.

No. I.

(REFERRED TO AT PAGE 207.)

[margin: ¹ Caledonia, vol I. p. 755, note (p).]

Chalmers,¹ in support of his allegation of "the custom of St Mungo," in the diocese of Glasgow, having been sustained by the Court of Session as late as 1633, quotes MS. Bisset's *Rollment of Courts,* Balfour's *Practique,* c. 44. But his last reference here should have been to p. 205, *ib.*, at least according to the edition of these *Practiques* published in Edinburgh in 1756, where we find the following, that must have been evidently in view :—" Gif any man be rentallit him alane in St Mungo's rental in ony lands and possessiounis, and decessis thairefter, his *wife* sall bruik and joise the samin for all the dayis of hir lifetime, by privelege of St Moungo's widow.—1st March 1532, *Relict of umquhile Alane Heriot, contra Mr Robert Heriot,* I.ᵗ. c. 416."

[margin: ² Acts and Decreets of Council and Session.]

This, abstracting from the curious specialty of Saint Mungo's widow (perhaps originally out of respect to *Centena,* his mother, whose name is still perpetuated in the neighbourhood), implies ordinary copyhold tenure, through entry in the Bishop's rental-books, of which the writer years ago saw the originals, in the possession of the late Bishop Cameron, a noted Roman Catholic Bishop in Edinburgh.² A payment or *grassum* was at the same time exacted on entry, constituting a valid title in the rentaller or copyholder. But the record, still extant, of the above process, quoted by Balfour in 1532 (not in 1633, as in Bisset's *Rollment of Court, ut sup.*), singularly renews our acquaintance with parties who have deeply attracted our attention. It bears to be an action of reduction before the Court of Session by "*Marion Fleming,* ye relict of umquhile *Alan Heriot,*" against "Archibald Dunbar of Blackcraig, bailie of ye barony and lordship of Glasgow, and others, being on the assize and inquest in ye action movit by Maister Robert Heriot and Gilbert Heriot, breyer" (*brothers*), "against ye said *Merion,* tuiching the lands of Ramshorne, Medofflat, &c." (in the barony foresaid, and yet known there), "quhilk sulde pertene to hir as *wedo* of the said umquhile Alan" (the inquest having repelled her just defence and decerned), "ye said Maister Robert Heriot to bruik the said lands." But the "Lordis of Counsale *cassis* and *annulis* ye said *rollment* and decreet" thereupon, "because Merion allegit that her husband was rentalit *him alane* in the *rental-buik* of Glasgow," being "callit and answerit for these *landis,* and be yat ryt *scho* suld bruik ye samin, be privilege of Sanct Mungo's *wedo.*"

[margin: ³ Ibid.]

And it transpires, by another process before the same Court, March 18, 1533,³ that the parties interested were "Dame Isabell Levingstoun, Lady Rosling; James Levingstoun, hir bruyer; Maister Robert Heriot; and Gilbert Heriot, bruyer to umquhile Alan Heriot," on the one side, and "William *Fleming of Boghall;* and *Marion Fleming,* relict of umquhile Alan Heriot; and *Robert Strievlin,* now *her spouse,* for his interes," on the other; and further, that there had been a compromise between them, in respect of Alan's "gudis movabil of airship," then in Marion's hands, whereby, on their delivery to Master Robert Heriot, his heir, the sum of one hundred and sixty merks was to be invested in lands for her behoof in liferent, and to Mr Robert in fee.

Here again, suddenly and curiously, reappear Robert Stirling of Letter, and his wife Marion Fleming, daughter of William Fleming of Boghall, both mentioned, at the end of the year of their marriage, in 1533 (which began on the 25th of March).[1] She must have been a good match, not only in point of family, but also as widow of a respectable proprietor of land—obviously well connected, too—in the barony of Glasgow (that comprised Cadder), of which, in law, she had been liferenter; while both parties illustrate a grave and interesting legal point, mooted by Sir James Balfour, Lord President of the Court of Session, in his *Practicks of the Law of Scotland,* and thought worthy of special comment by Chalmers in his *Caledonia.*

[1] See p. 58, where the dispensation for their marriage, dated June 11, 1533, is fully given.

No. II.

THE SEE OF GLASGOW A REGALITY OR REGAL BARONY, AND CADDER HOLDING OF IT, AS A BARONY, PROVED BY WHAT FOLLOWS.

(REFERRED TO AT PAGE 207.)

Charter by James II., 20th of April 1450, in favour of William, Bishop of Glasgow, constituting "*civitatem* Glasguensem *Baronium de Glasgu,* et terras vulgariter vocatas Bischope forrest in liberam, puram et *meram* REGALITATEM;" further, to be held *blench,* by the simple *reddendo* of a red rose "*si petatur,*"—thus devoid of, and abstracting from, all feudal service.[2]

On the 15th of November 1552, James Stirling "of ye Keir" raised an action against Andrew Hammilton, "baillie of the baronie of Glasgow, and John Johnston,"[3] stating that the latter had pursued him "before the baillie of ye baronie and his deputis," to receive "the same Johne, tenant to him of a mailing in *Cadder Culter*; howbeit ye said baillie and his deputis are *nawayis* competent to ye said James be resoune he *nalder* [neither] dwellis nor remains *weytin* ye said baronie, and *his saidis landis* are of CADDEN, haldin be him in *fre* [free] BARONIE be itself of ye *Metropolotine* and *Seit* [See] of *Glasgow,*[4] for service of three suittis at there heid courtis in ye year allanerlie, havand particular jurisdiction as BARROUNE yairfoir upon *all ye boundis* of ye samin, tenentis, inhabitantis, cottaris [cottars] yairof." Moreover, Keir urges that his predecessors (certainly the Stirlings of Cadder) were "infeft of *anld*—of his *fredome* and privilege of BARROUNIE and haldin of *courtis,* as his infeftment *shewin before the Lordis of Counsall proportis;*" and complains, too, that if the adverse plea or procedure of Johnston, as above, be sustained, then,

[2] Chartulary of Glasgow.

[3] Acts and Decreets of the Supreme Civil Court.

[4] Archbishopric of Glasgow or Metropolitan See.

instead of a *frie barroune*, as he was, (it) "sall mak *him* ane *thrall* (*slave*) tenent yairthrow, to his hevy dampnage and *skayt*" (*injury*). The process bears on the record to be continued, without apparently any result or decision, the evidence above thus formally submitted to the Court being probably held conclusive, and deterring the opposite party from taking further steps in the matter.

There were also the two following legal processes, to the same purport, and eliciting the same conclusion, by Keir against his tenants in 1576 and 1586 :—

[1] Records of the same Court, ut supra.

Action before the Supreme Civil Court in January 1576 by James Stirling of Keir, Knight,[1] against the tenants of Achwan, adjacent to the "landis and BARRONIE of *Cadder*," where it is stated that he and his PREDECESSORS had right to the *barony* of Cadder, "lyand in ya *regalitie* of Glasgow."

[2] Ibid.

Action also, 25th November 1586,[2] by the said Sir James Stirling, "lawful heretor of ye landis of ye BARRONIE of CAULDER, wyt tour, fortalice, and manerplace of ye samyn, lyand wytin ye BARRONIE of *Glasgow*," "aganis certain tenants, to remove from the Kirktoun of Cadder ;" it being requisite in a legal process thus to set forth the full title of the pursuer as proprietor of the *barony*. While no objection was taken thereto, this, coupled with what precedes, proves that the right, and the undenied—in fact, acknowledged—appellation of the fief were just and appropriate ; and Sir James, by thus maintaining Cadder, the ancient heirloom of the Stirlings of Ochiltree, &c., or of that Ilk, to be a barony in the barony and regality of Glasgow—*an imperium in imperio*—did the sole thing (among much detriment), in the course of his existence, seemingly respectful and agreeable to the former, as defending high rights and privileges once inherent in them, in virtue of a venerable fief and possession, though (however otherwise the Keir Performance has represented the matter) he clearly so far had but a legal right under a singular title, that, we may infer, weighed more with him than any such consideration.

No. III.

(REFERRED TO AT PAGE 209.)

The Ragman Roll in 1292 and 1296 would be an admirable and interesting *medium* through which, as a kind of nucleus or pivot, to convey more minute and valuable information about our families ; and it is therefore, in this view, with submission, suggested to the attention of our antiquaries.

Unfortunately now, in so advanced an age, when our records and writs of all kinds are so greatly increased, and made accessible to the public, affording good means and opportunities for the purpose, nothing of the kind properly or to its full compass has yet been attempted, while we have only a meagre publication of the Roll in question, under the auspices of one of our antiquarian clubs, without desirable or appropriate comments or illustrations by the editor, who was little of a genealogist, and thus in the main, it may be said,

WITH DRUMPELLIER'S EXPOSITION, &c.   221

unfitted for the undertaking. That peculiar gentilitial knowledge, including acquaintance with the interests, connections, names, and designations of our families, which last are often mistaken and misrepresented in the Roll, otherwise so valuable, owing to its English superintendence, or perhaps concoction, in a certain measure, must ever be indispensable requisites for the purpose.

No. IV.

SINGULAR INSTANCE of the KEIR EDITOR also in effect ignoring the WRITER and others on the occasion of the WINTON SERVICE in 1840, precisely as the leading features and merits of the Drumpellier case in the Keir Performance.

(REFERRED TO AT PAGE 217.)

The indeed very premature death of the late Lord Anderson, a most amiable person, and *collaborateur* with the writer in a high legal antiquarian case, which they, as the sole counsel, brought to a goodly end, and who then, though not greatly advanced in years, had attained the utmost eminence in his profession, with the promise of being even still more distinguished, the writer cannot refrain from adverting to. And most justly it is stated, in a recent number of *Notes and Queries*,[1] that his "unexpected demise was a source of deep regret to those who knew him, and a serious loss to Scotland; for a better or more upright lawyer never sat on the bench." The case in question involved the male representation by the present Earl of Eglinton of the ancient and noble house of Seton and Winton, from whom such a title of nobility flows in both kingdoms, and which the writer exclusively had the honour of *originating* as far back as 1825. It was then with his curators (who were *unaware* of the right) that he communicated during the minority of the Earl; and upon its being submitted for his opinion to that able and accomplished lawyer, Lord Corehouse, when at the bar (after one also by the writer), he decidedly advised its prosecution. This was the true groundwork of the subsequent procedure, which the writer, as sole counsel, in its various stages, directed and superintended till a later period, when he was happily conjoined, as his junior, with the preceding Lord Anderson; when they finally had the honour, December 22, 1840, of addressing one of the most dignified and intelligent inquests[*] who, it is believed, ever met on such an occasion, and who, after a full statement and adduction of the evidence, which was rather long and complicated, served the Earl in the status he claimed, identified with the Winton honours.

[1] December 3, 1859, Second Series, vol. viii. p. 458.

True statement of the origin and progress of the recent Winton claim and service in 1840.

From the strange partial way, however, which the editor of the *Memorials of the Montgomeries, Earls of Eglinton*,[2] privately printed in July 1859 (and of which time precludes further notice at present), the same with the editor of the Keir Performance, who has been the subject of so much comment, has there chosen to state the occurrence of the Winton service

[2] See vol. i. p. 139.

_____

[*] Several of their names will transpire in the sequel.

in 1840, one would be led to think that the late Lord Rutherford was its mainspring and conductor, *no other* counsel being *named* as employed. But this is palpably erroneous. He merely chanced, as a chamber-counsel, to give an opinion upon a point of forfeiture in the case, upon the strength of the old familiar precedent of Gordon of Park in 1750 and 1754, which, as the English law of forfeiture has been ours ever since the Union, was capable, in all its phases, of much riper and fuller illustration. Than this, Lord Rutherford, then of course at the bar (whose merits in other legal departments the writer is the last to question), did no more. The glimpse of him thus in private—for he made no public appearance in the matter—was quite *passager*. Like a shadow he came, and so departed; while the entire uncontrolled management of the case as counsel, both *in ovo* and otherwise, until the end, rested exclusively in the writer and Lord Anderson, who alike, by whomsoever suggested (of which they remained ignorant), did not descry the necessity of Lord Rutherford's casual or summary opinion, by which neither were they enlightened or influenced. Indeed, the writer partly demurred thereupon to the agent, with what effect he does not pretend to say, but at any rate his Lordship was as much subsequently in the case legally *nil* as he had been before.

<small>This case of Gordon of Park, too, did not relate to honours, which were in 1836 and 1840 mainly in question; and the case of Somerset, unnoticed in the opinion mentioned, was stronger, and more in point.</small>

The preceding account, though it is feared rather egotistical, and for which every apology is made, the writer has been induced to state in common justice to Lord Anderson, who deserved, in the work alluded to, from his peculiar situation, far more notice than the former—and indeed to himself.

Since the Winton service in 1840 was to be there introduced, it ought to have been in a full, correct way, adapted to the occasion. But it is evident, in the face of most obvious fact, and certain means of probation, that one only *nominatim* is represented as the ruling authoritative counsel, who, on the contrary, did not so figure, and did little or nothing. While those, on the other hand, who had the lead, and took the labouring oar —in fact, including the writer, who *originated* the case (which may be deemed *something*), and exclusively, without the least communing with Lord Rutherford, or aid from him, superintended, conducted, and successfully terminated it, in such very capacity, are thus ignored just as the leading merits and import of the Drumpellier claim in the Keir Performance. Whether there is justice and propriety in this—or why such conduct preferred by the Keir and Montgomerie editor—to what might be more eligible, the writer, without deigning to account for it, will leave the public to decide.* It may be

---

* For greater fairness, the following account of the Winton service in the work alluded to,[1] that has elicited the above remarks, shall be here literally given :—

"The representation of the Seton or Winton family having vested in Lord Eglinton, his Lordship was, on 22d December 1840, served nearest and lawful heir-male general, and also nearest and lawful heir-male of provision" (this was in reference to the *cardinal* grant of the Winton honours), " to George, fourth Earl of Winton, Lord Seton and Tranent. This service took place before the Sheriff of Edinburgh and a distinguished jury, including Lords Gillies, Moncrieff, and other Judges of the Court of Session, Mr Thomas Thomson, Advocate, and other gentlemen well qualified for legal and genealogical investigation. . . . . Previous to this service, Lord Eglinton had been advised by eminent counsel of his right to the Winton and Seton honours. Mr (afterwards *Lord*) *Rutherford* gave an *opinion* in

<small>[1] Vol. i. pp. 138, 139.</small>

only added, for otherwise it would be unknown, that Mr Dempster, the chief clerk of the agent, in the Winton service, well acquitted himself by his zeal and industry. As to the Keir editor, a clerk then in the same establishment, he can here speak for himself, as he has in fact done in the Preface to the *Memorials of the Montgomeries.*

1836, that Lord Eglinton has right to the honours of Winton, Seton, and Trauent, notwithstanding the attainder of George, fifth Earl of Winton. The case, adjudged in the House of Lords, *tempore* Lord Hardwick, is still of unquestioned authority, and must rule every case in the same circumstances. I see no ground of distinction between it and the present case. After expeding this service, Lord Eglinton assumed the additional titles of Earl of Winton, Lord Seton," &c.

No doubt, under the above description of "eminent counsel," the late Lord Corehouse—than whom a more accomplished gentleman and lawyer never sat upon the bench—together with the writer (if he may add), who originally advised the Winton procedure, as was shown, at a much earlier period (in 1825), and Lord Anderson, must be included, for there were no other counsel, excepting Lord Rutherford, who was but a momentary chamber one in 1836. But that avails nothing as to them, from the complete omission and strange withholding of their names, notwithstanding their especial situation, while so different a course is adopted in regard to his Lordship, who is pointedly named, and in effect as the sole legal oracle in the case, which tells by marked contrast to the prejudice of the former. As to the importance of publicly naming and specifying parties too, that they might be known and fairly defined, that has been already shown in a previous portion of the Exposition.[1]

[1] See p. 179.

CHAPTER VII.

BIOGRAPHICAL AND HISTORICAL SKETCHES AND NOTICES OF THE PRECEDING SIR JOHN STIRLING OF KEIR AND THOMAS BISCHOP, WHO ACTED SUCH IMPORTANT PARTS IN REFERENCE TO THE CADDER FAMILY AND OTHERWISE, BOTH PUBLICLY AND PRIVATELY.

I.—SIR JOHN STIRLING OF KEIR (1503-1539).

THE subject-matter of the case being exhausted, and in fact brought to a conclusion, in the previous chapter, it may only now remain for us to add a sort of supplementary one, for the purpose of laying before the public a few biographical sketches and curious historical notices connected more or less with the lives of those two extraordinary men, Sir John Stirling of Keir, Knight, and Thomas Bischop, who acted, as has been shown, such conspicuous parts in that drama—especially the latter, in concert, too, with Sir James, the son and heir of the former—in the course of which the chief patrimonies of the ancient family of Cadder passed out of their hands by a sort of legerdemain process, if we may use the expression, into those of the family of Keir. We will begin with what is known of the Knight.

As has been shown in a previous chapter (V.), the Stirlings of Keir have their origin in a "John de Strivelyn," who appears for the first and only time in a deed in 1338 as the husband of Mary, the aunt of John, then Lord of Lorn, who by the said deed grants to her and *her* heirs alone the comparatively secondary property of Rathoran in Lorn or Argyleshire. At this epoch nothing seems to be known of this John de Strivelyn, for, possessing no property, so far as yet transpires, we have no means of tracing him thereby, nor indeed in any way in connection with any known family. This alliance, however, with the Lords of Lorne, and his wife's property, may have imparted a certain degree of consequence to himself and his heirs. But the family do not seem to have progressed until the time of Luke, their representative in the next century, who acquired Wester Rathorne, together with other lands, actually the half of Keir, and hence may be held the founder of Keir. He, with acquisitiveness, appears to have evinced considerable talent and activity, if not also ambition, which qualities did not rest with Lucas, but were inherited by his successors. The first of these was Sir William of Ratherne, who, *inter alia*, acquired the other half of Keir, and thus completed the possession of that property. He died in 1471, and was succeeded by Sir William, his son, in whose time, in 1473, Keir was erected into a barony. But this favour of making the Keir estate baronial does not appear to have quieted his restless spirit, for his turbulence led him into an insurrectionary movement, in the course of which the tower of Keir was burnt, and his estate devastated, by the King or his adherents; whereupon, in feudal revenge, it is transmitted, he, Sir William, was accessory to, if not a main participator in, the slaughter of James III. in 1488, as detailed in a previous chapter.[1]

For this deduction see Keir Performance.

[1] See p. 178-80.

This Sir William Stirling of Keir died in 1503, and was succeeded by his son, Sir John, the subject of this memoir. He, too, was a remarkable person, and, like many within his own sphere in that age, was embroiled in nearly every private or public turmoil, hostile feud, and jarring affray, in political, and even in rebellious intrigues, while curiously combining the discharge of ordinary civil business with occasionally acting as procurator and advocate for parties, whose interests, however, for the most part, were nearly his own.* His power of ubiquity was surprising, and fully attested by various records of the time teeming with his name; and the characteristics of his family being strongly developed in him, he was eager to avail himself of every opportunity of aggrandising his family, and, *inter alia*, by adding to it the whole power and influence of the *fibulati Strivelienses*.

Sir John Stirling of Keir, a remarkable character, active and turbulent, while withal a lawyer.

Hence, the infant Janet (the only child of Andrew Stirling, the last direct male heir of Cadder), the heiress of Cadder, and representative of the direct line of the Stirlings of Cadder, from whom Sir John, as was shown, and upon what ground, is deduced by the Keir compiler, but as a remote cadet, became an object to him of especial concern and interest, and he immediately formed the design of uniting her family possessions, including the ancient fiefs of Uchiltree and Cadder, that are traced back to the remote and distinguished

Acts and Decreets of Supreme Civil Court.

* An instance or two may be given here: Summondis or action, 1530, at the instance of Andrew Striveling and Elizabeth Galbraith, against John Logan of Gartconnel, &c., John Striveling of Keir "*compeirand*" (thus quite *as an advocate*) for Andrew and Elizabeth;" and in like manner he *appeared* in another litigation in 1532-33, by Marion Fleming against Archibald Dunbar of Blakcraig.

Vicecomites de Strivelyn in the reign of William the Lyon, through a prospective marriage of the said lady, Janet, with his eldest son, James, then a pupil.

Accordingly Sir John made every effort, especially by the advance of a large sum, for which he mortgaged parts of his property, to purchase the wardship of the fief of Cadder from the superior, which, however, notwithstanding intervening grants in his favour, he did not succeed in fully accomplishing till 16th February 1524, shortly before which time Janet's mother, Margaret Cuninghame, had deceased, who, it may naturally be supposed, had been a stumbling-block in his way. As to Janet's *maritagium*, he did not, owing to some obstacles, secure it till 1529.[1]

Having been thus far successful in his designs against Janet and her property, the Knight, quick in his movements, immediately turned his attention to another party, with the view of performing a similar act there ; for in the ensuing month, March 16th, 1524, he obtained, as was formerly proved, another grant under the Privy Seal of the ward and marriage,[2] until the age of twenty-one years, of William Menteith, younger pronevoy (great-grandson) to William Menteith of Kerse or Carse, with the tenandries and baronies of West Ker and Alveth, both ancient Strivelin heritages.

His ward, William Menteith, doubtless designed for one of Sir John's daughters, was much *in pari casu* with Janet of Cadder, being lineally descended from Marjory Stirling, wife of John de Menteith, another Stirling heiress, daughter of Sir John de Strivelin, the last direct male descendant and heir of the great family of the Stirlings of the Carse and Alveth, who was dead in 1357.[3]

But the best-devised plans are not always crowned with success, and the Knight was doomed to see, for a time, the cup dashed from his lips. His feverish ambition and ardent temperament rendered it impossible that he could be passive in public affairs, or keep himself out of temptation when sedition presented itself, and he experienced the usual penalties for the cameleon course of treason, then so changeable in its hues, for which, in consequence, he was forfeited by Act of Parliament, November 19th, 1526 ;[4] and immediately on the 25th of the same month, there passed another Act confirming to George Douglas the "eschet of all landis and heritagis quhilkis pertenit to Johne Striveling, Knyt, sumtyme of ye Keir, wyt ye ward and mariage of ye air of Cadder."[5] The marriage, however, is here inserted *per incuriam*, for Sir John did not properly get a grant of it till the 22d of July

1529.[1] Janet thus slipped from his hands, and temporarily fell into those of by David Shaw (of Cambusmoor) and George Dreghorn, who both in 1541 had a respitt " for the slauchter of umquhile Johnne Striueling of ye Kere, Knicht."

226   COMMENTS ON KEIR PERFORMANCE,

Vicecomites de Strivelyn in the reign of William the Lyon, through a prospec-

¹ See Keir Performance, Chartulary, p. 320, No. 107.

¹ Ibid., p. 332, No. 119.

² Privy Seal Register.

³ See Keir Performance, Chartulary, p. 198-200.

Keir's plans prevented by an intervening forfeiture.

⁴ Acts of Parliament, vol ii. p. 311.

⁵ Ibid., p. 316.

mariage of ye air of Cadder."⁵ The marriage, however, is here inserted *per incuriam*, for Sir John did not properly get a grant of it till the 22d of July

1529.[1] Janet thus slipped from his hands, and temporarily fell into those of a Douglas, where she might have experienced a better fate.

But shortly afterwards the political surges rolled back again, and Sir John and his party proving the strongest, and therefore, of course, quite innocent, were restored against their forfeiture by Act, May 10th, 1527, to their lands and possessions.[2]

Having now got well free from all the public difficulties and perplexities he had involved himself in, and being once more a free agent, he lost no time in prosecuting and expediting his Cadder objects, which for a time had necessarily been suspended. His restoration or rehabilitation was, as stated, on the 10th May 1527; and actually on the 28th of that same month, Sir John entered into that solemn weighty contract with Robert, the particulars of which have been fully discussed and argued in the second chapter of this Exposition.[3]

Having by his success in this contract with Robert removed every obstacle to his designs upon Janet of Cadder and her property, Sir John,[4] in 1529, at length secured the grant of her *maritagium*, and on coming of age in 1534, she was infeft in her various fiefs, and thereafter married by Sir John to his son James.[5] But as is justly remarked so far in the Keir compilation, the parties seem to have been "ill assorted,"[6] and not suited; for on July 8th, 1535, the lady complained to the Supreme Civil Court both of the Knight and his son, especially of the hard, rigorous, and unwarranted conduct of the former, and with such frankness to the latter as to state that their marriage was "*pretendit*," and hence from the first illegal (as was afterwards so fully decided in law), and against her will.[7]

Sir John Stirling having now succeeded in handing over Janet of Cadder and all her possessions to her hard and unscrupulous husband, his own son, and thus secured the Cadder fiefs to the Keir family, nothing more is heard of him as respects them. But the Knight was not idle, for he was actively engaged after this time in other unwarrantable acts attended with difficulties in which he was involved, through his cruelty and oppression exercised towards some unfortunate Buchanans of Leny, when at length he met his match, and was slain on the Bridge of Stirling, according to Sir David Lindsay of the Mount, in his delectable poem of "Squire Meldrum," previous to November 5th, 1539, by David Shaw (of Cambusmoor) and George Dreghorn, who both in 1541 had a respitt "for the slauchter of umquhile Johnne Striucling of ye Kere, Knicht."

Mr Andrew Buchanan by his
"late Deed of Intail of Glasgow
acquired right to Lands of
Drumpellier & Longloan &c
Disposition dated from a
Deed-Colgrahamis London
of date 26 June 1735

Mr James Buchanan Esquire of
Drumpellier, grandson of above, succeeded
he in [illegible] in 1788 conveyed to
his sons of Drumpellier & others
to [illegible] Buchanan & others
all [illegible] & [illegible]
proprietors of Drumpellier in
as Trustees for his creditors who
in [illegible] 1782 sold and
conveyed them to Andrew
Stirling Merchant in Glasgow

In Nov 1868, Mr Andrew
Stirling also became insolvent
and conveyed his Drumpellier
and other estates in January 1807
and [illegible] land & [illegible]
&c to John Stirling Carlton
of the Royal Bank Glasgow
in Trust for his Creditors

who again carry, in practice, the Vacant lands to Donrau? Buchanan Esqr of Edward Vernon conforms to Difficile every state the Relation 1808. I am much interested that I now understand perfectly been in the hands of the Ancestors of Colonel Patrick Buchanan

Notes of Summing up
Lindy of Drymen
1826

This respite (besides what will be adduced as new in the matter in the sequel) first appeared long ago in the printed Drumpellier case in 1818, before its repetition in the Keir Performance, which strangely, though possessing, as one would think, the best sources of information, has yet nothing new to offer upon the event.

Strangely, indeed, again, in the emergency, it can only, after Keir's murder and the respite, add as follows, for which it is solely indebted to the preceding case, thus availing itself of it, when imagined to *serve* a purpose, though *vice versâ* otherwise:[1] "There was a *previous* feud with the Campbells of Auchinhowie, in which Allan Hamilton of Bardowie, Andrew Struieling of Bankeir, and Robert Struielyng in Cawder, were slain;" and here, with its usual carelessness and striking want of precision, it omits the date, though explicitly given in the case. But what earthly connection had this private feud between these alien parties, so far as can be proved, the Campbells of Auchinhowie and the latter, with the Keir catastrophe, though thus brought into exact juxtaposition with it? Nothing at all; nor was it adduced with such view by the Drumpelliers—there might as well have been here instanced any other feud in Scotland; and the same insertion is quite a *non sequitur* of a piece with others, and certain notable make-weights, that have been exposed in the Keir Performance. The above neither was a *previous* feud, but the sole one, and identical with that premised in the same page!

<small>See Keir Performance, p. 35.</small>

<small>Irrelevant make-weights and anomalies in the Keir Work. The term "previous" here carelessly used.</small>

It is mentioned, too, in the Drumpellier Abstract of Evidence in 1818, that Sir John Stirling of Keir "was murdered by Shaw of Cambusmore near Stirling, in a fit of compunction for having been the unworthy instrument of Keir in *assassinating Buchanan of Leny*, whose daughters, coheiresses, he had also stript of a great part of their estate. To this act he (Shaw) was instigated by the widow of Leny, who by Keir's machinations had been reduced to the lowest distress."

<small>See Exposition, p. 54, note ‡.</small>

The Keir compiler, after quoting the above, with the exception of the last sentence, forsooth exclaims—"This appears to be a *very partial* account of the slaughter of Sir John Stirling." In the Drumpellier Abstract it is simply introduced as a striking fact that had been transmitted, without bias or prejudice. But the compilation, while omitting, after its usual fashion, the last sentence in the quotation, though important as stating the cause of the assassination, though perhaps making against itself, does not hesitate here to charge the Drumpelliers with giving a "very partial account" of the transaction, though not very intelligibly or conceivably—recourse being had, as usual,

<small>See Keir work, p. 35.</small>

<small>Puny and unfounded attack by the Keir work against Drumpellier.</small>

again merely to unsupported oracular assertion. For the better comprehension of the affair, however, as well as vindication of the Drumpelliers from the charge of any partiality in their statements, it may be proper to adduce the authorities on which the present one is grounded, after which, it is conceived, they will be acquitted of partiality or injustice in drawing the character, or giving the incident as they have done, of Sir John Stirling, striking and remarkable enough in this part of the memoir. Fully refuted.

The first proof to be submitted, curiously enough, comes from the Keir repositaries, where the puny charge of implied unfairness recoils upon the assailant, who is here refuted by his own document, which he ought to have known, supplying full evidence of the material fact of Keir's cruelty to, and oppression and ruin of, the Buchanans of Leny, which, together with Schaw's first crime, as premised at Keir's instance, justifies the Drumpellier statement in 1818.

It is entitled "Account of the Family of Leny of Leny,* and Buchanan of Leny, sent by Robert Buchanan of Leny to the Laird of Keir, circa 1560."[1] [1] See Keir Performance, Chartulary, p. 413, No. 190.

"The Laird of Keir (the *James* in 1541) regards nocht my kindnes, ... quhowbeit the *hous* and *leving* (of Leny) be BROKIN, at the plesour of God, his *father*[2] and *himself being* the INSTRUMENTS." Patrick Buchanan, it is added, one of the house, "marcit the Laird of Buchquhananes doctir; scho buir him ane sone and *tway doctiris*. This *sone* was ane gud lyk man, callit *Walter*, and *wes slane* be ane sudden misfortonne† be David *Schaw*, aftir thai had been at ane curss of *hunting strive* for ane ra" (roe deer). Patrick Buchquhanane "had four doctiris, tway be the first wyfe Sempill . . . . the quhilk tway doctiris the Laird of *Keir gat* their richts, be the *quhilk* rychtis he has his tytill to the *lands* of Leny;" in other words, in the same way as Janet of Cadder, the family of Keir, here had stript these two other unfortunate females of their title-deeds and lands. [2] The preceding Sir John Stirling of Keir.
Sir James of Keir, son of the latter, accomplice, too, with his father in the ruin of the Buchanans.

And further still, the Keir Performance, by its imprudent and reckless intrusion of the topic and attack, has still more inculpated the latter by means of this document, which proves James the son to have been equally guilty, and an accomplice with Sir John his father in the ruin of the Buchanans.

---

* They were certainly ancient, and claimed the distinction of having originally held their lands by a peculiar tenure before the era of infeftments. A younger son of Buchanan of that Ilk came to represent them by marrying the heiress, and hence the Buchanans of Leny, who were thus well descended and connected. But what availed this to Keir, mainly here bent on pecuniary or landed aggrandisement?

† This is of course a delicate way of stating the murder. (See *afterwards*.)

The puny attack, too, upon the Drumpellier statement, has evoked another authority in vindication of the same, in the corroboration of it by Buchanan of Auchmar. This gentleman was not only a known Dumbarton antiquary and collector of old writs, but, what is more important, chief of the Buchanans, of whom those of Leny were near relations and cadets, and of course well versant in their history and traditions, so that he may be held an apt embodier and transmitter of all striking facts and incidents affecting them, like the present, which was not the least memorable, and must have left deep impressions. In fact, too, he wrote an "Historical and Genealogical Essay upon the Family and Surname of Buchanan," which, although certainly not legal evidence, yet, from the preceding exceptional reasons, may neither here be classed in the ordinary category of Scotch genealogists, but may have weight in the special matter in question.

[Marginal note: See Original edition, published in Glasgow in 1723, p. 99.]

In that work the author, after noticing the purchase, as he conceived, by Keir, of the liferent escheat of the Laird of Leny, adds that the former "reaped no advantage thereby, Lenny retaining possession of his estate by force, till, in the end, one *Shaw in Camsmore*, an intimate comrade of Lenny's, was *influenced*, as the story goes, by Keir, either to apprehend or kill Lenny. Shaw, judging the first somewhat impracticable, resolved upon the last method, which he *performed* while at the hunting with *Lenny*, by stabbing him behind his back and *killing* him. After which Keir *obtained possession* of *Lenny's estate*, but which he did not enjoy long; for Shaw, meeting *Lenny's lady* and children upon a time in a very *mean condition*, and the lady *upbraiding him* with her husband's *murder*, he was possesset with *such horrour of the fact*, and detestation of Keir his influence, as put him upon the *resolution of expiating Lenny's murder by that of Keir*, as he met him occasionally near Stirling;" and which he accordingly performed. (Altogether a very affecting story, and not ill adapted for a Scotch tragedy, which is to conclude the previous one here.)

[Marginal note: The compunctious incitement of Shaw to murder Keir.]

Taken with the preceding authority in 1560, what can be more corroborative, *in re antiqua*, of the Drumpellier statement in every tittle and particular—quite in keeping, too, with the bent and conduct of Keir, and seeing the Keir Performance—in its wretched fashion, contrary to all regular practice—does not condescend on a vestige of evidence in support of its unfair, while undefined and ill-devised charge, it at once must be disregarded and treated with contempt and indifference. It can never, after what has been unfolded, be said the Drumpelliers gave a partial account, or in any way endeavoured to aggravate the circumstances of the sad tragical affair in question.

It has already been mentioned that, in 1541, David Schaw and George Dreghorn obtained a "respitt" "for the slaughter of umquhile Johnne Striveling of ye Kere, Knicht." It will be well, therefore, to bring to light a new curious document connected with and confirmatory of the same untoward event. In 1543, before the "Lordis of Counseil," "compereit Johne Murray of Polmaise," and produced a writing subscribed by the Governor (*Chatelherault*) to the Chancellor and Lords, bearing "yat ye said John Murray of Polmaise became sourete and lauburrowis for David Schaw of Cambusmore, yat *umquhile* Johne Striveling of ye Keir, Knyt, suld be harmless and seatles of him *under* ye pane (*penalty*) of vi^c merkis; and ye said John, as souerte aforesaid, incurrit ye said pane through ye slaughter of ye said umquhile Johne, committet by ye said David, and was adjudged to pay the same."[1] But James V. (who died in 1542), it is added, had remitted the above sum or penalty to the party, provided the remission was registered in the books of Council and Session.

Sidenotes: See p. 227. The Government viewed Keir's murder in a mild light, and not only pardoned the murderers, but remitted the penalty incurred by the party who had been surety for Shaw's conduct towards Keir. [1] Acts and Decreets of the Supreme Civil Court.

So Murray here experienced the leniency of the Crown, as well as the murderers, evincing the crime not to have been very heinous, and possessing extenuating circumstances, probably owing to previous incentives or provocations, resolving into a modern case of manslaughter; while the heavy recognisances at the time in which Murray was bound for Shaw, 600 merks (then no small sum), bespeaks Keir's well-founded dread and guilty apprehension of the catastrophe.

The following entry in the original Act or Diet-book of the Official of Saint Andrews, that is new too, and in reference to some old transaction between Shaw and Keir, fixes the death of the former wretched individual —the *criminal but repentant tool of the latter* in the Leny atrocity, while its avenger against the alleged contriver—to have been not long after.

On 24th of March 1546, Young, procurator, "Willielmi Sterling, fratris germani, Jacobi Sterling de Keir, et Thome Leirmouth, executorum dativorum quondam Johannis Sterling de Keir, militis petiit quodam actum confectum per QUONDAM *David Schaw de Kammismur*, dicto quondam Joanni Sterling de Keir militi de et supra summam xxi^{lb} vii$^{s\cdot}$ monete Scotie in libris presentis, auditorii registratum, anno et 35°, cum omnibus juste secutis et

Sidenotes: Death of Shaw two years before, 24th of March 1546. Anno 1535.

sequendis in Alexandrum Schaw, tanquam heredi, dicti quondam David *passive*, transferri;" from which it, at the same time, transpires that David had died two years before. The object here has been to transfer the obligation of Schaw to Keir in 1533 (that no doubt, if preserved, had been curious) into the person of his heir, and make him liable.

<small>The marked features in Sir John of Keir's character. See also the well-known account of the affair by Pittscottie.</small>

Cruelty and tyranny, it may be said, without mercy, were ingrained in Sir John, and his leading characteristics, which he exercised with no hesitation in prosecution of his own peculiar selfish objects. His cotemporary, Sir David Lindsay, in his interesting and graphic poem of "Squire Meldrum" (whom the Knight waylaid and assaulted by overpowering numbers, with fifty to the five of the former, displaying as little gallantry as true valour on the occasion), indeed, no more than any one else, represents him in a different light, while he singularly never omits the epithet *cruel* in his regard.

<small>¹ See Chalmors's Poetical Works of Sir David Lindsay, under "Squire Meldrum," vol. ii. pp. 291-293, 297.</small>

He brands him as "ane cruell knicht," a "cruel knicht *full* of *invy*" (envy); talks again of the "crueltie of the knicht," of "this cruell *tyranne*" (tyrant), "that in his hart hes *na* mercie,"¹ which words he puts into the mouth of Lady Glencagles, and despatches him, and his final exit through his murder by David Shaw of Cambusmore at Stirling, in the same strains as follows :²

<small>² Also ibid., pp. 303, 304.</small>

"Bot efterward, as I hard say,
On Striviling brig upon ane day,
This knicht was slane with crueltie,
And that day gat na mair mercie

<small>³ Meldrum.</small>

Nor he gaif to the young *squire*.³
I say na mair—*let* him *ly thare ;*
For *cruell* men, ye may well see,
They end oftimes with crueltie.
For Christ to Peter said this word,
' Quha *ever straikis* with ane *sword*.
That man *sal be with* ane *sword slane*.'

<small>⁴ That saying is true.</small>

That saw is suith,⁴ I tell you plane ;
He menis *quha* strakis *cruellie*,
Agains the law *without mercie*."

Keir, in consequence of this atrocious and unwarrantable assault on Squire Meldrum in 1517, had been apprehended, and confined in Dunbar Castle, by the upright *De la Bastie*, a foreigner who was then deputy-governor of Scotland, but in consequence of whose lamented and premature catastrophe⁵

<small>⁵ As stated by Sir David Lindsay and other writers.</small>

shortly afterwards he was liberated, and enabled to re-enact his usual part at that turbulent period, chiefly during the minority of James V.

Another distinguishing feature, too, in Sir John's character, inherited from his ancestry, was a strong desire for acquisition; and if it be a virtue in a man to aggrandise his family at whatever cost, then surely his descendants owe a deep debt of gratitude to him, not overlooking either Sir James, his son, of Cadder notoriety, who followed so closely in his footsteps, and further aggrandised them even still more exceptionably by the spoliation of the unfortunate heiress of that house. If authority be required as to the extent of the acquisitions by the former, the Keir Performance may be referred to,[1] which somewhat boastingly states that "*this* laird (the *same* Sir John of Keir) added largely to the family estates." Then follows a long list of nearly thirty properties, some of them of considerable value, added by him between the years 1517 and 1535. How he had accomplished this, must be left to the reader's imagination. It does not appear probable that it could have been by purchase, for he was evidently but slender in his means, having had to borrow the money on wadset or mortgage to pay for the wardship of the Cadder estates; and even Auld Keir, it is proved, his ancient family patrimony, was thus held in warrandice by the Drumpellier ancestors for three generations, dating from 1527. The Knight of Keir was well hackneyed in *the law* at the *time*—more so than impressed with the higher sentiments of gallantry and chivalry—and not very scrupulous (for example, as in the striking Leny instance) in the means adopted when he wished to carry a point.

<small>Acquisitiveness of the Knight and his family.</small>

<small>[1] See p. 31.</small>

He left several sons, of whom one, "Mr David," is quite unknown to the Keir Performance, though having access to the best means of information. On the 26th of July 1547, in the court of the Official of St Andrews, "Magister David Striveling," "styled *filius legitimus*" of the late Sir John Stirling of Keir, claimed to be his executor dative, which that judge deemed accordingly in his behalf, "*tanquam* PROPINQUIOREM *de sanguine.*" What his precise legal standing or seniority among his brothers was, has not otherwise been made clear. On a literal interpretation at least of the finding, through this description "PROPINQUIOREM *de sanguine,*" he might be held *nearer* than any, and hence the eldest son and heir at common law, in which event there must have been another disinheritance, to his prejudice, as in the case of John of Wester Bankeir, eldest lawful son of his brother James. Mr David, at any rate, by this procedure, made up titles to the executry.

<small>Original Act and Diet Book (formerly adduced) of the Official of St Andrews. Unfolding new offspring of Keir.</small>

2 G

Having thus discussed Sir John of Keir—for we have nothing more worth stating about him—we now come to

II.—THOMAS BISCHOP, "ARMIGER."

To account for the introduction of this person in a work mainly concerning the Stirlings and their representation, it is only necessary to bear in mind, together with his connection by marriage with them, the very important, though no doubt to a great degree blamable part he played at an eventful and critical period of the Cadder history, added thereto the erroneous impressions of his character and position in society likely to be conveyed by the brief, as usual unauthenticated, and disparaging notices of him in the Keir Performance—from whence so little in the main is to be gathered.

The editor, from his marked want of ordinary research, it may be concluded, and inability to act otherwise, says as little as possible about this gifted and extraordinary individual—supplying no genuine information about his parentage and original *status;* and so hard is he driven in this respect, as to make a signal merit in giving his seal and autograph subscription in 1541—for which he interrupts the course of his Preface.[1]

But not only are his accounts of him meagre, they also would imply Bischop to be almost beneath notice ; for instance, the editor on one occasion calls him " tailor, and a *servant* of Keir "[2]—just as if he was a tailor by profession (which after all, as will be seen, would not prejudice his rank at the time), and a low menial, using, as we may infer, the term "servant" in the modern sense.[3] And he likewise is gratuitously charged in effect with ill treating his wife, the only evidence adduced for the first of these facts being wretched doggerels, probably but of modern origin, which are no evidence at all, and cannot even in the least be twisted as to have reference to the latter charge, which rests upon the editor's sole assertion. Indeed, it is remarkable that none of the charges prejudicial to Janet of Cadder, including that of her "dishonour,"[4] so coolly and recklessly made against her in the Keir work, and that has been so fully exposed, can be established by proper evidence, or what may even approach to it ; for the writer cannot here admit within such category the clandestine, most suspicious, and strange transaction in 1541, which neither can the above fairly own, and has also been commented upon, in the obvious default of which the Keir family and their adherents have been driven to stoop to low scandal, and to loose and unfounded fabrications.

Perhaps, therefore, in reference to Bischop, the best method to disabuse the public mind on this head will be to give an account of all that is justly and fairly known to the exponent concerning him. At the same time, it is but fair to admit that if the Keir editor carried his researches no further back than the Drumpellier printed abstract of evidence in 1818, he may be in some measure excused in forming his present opinion of Bischop. At that time the Drumpellier family had no object in prosecuting minute researches into his career, but they have since done so, and have found good reason in a considerable degree to qualify or alter their opinion as to the man, as will be seen in the sequel. But that of Keir, in gratitude to the memory of him to whose assistance and co-operation and address they are exclusively indebted[1] (having no claims by relationship) for "the valuable estate of Cadder" (as the Keir Performance styles it[2]), besides other also valuable Stirling of Cadder inheritances, which they chose to alienate, might, in gratitude to his memory, have been at more pains to trace out his career.

[1] See Expos., p. 67, No. 9.
[2] See ibid., p. 36.

Thomas Bischop, originally of Mid-Lothian, and having at first nothing to do with Cadder and the west, was son of Robert Bischop, "*alias* Huntrodes" (as so styled), a burgess of Edinburgh, and possessor of certain particates and portions of land within the burgh, thought worthy of a royal confirmation to the family in the year 1577, and which likewise proves his filiation.

Fully proved by a charter in the Great Seal Register, that will be adduced at a more fitting time in the Memoir.

Robert, the father of Thomas Bischop, seems then, from the property he held, to have been a person of some importance; and Edinburgh burgesses in those days were the first in the kingdom, carrying on a considerable traffic with the north of Europe, but more especially with France, the great mart of supply. Division of labour or occupation was little practised at the time, or for long afterwards, so that merchant burgesses then dealt in everything from "a needle to a sheet-anchor," *inter alia*, professing to be cloth-merchants and tailors, which, in fact, was no degradation. It was, of course, the most respectable and well-doing of the citizens who attained the rank of burgesses of Edinburgh, in right of which (as proved by their records) they were expected to be always duly armed, and to be the military defenders of the city. Many of them became opulent men, figuring in good society, and their offspring high lady-killers;[3] while, moreover, ancestors, as could be proved, of noble and knightly houses. Several even originally were of good family; for, with the exception of foreign military service and the Church, there was no outlet for the enterprise and activity of the younger sons of the

[3] See Addenda, No. 1.

nobility and gentry. There was no standing army, no colonies then, or for long afterwards, so that many of them, for their own support, took refuge in towns, and followed what might be thought humble or servile professions; and, what is very singular, the practice continued even to last century.[1]

<small>¹ See here in proof, the instances adduced in the ADDENDA, No. II.</small>

Hence it might be inferred that "*Huntrodes*," in the way of his occupation, may have been something in the tailoring line; and possibly Thomas Bischop, his son, even once his assistant, which, after the instances just quoted, would have done him no discredit, though we have not a vestige of proper evidence for the fact—nothing but the doggerel lines which, in the total absence of what was relevant and better, the Keir Performance is too happy to cite. But from all we can learn truly and correctly, Bischop's youth and earlier years must have been very differently occupied by the successful prosecution of a learned education, for which Edinburgh was so peculiarly adapted, indispensable to qualify him for the profession of the law, the only one, besides the highest State offices and duties, he is proved acutely to have discharged.

<small>The earliest proper evidence prove Bischop first a lawyer and legal officiary alone.</small>

This will fully transpire by tracing him *ab ovo*. Thomas Bischop, then, as we may hold, young, and in the capacity of "Notar Public," is witness to a grant by John Halliday of lands, and also to its confirmation by Mathew, Earl of Lennox, in 1532; while a decreet or judgment in the same year by William Strivelin of Glorat, Sheriff-Depute of Dumbartonshire, bears to be "extractum de libro actorum dicte curie" (of this court), "per me, Thomam Bischope, notarium publicum CLERICUM ejusdem sub meo signo et subscriptione."

<small>Kilsyth writs and papers. Adduced in Erskine's Institutes, edit. 1803, Appendix, No. V., and there said to be from the original in the hands of Archibald Stirling of Keir, but it is not in the Keir compilation.</small>

These are the earliest notices we have of Bischop, and we thus find him, at the commencement of life, figuring in a legal capacity, and in the situation of Notary-public and of Sheriff-clerk, even at the present time filled by respectable and able practitioners. While, at the former period, some of our higher barons could not write, Bischop was a good scribe, as evinced by a fac-simile of his seal and subscription (in a technical business style, quite alien to a tailor's) to a material deed in 1541 in the Keir compilation.[2]

<small>² See Preface, p. x.</small>

We have again Thomam Bischope, *Notarium Publicum*, in 1533, as witness to a deed affecting Sir John Stirling of Keir in the Official book of the Bishopric of Dunblane; and there is retrospectively mention in a litigation in 1542 of Thoma Bischop, "*servand* to the Laird of Keir for the tyme"—that is, Sir John Stirling of Keir, who predeceased in November 1539, and which denotes, in the circumstances, that he was his law-clerk and family agent—a duty or vocation also now often united in a county with

<small>Acts and Decreets of Council and Session.</small>

the clerkship of the Sheriff-Court, while an object of ambition with such legal practitioners. After which we have "Extract furth of the Commissaris Court of Dumblane of ane instrument of seising to James Strivelin of Keir, as air to the said umquhile Sir John Strivelin, his father" (he being previously mentioned), "of the lands and baronie of Keir," dated 5th November 1539, where, again, "Thomas Bischop, Notar," legally acts as notary, and, of course, as may be presumed, the family law-agent when attesting this material Keir investiture ; which precise situation, too, under the designation of "*servitor*" to James (that denoted a law-clerk even as late as last century, associated with notary-public, as before), he is proved to have filled, by the noted instrument in 1541.[1]

<small>Excerpt from an old quarto inventory *james familiam de Balcarres*.</small>

<small>[1] See again Expos., p. 67, No. 1.</small>

Such then was the status and vocation of Thomas Bischop ; respectable certainly—not low or secondary. But it might follow from the terms "servitor" and "servand,"[2] applied to him in the Keir Performance, and its drift, that he was a humble menial or domestic servant, as if further to degrade the Cadder lady to whom he was united in 1541.

<small>[2] See ibid., p. 34.</small>

It is only necessary here, in refutation, to quote from the reports in 1701 of the decisions of Sir John Gilmour, President of the Court of Session from 1661 to 1666, where the learned publisher thus addresses his brethren :—

<small>Also published in 1701. See Preface, p. 7.</small>

"It must be owned that the young men of this age, in point of painfulness, come far short of their ancestors. It is true that the encouragement which the professors of the law then had, *and the respect paid them, was greater than it is at present.* Places and preferments were bestowed according to merit ; every man had an employment according to his skill. The candidates of the law were CLERKS *and* SERVANTS" ("servientes ad legem" as they were styled in England) "to the experienced advocates, and had an opportunity of learning, at the same time, both the civil and the municipal laws. When those advocates were either advanced to the bench or deceased, the *young students*" (certainly *the servants ut supra*), "who by that time were fitted for business through their attendance at Gamaliel's feet, did presently get into employment and a competent living," &c.

We thus see what "servand" and "servitor" (which are synonymous) meant in reference to the law, even as late as 1701—the sole original profession of Bischop. It merely denoted a legal graduate or clerk, as he first was, and in such capacity he would be styled servant or legal ministrant to Keir ; and he could not have acquired a knowledge of his profession under a more resolute

<small>Complete misapprehension now as to import of term "servant," identical with "servitor" formerly, and applicable to parties like Bischop in the course of their legal career.</small>

master, or one less troubled with uneasy scruples. He may, also, under such a master, have acquired those unscrupulous habits of intrigue and high daring, tempered, perhaps, with more skill and judgment, that afterwards enabled him in his political sphere to soar so far above his teacher.

It is by no means intended unduly to elevate Bischop, or to stand up for his moral character, but only to present him in his true light. He was certainly not the low menial he was represented, but a man of good education for his times, and endowed with natural abilities in no common degree.

<small>¹ Great Seal Register.</small>

The next notice we have of him upon record is a royal confirmation, October 2, 1540,¹ of a grant by James Stirling of Keir, the proprietor,² the previous 27th of September, to Master Thomas Majoribanks, burgess of Edinburgh, his wife and son, of thirty-six carrucates of land in the village of Ratho, a few miles from that city, with the lake of Ratho, &c., "quas Magaretta Wilky, relicta quondam Jacobi Winram, Georgius Wilky, THOMAS BISCHOP, Walterus Wilky," &c., "*nunc occupant.*"

<small>² There is no notice whatever of this or the property in the Keir compilation.</small>

<small>³ The modern orthography of the surname.</small>

Of such Wilkies,³ co-rentallers with Bischop, sprung those of Ratho-byres, comprising men of high endowments, such as Wilkie the poet, author of the "Fables" and the "Epigoniad" (truly a rough diamond); and Sir David Wilkie, the Scotch Apelles, and first painter, either in Scotland or elsewhere, in his peculiar sphere. In such hotbed of genius, therefore, in Mid-Lothian, which he also was curiously and remarkably to illustrate as an historical character, Bischop, as rentaller, held property, showing him not to have been originally so insignificant and low in his means as has been imagined. It is not unlikely that the interest of Bischop in Ratho that thus existed, and may have long previously, originated his more intimate connection, as explained, with the Keir family, on whom he was there dependent.

<small>Bischop may have come from a quarter eventually the hotbed of genius, where he also had an interest.</small>

In this way, therefore, Bischop for some years held a position in the Keir family of no small importance, acting, besides, in the public capacity of Notary-public and Sheriff-clerk of Dumbartonshire, sometimes as law-agent, and at the same time as factor in the management of the extensive properties of Keir and Cadder. This naturally brought him into very intimate and confidential communication with Sir John Stirling while he lived, and especially with James, his son, who availed himself of his talents and legal knowledge or address as an instrument to despoil Janet of Cadder of her property, and at the same time to get rid of herself. Of course, Bischop would join warmly in the conspiracy—adroitly masked—with which his interest was as much concerned—exemplified in the notable private agreement or settlement, it may be said, between the two conspirators, against Janet, in 1541,[1] which the Keir Performance does not venture to own or adduce from the Keir charter-chest. It insensibly reminds us of the partition of booty in requital, or for co-operation of mutual services between two foreign *condottieri*, equally clandestine, and with objects not very dissimilar. This lamentable and discreditable subject has been so fully dilated upon elsewhere, that it is unnecessary to say anything more upon it here.

[1] See *ut ante* repeatedly.

The divorce of James of Keir and Janet of Cadder took place last of January 1541,[2] and on 21st April 1543 there was a summons raised before the Supreme Civil Court, "at ye instance of Janet Striveling, Thomas Bischop, hir *spouse*," against "Johne Kincaid, and his spouse," in reference to the lands of Over Carloury, formerly her heritage, and part of the Cadder estate. Janet had thus been married to Bischop before this—probably in 1541.

[2] See Exposition, p. 65.

Acts and Decreets of Supreme Civil Court.

The above lawsuit, April 1543, is the last notice we have of both parties together in Scotland. Bischop's restless activity of mind and body did not allow him to remain long at ease in comparative idleness. He required something more exciting than domestic comfort or rural occupation could afford to fill up his time and his thoughts, for we find in the following year, in April 1544, a letter to Henry, Lord Methven, of the "escheat of all cornis, cattel, &c., quhilkis pertenit to Thomas Bischop of Ochiltree (which is scored out, though completely identifying him), throw his being at the horne for not *underlying* the law for the *slauchter* of umquhile Andrew Johnston."[3]

Bischop, now husband of Janet of Cadder, his main object being attained, begins his active public career.

[3] Privy Seal Register.

From the daring spirit of hostile enterprise and adventure, probably the cause of the act, and from his qualifications and address, he was preferred to the elevated position of private secretary to the noted Mathew, Earl of Lennox, who, besides being a male Stuart, was descended from Mary, sister of James IV., in virtue of which, coupled with some special arguments, he competed with the house of Hamilton—between whom, therefore, and his own there was much enmity and rivalry—for the eventual right to the crown of Scotland. He was father of Henry Lord Darnley, grandfather of James VI., and, moreover, himself Regent of Scotland.

He obtains the high situation of private secretary to the princely Mathew, Earl of Lennox, afterwards Regent of Scotland.

The Earl had recently returned from France, having distinguished himself abroad, especially in the wars in Italy ; and being discerning, and versed in public affairs, his selection of Bischop to a situation no doubt coveted by many, must have been highly creditable to the latter. How the acquaintance first began seems unknown, but probably from JANET, Bischop's spouse, the *ci-devant* Cadder heiress, and her ancestors having held the land of Lettyr (afterwards the heirloom of Drumpellier), of the house of Lennox. This implied a feudal connection, which Bischop's sagacity may have turned to account, together with his other endowments and qualifications.

The very first step or procedure of Earl Mathew in his negotiations with England for assistance and redress against Arran the Governor (the head of the Hamiltons, and, of course, his enemy) and Cardinal Beatoun, of whom he bitterly complained as injuring and oppressing his country, and denying him his due rank and influence, is an especial commission, April 8, 1544, to "Thomas Bischop, our *Secretaire*,"[1] and Hew Cunninghame, "our verray lauchful and undowtit Procuratoris," &c., to "convene" and treat accordingly at Carlisle with "my Lord Whartoun, Lord Wardane of the West Merchis of Ynglande, and Sir Robert Bowys, Knyght—Commissionaris," &c., for "the Kingis Majesty (Henry VIII.)," public characters well known in history.

Then actually at Carlisle, on the evening of the 17th of May, there followed solemn indentures of agreement between the English commissioners on the part of Henry, and those on that of the Earl—viz., "William, Erle of Glencarne ; Robert, Bischop-elect of Caithnes, brother to the Richt Honorable Matthew, Erle of Levenax (Lennox) ; as also *Thomas Bischop* and Hew Cunyngham, commissionaris nemmit" by a "commission maid under the selis, &c., of the saidis Erlis of Levenax and Glencarne."

They contain important conditions for the general behoof and state, *inter alia* that Lennox "by his SECRETARY" (*Bischop* of course, thus his confidant and plenipotentiary) had "maid suit unto the Kingis said Majestie (Henry VIII.) to have in mariage my Lady Margarete Dowglas, His Majisteis neice." Here Bischop had the honour of personally negotiating and promoting a marriage, subsequently concluded, between these high parties, in the terms of the above, by which Henry, Lord Darnley, their son, became next heir to the English throne (some thought, from being born an Englishman, a preferable one) after our Queen Mary, and which chiefly led to their union. Further still, by another clause, Bischop, as one of the commissioners, is to do all in his power to get "the young Quein of Scotland" (the latter) "in thair keiping," and afterwards deliver her to Henry VIII. to be nourished "at his Hienes order until (the most weighty affair notoriously at the time) the marrage quhilk his Majeste determynit betwein his Hienes maist excellent

Prince Edward, his Grace's sone, and her Grace, may tak effect." To which, and much more, Bischop, as a high diplomatic functionary, appends his subscription with the rest.*

On the 26th of June following there was a fresh political treaty,¹ with many clauses, between the said Earl of Levenax and Lord Wryothesley, Lord Chancellor of England; Charles Duke of Suffolk, Lord Great Master of the King's Hienes most honorable household (brother-in-law of Henry VIII.), &c.; and Sir William Paget, one of the King's Secretarys of State, where again Lennox becomes bound "to hold firme and stable" what had been concluded *ut supra* at Carlisle, May 17, 1544, by William, Erle of Glencarne; Robert, elect Bischop of Caithness (brother to the said Erle of Levenax); "Thomas Bischop," and Hugh Cunningham.

Nothing can more strongly evince the high position occupied both in politics and in the family of an Earl, whom Buchanan celebrates as—

> "Regis avus, Regis pater alto e sanguine Regum
> Imperio quorum terra Britannia subest."

And who, besides, makes him posthumously exclaim—

> ———— "famam virtute refelli
> Arma armis vici, concilioque dolos,
> Gratus in ingratos, patriam justeque pieque
> Cum regerem, hostili perfidia cecidi."²

But this is not all of one whose case has been so little understood by the Keir party and others. On July 6, Henry VIII. granted "prædilecto consanguineo nostro Matheo Comiti Lynox"³ special letters of indigenation, or naturalisation, by which he became a free English denizen, as if born in England. Neither was Bischop Lennox's *alter ego* to be overlooked on this occasion, but to participate also in the same favour, for in Rymer's *Fœdera*, from whence the above is taken, under the title of "Pro *Secretario* predicti *Comitis*,"⁴ there immediately follows other identical letters of indigenation, "Thome Byshop, ARMIGERO, *Secretario* prædilecti consanguinei nostri Mathei Comitis Lynox"—to which honour of ARMIGER, or squire, having then in chivalry an admitted general application or import throughout Europe, he had thus been

¹ Rymer's Fœdera, p. 29 *et sq.*

² Alluding to his violent and premature death in 1571.

³ Rymer's Fœdera, p. 37.

⁴ Ibid., p. 38.

Highest honour and favour shown by the Crown to Bischop in England, who especially is made an Esquire by Henry VIII.

* There is also this clause affecting *Lennox*, and agreed to, that Henry VIII. should maintain "his *titule*" (conceived preferable *status* and right to the Crown) "agauis the Erle of Errane" (Arran, the Regent and Governor), in elucidation of a former remark.

242   COMMENTS ON KEIR PERFORMANCE,

> See Confirmation in 1414 by Countess Euphemia to Luke, "*dilecto armigero* NOSTRO; *pro servitio suo nobis impenso*," Keir Performance, Chartulary, pp. 206, 207, under No. 10.

raised, by the highest authority, a sovereign prince, Henry VIII., who accordingly so expressly recognises and names him in his grant. Nor is it a little remarkable that Bischop thus held a higher style and grade than Luke Stirling of Ratherne, the Keir ancestor, who was only "*armiger*" of a female subject, Euphemia, Countess of Stratherne (rather of a peculiar sort, and how made, unknown), without a royal interposition, as in the prior instance. Du Cange, Cowel, and Spelman, may be here, *sub voce*, consulted.

> [1] See Scotch Acts of Parliament, vol. ii. p. 455-459.

But Bischop, having thus warmly espoused the cause of the Earl, and identified himself with English interests, naturally experienced the consequences in company with his master, who (after the example of most of his equally rebellious brethren) had so far led him astray, and was more blamable than his faithful dependant, who might thus have an apology for following in his track; and under the title of "Uchiltree," the former was expressly forfeited by an Act of Parliament, 1st of October 1545,[1] for conspiring and co-operating with the English in their expedition, in 1544, against the west of Scotland, which they hostilely invaded and devastated.

> Bischop is forfeited with Louuox in 1545, by which mischance Keir absolutely and luckily acquires right to Uchiltree.

It is an ill wind, however, that blows nobody any good, for Sir James Stirling of Keir afterwards was enabled to profit by this event, by securing to himself absolutely, through proceedings before the Supreme Civil Court in 1562 and 1563, with a decree thereupon, the above ancient Cadder heritage of Uchiltree, which had before been settled by him, with Janet of Cadder's indispensable consent, upon Bischop, under reversion of two thousand merks.*

In 1562-3 Bischop was out of the kingdom. Janet was so too, that

> Act and Decreet, Register of Supreme Civil Court.

* Action, December 19, 1562, by James Strivelling of Keir, against "Thomas Bischop, pretendit heritable possessor (as he is styled) of, the lands of Uchiltree—sauld be ye said James to ye said Thomas, his aires and assignees," and other defenders. The sum for the reversion is just that specified in the noted disposition and assignation in 1541 by the former to the latter;[2] and being of an onerous character, the transaction is thus held a sale—not the less applicable, too, as *Janet* and the *lands* were thereby, in return for her soliciting, and obtaining from her the conveyance of Cadder to Keir, actually sold, as a *quid pro quo*, to Bischop. Such was the arrangement and settlement of this notable and baneful conspiracy. There was a later action before the same tribunal in 1563, by Keir against Thomas Bischop, about

> [2] See Expos., p. 57, No. 9.

> Acts and Decreet Register, *ut sup.*

Uchiltree also, stated to have been sold to the latter under reversion, and other defenders. Thomas, being "then out of the realme," did not appear, and the Court find they had been lawfully redeemed by Keir, thus deciding in his favour. Upon this head as to his final absolute title to Uchiltree, the Keir Performance can only vaguely say that "*on the forfeiture*[3] of Bischop, Sir James Stirling (he was not then a knight, by the way) re-acquired Ochiltree, from the Crown *donatar*," which is not borne out by the preceding *conclusive* lawsuits in 1562-3, while the forfeiture was long previous in 1545; and the Performance, in its usual careless manner, and against the practice of every regular discussion, does not state the date, or aught in support of such alleged re-acquisition, which hence may be questioned.

> [3] Keir Performance, p. 30.

> Other instance of extreme carelessness and imprecision here in the Keir work.

unfortunate lady having obtained, long before, a "licence" or safe-conduct for England from the Regent Arran, that was renewed by Queen Mary with his consent by another, March 28, 1547, where the Queen, moreover, and Governor "ratefey and apprevis all rychtis maid sene her departing furth of our realm, and procuratories to James Striveling of the Keir, and to be maid during the tyme of this licence to ryn."[1] Very probably Keir was very glad to have her out of the kingdom, independently of this further eligible guarantee as to Cadder in his favour. [1] See Keir Performance, Char- tulary, p. 395, No. 173.

There is a curious and interesting letter, under the Privy Seal, by Queen Mary, first only adduced in this Exposition,[2] dated October 8, 1551, to Matho Hamilton of Mylnburn, that completes all upon this subject "of ye escheit of all gudis, soumes of money, actis, contractis, jowellis, gold, silver," &c., "whilkis parteinit to   .* Striveling, sumtyme Lady Caldoure, and now ye spous of Thomas Bischop, and now partening, &c., to our soverane Lady," because she was in England remaining "wyt ye said Thomas, her spous, rebell and traitour, &c., helping and supporting him." She still remained faithful and attached to him, which naturally may have had a corresponding return on his side, and refute any ill treatment to be inferred from what is vaguely and gratuitously again charged against Bischop in the Keir work.[3] [2] See p. 26. Last notice of the unfortunate Janet of Cadder in 1551, then in England. [3] See p. 38, note.

Janet's career was, indeed, a baneful and partly a ruinous one to her ancient house, and its lawful heirs and representatives, who have so unmeritedly suffered in consequence, and may be held the chief victims.

In the earlier part of Bischop's career, his conduct certainly merited reprehension, but his political life thereafter was in a great measure laudable and consistent. He devoted the *fervidum ingenium* of a Scotchman to the advancement of Lennox, as well as of the cause of the Queen. He could never stimulate that nobleman sufficiently (whose secretary and confidant he was, and over whom he even exercised authority) to take steps he thought conducive to his advantage. Even the royal Margaret Douglas (daughter of Margaret of England), whose marriage with the former he had personally negotiated and promoted,[4] was nothing when weighed in the scale of her husband, and his own, that was actually the royal cause. [4] See afterwards, p. 245.

He was so far a political zealot; but at the same time this remarkable person, though it is admitted unscrupulous, artful, and intriguing from his youth, nevertheless was warlike withal, and chivalrous, being, in return for his

* So blank in the original.

bold and military services in his noted expedition with Lennox against the west of Scotland in 1544, honoured, and even embraced, by Henry VIII., that haughtiest of monarchs, in presence of his whole Council in France, after formally reporting to him the details.

We give literally Miss Strickland's account[1] of this striking occurrence,—we may conclude, on good authority : " He, *Bischop*," she states, " was sent with despatches to Henry VIII., who had just taken Boulogne, with the account of the proceeding of the naval force in its descents on the western coast of Scotland. Tom Bischop, who had distinguished himself in this warfare, says, ' I was embraced in the King's Majesties armes before his whole Privy Council in his privy chamber.' A curious fact this," the former here adds, " illustrative of the popular and hearty manner of bluff King Hal in testifying his approbation of those who rendered him important services."[*] This is pretty well for Miss Strickland,[2] with whom Bischop is far from a favourite ; and who, like his political opponents, inveighs against his interference and officious concern in the affairs of Lennox and his wife (whom he openly, but honestly, as will be seen, thwarted and opposed), as well as his influence over the Earl and her royal relatives. But these feats, in that age, are sufficient to commemorate him, evincing his superior power and address.

Though forced, as we have seen, from circumstances, to reside in England, where he, with Lennox, was identified with English interests, he nevertheless kept his eyes constantly on Scotland and the Stewarts, and communicated to them what might be pleasing or advantageous to their cause.

Thus, in 1555, he communicates, with interest, to the English Secretary of State (who coincided with and furthered Lennox's politics), that Elder, the well-known tutor of Lord Darnley, had been with him, and told him " he had letters from my Lord Aubigny to my Lord Lennox, my Lord Darnley, and as, I think," he adds, " to my Lady,"[3] and that " he showed the Queen of Scots (in France) my Lord Darnley's hand which he wrote, being eight years of age :" and in respect to which Miss Strickland pertinently says, " This was perhaps the first time Mary's attention was called to her youthful kinsman's

---

[*] On a critical occasion, when Lennox and Bischop, in 1544, had nearly been surprised in Dumbarton Castle, and the former hastened to escape, Bischop writes (see Ap., *Maitland Club Miscellany*, " I *willed* (*wished*) the Earl of Lennox a marrishly *pike*, and *fight*, rather than return with shame in England ;" thus preferring the bold and gallant acts of a soldier in the emergency to what in the least savoured of recreancy and military dishonour.

existence, except, perhaps, as a person likely to be set up by her royal cousin of England as a rival to her claims in the succession of the sister realm."[1]

The career of this extraordinary man lay far more in England in the highest society than in Scotland, being there involved in a whirlwind of plots and intrigues, public and domestic, but not altogether for bad purposes.

Notwithstanding the representations of some, he was ever essentially attached to Lennox, and laudably exerted himself to keep him a Protestant;[2] while the Lady Margaret Douglas, who, in consequence, called Bischop a heretic, did all she could to keep him a Papist, so that there was no love lost between these two parties, which accounts for his opposition to her. He is even said, or inferred, to have denounced her to his patron Henry VIII.[3]

But what is most remarkable, and evinces the highest talents and address, either when we weigh his conduct in the indeed suspicious affair of Janet of Cadder, or as coupled with his being held, or shown to be, an "expert mischief-maker" at court by Miss Strickland,[4] who is little favourable to him, he would appear to have had more weight with the *Popish Mary*, Queen of England, than even Margaret. In a letter of Bischop, adduced by the same female writer, to whom we are beholden for such curious and original information, always to be so greatly prized in our history, he says,[5] "Queen Mary, though my Lady Lennox (Margaret) told her I was an heretic, gave me, unbeknowen of her, who would have had me forsaken, livings here to have followed her army into Scotland, my pension *anew*, with the addition of the word *lakking*,* and to the end of her Majesty's days in the affairs of Scotland, *trusted me*, where she did not her *deare cousing of Levenax.*" So withal he, a Protestant, enjoyed a pension, with promise of its being renewed, from the Popish Queen, besides the influence he exercised, to the exclusion of her royal Scotch relatives, over this bigoted sovereign.

Two incidents in Bischop's public life, ever consistent as before, present him in very favourable colours.

In the first place, Sir James Melville, in his Memoirs,[6] after noticing the

[1] Queens of Scotland, vol. iii. pp. 53, 54.
[2] Extraordinary influence of Bischop in England, while ever consistent in his Stewart or the royal politics.
[2] See ibid., vol. ii. p. 327.
[3] Ibid.
[4] Ibid.
[5] Ibid., p. 357.
[6] Bannatyne Club edition, pp. 175, 176.

---

* Miss Strickland here explains this word as the same with "*lacking;*" meaning that the Crown was indebted to him for arrears of the said pension, which seems just enough. This female author, as was remarked, is unfriendly to, and biassed against Bischop, as also are some others, ignorant of his precise position and status in society, formerly humbly including the present writer: but he must confess, after more deeply considering the matter, together with additional evidence, that he now views it rather differently, especially in one respect, as will be immediately evident.

Highly commendable conduct of Bischop in the case of Queen Mary. Adopts here that laudably pursued by the patriotic Lord Herries, while always consistent in his Stewart politics.

"bruit" or rumour of Mary's marriage to Bothwell, which "my Lord Heres, a worthy nobleman," he states, "most humbly upon his knees," dissuaded her from; informs us also that "in the mean tym there came a letter to *me*" (*Sir James*), "fra ane Thomas Bischop, a Scottis man that had been lang in England, and was a *gret* persuader of many in England to *favour her Majesties title*, and used to wret oft unto my brother and me information and advertisements;" while he adds, "at this tyme he used even the lyk language that my Lorde Heres had spoken, but mair freely, because he was absent in another cuntre. He aduised me to schaw the said letter unto her Maiestie, declairing how it was bruited in England that her Maiestie was to marry the Erle of Bodowell, wha was the mourther of her husband, and other crymes, a man full of reproch and grangoir, with many uther reproches that he allegit; quhilk bruites he wald not believe, be resone of hir noble wit and qualities, and of the honorable mark that scho schot at. And in case sche married hym, sho wald tyn the favor of God, hir awen reputation, the kingdomes England, Yreland, and Scotland, with many other dissuasions and *examples* of *histories*, quhilk wald be our lang to reherse. I had been absent, and past to the court to schaw this letter unto her Majestie, protesting scho wald tak it in gude part.

"Efter that hir Majestie had sed (seen) the said writing, sche gaif it to me again without mair speach, but callit upon the Secretary Liddington, and said to him that I had schawen hir a strange writing, willing him also to se it. He askit what it culd be; scho said a device of his awen, tending only to the wrak of the Erle of Bodowel."

So spoke the here infatuated Mary (like others of her sex on similar occasions), dissembling after a French fashion, and affecting to undervalue and despise such weighty, honest, and salutary advice—which, if she had followed, it would have been far better for her—while curiously betraying her love in the fear of "the *wrak*" (*wreck*) "of the Erle of Bodowell," the object of her affections. But the Secretary, also after perusing Bischop's letter, seriously asked Melville what was "in his mind," or he about, for he added, "that so soon as the Erle heard of his act, he will not fail to sley you," and that Melville, in his repugnance to "se that gude princes run till utter wreck, and nobody to forewarn her, had done mair honestly nor wysely."

With all submission, Bischop here is entitled to the highest commendation, being actuated by the best motives—religious withal—zealous for the Queen's

English interests, which he could better advance where he was obviously, too, not without risk; and unconsciously adopting the very conduct of the patriotic Lord Herries. Neither can it escape attention, from Melville's account, that Bischop must have been an educated man, and versed in history, from the precedents he drew from thence in opposition to Mary's projected union, no doubt enforced in language sufficiently strong and eloquent. This and other facts stated, evince him not to have been the low secondary person, as some of the Keir faction both ungratefully and injudiciously would make him.

The above very striking incident in Melville's Memoirs may not have met the attention it deserved.

Secondly, in December 1568 there was circulated a celebrated "Ryme," or poem, "in *defence* of the Queen of Scots *against* the *Erle of Murray*," by one styled "Tom Trouth," of some length, and, according to Chalmers, "full of historical and useful truths,"[1] upon which the espousers of Mary's innocence, and inculpators of Murray, confidently found. It is a remarkable production every way, classical enough, and could only have been written or compiled by an educated Scotchman well versed in Scotch affairs.[2] It occasioned a sensation even in London, the immediate consequence of which was the actual apprehension of Thomas Bischop as the author, by Cecil, the English Secretary, the warm protector of Murray; and his confinement for a time in the Tower of London, in which place, in 1569, he was subjected to interrogations, based upon his acquaintance and influence with the highest leading characters, especially on *his* side of politics. He was pointedly questioned "who were they yat made ye book" (the *Ryme* in question) "agaynst the Erle of Murray, and *what part* did *yourself* (Bischop) make or minister to ye makers?" with more of the kind specifically as to this *brochure*. Bischop's answers unfortunately are not transmitted; but combining all, he may be fairly concluded to have more or less had a hand in the work, which subjected him, as a state prisoner, to considerable trouble and prosecution.

Thus, while, like public characters in general, he may have been occasionally misrepresented and exposed to much obloquy, he was here (unlike many even the most meritorious) still as consistent as ever, his ardent zeal for his royal mistress and her cause making him the determined enemy of one who has been loudly charged with ingratitude and unnatural conduct towards her.

Writers ignorant of Bischop's life, and his forced and protracted residence in

[1] See his Life of Queen Mary, vol. ii. p. 143, where he has been at pains fully to give the interesting "Ryme" in question.

[2] It is preserved in the Cotton Library; see Chalmers, *ut supra*, pp. 449, 450.

England, have deemed him some subaltern emissary or clandestine spy, maintained by a narrow faction to serve their purposes, when, in fact, he was nothing of the kind, but merely continued in a foreign land (where he held, too, the high official situation of secretary and confidant of an influential nobleman, the Earl of Lennox, afterwards Regent of Scotland, while in communication with the first personages) the uniform consistent tenor of his political career, and did what he could, by active correspondence in both countries, with the espousers of the same cause, by giving and obtaining useful information, to assist and promote it. He has been stigmatised as a plotter and intriguer, not without cause; but as it may have been chiefly on the right side, surely it is not fair to select him as the only politician obnoxious to such imputations? Were they not, it may be asked then, besides many now, nearly all so?

<small>Bischop not a common spy or subaltern emissary, as unfoundedly represented.</small>

On the 12th of August 1575, James VI. granted a charter[1]—"Agnete *Bischop*, filie legitime quondam *Roberti* BISCHOPE, *alias* HUNTRODDES, *burgensis* de Edinburgh, suis heredibus et assignatis"[2]—of certain lands there formerly specified, "que quidem (it is added) pertinebant, saltem *pertinere* debuerunt THOME BISCHOPE FRATRI dicte *Agnetis* perprius hereditario, et nunc *nobis* pertinent nec non in manibus charissime *nostre matris* regine pro tempore devenerunt, et nunc in manibus nostris *ratione eschete ob processum* FORIS FACTURE *contra* dictum *Thomam* pro certis *proditionis* et *lese magistati criminibus* per cum commissis legaliter *deductum* de quibus *in parliamento convictus fuit.*"

<small>[1] Great Seal Register.
[2] See p. 235.</small>

<small>[3] See p. 242.</small>

The above family property, it may be concluded, that had of course also been escheated to the Crown by the forfeiture of Thomas in 1545, here especially alluded to, was thus kindly bestowed by it on behalf of James, the grandson and heir of Mathew, Earl of Lennox, the patron of the former, upon Agnes his sister—bating the forfeiture—probably his heir, and last of his race. The grant quoted in substance necessarily proves the filiation of Thomas (clearly the same with him of *Ochiltree*, attainted in 1545) through the exactly corresponding status or descent of Agnes his *sister*; for if she, as above, was daughter of Robert Bischop, he infallibly too was his son.

<small>Filiation proved of Bischop, and favour of the Crown to his sister.</small>

The Crown probably here intended a favour to Bischop in the person of his sister, *nominatim*, in return for his services, in the only way practicable, it not yet being expedient to restore him against his forfeiture.

Still keeping to the favourable side of the case, Bischop's political career, irrespective of what has been expressly admitted otherwise to his prejudice and tarnished his character, we may close the subject with the following final account of him (for we learn nothing more of Janet of Cadder), by an amiable and accomplished gentleman, the late William Stirling of Drumpellier* (who so prominently figured in the collision with the Keir in 1818), the son and heir of Andrew Stirling of Drumpellier, who obtained his important service in 1818. It is derived from other Stirling and Cadder collections and reminiscences, in which he much delighted, still extant in his repositories.

"He (Bischop) became a strenuous partisan of that unfortunate Princess (Queen Mary) in her riper years, and there are various notices of his efforts in her favour from the period above mentioned to that of her death, soon after which, being then advanced in years, he returned to his native country under the protection of a *Remission* from her son James VI., in which honourable mention is made of his faithful services to his deceased sovereign."

This last information as to James's Remission against his forfeiture in 1545, and in consequence his return to Scotland, there ending as well as commencing his indeed strange and varied existence, is new and interesting, and for which we are indebted to the preceding Mr William Stirling, who was too candid to withhold merit where it was due, in any event, even from such a person, the mainspring of the ruin and calamity that temporarily befel his house.

---

* In addition to good mental endowments and a high spirit, nature had been lavish in moulding him in her best form, which, joined to cultivated manners, in the best society, with general information, rendered him especially attractive and agreeable. None, in prepossessing qualities and appearance, could have been a better Stirling of Cadder representative, which in truth he was; and the writer is most happy in contributing this merited eulogium and tribute to his memory.

ADDENDA TO CHAPTER VII.

No. I.

REMARKABLE INSTANCE, in the seventeenth century, of the dangerous influence and attractions of sons of Edinburgh burgesses with the higher and most beautiful of the fair sex.

(REFERRED TO AT PAGE 235.)

In MS. Historical Notes by him in the British Museum.

Mr David Simpson, Historiographer of Scotland to Queen Anne, informs us that "upon the 13th of September 1633," " the sinful presumption of Maister Robert Menteith, *sone* *to Alexander Menteith, merchant burgess of Edinburgh*, came to light by *falling** with ane *honorable* ladie, Dame Annas Hepburn, dochter to the Laird of Wauchton, and spons to ane worthie and nobill man. Sir James Hamilton, son to Sir Thomas Hamilton, who was President of Scotland.† True it is, the foirsaid Mr Robert Menteith was minister in Dudingston, where this noble woman was one of his parochinaris, for sche dwelt in Priestfield. Her worthie husband being *out of the countrie*, he inticed this *worthie* and noble woman to   , ‡ and begat on hir two children; which, when

¹ See, in corroboration of this cotemporary authority, at p. 253 of the Exposition.

it came to his eares *at his home-coming*,§ it bred a great grief in his heart, and he persewed devorcement against hir, which he obtained, and sua put hir away, *who was the maist beautiful woman that was in our country*. The saide Mr Robert Menteith was charged at the Croce of Edinburgh to compeir and answer to the lawes of the country, but did not appear.¹ The Lord forgive him, for he has been a great scandal to our Kirk."

Mr Robert, the paramour in question—a remarkable and talented person, somewhat on a *par* with Thomas Bischop—fled to Paris, where he turned Jesuit, and became the friend and confidant of Cardinal Retz (on a *par* again with the Earl of Lennox in the case of the latter), who gave him good church preferment. He came to be styled " *le Sieur de Salmonet*," and under such designation is described by another adherent of the Cardinal ‖ as " *pretre Eccossois homme savante et de merite*." With his religion (where he certainly was not a *little* in *default*) he changed his former habits, being afterwards reverenced and highly esteemed by many of his cotemporaries, including Balzac and Maresius. He figured, withal, as a writer of repute, and addressed a humble remonstrance to Charles II. on the state of his affairs in 1652, but is better known as author of the *History of the Troubles of Great Britain from 1633 to 1649*.

* *i. e.*, by his *faux pas*.
† That is, President of the College of Justice, or Court of Session, no other than the first Earl of Haddington, so justly celebrated.
‡ A blank here.
§ He seems to have been oblivious of the salutary maxim, "Cleave to your wife"—who would seem to have had sufficient attractions to arrest his gadding abroad and leaving her to herself,—"that heritage of woe."
‖ Joly, in his *Memoirs*, edit. *Petitot*, pp. 310, 311.

No. II.

RESPECTABILITY formerly of TAILORS in SCOTLAND, and cases of members of good and even high families following, even as late as last century, secondary professions and trades, restricted now to the lower orders.

(REFERRED TO AT PAGE 236.)

Tailors of old were cherished with us, and in high repute. James III., who had somewhat of the same *penchant* with a recent British monarch for dress and habiliments (or "*abulzementis*," as we styled them), and cultivated the fine arts, highly appreciated, and evinced the utmost affection for, *Hommyl*, his esteemed "*sartor*" or tailor. And being resolved that he should be comfortably lodged, issued in 1477 a special order for the payment to the same party, therein styled "Jacobo Hommyl," "ad *reparationem et edificationem* domus sue." This too, as proved by the same authority, was independently of the "vigini libras" that he received annually, "pro feodo suo in *officio* sartoris" to the monarch.[1]

We are here, coupled with an authority in 1474,[1] supplied, too, with the Christian name of this worthy, whose merits excited envy, and hastened his exit (with others) in

——— "Lauder's dreary flat,"[2]

where the higher orders ungratefully despatched him, doubtless to save payment of his bills.

Mantua-makers likewise—equivalent to the same profession in the female sex, even well-descended, will be shown, too, by an instance at a much later epoch, to have been patronised by the great. And the parties last century, next to be noticed, though of high and ancient families, were yet but ordinary tradesmen and burgesses and shopkeepers.[3]

The Mowbrays of Cockairney, in virtue of a descent as far back as the reign of James III., may be justly held the heirs-male of the ancient and distinguished house of Mowbray of Barnbougal, subsequently to the transmission of the direct representation through Sir Bartholomew de Loen, a foreign knight of family, who, before the middle of the fourteenth century, had married Philippa de Mowbray, the heiress of the original Mowbrays,[*] and

---

[*] The writer may here adduce an original royal Mowbray document in 1360-61, which he saw, with other ancient Mowbray writs, in a private charter-chest,[4] as it partly supports his remarks upon an incident in the Keir pedigree and succession, bearing against the notion of their Cadder descent. It is a charter by David II., dated at Aberbrothock, January 6, 1360-1, in the thirty-second year of his reign, confirming "dilecto et fideli nostro Bartholomeo de Loen, militi, ac nostre dilecte *consanguinee* Philippe de Mubray, spouse sue, totam terram de Barnebugall; et quam baroniam, &c., Johannes de Grahame, Comes de Meneteth, et Maria, sua spousa" (had resigned) "in concilio meo, at Perth," (seventeenth year of our reign, 1345-6), "pro acquietantia et remissione a nobis petitis de duobus millibus marcarum Sterlingorum,[5] &c., quibus supra dictus Johannes et Maria ratione maritagii et relevii nobis strictius tenebantur." The latter transaction is interesting and new, as well as the charter itself—not

---

[1] Proved by an original Exchequer Roll in Her Majesty's General Register-House, Edinburgh. The original accounts of the Lord Treasurer for that year.
[2] See Pinkerton, vol. II. p. 289, 308; and Scott's Marmion, cant. v., xiv.
[3] See Expos., pp. 252, 253.
[4] See Expos. p. 181.
[5] This was a large feudal fine or exaction then, evincing the high value and importance of Barnebugall.

thus continued the line—the more immediate ancestors of the former,—and of course long prior, again, to its second devolution upon such heir in the person of Barbara Mowbray (that surname being always preferred), who was matched before 1527 to Robert Barton, of a family more famed for valour and sea exploits than descent.* In consequence of this, they were empowered, by an Act of Parliament in the above year,¹ to take the surname of Mowbray, which he and his descendants through Barbara did accordingly. Yet Robert Mowbray, brother-german of John Mowbray of Cockairney, the heir-male and representative of the preferable De Loen Mowbray stock premised, who figured in the earlier part of last century, did not scruple to be King's wright, master-carpenter, and Convener of the Trades of Edinburgh,—thus completely a burgess in that city. And further, as if glorying in his trade, he took as indicative of it, for his crest, a most effective "handsaw," with the corresponding humble motto, "*Labore et industria*,"² to the exclusion of any high chivalrous Mowbray emblem or device, such as the mulberry of the Mowbrays in England, who notoriously were of paramount rank and importance.

Though highly disreputable, and otherwise unworthy of mention here, the notorious William Brodie, "Deacon of Wrights and Masons" in Edinburgh,³ who justly expiated his crimes by his public execution there in 1788, was, as can be proved, through his father, a respectable person, and who had followed much the same profession, well descended, and actually an heir under settlements of the ancient and eminent family of Brodie of Brodie in the north. This fact came out several years ago in a consultation the writer had along with a brother advocate touching the Brodie succession.

Further still, there existed in 1750 "Mr John Seton, *upholsterer*, corner of Drake Street, Red Lyon Square, London"—who was so uniformly addressed—and no other than a cadet of the knightly family of Seton of Garleton, directly sprung from the ancient and noble house of Seton and Winton—of which John, moreover, had there been existing male descendants, they now, to the exclusion of all others, would have been the male heirs and representatives of that distinguished house, and occupied the high status now vested, owing to their failure, in the present Earl of Eglinton and Winton.

That active and spirited lady, Margaret, Duchess of Douglas, when in 1762 she benevolently prosecuted inquiries in France on behalf of the successful party in the celebrated Douglas cause, took, as French interpreter with her, necessary for the purpose, a Miss Primrose, proficient in that language, and to whom, in return (as stated in the evidence),⁴ adduced in any Cockairney pedigrees, though bearing grants in different years of Mowbray property to the same grantees. Here, then, the royal relationship, through the ordinary term "*cousin*," is pointedly stated; and hence, if any had subsisted between Luke Stirling of Ratherue and William Stirling of Caldor, it could not but have been similarly mentioned, through use of the same term "cousin," in the settlement of Ratherne by the former upon the latter in 1414, whose absence there, it may be inferred, bespeaks them strangers.⁵

* She has erroneously by genealogists been made to marry Drummond of Stobhall, which mistake may have been occasioned by the Barton-Mowbrays having quartered with Mowbray three bends (or bendlets) wavy, most technically to denote their services at sea, which correspond, too, with the Drummond arms.⁶ The fact of such quartering by the above is proved by their seals in 1545.

"besides the expence of her journey and residence in France, the Dutchess gave . . . . a gown or two, and some other small presents, for her trouble and loss of time in being absent from her *business* as a *mantua-maker* in London."[1] One would infer from this that the latter was some secondary individual, and of humble descent; but yet she is explicitly designated in the same case, "Miss Fleming Primrose, daughter of the late Sir Archibald Primrose, *Baronet*," "mantua-maker!"

[1] Proof for the Defender in 1766, p. 357.

Here, from her profession, is an analogous instance in the female sex to that of a tailor in the male, and equally illustrative, while indicating a state of society rather different from the present, and of which other examples might be cited.

These precedents inculcate a salutary caution, too, in questions of descent, against inferring what may be derogatory to the *status* and descent of a party from subaltern or inferior professions formerly exercised by his ancestors.

[In reference to Mr Robert Menteith, ex-minister of Duddingston (see under previous page, 250), there is a grant, 16th of November 1633, to George Douglas, in the Canongate, and his heirs, of the escheat of Mr Robert Menteith, minister at Duddingston, denounced rebel, 7th of October 1633, by letters of horning, at the instance of Sir Thomas Hope of Craighall, advocate, "and of Sir James Hamilton of Priestfield, knight, as *informer* to his said hienes advocat," for 'not finding caution to "compeir before the Justice Clerk on the 7th of November, and underly the lawes" (for his "DOUBLE *adultery*," expressed in the usual way at the time, and hence showing *he* also was a married person), "committit be the said Mr Robert Menteith, with Dame Annas Hepburne, *sumtyme* spous to the said Sir James."]

Privy Seal Register.

COMMENTS ON KEIR PERFORMANCE, &c.

No. I.

DRUMPELLIER, BANKEIR, AND LETTYR PEDIGREE.

(REFERRED TO, "EXPOSITION," PAGE 49, NOTE *.)

I. ROBERT STIRLING, styled "in CADDER" and of BANKEIR (his Cadder appanage), LETTYR, and AULD KEIR (the *ancient Keir* patrimony, in which Sir John of Keir, the *Cadder* Wardator, was forced to infeft him and his heirs, in warrandice of their claims), and actually proved, in 1541, Janet of Cadder's nearest heir collaterally. Died in 1537. M⁴ Marion, daur of William Fleming of Boghall, cousin of Malcolm, Lord Fleming, who was curator to their children.

II. JOHN STIRLING of LETTYR, BALQUHARAGE, and AULD KEIR, the Cadder heir and lawful representative. M⁴ 1ᵃ. Beatrix, daur of Geo. Elphinstone of Blythswood; 2⁴ Beatrix, daur of James Chisholm of Glassingall; died 1585.

WILLIAM of WESTER BANKEIR. M⁴ Eliz^th. Stewart, daur of John Steward of Bowhouse, whose second husband was John Stirling, also styled of Wester Bankeir, the elder and direct heir-male and at common law of Keir; died 1575.

JANE.

III. ROBERT STIRLING of LETTYR, BALQUHARAGE, and AULD KEIR, (in which last the family was still infeft), 1585-1606. Sold his estates. M⁴ Jean, daur of John Stirling of Glorat, by whom he had no issue.

WALTER STIRLING lived previous to 1585, and down to 1656.

IV.

JOHN STIRLING. Born 1615, and predeceasing his father, died in 1648.

V.

JOHN STIRLING. Born 1640, died 1709.

VI. JOHN STIRLING. Born 1677, died 1736.

Dr WILLIAM STIRLING. Born 1682, died 1757. The evidence afforded by his Family Bible has been fully stated.

VII. WILLIAM STIRLING. Born 1717, died 1777.

VIII. ANDREW STIRLING of DRUMPELLIER, &c. Served heir-male (in 1818) to his direct ancestor ROBERT STIRLING of BANKEIR and LETTYR, &c., who died in 1537 (see here under No. I.), and who was father of John of Lettyr, &c.

IX. WILLIAM of DRUMPELLIER, died 1850; no issue.
X. WALTER of DRUMPELLIER, *present representative*.
JOHN, died 1854; issue.
CHARLES of MUIRAVONSIDE; issue.
Sir JAMES, K⁺ Vice-Adm^lᵗ; issue.
ANDREW, R.N.; died.
ROBERT, Captain 3⁴ Reg^t; died.
EDWARD, H.E.I.C.S.

STIRLINGS OF KEIR AND THEIR FAMILY PAPERS,"

I. Sir A
Styled "d

"dom

[The link between Sir William and John de Strivelin, in 1338, the *first admissible* Keir ancestor only, is confidently maintained by Drumpellier to be quite fabulous and ideal, and is here, therefore, marked in red ink.]

JOHN.   WILLIAM.   LEWIS.

WILLIAM.

[Mr DAVID, a *new* character, decerned, in 1547, executor-dative, as "PROPINQUIOREM *de sanguine*" to Sir John, his father, and hence literally *ex verbis* his heir-at-law. He thus might have been eldest of these four brothers.]

WILLIAM,   LUCAS.
ancestor of the knightly
family of Ardoch.

Sir ARCHIBALD,
2d and YOUNGER SON,
by Jean Chisholm, daur. of William Bishop
of Dunblane, upon whom, 1579, *nominatim*,
though not his heir, he entailed both Keir
and Cadder.
ANCESTOR of the PRESENT FAMILY of
KEIR.

n the Keir Performance the writer is not answerable.
r Dankeir, their son, was lawful (as admitted on all hands), obviously alone owing

No. I.

DRUMPELLIER, BANKEIR, AND LETTYR PEDIGREE.

(Referred to, "Exposition," Page 49, Note *.)

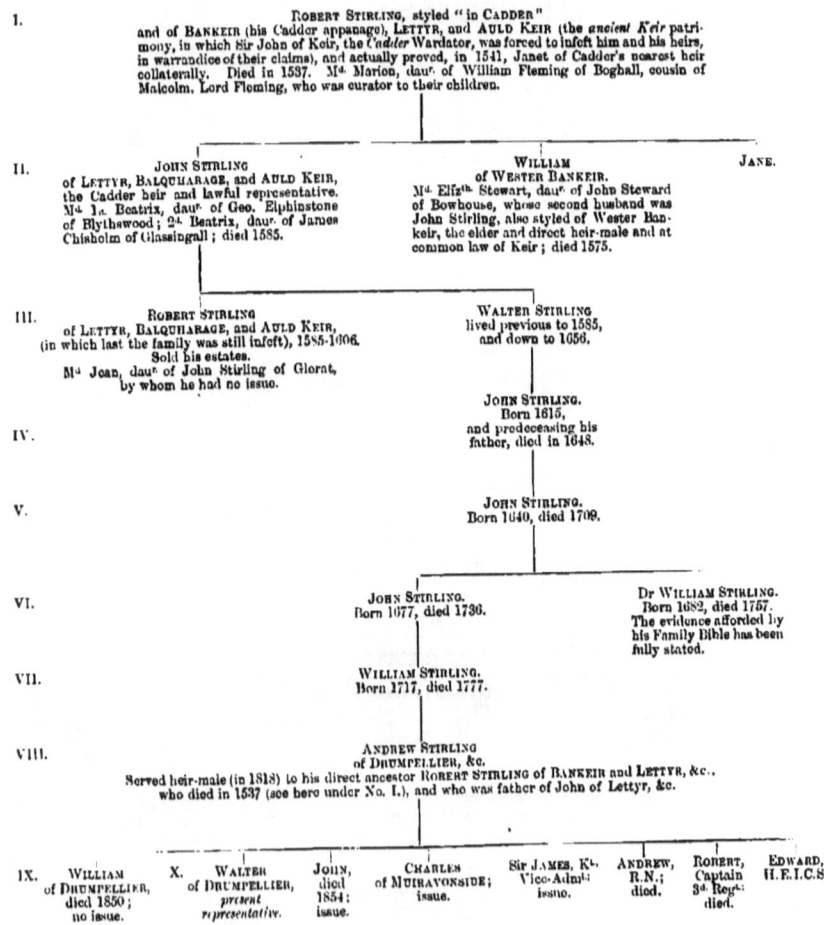

I. ROBERT STIRLING, styled "in CADDER" and of BANKEIR (his Cadder appanage), LETTYR, and AULD KEIR (the *ancient Keir* patrimony, in which Sir John of Keir, the *Cadder* Wardator, was forced to infeft him and his heirs, in warrandice of their claims), and actually proved, in 1541, Janet of Cadder's nearest heir collaterally. Died in 1537. M⁴ Marion, dau⁽ of William Fleming of Boghall, cousin of Malcolm, Lord Fleming, who was curator to their children.

II. JOHN STIRLING of LETTYR, BALQUHARAGE, and AULD KEIR, the Cadder heir and lawful representative. M⁴ 1˂ Beatrix, dau⁽ of Geo. Elphinstone of Blythswood; 2⁴ Beatrix, dau⁽ of James Chisholm of Glassingall; died 1585.

WILLIAM of WESTER BANKEIR. M⁴ Eliz^th Stewart, dau⁽ of John Steward of Bowhouse, whose second husband was John Stirling, also styled of Wester Bankeir, the elder and direct heir-male and at common law of Keir; died 1575.

JANE.

III. ROBERT STIRLING of LETTYR, BALQUHARAGE, and AULD KEIR, (in which last the family was still infeft), 1585-1606. Sold his estates. M⁴ Joan, dau⁽ of John Stirling of Glorat, by whom he had no issue.

WALTER STIRLING lived previous to 1585, and down to 1656.

IV. JOHN STIRLING. Born 1615, and predeceasing his father, died in 1648.

V. JOHN STIRLING. Born 1640, died 1709.

VI. JOHN STIRLING. Born 1677, died 1736.

Dr WILLIAM STIRLING. Born 1682, died 1757. The evidence afforded by his Family Bible has been fully stated.

VII. WILLIAM STIRLING. Born 1717, died 1777.

VIII. ANDREW STIRLING of DRUMPELLIER, &c. Served heir-male (in 1818) to his direct ancestor ROBERT STIRLING of BANKEIR and LETTYR, &c., who died in 1537 (see here under No. I.), and who was father of John of Lettyr, &c.

IX. WILLIAM of DRUMPELLIER, died 1850; no issue.

X. WALTER of DRUMPELLIER, *present representative.*

JOHN, died 1854; issue.

CHARLES of MUIRAVONSIDE; issue.

Sir JAMES, K^t Vice-Adm^lt issue.

ANDREW, R.N.; died.

ROBERT, Captain 3⁴ Reg^t died.

EDWARD, H.E.I.C.S.

[253-256]

No. II.

GENEALOGICAL TREE, as relates to the more immediate subject, deduced partly from STATEMENTS in a RECENT WORK—"THE STIRLINGS OF KEIR AND THEIR FAMILY PAPERS," and other Authorities referred to and explained in Exposition, p. 49, note*.*

I. Sir ALEXANDER DE STRIVELING of CADDER, Knt.,
styled "*del rende de Leuenax*" in "Ragman R-ll,"
1272-1306.
|
JOHN,
1306-1333.
|
Sir JOHN,
dominus DE CADDER" and REDINGTON,
1333-1406.
|
WILLIAM,
"LORD OF CADDER,"
1406-1425.
|
Sir WILLIAM
of CADDER and REDINGTON,
1425-1468.
|
WILLIAM ——— HUMPHREY. ROBERT. ANDREW. WILLIAM,
of CADDER,   conceived illegitimate.
1467-1505.
|
WILLIAM
of CADDER,
m. Elic Bartonne,
1505-1517.
|
ANDREW
of CADDER and OURHOUSE,
m. Marjory Cunningham,
1517-1562.
|
JANET
of CADDER, OURHOUSE, BANKIER, &c.
in 1562 and thereafter the direct CADDER
Letters and representative [of whom the
family of the presenting Robert Stirling
of Bankier and Letter, the Dunpacker
ancestor (see under previous Genealogical
Tree, No. I.) were entered collaterals below.]

II. Sir JOHN DE STRIVELING, Knt.,
Lord of CARSE and ALVA.
|
MARJORY,
had been married in 1332 to John Montieth,
from whom came down her son Maurice of Carse.

III. Sir WILLIAM DE STRIVELING,
1270-1290.
Promoted in Keir work, but not on the
least ground, to be father of †
|
"JOHN DE STRIVELING," in 1330,
as yet unappropriated and without his
further by that year as husband of Mary
Avent of Johne, Lord of Lorne, upon
whole clear and her heirs the properly
timely monastery property of Bankier
was then united.
|
(?)
WILLIAM RAYMOND,
presumptive heir of Mary, and hence, †
is to be presented of John, but provid-
ble between him and these parties un-
proved; died in 1363.
|
LUCAS,
property the KEIR PURCHER,
who acquired "RATHERHEN or QUYLTON,
and afterwards half of KEIR, from George,
Lord Levis, 1370-1415.
|
Sir WILLIAM, Knt.,
of RATHERHEN and KEIR,
of which he acquired the other half,
1420-1471.
|
Sir WILLIAM of KEIR, ——— JOHN. ——— WILLIAM. ——— LUKE.
required superiority of James III.
Keir entail into a barony, in 1473;
1471-1503.
|
Sir JOHN, Esqr., ——— WILLIAM.
of KEIR,
1503-1528.
|
the JAMES, Esqr., ——— Sir DAVID, a new character, deceased, ——— WILLIAM, ——— LUKE.
of KEIR,   in 1547, executive deceive, as "procure-   ancestor of the knightly
acquired Cadder [by a slender title only, STURAGE of *nonlete*" to be John, his   family of Arduck.
and not by purchase, to great reputation- father, and hence legally or *cristably* his
bly asserted in the Keir Peerages];   brother. The first might have been elded
| of these four brothers.]
JOHN,
of Wester Bankier,
his eldest Son and heir,
direct male Heir Presumptive [and
common heir, as heir of all lands, with
right of the successive and inheriting]
inferred Sex *Shirr* Stewart, widow of
James Wilson Stirling of Wester Bankier,
a cadet of the family of Drumpeller;] and
commonly, Burgess Culquhoun.
|
Sir ARCHIBALD,
3d and 2nd son,
by John Chisholm, dept. of William Bishop
of Dumblane, upon whom, 1579, conveniently,
though not his heir, he entailed both Keir
and Cadder.
|
Ancestor of the PRESENT FAMILY OF
KEIR.

* The material additions to particulars, which here here in this Tree, № *[for Exemption, are established by legal evidence; but for the validity of what is here derived from the Keir Papers, even the author is not answerable.
† James's putative marriage with Janet, the heirs of Cadder [in 1532] we know not have mentioned, was lasted, in 1541, null and void from the beginning; but John of Wester Bankier, their son, was levied (as attached on all hands), obviously above acting to a legal spurnity, for which see Exposition, pp. 169, 180, and 19

GENERAL APPENDIX.

[*Want of room, and more important subjects, have necessitated in this place the abbreviation of the two articles that follow under Nos. I. and II.—especially of the former, in a great degree—which had been reserved for it.*]

No. I.

EXPOSITION of the ERRORS, DISHONESTY, and MALPRACTICES of DOUGLAS, the Peerage Writer, in his Statements and Deductions of Scottish Pedigrees.

(REFERRED TO AT PAGE 3, NOTE.)

PERHAPS, too, independently of the preceding weighty motive, this was not so incumbent, from the samples that Chalmers (besides the writer) has given of the above in his *Caledonia*, to which references may be made,[1] and whose further detection is not difficult to any Scotch antiquary who begirds himself to the task.

One additional instance, however, the writer may cite. The notable author in question, in the account of the noble family of Sempill in his *Peerage*[2] (that did not, from its high rank and influence formerly in Renfrewshire, stand in need of exaggeration), actually multiplies one Robert Sempill, figuring early in the fourteenth century, through his mere gratuitous fancy and assumption, into no less than three Robert Sempills, taking each in succession *seriatim* after the other: while, still more flatteringly to elongate the pedigree—precisely like the Keir editor in the Keir instance—the first of these *ideals* is made co-existent with the year 1246, and even earlier. All this, too, will be easily discovered, when tested by ordinary research and investigation.

[1] See ibid. vol. i. pp. 509, 534, 535, 536, 547, 549, 565, 579, &c.

[2] See that work, published in 1764, p. old.

No. II.

ORIGINAL EVIDENCE of the first HAMELDON or HAMILTON settler in Scotland, and his possessing lands there, with INCIDENTAL REMARKS about the ORIGIN of the SCOTCH HAMILTONS, &c.

(ALSO REFERRED TO IN EXPOSITION, PAGE 3, NOTE.)

"Hameldun" or "Hamelton" may be held an English surname, but the precise origin of the Scotch Hamiltons—English, also, we may at least conclude—who became so great and distinguished with us, has not, like that of the Stewarts, been further illustrated in our days. The putative Leicester descent ascribed to them is unworthy a moment's attention; and "Walter Fitzgilbert de Hameldon," who swore fealty to Edward I. in 1296, is at present their only certain ancestor; for we must efface from the discussion the antecedent *Gilbertus de Hambleton*, the obscure *clericus* or monk in 1272—equally with the cotemporary Gilbertus de Strivelin, *clericus*, elsewhere, whom Douglas and the Keir editor respectively, withholding their clerical designations, affix in the guise of laics on the higher stems of the Hamiltons and De Strivelins.[1]

[note 1: See p. 2, note; and Expos., pp. 203, 204.]

[note 2: See Bannatyne printed copy, vol. i. p. 207.]

The next EARLIER individuals who claim our attention are *Robert* and *Roger de Hameldons*, who witness a deed in the Chartulary of Melrose shortly after 1223;[2] but it would appear to refer to Northumberland, and involve interests there irrespective of Scotland; however, the authority may bring the surname much nearer to that country, which once included the former.

But who, then, was the *first* Hameldun or Hamelton who *actually* held lands and had thus *settled* in Scotland *anterior* to Walter Fitzgilbert de Hameldun, the hitherto earliest discovered founder of the family? This may be a material preliminary to fixing their original ancestry, and, as it happens, is all *in hoc statu* that we may be enabled to ascertain.

[note: Preserved among the writs and documents of that English religious house.]

The writer believes he can answer the preceding question by adduction of an original *quit-claim* by "*Roger de Hameldun*" of his right to a carrucate of land in *Oxenham*, in Roxburghshire, which held of the Crown of Scotland, to John, Abbot of Whitby, in Yorkshire. It is without date, but must have been between 1245 and 1258, when the latter can be proved to have been Abbot.

The preceding we may conclude also to have been the "Roger de Hameldun," who is established by other Whitby deeds to have possessed *Geker in "Hamelton*," along with the woods of "Hamilton," which formed a manor in Yorkshire, and hence must have been the *foyer* of these Hamiltons; while they further disclose, as we may infer, a previous *kindred* Roger, son of a William de Hamilton.

It hence follows that the first of the surname (for there is no prior notice of it there elsewhere) who had settled and actually held lands of the Crown in Scotland, was the preceding "Roger de Hameldun," as proprietor of *Oxenham*, in Roxburghshire, between 1243 and 1258 ; and, singularly, of an English family, who, precisely like the Scottish eventually, had an estate named Hamilton, and who, in Scotch parlance, might be styled the Hamiltons *of that Ilk* in Yorkshire. This Roger may have been cotemporary with the "Roger de Hameldun" already mentioned, who (with his brother Robert) test a deed, though only connected with Northumberland, shortly after 1223, in the Chartulary of Melrose—a coincidence worth remarking, though not yet identified with him.

The above, consistently with what was stated, is all that can as yet be safely offered touching the origin of the Anglo-Scoto Hamiltons, we not being able to connect the same Roger or his kindred with the Walter Fitzgilbert de Hameldun in 1296, though they possibly enough—considering, too, the extreme rarity then of this English surname in Scotland—may have been related.

The writer is not generally partial to what are styled Scotch *birth-brieves*, but it may be added that one in 1680, in favour of Sir James Hamilton, "*centurionis*," of the family of Abercorn, both at the time and now the Hamilton heirs-male, while wisely ignoring the fabulous Hamilton-Leicester descent, and the equally visionary one from the English refugee knight in the reign of Edward II., actually represents the progenitor of Gilbert de Hameldun (not the *clericus*, but father of the Walter who swore fealty to Edward I. in 1296) as having come to Scotland with his cousin, Robert Bruce (Lord of Annandale), the grandfather of Robert I. All that can be said is, that this is not improbable, while the account and period tally with the first legally proved appearances, as shown, of the Hamiltons in Scotland. Great Seal Register.

The intimation in the Sadler state papers that they were descended from the English "Hamptons" may only go to support their English origin. 1 See vol. i. p. 693, note.

Wood, in his edition of Douglas's *Peerage*, says that "neither" Walter Fitzgilbert in 1296, nor David, his heir, "had the surname of Hamilton ;"[1] but this is palpably refuted by an original grant, probably in 1369, witnessed by the latter as "Dominus David, filius WALTERI *dicti de Hamilton*."[2] 2 See Andrew Stuart's Gen. History of the Stewarts, p. 76.

The question in the case of Riddell against Brymer, in 1811, was "whether a lady who was alleged to have been privately married, having afterwards, during the lifetime of her husband, contracted a second marriage with a gentleman *ignorant* of the *first*, the child of that *second* marriage *was or was not legitimate*, on account of the *bona fides* or *ignorance* of the father ?" Explanatory Note as to a modern case in 1811, cited in the Exposition, see p. 106, note *.

The father here, in a legal view, was in the same situation with James Stirling of Keir, when married *de facto* to Janet of Cadder,[3] who also is proved, by their 3 See Report of the divorce in 1541, on the ground of original nullity, to have been ignorant of the legal impediment to their marriage, owing to which it relevantly followed on account of his *sole* ignorance or *bona fides*, in like manner—though the marriage *ab initio* was quite a nullity and inept—that John Stirling of Wester Bankeir, their offspring, behoved to be legitimate, as in truth he confessedly was.[1]

<small>case given, without the names of the parties, by Robert Dell, Advocate, published in 1825.</small>

The Court of Session, in the antecedent case in 1811, it must be added, were equally divided in their opinion, while the premature death of the child in question of the second marriage precluded a final judgment; but still, it may be fairly maintained that the weight and talent of the bench preponderated in favour of its legitimacy, in virtue of the specialty stated.

<small>[1] See Expos., pp. 106, 107, 108.</small>

But that the same legitimating consequence and effect merely through such ignorance or *bona fides* of *one* of the parties, obtained in Scotland, in modern times at least, long after the abolition of Catholicism in 1560, is clenched by the opinion which follows of Sir James Stewart, Lord Advocate to Queen Anne, certainly one of the first and most experienced lawyers of his age:—

"*Tho'* a marriage be *unlawful*" (and hence null and void, he broadly inculcates),[2] "yet, if *either* of the *parties* be *in bona fide*, it *should legitimate the children;* and if once legitimate, they should succeed with the *other* children of a *lawful* marriage. For the legitimation should be *ad omnes effectus*, and even to succeed to the *other* kinsmen."

<small>[2] Answers to Direlton, Edit. 1715, p. 200.</small>

This precisely meets the case of James Stirling of Keir in 1541, and John Stirling of Wester Bankeir, his offspring. And independently of the above concurrent modern doctrine, too, the status of the last must be entirely ruled by our law before the Reformation (in 1560), which, as is maintained in the text, was quite fixed and established upon the point.

If it had not been for such legal ignorance, in 1541, on the part of James Stirling, the said John would assuredly have been illegitimate, which might casually have been thought by the legally uninitiated, and those unaware of this nice protecting specialty, especially of parties to whose interests his legitimacy was prejudicial; owing to which, in transactions, he was, as has been proved, by *one* of the *latter*, styled "*natural* son" of his parent,s who capriciously, from other motives, as stated, may have come to view, or rather affected to view him in the same light.

<small>[3] See Expos., pp. 110, 111; also, 106, 107, 108.</small>

THE END.

www.ingramcontent.com/pod-product-compliance
Lightning Source LLC
Chambersburg PA
CBHW031333230426
43670CB00006B/336